No. 2116
$19.95

UNDERSTANDING AUTOMOTIVE SPECIFICATIONS AND DATA

JAMES M. FLAMMANG

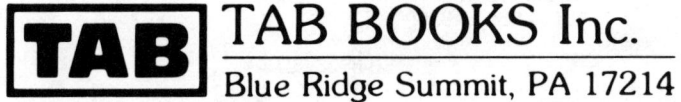
TAB BOOKS Inc.
Blue Ridge Summit, PA 17214

FIRST EDITION
FIRST PRINTING

Copyright © 1986 by TAB BOOKS Inc.
Printed in the United States of America

Reproduction or publication of the content in any manner, without express permission of the publisher, is prohibited. No liability is assumed with respect to the use of the information herein.

Library of Congress Cataloging in Publication Data

Flammang, James M.
Understanding automotive specifications and data.

Includes index.
1. Automobiles—Specifications. 2. Automobiles—Maintenance and repair—Specifications. I. Title.
TL154.F55 1986   629.2′222′0212   85-27696

ISBN 0-8306-0916-4
ISBN 0-8306-0316-6 (pbk.)

Contents

Introduction   vi

An Important Note on Sample Spec Tables   viii

1 Nice Numbers   1

Numbers Large and Small—A Few Basics—Decimals Versus Fractions—Battle of the Units: The Metric System—Length and Diameter—Area and Volume Measurements—Elbow Room—Thousandths or Tighter—Proportions, Ratios, and Angles—Ranges and Absolute Values—Numerical Style—Numbers Don't Have to Be Numbing

2 Specifications   14

Sources of Specs—Data Formats—Specs You'll Need to Know—Which Line Is It?—Notice all the Footnotes?—Unraveling the Maze—Early Model Spec Problems

3 Identifying Your Engine   27

Such a Selection!—Most of the Time, It's Easy . . .—Vehicle Identification Number (VIN)—Identification Plates—Color Codes and Stickers—Models and Body Styles—Identity Problems—When You're Not Sure

4 Engine Size and Style   36

Engine Styles—Number of Cylinders—Bore and Stroke—Displacement: The Prime Measurement—Monsters, Minis, and Guzzlers—Adding Inches—Compression Ratio

5 Power, Torque and Rev's   50

Power and Work—Torque Comes First—Brake Horsepower: The Number One Rating—Gross Versus Net Horsepower—Other Horsepower Ratings—The Power/Torque Relationship—Efficiency and Power Loss—The Fifties Horsepower Race—Adding Horses in Midstream

6 Electrical Values and Measurements — 63
Electrical Circuits—Volts, Amps, and Ohms—Test Instruments—Ohm's Law—Electrical Power—Voltage Drop—Voltage Drop as a Troubleshooting Technique—Shorts and Fuses—Battery Ratings—Starter Specs—Alternator and Regulator Data—DC Generators

7 Ignition Tune-Up Specifications — 79
The Ignition System—Spark Plugs: Type and Gap—Distributor Point Gap and Dwell Angle—High Tension: The Ignition Coil—Firing Order—Ignition Timing—Centrifugal Advance—Vacuum Advance—More Distributor Data—Electronic Ignition: What's New?

8 Finishing the Tune-Up — 93
Idle Speeds—Idle Mixture—Fuel Pump Pressure—Compression Testing—Valve Clearance—Valve Timing: Duration and Overlap—Diesel Data

9 Engine Pressures and Temperatures — 101
Atmospheric Pressure—Compression and Combustion—Oil Pressure—Coolant Pressure—Fuel and Other Pressures—Engine Temperatures: A Mass of Heat—Overheating: Curse of the Older Auto

10 Vacuum, Carburetion and Emissions — 107
Vacuum: It Lets the Engine Run—Fuel Supply—Carburetor Capacities—Boosting the Air Supply—Air/Fuel Ratio—Gasoline Octane—Carburetor Adjustments—Choke Settings—Fuel Injection—Emissions Control

11 Computer Control and Testing — 120
Computers Under the Hood—On-Board Computer Diagnostics—Future Dashboards—Computers in the Shop

12 Inside the Engine — 127
Valve Trains: Running at Half Speed—Pistons and Rings—Crankshaft Data—Elsewhere in the Engine

13 How Worn Is Worn? — 138
Valve Train Wear—Piston and Cylinder Wear—Crankshaft and Camshaft Journal Wear—Wear Elsewhere in the Engine

14 Precision Tools and Measurements — 143
The "Feel" of a Thousandth—Outside Micrometers—Reading a Micrometer—Inside Micrometers—Calipers—Hole Gauges—Dial Indicators—Feeler Gauges and Shims—Plastigage for Bearing Clearances—Special Measuring Tools—Tips and Techniques—Can You Measure It Yourself?

15 Hardware — 153
Screw and Bolt Sizes—Measuring the Thread—Fitting the Nut—Threaded Fastener Styles—Tensile Strength—Pipe Threads—Special Threads and Substitutions

16 How Tight is Tight? — 159
Foot-Pounds and Newton-Meters—Torque Wrenches—Parts That Must Be Torqued—Parts That Should Be Torqued—Guessing at Torque—Rust, Dirt, and Oil—Torque Tricks

17 Fluid Capacities — 164
Motor Oil—Oil Viscosity and Classification—Gasoline and Diesel Fuel—The Cooling System—Driveline and Chassis Fluids

18 Driveline Data — 168
Total Gear Reduction—Calculating a Gear Ratio—Final Drive: High or Low Ratios—What Size Is the Rear End?—Manual Transmission Gearing—The Automatic Transmission—Effect of Tire Diameter—

Gearing Down for Performance or Economy—Clutch Specifications—Driveline Adjustments—Forgotten Specs

19 Chassis and Body Measurements   **175**

Vehicle Size: Wheelbase to Trim Height—Vehicle Weight—Brake Specifications

20 Aiming the Wheels   **180**

Wheel Alignment Geometry—Rear Wheel Alignment—Understeer and Oversteer—Wheel Balancing—Tire Sizes and Ratings

21 Performance   **188**

What Do Published Road Tests Tell Us?—Fuel Economy: From Guzzlers to Misers—Braking Distance

Appendix: Sources for Service Manuals   **193**

Index   **195**

Introduction

THIS BOOK IS ABOUT NUMBERS. NOT DULL, OR-dinary numbers, but the ones that apply to automobiles. We'll be studying the immense variety of specifications, sizes, ratings, and other essential data that help describe any car's operation, maintenance, and repair duties.

Auto enthusiasts, mechanics, and motorists are bombarded by figures. We read and hear about them all the time: a 4 1/2-liter engine, 259 cubic inches, 9-to-1 compression, 3.625-inch bore, 120 horsepower. Both amateur and professional mechanics also come across a mass of tiny numbers: clearances measured in thousandths of an inch or less.

What do they all mean? Who needs to know? When is that knowledge necessary?

Indispensable as they are in servicing autos, specifications are not universally loved. Or understood. Nearly every do-it-yourselfer owns a manual or two containing specification tables and charts. No professional shop worthy of the name can survive without dozens of such volumes. Yet countless novice and amateur mechanics—and more than a few old pros—shy away from the arrays of figures.

Oh, they use the figures all right. They have to. Still, each encounter with a spec table is likely to result in grumbling and distress—even cursing and table-pounding.

Many of us, then, are mystified by some—perhaps many—of the numbers we confront. The books and manuals that *give* you the essential specifications seldom tell you much, if anything, about them. They assume you already know or they offer explanations more appropriate for engineering students. All you get are the plain, cold facts and figures.

This book is meant to fill that "information gap," providing aid to motorists and mechanics who've been intimidated by data. It gives clear, concise explanations of the figures and numerical concepts you might encounter around the car engine and chassis. Technical jargon, while impossible to avoid, is minimal. Before we're through, you should have enough background to understand the significance, history, and measurement methods of nearly all the numbers you'll find in print. Not only what they mean, but what to do about them.

Most of that data consists of mechanical or electrical specs needed by persons doing tune-ups, overhauls, or adjustments. But we also take a close look at important general information dealing with engine size, power, economy, and similarly intriguing matters. To the extent possible, I have shown:

1. What each specification means.
2. What units are commonly used to measure it (inches, rpm, cubic centimeters, etc.).
3. What value you're likely to find for the spec on a typical modern car, on an older car (say 10-20 years old), and on an early model vehicle.
4. Who needs to know about this spec, when, and why.
5. How it's measured (and by whom).
6. How it relates to other specifications.
7. How it affects performance, economy, reliability, or car life.
8. How it might change as the car ages.
9. How much variance might be permissible from the published figures.

A certain ease with numbers is essential for the amateur or professional mechanic, helpful to enthusiasts who want to know more about their vehicles—and more useful to everyday motorists than they might realize. When delving into serious tune-up duties and machinist skills, and working to close tolerances, an easy intimacy with figures is vital.

Even if your own do-it-yourself efforts are minimal, it certainly doesn't hurt to know a bit about compression ratio, camber, valve overlap, and a few hundred other figures that pop up. Americans love to talk and read about their cars, and technical details are part of the appeal.

Many of these explanations will, oddly enough, be more valuable to owners of older vehicles than for the current crop of Detroit offerings. Why? Because there's more work to be *done* on some of the old buggies—work that can be performed without a garage full of sophisticated equipment.

Some of you are professional mechanics or perhaps you are aspiring to that status. This book can help you by serving as a handy reference, or explaining certain details that are a bit vague in the textbooks.

We can't evade the spec tables and charts, but let's see if we can at least make those mazes of figures and footnotes a little less ominous. Maybe even friendly.

Let me assure you that the math won't be painful. We won't get into anything more complex than decimals and fractions—plus a handful of basic formulas that help create a foundation of understanding (but few of which you'll ever actually have to use). What you learned in grade school and high school, even if dimly remembered, will be sufficient preparation. We'll be talking about four levels of data:

1. Figures found in nearly every specification manual needed for tune-up, repair, maintenance, or overhaul.
2. Seldom-used data that are in the tables anyway.
3. Useful figures found in some, but not all, manuals.
4. Figures you won't come across in any tables, but are nevertheless important.

Naturally, we can't cover everything. Only the most commonly found, most useful specs can receive full attention. Once you grasp the meaning of these vital figures, however, any others you might encounter are sure to be clearer, too.

Numbers need not be frightening. It might come as a surprise to many, but numbers actually can be fun. Whether you're actively involved in maintenance and repair (or want to be), or simply enjoy everything about automobiles, I hope this book helps you understand the facts and figures about your favorites. Even if the mathematical aspects of your automotive work never quite qualify as fun, let's hope they can become a bit less like drudgery—and a lot more comprehensible.

Good luck.

An Important Note on Sample Spec Tables

AT THE BEGINNING OF MOST CHAPTERS, you'll find a small sample table of typical specifications that illustrate the chapter topic. Another table may appear later in the chapter, covering a subtopic. They're meant for study—not for actual use. They show different ways in which a given spec might be displayed in a table and demonstrate some typical values for each one.

The tables are hypothetical, but their figures are taken from actual vehicles of varying vintages and types. They're consistent, too. Each value in any line of a sample table applies to a single vehicle. Those from newest vehicles are at the top. The example on the next page, for instance, contains specifications for (top to bottom): a 1985 Chevrolet Cavalier four-cylinder, 1985 Ford V-6, 1984 front-wheel-drive Chrysler four, 1984 Buick V-6, 1983 Honda, 1979 Pontiac V-8, 1972 Plymouth six, 1959 Ford V-8, 1953 Packard straight eight, and 1940 Chrysler. The car year and engine type are given in the left-hand columns of some, but not all, of the sample tables.

Typical Non-Ignition Tune-up Specifications.

Engine	Curb Idle Speed (rpm)		Fast Idle Speed (rpm)		Fuel Pump Pressure (psi)	Valve Clearance (Inches)	
	MT	AT	MT	AT		Intake	Exhaust
4-112	800	700	—	—	—	Hydraulic	
V6-232	—	500-600D	—	—	40-45[1]	—	—
4-156	See sticker				4.6-6.0	.006	.010
V6-231	Controlled		—	2200	4 1/4-5 3/4	Hydraulic	
4-1.3L	650-750	—	3000	—	—	.006C	.008C
V8-403	—	500/600D[2]	—	1000	5 1/2-6 1/2	—	—
6-225	750	750N	2000	1900	—	—	—
V8-332	600	—	—	—	5.5	.026H	.026H
8-327	400	400	—	—	—	Zero	Zero
8-323	300	—	—	—	—	.008H	.010H

[1]Frame mounted pump. [2]Higher figure with solenoid energized.

Nice Numbers

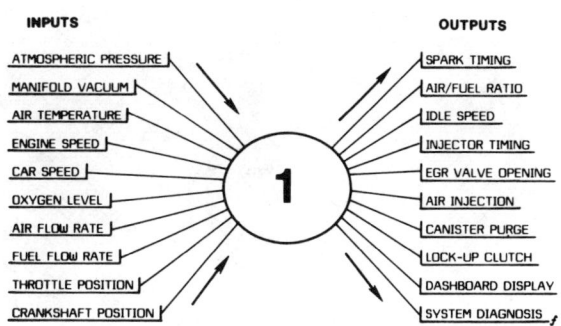

BEFORE LEAPING ABRUPTLY INTO THE SEA OF actual automotive specifications, we need to take a quick look at measuring units—from inches to psi, degrees to foot-pounds, etc. A couple of formulas, too.

We'll also consider a few uses for each unit and formula, specifying the chapter(s) in which they will appear again, discussed in greater detail and ready for serious business. The formula for calculating the volume of a cylinder, for example, is explained in this chapter—but becomes useful in Chapter 4, in order to compute engine displacement.

This chapter concentrates, for the most part, on measures of linear (straight-line) distance and size: length, volume, and so on. Units that measure pressure, torque, and other significant automotive values are described fully in the chapters where they're needed.

You probably learned the basic formulas, and made use of many numerical units, in your early school days. Most of them should be familiar. In the years following departure from scholastic endeavors many of us have managed to forget a lot of the elementary math and physics we learned. This introductory chapter is a sort of refresher course for those whose memories need a bit of jogging. It also tells how some very familiar measurements are used in automotive applications.

NUMBERS LARGE AND SMALL

Every automobile description is packed with sizes and measurements (Fig. 1-1). Some are large: 350 cubic inches (engine displacement), 4500 rpm (rotational speed), or 40,000 volts (spark plug voltage). Others are extremely small: the tiny clearances between a connecting rod journal and its surrounding bearing, or the jet size in a carburetor, measured in thousandths of an inch.

More important than the actual sizes involved, however, are the relationships between components. Automotive math deals not only with absolute sizes, but with shapes, positions, spaces between moving parts, proportions, ratios—values that have little or nothing to do with inches or millimeters.

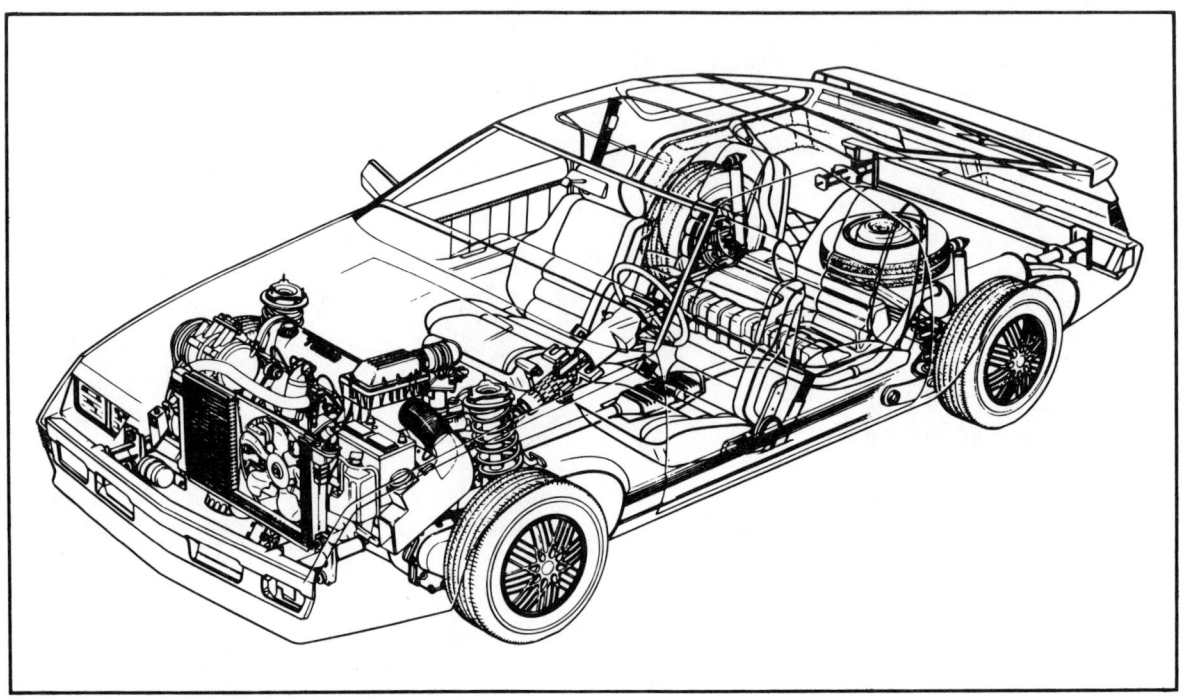

Fig. 1-1. Inside the engine and throughout the chassis, every automobile is a mass of numbers: sizes, clearances, ratings, ratios and more. (Chrysler Corp.)

Precisely measured sizes and spaces are crucial to the automotive mechanic and machinist in the course of their work. A grasp of the relationships is important to every motorist. For instance, understanding how tolerances allow an engine to run efficiently for many years is valuable even if you rarely (or never) actually have to measure one.

A FEW BASICS

In the course of our study, we'll work with a variety of decimals and fractions, manipulating them now and then. Do you need to do these computations on paper? Of course not. Calculators are perfectly acceptable so long as you understand what's being calculated. For that matter, only occasionally will you need to perform any real calculations. The important thing is that you grasp the meaning and importance of a formula or size, and how it's computed or measured. Doing it yourself isn't always essential to learning.

In the simple formulas that pop up, multiplication is sometimes denoted by X or $\times$ ($3 \times 2 = 6$, or $3 \times 2 = 6$). There might or might not be space between the digits being multiplied. In math books, the multiplication symbol is a dot ($3 \cdot = 6$). When letters are used in a formula, there probably is no symbol at all: $E = IR$ means E is equal to I multiplied by R.

For clarity, parentheses are often used to show multiplication of several numbers or complex numbers. Example: (346) (21) (2), which equals 14,532. The parentheses mean the same thing as a dot or X sign.

Division is indicated by $\div$ or, more often, a diagonal line (slash): $8 \div 4 = 2$, or $8/4 = 2$. For larger numbers, it can instead be a horizontal line:

$$\frac{624}{2} = 312$$

The (+) symbol means addition, of course; the (−), subtraction. Plus and minus. In referring to electrical parts, they indicate positive and negative polarity, respectively.

Powers of a number refer to multiplying that number by itself a specified number of times. In automotive work, you may have occasion to compute (or understand) *squares*. That's not a derisive term for folks who haven't kept up with the latest trends in music and dress. It simply means a number multiplied by itself one time—a power of 2. The number 3 squared (written 3^2) is 3 times 3, or 9. Squaring a number is important in determining engine size (Chapter 4).

Cubes are the next step; they are numbers to the third power. The number 3 cubed would be 3 times 3 times 3 ($3 \times 3 \times 3$), or 27. Cubing and higher powers (they go all the way up, as high as you'd like) are generally needed only by engineers. But as we shall see with the prefixes used for metric equivalents and with decimals, a little knowledge of powers helps in understanding the relationships between units. For the moment, just note that a number to the first power is that number itself ($10^1 = 10$); to zero power, it's always one ($10^0 = 1$).

Negative powers form fractions, with a one as the numerator (top portion), and the base number to a given power as the denominator. How's that? Well, 10^{-2} (10 to the minus two power) is equal to $1/10^2$. That's 1 divided by 10 squared, or 1/100. 10^{-3} would be $\frac{1}{(10)(10)(10)}$, or 1/1000. And on and on. Does it matter to you? Only in terms of those decimal/metric prefixes.

Negative numbers (those less than zero) seem to appear in wheel alignment specifications. But a camber reading of $-1/2$ isn't really negative. They're used as a convenience to show whether a part inclines one way or the other away from vertical, which is considered to be zero.

Confused? Don't worry about it. All will become clear as we get into some real figures.

DECIMALS VERSUS FRACTIONS

A few specifications, especially for earlier engines, appear in fractional form: 3 1/4-inch cylinder bore, 3/8-inch valve stem diameter, and so forth. Decimals are more common, however; they are standard for precision tolerances.

Automotive work, for the most part, deals with figures given in thousandths of an inch. That's 1/1000 as a fraction or .001 as a decimal. A specification for cylinder bore might be shown as 3.625 inches. This translates to 3 and 625 thousandths, and happens to be equivalent to exactly 3 5/8 inches. For numbers less than one, a zero often, but not always, precedes the decimal point (0.375 is the same as .375).

Any mechanic should know without thinking that 3 1/2 is the same as 3.5, and that the figure could be given with additional decimal places (3.50, 3.500, etc.) to show increased accuracy. Converting 3 1/4 to 3.25, even 3 5/8 to 3.625, is easy enough. Beyond that point, most of us tend to forget the fraction/decimal equivalents.

Table 1-1 gives decimal and metric equivalents for fractional dimensions down to 64ths of an inch. If you ever have to convert a fraction to a decimal, it's not too difficult. All you do is take the numerator (top number of the fraction) and divide it by the denominator. The fraction 3/8, then, is 3 divided by 8, or .375. A 3 5/16-inch bore amounts to 3.3125 inches (3, plus 5 divided by 16) in decimal form. After figuring the decimal equivalent of the fraction, just tack it onto the whole number ahead of it, at the right of a decimal point.

More complex fractions, such as 63/64, are just as easy when using a pocket calculator. With pencil and paper, they take a bit more time. Nevertheless the idea's the same.

Converting a decimal to a fraction, unfortunately, is not so simple. A conversion table in the garage might come in handy. In real life, though, few of us have many occasions to use such tables.

BATTLE OF THE UNITS: THE METRIC SYSTEM

The battle has been furious in some circles, and nearly unnoticed (or forgotten) by others. Bystanders can perhaps be excused for believing that metrics have lost because the verbal war between advocates and opponents seems to have halted. In reality, metrics have crept into our lives, part of the way, rather than taken over as predicted.

Engine displacements, for example, are commonly shown in specification tables with both U.S. standard and SI metric figures. ("SI" is a French abbreviation for International System: Systéme International d'Unites). In textbooks, articles and

Table 1-1. Decimal and Metric Equivalents of Fractional Sizes to 1 Inch.

Fraction	Decimal	Millimeters	Fraction	Decimal	Millimeters
1/64	0.0156	0.3969	33/64	0.5156	13.0969
1/32	.0312	0.7938	17/32	.5312	13.4938
3/64	.0469	1.1906	35/64	.5469	13.8906
1/16	.0625	1.5875	9/16	.5625	14.2875
5/64	.0781	1.9844	37/64	.5781	14.6844
3/32	.0938	2.3812	19/32	.5938	15.0812
7/64	.1094	2.7781	39/64	.6094	15.4781
1/8	.1250	3.1750	5/8	.6250	15.8750
9/64	.1406	3.5719	41/64	.6406	16.2719
5/32	.1562	3.9688	21/32	.6562	16.6688
11/64	.1719	4.3656	43/64	.6719	17.0656
3/16	.1875	4.7625	11/16	.6875	17.4625
13/64	.2031	5.1594	45/64	.7031	17.8594
7/32	.2188	5.5562	23/32	.7188	18.2562
15/64	.2344	5.9531	47/64	.7344	18.6531
1/4	.2500	6.3500	3/4	.7500	19.0500
17/64	.2656	6.7469	49/64	.7656	19.4469
9/32	.2812	7.1438	25/32	.7812	19.8438
19/64	.2969	7.5406	51/64	.7969	20.2406
5/16	.3125	7.9375	13/16	.8125	20.6375
21/64	.3281	8.3344	53/64	.8281	21.0344
11/32	.3438	8.7312	27/32	.8438	21.4312
23/64	.3594	9.1281	55/64	.8594	21.8281
3/8	.3750	9.5250	7/8	.8750	22.2250
25/64	.3906	9.9219	57/64	.8906	22.6219
13/32	.4062	10.3188	29/32	.9062	23.0188
27/64	.4219	10.7156	59/64	.9219	23.4156
7/16	.4375	11.1125	15/16	.9375	23.8125
29/64	.4531	11.5094	61/64	.9531	24.2094
15/32	.4688	11.9062	31/32	.9688	24.6062
31/64	.4844	12.3031	63/64	.9844	25.0031
1/2	.5000	12.7000	1	1.0000	25.4000

even newspapers, metric equivalents appear in parentheses following a bit of technical data. Sometimes it is the reverse with the U.S. version in parentheses. More and more often, a metric figure alone is used. This is especially true when referring to engine sizes in liters.

You've probably encountered millimeters, liters, and a few other such units in your work. Other metric units haven't taken over quite so easily. Not many of us are comfortable with pressure readings in kilopascals rather than pounds per square inch, or kilograms instead of pounds to specify weight. We don't usually think of a car as being 5000mm long, delivering 15 l/km mileage from a 110kW engine. In the spec tables, larger sizes (bore, stroke, displacement) may be given with metric figures, but the small ones still tend to use inches—not millimeters.

The metric system is based on relationships of 10, using the following prefixes ahead of any measurement unit:

mega (M) = 10^6 = one million (1,000,000)
kilo (k) = 10^3 = one thousand (1000)
hecto (h) = 10^2 = one hundred (100)
deca (da) = 10^1 = ten (10)
deci (d) = 10^{-1} = one tenth (1/10, or 0.1)
centi (c) = 10^{-2} = one hundredth (1/100, or 0.01)
milli (m) = 10^{-3} = one thousandth (1/1000, or 0.001)
micro (μ) = 10^{-6} = one millionth (1/1,000,000)
nano (n) = 10^{-9} = one billionth (1/1,000,000,000)
pico (p) = 10^{-12} = one trillionth (1/1,000,000,000,000)

Only a few of these prefixes find common use in auto specifications: kilo-, centi-, occasionally micro-, and milli-. Every U.S. standard unit has an equivalent in the metric system. Some of the most common measurements, with formulas for changing between the two systems, are shown in Table 1-2.

We don't always think of it, but decimals are based on a "tens" relationship too. The difference is that we don't use prefixes. Instead, we speak of small numbers in hundredths (.01) or thousandths (.001) of some unit.

LENGTH AND DIAMETER

Among the most common dimensions are those for length, width or height, and diameter mea-

Table 1-2. Metric and United States Equivalents for Common Automotive Measurements.

Measurement	When you Know	Multiply by	To get an equivalent in
Length	inches (in.)	25.4	millimeters (mm)
	inches	2.54	centimeters (cm)
	miles	1.609	kilometers (km)
	millimeters	0.03937	inches
	centimeters	0.3937	inches
	kilometers	0.6214	miles
	kilometers	3280.8	feet (ft)
Area	square inches (sq. in.)	645.2	square millimeters (mm^2)
	square inches	6.4516	square centimeters (cm^2)
	square millimeters	0.00155	square inches
	square centimeters	0.155	square inches
Volume	cubic inches (ci)	16.387	cubic centimeters (cc)
	cubic centimeters	0.061	cubic inches
	liters (1 l = 1000 cc)	61.0237	cubic inches
Fluid Volume	quarts (qt)	0.946	liters (l)
	gallons (gal)	3.785	liters
	liters	1.057	quarts
	liters	0.264	U.S. gallons
	liters	0.22	Imperial gallons
	Imperial gallons	4.546	liters
Weight	pounds (lb)	0.4536	kilograms (kg)
	ounces (oz)	28.35	grams (gm)
	kilograms	2.2046	pounds
	grams	0.035	ounces (avoirdupois)
	metric tons (1 t = 1000 kg)	2204.6	pounds
Force	ounces (oz)	0.278	Newtons (N)
	pounds (lb)	4.448	Newtons
	Newtons	3.5969	ounces
	Newtons	2.248	pounds
Engine Torque	pound-feet (lb-ft)	1.3558	Newton-meters (N·m)
	Newton-meters	0.7376	pound-feet
Hardware Torque	foot-pounds (ft-lb)	0.138	kilogram-meters (kg-m)
	foot-pounds	1.3558	Newton-meters (N·m)
	inch-pounds (in-lb)	0.113	Newton-meters
	kilogram-meters	7.23	foot-pounds
	Newton-meters	0.7376	foot-pounds
	kilogram-meters	9.807	Newton-meters
	Newton-meters	0.102	kilogram-meters
Pressure	pounds per sq. inch (psi)	6.895	kilopascals (kPa)
	kilopascals	0.145	pounds/square inch
Power	horsepower (hp)	0.746	kilowatts (kW)
	kilowatts	1.341	horsepower
Velocity	miles per hour (mph)	1.609	kilometers per hour (km/h)
	kilometers per hour	0.621	miles per hour
Fuel usage	miles per gallon (mpg)	0.425	kilometers per liter (km/l)
	kilometers per liter	2.353	miles per gallon

surements of circular components. A car's wheelbase might be 108 inches (length). Its width from center to center of front tires (tread) could be 57 inches, ground clearance 5.4 inches (height).

Diameter is the distance across a circle (Fig. 1-2). It's used in specifications for cylinder bore, crankshaft journal size, piston diameter, and various other measurements inside the engine. Outside diameter (O.D.) is measured across a solid object and inside diameter (I.D.) is measured across a "hole" of some sort. *Circumference*, the distance around a circle, comes up far less often in auto specs.

In the familiar U.S. standard system, lengths and diameters are measured in inches, feet, yards, or miles:

12 inches = 1 foot
36 inches = 3 feet = 1 yard
5280 feet = 1760 yards = 1 mile

Nothing strange there. In metrics, based on relationships of 10:

1 centimeter = 10 millimeters
1 meter = 100 centimeters
1 kilometer = 1000 meters = 100,000 centimeters

For convenience, just remember that a centimeter equals about two-fifths of an inch (Fig. 1-3). Nearly all internal engine measurements are given in inches and/or millimeters (sometimes centimeters). The meter is used where the foot would otherwise serve. Kilometers are the metric substitutes for miles.

AREA AND VOLUME MEASUREMENTS

In automotive work, areas don't come up too often (only for such things as exhaust pipe capacity or glass surface area). Area is the amount of surface, measured in square units, bounded by specified borders. It's often used to show cross-sectional space (the amount of room for fluids to move through a pipe, for instance).

Area of a rectangle, or a square, is equal to its length times its width. A 5-by-3-inch rectangle has an area of 15 (3 times 5) square inches.

Area of a circle (Fig. 1-4) makes use of *pi* (π). Pi is the ratio of the distance around any circle (cir-

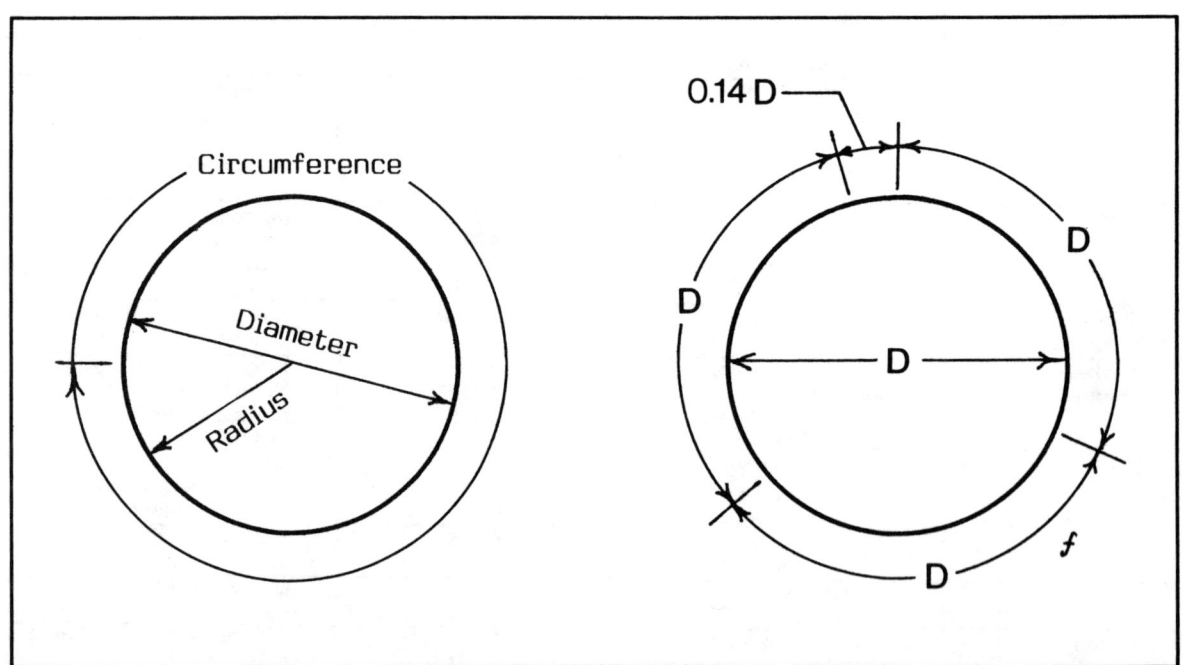

Fig. 1-2. Circumference is the distance around a circle and diameter is the distance across. Radius equals half the diameter. Pi (right) is the ratio between circumference and diameter of any circle: approximately 3.14.

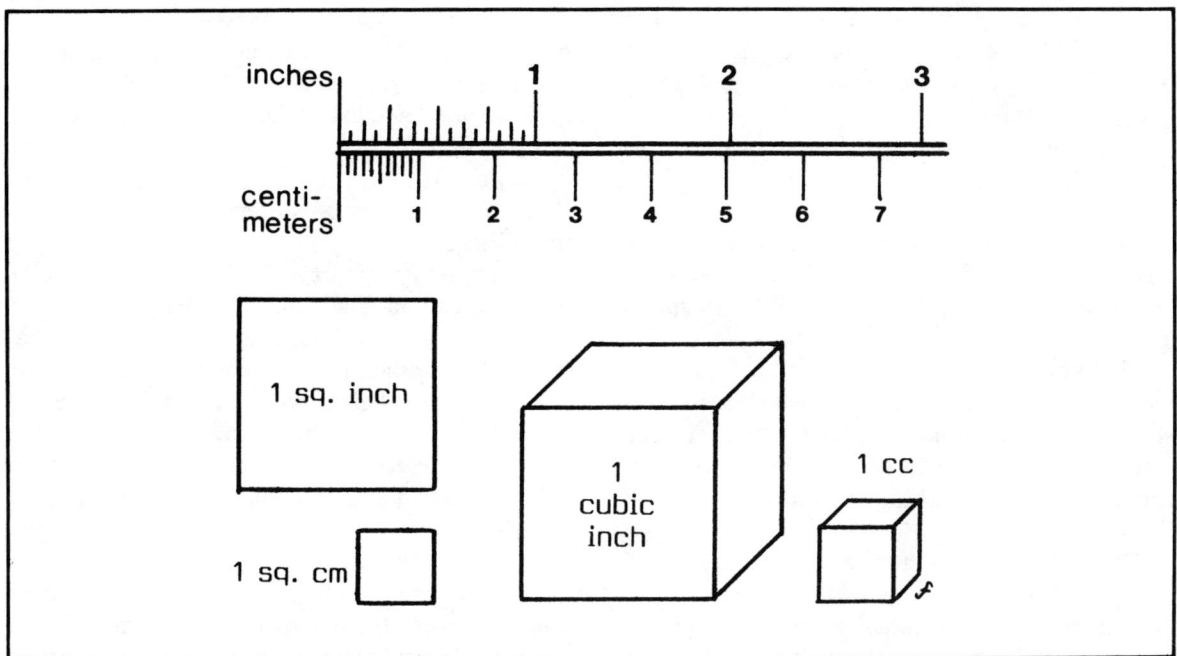

Fig. 1-3. Linear measurements of length, area, and volume are made using United States (inch) or metric units.

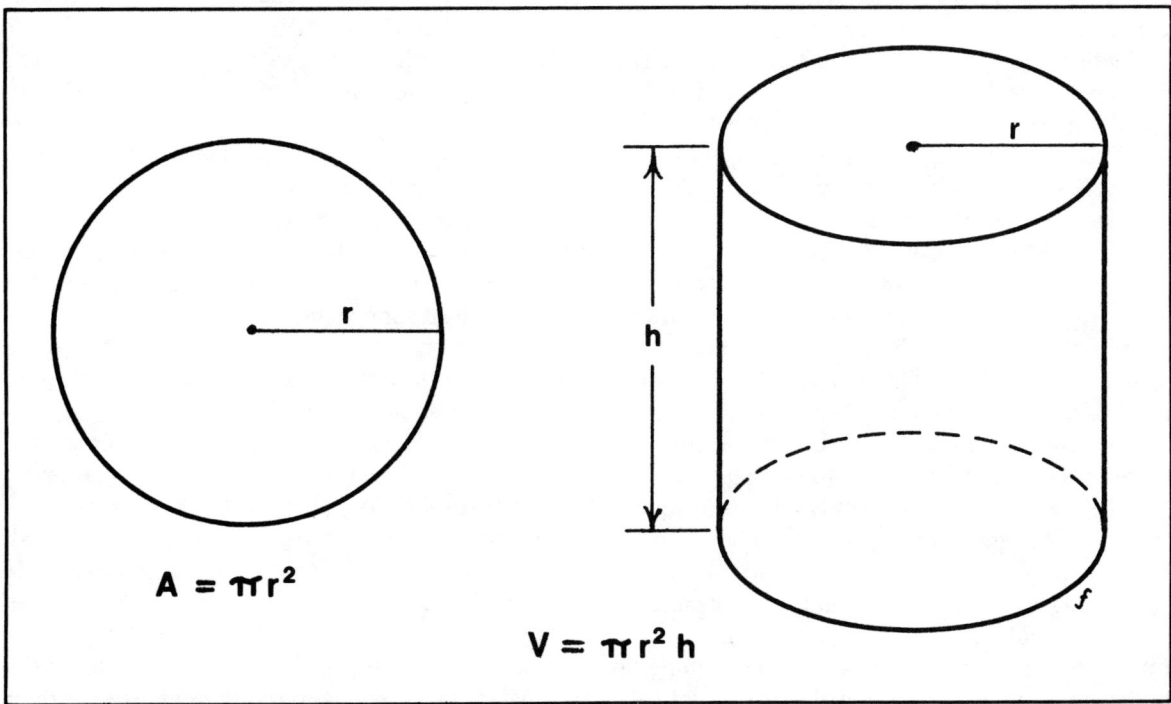

Fig. 1-4. Area of a circle (left) equals pi times the square of its radius. Volume of a cylinder (right) equals the area of the circle forming its shape, multiplied by its height.

cumference) to its distance across (diameter). Pi is a transcendental number having the value of 3.14159 . . . For our purposes, rounding off pi to 3.1416, or even 3.14 is sufficient.

Circular area equals pi multiplied by the square of the circle's radius (πr^2). Radius is half the diameter.

Example. A circle with 4-inch diameter has a radius of 2 inches (half of 4). Its area equals pi (3.14) times the square of 2 (4), or 12.56 square inches.

Volumes have a more direct application under the hood. Volume is the capacity within a solid object, measured in cubic units. The volume of an actual cube or a rectangular prism (box-shaped object) equals its length, times its width, times its height: $V = L \times W \times H$.

Far more useful is the volume of a cylinder (tin can shape). Volume is needed to compute a cylinder's displacement. Volume of a cylinder equals pi (3.14 again) multiplied by the square of the radius to obtain the area of the circular base. Then that answer is multiplied by the cylinder's height. In the engine, radius is one-half the cylinder bore. Height is identical to stroke (as we'll see in Chapter 4). The formula applies to any cylinder: $V = \pi r^2 h$.

Example. A cylinder with 3.5-inch-diameter (bore) and 3-inch height (stroke) has a volume of about 28.85 cubic inches. That's pi (3.14) multiplied by the square of the radius (1.75 times 1.75, or 3.0625), all times the height (3).

Note that, whether measured in cubic inches or cubic centimeters, actual cube shapes of air or anything else could hardly fit neatly into a circular cylinder. What we're talking about is an equivalent number of cubic units. It's as though we could pour out the contents of that engine cylinder and put them in a squarish container to be measured.

Automotive areas are nearly always in square inches, millimeters, or centimeters. Volumes are in cubic inches or centimeters (or liters). Trunk capacity is one exception (in cubic feet or meters).

Fluid volumes are different. Those are measured in quarts or gallons (U.S.), imperial quarts or gallons (Britain), or liters (metric).

ELBOW ROOM

In any discussion about automobile engines, the emphasis leans toward large numbers. We talk about motors with 350 cubic inches, 240 horsepower, 9:1 compression. Yet when long, trouble-free engine life is the goal, little numbers—the tiny clearances between moving parts—deserve the utmost attention (Fig. 1-5).

Each moving part, whether it's rotating or traveling up and down, needs a certain amount of freedom: a specified distance, or clearance, between it and adjoining components. Without that elbow room, the heat produced by friction between mating parts would halt any engine in short order. Too much clearance, on the other hand, results in noisy operation and, eventually, damaged or broken parts.

Linear clearance is the distance between one flat surface and another. It might be constant or measured when the two surfaces are farthest apart from (or closest to) each other. Circular clearance is the distance between two round objects, one fitting inside the other. That's the most common clearance measurement in engines. Either clearance might be the space between two moving parts, or between a moving and an adjoining stationary part.

Clearance isn't merely a matter of supplying a little air space for a part to slide or rotate freely. Nearly all moving parts operate with a thin film of oil on contacting surfaces. The oil provides lubrication and cooling. Insufficient oil leads to excessive friction, heat, and rapid wear. A surplus is likely to wind up out the exhaust pipe. Precise clearances allow oil to flow freely between parts, keeping oil films at their most effective thicknesses.

Perhaps I can clear up a common misconception about the clearance between two circular parts: a valve stem in its guide, or a bearing around its crankshaft journal. In theory (and in reality, if all is well), the smaller part rides surrounded by a cushion of oil—right in the center of the circular space. The two never touch.

But clearance specifications do not refer to the actual distance between the two, all around their

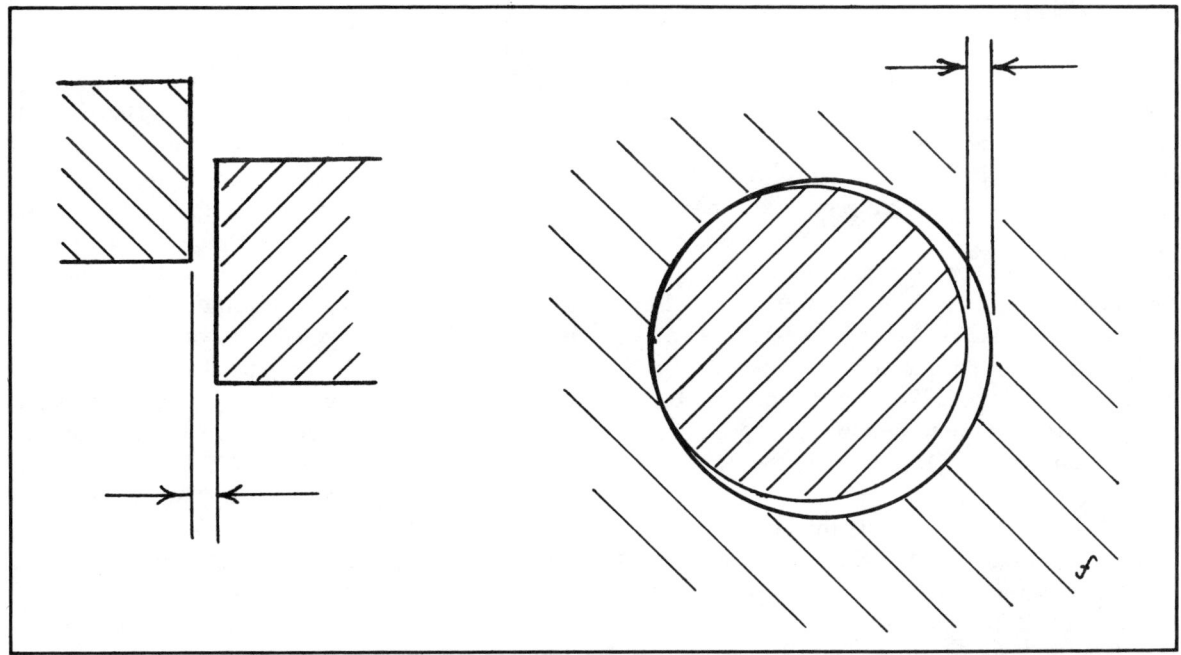

Fig. 1-5. Clearances may be linear (left), between parts with flat surfaces that slide against each other. In automotive work, circular clearances (right) are most common.

circumferences, in this ideal state. Instead, it's measured with the smaller (inner) part pushed all the way to one side, creating the largest possible space at the *other* side. A bearing clearance of .002 inch actually means there is half that distance (.001) between bearing and journal as the bearing sets perfectly centered.

Clearance is also essential to allow for the normal thermal (heat) expansion that occurs, in various metal parts, as the engine approaches operating temperature. Without sufficient clearance, an inner part could expand too much—perhaps binding or seizing. Big troubles.

Because metals expand at varying rates, clearance can change quite a bit as any engine warms up. It must be large enough to keep adjoining parts separated at all times. A piston with inadequate clearance in its bore could conceivably expand to the diameter of the cylinder, and then try to grow even larger!

Thermal expansion can be controlled in another way: by using a gap in a part. Piston rings are the best example. Unless a ring has enough space (gap) between its ends when cold, it will try to expand past the cylinder diameter, probably breaking.

Gap, then, is a linear clearance between flat surfaces. The term is most often used, though, to describe an adjustable or changing space between parts or portions of a single part. Anyone doing tune-ups is familiar with a couple of gaps: between spark plug electrodes or old-fashioned breaker point contacts. These have no relation to oil flow or thermal expansion.

We'll have a lot more to say about clearances when we peek inside the engine (Chapters 12-14). They also pop up around the carburetor (Chapter 10) and elsewhere.

THOUSANDTHS OR TIGHTER

Throughout the engine, thousandths of an inch is the standard tolerance for precision measurements. A bearing-to-journal clearance might be .002, or two thousandths of an inch; in fractional form that means 2/1000. That journal's diameter might measure 2.124 inches.

We speak of these measurements as being "to three decimal places," or "three places." Occasionally, a thousandth is called a "mil." Whatever the term, it's a size far too small to be measured without instruments or to discern with the naked eye.

Quite a few specifications, in certain manuals for modern engines, are given to even closer tolerance: in "tenths," or ten-thousandths of an inch. That's .0001 (four places) in decimal form, 1/10,000 as a fraction. To give some idea of the size, the page you are now reading is approximately .0025 inch thick (2 1/2 thousandths or 25 ten-thousands).

A "tenth," then, is mighty thin. But some commonly used instruments are quite capable of measuring with such accuracy, as we'll see in Chapter 14. In practical work, however, the ten-thousandth figure is often overlooked (with parts fitted to the nearest thousandth). A specification calling for .0022-inch clearance can usually be set to .002 without notable harm (or perhaps made just a hair larger).

Precision measurements of this sort are, of course, needed at the factory to produce internal engine specs (as discussed in Chapter 12). They're also needed for checking wear (Chapter 13) and making actual repairs. Outside the motor, the need for such precision isn't quite so pressing.

PROPORTIONS, RATIOS, AND ANGLES

Percentages come up when measuring emission levels. A car's exhaust might contain 0.1 percent (%) hydrocarbons. Because 1 percent equals one hundredth (1/100), 0.1 percent is one tenth of that, or one thousandth.

Proportions are far more common. We use them in talking about fuel economy and road speed. When you see a phrase with so many units of A *per* B, that's a proportion. Miles per hour (mph) is the most basic (the number of miles covered in one hour).

Speed of a car can be measured in miles or kilometers per hour (that of a working engine in revolutions per minute, rpm). Rotational engine speed measurements are important in discussing horsepower and torque (Chapter 5), carburetor adjustments, and ignition timing advance (Chapters 7-8).

Miles per gallon is, of course, the number of travel miles delivered by 1 gallon of fuel. Many motorists have a bit of trouble calculating mpg on a trip. Computation is foolproof, really: it's the number of miles traveled (shown by odometer), divided by the number of gallons *added* during the trip. Before starting out, though, you must begin with a full tank, and top it up again upon arrival at your destination. The amount you put in to fill up before departure is irrelevant. MPG could also be figured by starting out with a totally empty tank, but that's hardly practical. More on economy in Chapter 21.

You'll come across one other proportion, parts per million (ppm), in the discussion of emissions in Chapter 10. This refers to the number of units of a certain substance (by volume) in each million parts of the whole. One ppm equals about one drop in 16 gallons. That is a very small amount, to be sure, but with some noxious pollutants it doesn't take much to do harm.

Ratios exist between many engine and chassis parts. They're most important in describing gear action (Chapter 18) and the engine's air/fuel mixture (Chapter 10). A ratio is similar to a proportion. It shows a relationship between two amounts that are always expressed with the smaller equivalent "to one." An 18:1 ratio means the first measurement is 18 times the second (Fig. 1-6), whether in size, volume, or some other comparison.

Angles are important for understanding the relationship between piston travel, time of firing, and sequence of valve opening (Chapters 7-8). They also come up in describing the shape of a V-type engine. Small angular measurements are needed for wheel alignment (Chapter 20).

A circle, you'll recall, has 360 degrees (Fig. 1-7). One degree, then, equals 1/360th part of a circle. A right (square) angle is 90 degrees. And an

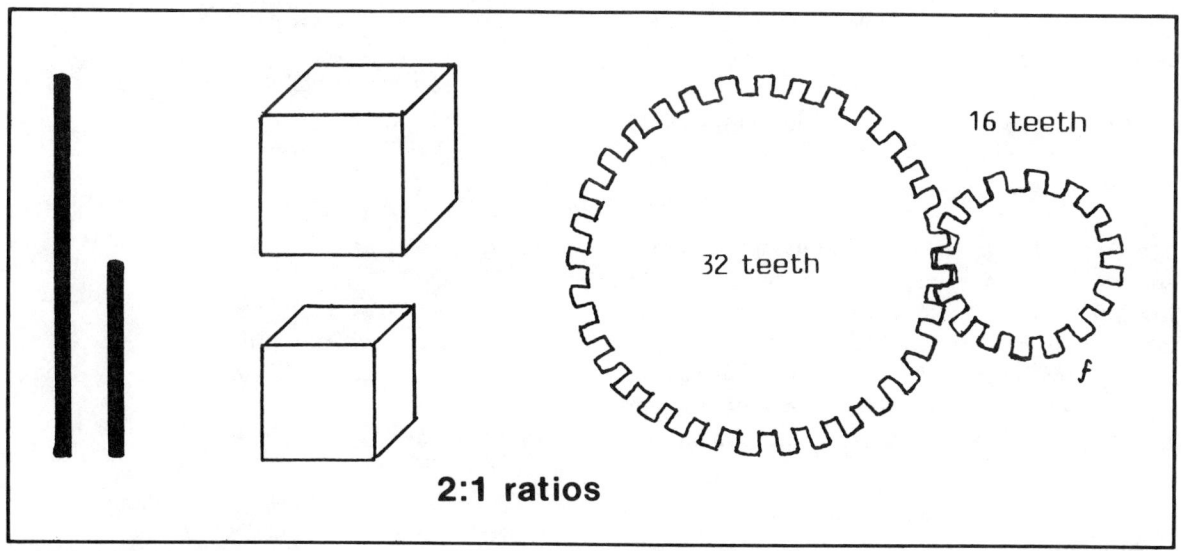

Fig. 1-6. Ratios show the relationships between two objects according to their size, weight, number of (gear) teeth or other comparative units.

engine crankshaft for any 4-cycle motor turns twice around (two times 360, or 720 degrees) for all of its cylinders to fire.

RANGES AND ABSOLUTE VALUES

Specifications are supplied in either of two modes:

1. As a single figure, which the mechanic or machinist should try to match as closely as possible in the course of repair or maintenance work.

2. A range of figures, so any measurement that falls within the stated limits is considered acceptable.

A specification for piston clearance within its cylinder, for example, might be given as .002 inch: a single figure, the "ideal" goal. Or it might be shown as .001-.003, suggesting that clearance as

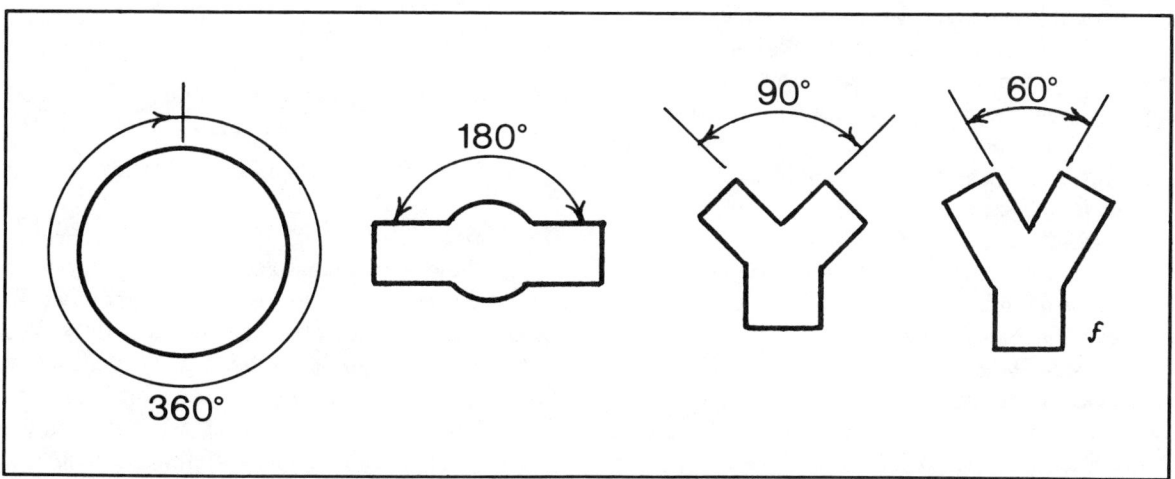

Fig. 1-7. A circle contains 360 degrees. Most modern V-6 and V-8 motors have a 90-degree angle between their banks; some have 60 degrees. Horizontally opposed engines have 180 degrees between banks (straight across).

tight as .001 inch, or as loose as .003 (a range of two thousandths) is acceptable for this engine.

Some figures, such as those for ignition timing, are nearly always given as a single figure. Others can be found as a single figure in one manual or a range in another. In those cases, it's generally wisest to shoot for the single (absolute) figure. But don't panic if your best efforts cannot produce a result precisely "on the money," so long as it's within the limits of a range stated elsewhere. Some ranges are given in ten-thousandths, such as .0013-.0025 inch, giving leeway of .0012 (more than a thousandth). The working mechanic is generally content with a reading around the middle of any range.

NUMERICAL STYLE

Abbreviations differ. Even the terms used for each unit can vary. Any dimension or specification might appear in one of several different ways in one manual or another.

The most basic example is the inch. Sometimes you will see a dimension given as 3 1/2 inches or it might be 3 1/2" (the usual symbol). In a table, the word "inch" or an abbreviation "in." might be in the column heading, rather than next to the figure itself. Periods are usually omitted from abbreviations unless the shortened version forms an actual word (as "in" does).

Metrics nearly always seem to appear with the standard abbreviation or are spelled out completely: volume, for instance, usually appears as either cc or cubic centimeter. Other measurements are not always standard. So here's a list of some common abbreviations and alternate terms (both correct and not quite) that you might encounter.

Inch: in. in In. In "
Foot: ft ft. Ft. Ft '
Mile: mi m (as in mpg) M Mi
Diameter: dia. diam.
Inside Diameter: I.D. ID
Outside Diameter: O.D. OD
Cubic Inch Displacement: cubic inch cubic-inch cu. in. in^3 CID cid ci -inch cubes (slang) inches (slang)
Cubic Centimeter: cc cm^3 cu. cm
Liter: Litre l L

Horsepower: hp h.p. HP H.P. -horse (slang) horses (slang)
Brake Horsepower: bhp BHP B.H.P.
Compression Ratio: comp. ratio c.r. C.R. cr c/r CR C/R compression
Compression Ratio (the actual ratio): 9:1 9-to-1 9 to 1 9.0 to 1 9.0:1 9 (incorrect)
Revolutions per Minute: rpm RPM revs (slang) rev/min
Miles per Hour: mph mi/hr
Feet per Second: fps ft/sec
Degree (angular): 45-degree 45° 45-deg. 45-deg
Pounds per Square Inch: psi lb/in.^{2} lbs/sq. in. pounds (incorrect but common)
Foot Pound: ft-lb ft.-lb. ft/lb pound (incorrect but common)
Pound Foot: lb-ft lb.-ft. lb/ft pounds (incorrect)
Ounce Inch: oz-in. oz.-in. oz/in.
Percent: % per cent
Number(s): No. # Nos.
Barrel: bbl bbl.
Kilogram: kg kilo
V-8 Engine: V8 V-eight vee-8
Alternating Current: AC ac a.c.
Direct Current: DC dc d.c.
Ampere: A -amp amps
Microfarad: μF mfd
Candlepower: cp c.p.

Stay alert when studying the spec tables. Be sure you know just what unit is used for each measurement, and whether its abbreviation is right or not. Some curious terms manage to crop up.

NUMBERS DON'T HAVE TO BE NUMBING

Strange how so many auto enthusiasts understand and use a variety of technical data for service work, yet are totally turned off by math in any form. We tend to learn the fear of numbers early. While a few manage to develop a love for figures (often in spite of their educational experiences), millions of otherwise capable people retain a lifelong distaste for numerical concepts.

No doubt, the national disdain for figures is

largely to blame. Even though we're hustling headlong into the computer age, bombarded by data from every direction, millions of Americans are uncomfortable with figures. They automatically doubt their abilities to decipher seemingly complex tables and charts. Underneath, many secretly may yearn for the "good old days" when ignition points were set with a business card, tappets "by ear."

In those days, nobody needed a pocket calculator to unravel the mysteries of the neighborhood supermarket.

Those days never will return. No one can tune or overhaul a modern engine without consulting the tables. Some of those tables are so awesome they are likely to give even ardent math lovers a headache.

Still, with a little patience, any of us can learn to understand and appreciate the data we have to deal with on the car and throughout our daily lives. Relax, and try to enjoy the figures. They're not here to do harm; they're here to help you with automotive tasks that should be a pleasure.

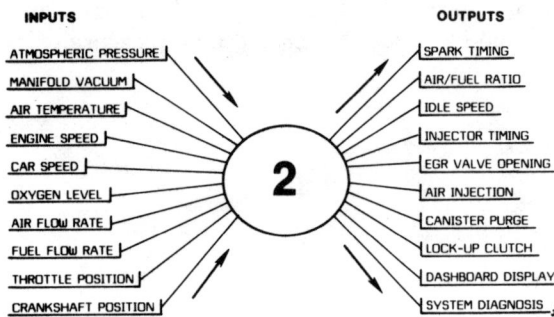

Specifications

WITHOUT A SELECTION OF SPECS, LITTLE mechanical work can be done on any engine or chassis. What is a specification? It's a published numerical value that shows the desired rating, size, speed, clearance, limit, level, or other piece of data pertaining to the car or one of its component parts.

Specs are determined, at the factory, as the car is designed and manufactured. Everything from the best idle speed for efficient operation and minimal exhaust emissions, to the size of the spark plug electrode gap that gives the most potent spark, to the preferred clearance between a bearing and journal that ensures correct oil flow, is a specification. Any mechanic who ignores a published spec does so at his or her peril. They're crucial. For modern autos, specifications are indispensable.

You'll need a set of specs when doing a Saturday-morning tune-up (Fig. 2-1) or other maintenance work. Trying a full or partial engine overhaul without specs would be disastrous. Finally, specs are nice to know about just to give a better idea of what's going on under the hood, and what can be done to enhance your car's life and reliability.

SOURCES OF SPECS

Data for performing tune-ups, overhauls, and general maintenance duties are found in a variety of manuals and other publications (Fig. 2-2). The figures themselves appear in a variety of formats. Some are fairly easy to decipher while others are guaranteed to throw the neophyte spec-searcher into a tizzy.

Factory Service Manuals

As a rule, the most definitive and thorough information comes from the car's very own factory shop (service) manual. This large manual does not come with the car when it is purchased new at the showroom. The manual must be bought separately, either through the car dealer or from a mail-order supplier associated with that automaker. In the case of earlier models, manuals can be obtained from a specialist dealer in auto literature.

Fig. 2-1. Whether performed by an amateur or professional mechanic, a tune-up demands close attention to specifications.

Fig. 2-2. Popular manuals (top) give specifications for all standard U.S. or imported car makes. Factory service manuals (bottom) contain detailed data for vehicles made during a single model year.

In addition to thousands of specs, factory manuals contain exploded drawings of operating systems, troubleshooting charts, 1-2-3 descriptions that tell how to disassemble everything, and much more. The factory book might be the only source for locations of hidden bolts, detailed wiring diagrams, information on special tools needed for certain jobs, and other crucial information.

Nowadays, it's not just one manual you have to buy. You might need (or want) a whole set. To begin with, there are always separate manuals for chassis and body work. The chassis manual usually contains data on the engine, drivetrain, steering, suspension, brakes, etc. There might be a third manual, covering accessories and electrical devices, and also a supplement (especially when one model is produced for some years). The basic manual has preliminary data for the introductory year, and supplements cover any changes made in succeeding years. There might also be supplements for high-performance or special models.

Naturally, purchasing a complete set could get expensive, but you might need only one book for the types of jobs you do yourself. Be careful to order the manual(s) that pertain to the specific car model you have. Each manufacturer puts out several sets of manuals. Once upon a time, a single manual covered all Fords in a particular year; not any more.

Although quite complete and comprehensive, the "factory" manuals are often not the easiest to use. Some are downright exasperating and confusing. If anything, there's too much information to wade through while trying to find one needed bit of data or information. That's true even though a factory manual covers only one, or a few, engine types and car models produced in a single year.

Their basic data might appear in tables, charts and lists (often the latter). Nevertheless, all the facts needed to perform a tune-up aren't always found in a single handy table. Related charts could be scattered among several sections of the manual. Some specs might be written into the text.

Worse yet, some indexes offer little help in trying to locate all the information on a specific topic. Factory manuals generally have a broad table of contents at the front. Each section is numbered and subtopics get a number within that section (6-1, 6-2, 6-3, etc.). You should also find a more detailed table of contents at the beginning of each major section and, if you're lucky, an overall index at the back of the volume. All too often, though, these "helpers" are missing or so vague that they help not at all.

Before buying any factory manual, you might want to take a good look at an example from your car's manufacturer. Many large public library systems keep at least a few current or recent factory service manuals in their automotive departments. You might ask your local dealer to let you thumb through one of its service department's copies.

Non-Factory Manuals and Charts

"Multi-make" manuals are generally easier (and cheaper) to use. Those published by Motor and Chilton are doubtless the most popular and familiar. New editions are issued each year that contain information for all American autos made during the previous seven years or so. Editions for imports and early model cars are also published.

Each volume includes nearly all the essential data for tune-up, valve work, wheel alignment, and most other chores, including total overhauls. All are found in one handy section for each car make or model. Naturally, they're not nearly so thorough as the factory books, but they are not overwhelming either.

Mult-make manuals are ordinarily arranged mainly by car make/model. Spec tables come at the beginning of each make's section, followed by repair instructions and other information. But specs for certain components—carbs, starters, alternators, brakes—may be in a separate "unit" section (not included with information for each car make). Some multi-make books are arranged by topic or system, and then subdivided by car make and year within each topic group.

Most of their specifications are in tabular form: one table for each of a dozen or so major topics (from tune-up to cooling system to valve specs). The large Mitchell manuals used by professional mechanics, as well as older National Service Data and Chilton volumes, offer lists of data under each heading rather than tables.

Chilton's and Motor's manuals are available at nearly any bookstore. The manuals are even available in a few discount stores at reduced price, especially after the new editions come out. Most libraries carry one or both. Other manuals are generally sold only to professionals (at hefty costs).

Tune-up and overhaul specs are also published in countless smaller books and charts (Fig. 2-3). Many are distributed by oil companies, aftermarket parts suppliers, test equipment manufacturers, and sundry service organizations. Some contain data for the most recent American car models, covering a specified period of years. Others contain data only on certain components (ignition or pistons), or cover only a single year or model.

Quite a few of these smaller books are given away to professional mechanics. Others are startlingly expensive. Attendees at service trade shows can wind up with several shopping bags full of such data—absolutely free. They're eagerly given by parts company representatives, hoping the recipient will be induced to use the brand name of parts advertised therein.

Some of these supplementary information sources are particularly important to owners of older models, containing data that would otherwise be hard to find. Although originally published for use in gas stations and garages, they eventually wind up in the hands of literature dealers and old-car hobbyists.

The owner's manual that comes with a new car, incidentally, has only limited value out in the garage. Years ago, when motorists did most of their own work, they contained far more data and facts, acting as combination operating/service manuals.

Fig. 2-3. Tune-up and repair specifications appear in a variety of smaller publications in addition to the big manuals.

In the appendix of this book, you'll find a list of service manual sources. Included are suppliers of factory manuals, publishers of multi-make volumes, and magazines containing ads for dealers offering early model manuals. There might also be an order blank for service manuals in the back of your car's owner's manual or you can order through the dealer.

DATA FORMATS

Specs come in several forms. Most appear in tables (Fig. 2-4). In multi-make manuals, a single table might contain all the data needed for a certain job for one car make over a several-year period. One table, for instance, could have all the tune-up specs for compact Chevrolet vehicles over a seven-year period. For valve specs, or piston clearance information, you must turn to a different table. Same thing if you want Ford information or that of a different Chevrolet series.

At the left of each table are one or more columns that list the various engine types, model

CHRYSLER CORP.—Rear Wheel Drive

VALVE SPECIFICATIONS—Continued

Year	Engine/V.I.N.	Valve Lash		Valve Angles		Valve Spring Installed Height	Valve Spring Pressure Lbs. @ In.	Stem Clearance		Stem Diameter	
		Int.	Exh.	Seat	Face			Intake	Exhaust	Intake	Exhaust
CHRYSLER & IMPERIAL—Continued											
	V8-318⑩⑪	Hydraulic①		45–45 1/2	44 1/2–45	1 11/16	177 @ 1 5/16	.001–.003	.002–.004	.372–.373	.371–.372
	V8-318⑧⑪	Hydraulic①		45–45 1/2	44 1/2–45	1 21/32	193 @ 1 1/4	.0015–.0035	.0025–.0045	.3715–.3725	.3705–.3715
1984	V8-318	Hydraulic①		45–45 1/2	44 1/2–45	1 11/16	177 @ 1 5/16	.001–.003	.002–.004	.372–.373	.371–.372
DODGE & PLYMOUTH											
1977	6-225/C,D	.010H	.020H	45	②	1 11/16	144 @ 1 5/16	.001–.003	.002–.004	.372–.373	.371–.372
	V8-318/G	Hydraulic①		45	②	1 11/16	177 @ 1 5/16	.001–.003	.002–.004	.372–.373	.371–.372
	V8-360/K,J	Hydraulic①		45	②	1 21/32	193 @ 1 1/4	.001–.003	.002–.004	.372–.373	.371–.372
	V8-360/L③	Hydraulic①		45	②	1 21/32	193 @ 1 1/4	.0015–.0035	.0025–.0045	.3715–.3725	.3705–.3715
	V8-400/N, 440/T	Hydraulic①		45	45	1 55/64	200 @ 1 7/16	.0011–.0028	④	.3723–.373	⑥
	V8-400/N, 440/U③	Hydraulic①		45	45	1 55/64	246 @ 1 23/64	.0016–.0033	⑤	.3718–.3725	⑦
1978	6-225/C,D⑨	.010H	.020H	45	②	1 21/32	144 @ 1 5/16	.001–.003	.002–.004	.372–.373	.371–.372
	V8-318/G,H	Hydraulic①		45	②	1 21/32	177 @ 1 5/16	.001–.003	.002–.004	.372–.373	.371–.372
	V8-360/K,J	Hydraulic①		45	②	1 21/32	177 @ 1 5/16	.001–.003	.002–.004	.372–.373	.371–.372
	V8-360/L③	Hydraulic①		45	②	1 21/32	193 @ 1 1/4	.0015–.0035	.0025–.0045	.3715–.3725	.3705–.3715
	V8-400/N, 440/T	Hydraulic①		45	45	1 55/64	200 @ 1 7/16	.0011–.0028	④	.3723–.3730	⑥
	V8-400/N, 440/U③	Hydraulic①		45	45	1 55/64	246 @ 1 23/64	.0016–.0033	⑤	.3718–.3725	⑦
1979–80	6-225/C,D	.010H	.020H	45	②	1 11/16	144 @ 1 5/16	.001–.003	.002–.004	.372–.373	.371–.372
	V8-318/G,H	Hydraulic①		45	45	1 11/16	177 @ 1 5/16	.001–.003	.002–.004	.372–.373	.371–.372
	V8-360/K,J	Hydraulic①		45	45	1 11/16	177 @ 1 5/16	.001–.003	.002–.004	.372–.373	.371–.372
	V8-360/L③	Hydraulic①		45	45	1 21/32	193 @ 1 1/4	.0015–.0035	.0025–.0045	.3715–.3725	.3705–.3715
1981–83	6-225/E,H	Hydraulic①		45	②	1 11/16	144 @ 1 5/16	.001–.003	.002–.004	.372–.373	.371–.372
	V8-318/K,M,P	Hydraulic①		45–45 1/2	44 1/2–45	1 11/16	177 @ 1 5/16	.001–.003	.002–.004	.372–.373	.371–.372
1984	V8-318	Hydraulic①		45–45 1/2	44 1/2–45	1 11/16	177 @ 1 5/16	.001–.003	.002–.004	.372–.373	.371–.372

①—No adjustment.
②—Intake 45°, exhaust 43°.
③—High Performance.
④—Hot end .0021–.0038, Cold end .0011–.0028.
⑤—Hot end .0026–.0043, Cold end .0016–.0033.
⑥—Hot end 3713–.372, Cold end .3723–.373.
⑦—Hot end .3708–.3715, Cold end .3718–.3725.
⑧—With Electronic Fuel Injection.
⑨—Some Aspen & Volaré models w/6-225 2 bar. carb. will be equipped w/hydraulic lifters which cannot be adjusted.
⑩—Less Electronic Fuel Injection.
⑪—Refer to General Engine Specifications for V.I.N. code.

Fig. 2-4. A typical valve specification table from a multimake manual. (Reproduced from MOTOR Auto Repair Manual Copyright © 1984 by permission of Hearst Business Publishing, a division of the Hearst Corporation.)

SPECIFICATIONS

GENERAL SPECIFICATIONS

DISPLACEMENT	2 3L
NUMBERS OF CYLINDERS	4
BORE AND STROKE	3.780 x 3.126
FIRING ORDER	1-3-4-2
OIL PRESSURE (HOT @ 2000 RPM)	40-60
DRIVE BELT TENSION	1

CYLINDER HEAD AND VALVE TRAIN

COMBUSTION CHAMBER VOLUME (cc)	59.55-62 55
VALVE GUIDE BORE DIAMETER	0.3433-0.3443
VALVE SEATS	
Width — Intake	.060-.080
Width — Exhaust	.070-.090
Angle	45°
RUNOUT LIMIT (T.I.R. MAX.)	0.0016
VALVE ARRANGEMENT (Front to Rear)	E-I-E-I-E-I-E-I
VALVE LASH ADJUSTER BORE DIAMETER	0.8430-0.9449
VALVE STEM TO GUIDE CLEARANCE	
Intake	0.0010-0.0027
Exhaust	0.0015-0.0032
Service Clearance Limit	0.0055 Max.
VALVE HEAD DIAMETER	
Intake	1.730-1.740
Exhaust	1.49-1.51
VALVE FACE RUNOUT LIMIT	0.002 Max.
VALVE FACE ANGLE LIMIT	44°
VALVE STEM DIAMETER (STANDARD)	
Intake	.3416-.3423
Exhaust	.3411-.3418
(0.015 Oversize)	
Intake	.3566-.3573
Exhaust	.3561-.3568
(0.030 Oversize)	
Intake	.3716-.3723
Exhaust	.3711-.3718
VALVE SPRINGS	
Compression Pressure (Lb. @ Spec. Length)	
Intake and Exhaust (Installed Load)	71-79 @ 1.52
Exhaust and Intake Valve (Open Load)	1.52-1.56 @ 1.52
Free Length (Approximate)	1.877
Assembled Height	1-17/32" - 1-19/32"
Service Limit	5% Pressure Loss @ Specified Length
Out of Square Service Limit	5/64 (0.078)
ROCKER ARM (Cam Follower)	
Ratio	1.64:1
VALVE TAPPET, LIFTER OR ADJUSTER	
Diameter (Standard)	0.8422-0.8427
Clearance-to-Bore	0.0007-0.0027
Service Limit	0.005 Max.
Hydraulic Leakdown Rate ②	2-8 Seconds
Collapsed Tappet Gap	
Allowable	0.035-0.055 @ Cam
Desired	0.040-0.050 @ Cam

CAMSHAFT

LOBE LIFT	
Intake	.2381
Exhaust	.2381
Allowable Lobe Lift Loss	0.005 Max.
THEORETICAL VALVE LIFT @ ZERO LASH	
Intake	.390
Exhaust	.390
END PLAY	0.001-0.007
Service Limit	0.009
JOURNAL-TO-BEARING CLEARANCE	0.001-0.003
Service Limit	0.006

CAMSHAFT (Continued)

JOURNAL DIAMETER	
#1	1.7713-1.7720
#2	1.7713-1.7720
#3	1.7713-1.7720
#4	1.7713-1.7720
Runout Limit	0.005 Max. T.I.R.
Out-of-Round Limit	0.0005 In. Max.
Front Bearing Location	③ 0.000-0.010

CYLINDER BLOCK

HEAD GASKET SURFACE FLATNESS	0.003 in any 6"-0.006 overall
HEAD GASKET SURFACE FINISH (RMS)	60-150
CYLINDER BORE	
Diameter	3.7795-3.7831
Surface Finish (RMS)	18-38
Out-of-Round Limit	0.0015
Out-of-Round Service Limit	0.005
Taper Service Limit	0.010
MAIN BEARING BORE DIAMETER	2.5902-2.5910
DISTRIBUTOR SHAFT BEARING BORE DIAMETER	.5155-.5170

CRANKSHAFT, FLYWHEEL AND CONNECTING ROD

MAIN BEARING JOURNAL DIAMETER	2.399-2.3982
Out-of-Round Limit	0.0006 Max.
Taper Limit	0.0006 Per Inch
Journal Runout Limit	0.002 Max.
Surface Finish (RMS)	12 Max.
Runout Service Limit	0.005
THRUST BEARING JOURNAL	
Length	1.2010-1.1990
CONNECTING ROD JOURNAL	
Diameter	2.0465-2.0472
Out-of-Round Limit	0.0006 Max.
Taper Limit	0.0006 Per Inch Max.
Surface Finish (RMS)	12 Max.
MAIN BEARING THRUST FACE	
Surface Finish (RMS)	35 Front 25 Rear (Max.)
Runout Limit	0.001 Max.
FLYWHEEL CLUTCH FACE	
Runout Limit	0.005
FLYWHEEL RING GEAR LATERAL RUNOUT (T.I.R.)	
Standard Transmission	0.025
Automatic Transmission	0.060
CRANKSHAFT FREE END PLAY LIMIT	0.004-0.008
Service Limit	0.012
AUXILIARY SHAFT END PLAY	0.001-0.007
CONNECTING ROD BEARINGS	
Clearance Crankshaft — Desired	0.0008-0.0015
— Allowable	0.0008-0.0026
Bearing Wall Thickness (Standard) ④	0.0619-0.0624
MAIN BEARINGS	
Clearance to Crankshaft — Desired	0.0008-0.0015
— Allowable	0.0008-0.0026
Bearing Wall Thickness (Standard) ④	0.0956-0.0951
AUXILIARY SHAFT BEARINGS	
Clearance to Shaft	0.0006-0.0026
CONNECTING ROD	
Piston Pin Bore Diameter	.9096-.9012
Crankshaft Bearing Bore Diameter	2.1720-2.1728
Out-of-Round Limit	0.0004
Taper Limit	0.0004
Length (Center-to-Center)	5.2031-5.2063
Alignment (Bore-to-Bore Max. Difference) ⑤	
Twist	0.024
Bend	0.012
Side Clearance (Assembled to Crank)	
Standard	0.0035-0.0105
Service Limit	0.014

Fig. 2-5. A typical engine specification chart from a factory service manual. Note the detailed information. (Reproduced by permission of Ford Motor Company.)

years, or other factors that differentiate one car from another. Across the top are column headings for the specs themselves. You have to isolate the line in the table that applies to your vehicle, and then follow across to the column that gives the figure you need.

Tables seem to stump some mechanics, but with a bit of practice, they're actually the most convenient formats to read and use. Once you're familiar with locating information in a table, extracting similar data from a chart or other listing is a snap. We'll be concentrating on the tabular formats. Learning to determine which horizontal line in a given table will yield the information needed, and what the values and terms in each column mean.

Other manuals use charts of various types to supply the data (Fig. 2-5). Same idea but without the need for following a maze of figures across many columns. Information is separated by car make and model, and by category of work, just like a table. But the figures themselves are listed below separate headings for spark plug gap, camber, charging voltage, or whatever. Some mechanics prefer charts. If you're one of them, select a manual using that style.

In certain manuals, some specifications aren't in any type of table or chart or list, but are buried in the text. That's not a problem if you have the time and interest to study it all, but it is frustrating when you simply want to locate a certain figure.

SPECS YOU'LL NEED TO KNOW

Such a variety in the spec tables! Dozens of tiny clearances inside the engine; gaps and spaces to be measured and adjusted; voltages and resistances; engine speeds and gear backlash. An awful lot of figures. How many do you really need?

The list begins in Chapter 4 with some general facts that every knowledgeable motorist should know about: engine size, cylinder bore and stroke, compression ratio. Few of us ever have to do anything about these general specs. They simply aid in identifying the engine we're working on, and tell how it compares with others. Chapter 5 goes a step further by explaining the measurement of horsepower, torque, and related data.

Tuning a modern engine is impossible without specs. These include figures for spark-plug gap, firing order, ignition timing, idle speeds, fuel pump pressure, and valve lash. They're covered in Chapters 7 and 8.

Electrical tests and problems have a set of figures of their own: voltages, current flow, battery capacities, resistances, starter and alternator ratings. Chapter 6 gets into those.

Chapter 10 deals with details of the carburetor beyond mere idle speed adjustments. Chapters 12-14 take you inside the engine for a look at the precision measurements involved with valves, pistons, bearings, camshafts and crankshafts. They're essential for overhauls.

Finally, specifications outside the engine. They're needed when dealing with the driveline (transmission, clutch, rear end), steering, and brakes. Most of these consist of adjustments, and checking for wear.

Although specs are crucial today, their importance wasn't always so apparent. Tolerances have grown far tighter during the past few decades. Guesswork that might have been acceptable 20, 40 or 60 years ago just won't do any longer.

As crucial as clearances are, for example, they haven't always received serious attention from mechanics—or even from the factories. In the early days of motoring, precise clearance specifications weren't even published in service manuals. Ford, for one, advised owners and mechanics working on Model T engines to adjust crankshaft bearings by "feel," tightening them just enough to feel a bit snug when cranking the engine by hand. Point gaps and tappet clearances were routinely adjusted to the thickness of a business card or a dime.

The importance of measured clearances was hardly unknown. And the desirability of interchangeable parts, produced to specified, precise sizes (rather than being individually hand-fitted) had been clearly demonstrated in 1908. In that year, Henry Leland astonished the Royal Automobile Club of England by having three Cadillacs disassembled, mixing their parts, and putting them back together. All three ran beautifully in a 500-mile endurance run.

Nevertheless, considerable leeway in measurements—in the field if not at the factory—remained the rule for some years even for engines far more complex than the Ford four. By the 1920s and 1930s, though—as machining techniques advanced and engineers determined optimum clearances for closer-fitting engine parts—manuals were supplying more and more data. Shop manuals for recent models contain precise specifications for virtually every mechanical part.

WHICH LINE IS IT?

Thirty years ago or more, auto service manuals were a lot easier to understand and use. Perhaps, in a similar way, life was considerably less complex. Each automaker offered only a few engine types (maybe just one), one or two transmission choices, a limited selection of drive gear ratios, and so on.

That car's shop manual contained a far smaller array of figures to reflect the more limited choices. So did the multi-make service manuals of the day. Locating the correct line in a table, or the appropriate paragraph in the text, was quite a bit simpler.

By the 1960s, the manufacturers were offering a big selection of engine styles and sizes, plus a huge variety of options that affected specifications. Thus, a spec table had to contain many more lines, many more figures—and the repair person had to worry more about finding and using the right one.

The secret? Nothing mysterious of course. To begin with, you simply had to know exactly which engine was in the car setting in front of you. If it's your own car and you've done some work on it before, you probably know the answer without a doubt. If you're working on someone else's vehicle or on a newly purchased car, some investigation is in order before picking up a wrench for the first time.

As we shall see in Chapter 3, identifying most engines and car models isn't too difficult. It's just a matter of deciphering its serial number. Actually, mechanics in the old days sometimes had far greater problems when facing an unfamiliar auto. The serial numbers contained nothing but—well, serial numbers.

Modern manuals offer one other bit of confusion that didn't exist in the past. Because so many automakers offer the same basic car under different names, a single table may be used for half a dozen different makes—all with the same specs, or perhaps with minor differences. Years ago a Ford was a Ford; a Plymouth a Plymouth. There were similarities between a full-size Chevrolet and a Pontiac, let's say, but their specs were different, and the specs were found in different places.

It's different for manuals of the 1970s and 1980s. These vehicles that use the same basic chassis and/or body structure, regardless of make, might be grouped together into one factory manual or one section of a multi-make manual (Fig. 2-6). One volume or section may contain all GM full-size models, another its intermediates, yet another the subcompacts under the GM banner. The GM "A" and "X" bodies could be in one section, "F" bodies in another, and so on. All the brand names for each style are bunched together. Any exceptions that apply to certain makes/models are indicated as footnotes.

Chevrolet's Cavalier, for example, has far more in common with Buick's Skyhawk, Cadillac's Cimarron, the Olds Firenza and Pontiac Sunbird than it has with other Chevrolet models. Its specs, then, are often found in a section of the manual devoted to all five subcompact makes.

Overlap between model years presents some problems, too. Some specifications might differ between a 1983, '84 and '85 Cavalier. Other specs could be the same for all three, appearing on a single line in a table. Certain specifications remain the same year after year; others change with each new model.

High-performance and special models have their own problems. Data might not appear in a basic spec table for that make; it might be preliminary (and inaccurate) or incomplete. At times, a manual from a later year gives better information. Select-

FORD MUSTANG & PINTO • MERCURY BOBCAT & CAPRI
TUNE UP SPECIFICATIONS—Continued

The following specifications are published from the latest information available. This data should be used only in the absence of a decal affixed in the engine compartment.

★ When using a timing light, disconnect vacuum hose or tube at distributor and plug opening in hose or tube so idle speed will not be affected.
● When checking compression, lowest cylinder must be within 75 percent of highest.
▲ Before removing wires from distributor cap, determine location of the No. 1 wire in cap, as distributor position may have been altered from that shown at the end of this chart.

Spark plug types shown in this chart are recommendations of the original vehicle manufacturer and not MOTOR. Check local sources for other spark plug manufacturers listings.

Year & Engine/V.I.N.	Spark Plug Type	Gap	Firing Order Fig. ▲	Ignition Timing BTDC①★ Man. Trans.	Ignition Timing BTDC①★ Auto. Trans.	Mark Fig.	Curb Idle Speed② Man. Trans.	Curb Idle Speed② Auto. Trans.	Fast Idle Speed Man. Trans.	Fast Idle Speed Auto. Trans.	Fuel Pump Pressure
1982—Continued											
4-140/A Calif.⑦⑬	AWSF-42	.034	G	4°	12°	E	850	800D	1600③	1800③	5-7④
4-140/A High Alt. ㉜		.034	G	6°	12°	E	850	800D	1800③	2000③	5-7④
6-200/B	BSF-92	.050	A	—	㉘	B	—	450/600D	—	2000③	5-7
V8-255/D Exc. High Alt.	ASF-52	.050	D	—	8°	C	—	500/700D	—	1500③	6-8
V8-255/D High Alt.	ASF-52	.050	D	—	14°	C	—	500/700D	—	1600③	6-8
V8-302/F	ASF-42	.044	I	12°	—	C	700/900	—	1500③	—	6-8
1983											
4-140/A㉓	AWSF-44	.044	G	9°	9°	E	850	800D	1800③	2000③	5-7
4-140/W㉖	AWSF-32	.034	G	10°	—	E	825-975㊵	—	㉝	—	—
V6-232/3 Exc. Calif. & High Alt.	AWSF-52	.044	J	—	10°	K	—	㉝	—	2200③	6-8㊸
V6-232/3 Calif.	AWSF-52	.044	J	—	8°	K	—	㉝	—	2200③	6-8㊸
V6-232/3 High Alt.	AWSF-52	.044	J	—	18°	K	—	㉝	—	2100③	6-8㊸
V8-302/F	ASF-42	.044	I	10°	—	C	700	—	2400③	—	6-8
1984											
4-140/A㉓	AWSF-44	.044	G	—	—	E	850	750D	—	—	5.5-6.5
4-140/W㉖	AWSF-32	.034	G	—	—	E	—	—	—	—	—
V6-232/3	AWSF-54	.044	J	—	—	K	—	—	—	—	㉝
V8-302/M㊹	ASF-42	.044	I	—	—	C	700	—	—	—	6.5-8.0
V8-302/M㊹	ASF-42	.044	I	—	—	C	—	—	—	—	—

①—B.T.D.C.—Before top dead center.
②—Idle speed on manual trans. vehicles is adjusted in Neutral & on auto. trans. equipped vehicles is adjusted in Drive unless otherwise specified. Where two idle speeds are listed, the higher speed is with the A/C or throttle solenoid energized.
③—On kickdown step of cam.
④—With pump to fuel tank line pinched off & a new fuel filter installed.
⑤—On high step of fast idle cam.
⑥—Except calibration code 1-12B-R10, 10° BTDC; calibration code, 1-12B-R10, 12° BTDC.
⑦—Refer to engine calibration code on engine identification label located at rear of left valve cover on V6 & V8 engines, on front of valve cover on inline 4 & 6 cyl. engines. The calibration code is located on the label after the engine codes number & is preceded by the letter C & the revision code is located below the calibration code is preceded by the letter R.
⑧—Except calibration code 7-2B-R16, 1600 RPM; calibration code 7-2B-R16, 1800 RPM.
⑨—Except calibration code 7-2N-R1, 800/850 RPM; calibration code 7-2N-R1, 650/850 RPM.
⑩—Calibration code 7-1X-RO, 550/750D RPM; 7-1X-R10, 550/800D RPM.
⑪—Calibration code 7-1X-RO, 1800 RPM; 7-1X-R10, 2000 RPM.
⑫—Calibration code 7-3A-R2.
⑬—Calibration codes, man. trans. 7-3A-R10; auto. trans. 7-4A-R2.
⑭—Calibration code 7-11X-R2.
⑮—Calibration codes 7-11X-R4 & 7-11X-R6.
⑯—Calibration codes, man. trans. 8-2A-RO & 8-2A-R10; auto. trans. 8-1A-RO & 8-1B-R10.
⑰—Calibration code 8-2A-RO, 850 RPM; 8-2A-R10, 900 RPM.
⑱—Calibration codes, man. trans., 8-2B-RO auto trans., 8-2B-RO & 8-2B-R11.
⑲—Calibration codes, man. trans., 8-2N-RO & 8-2N-R11; auto. trans., 8-1N-RO.
⑳—Calibration code 8-2N-RO, 650/900 RPM, & 8-2N-R11, 600/850 RPM.
㉑—Calibration codes, man. trans. 8-2P-RO & 8-2T-RO; auto. trans., 8-1R-R1.
㉒—With throttle solenoid energized. Higher idle speed is with A/C on & compressor clutch de-energized, if equipped.
㉓—Calibration codes 8-10A-RO, 900/975 RPM; 8-10A-R10, 800/875 RPM.
㉔—Calibration codes 8-31A-RO, 700/775D RPM; 8-31A-R10, 700/825 RPM.
㉕—Except turbocharged engine.
㉖—Turbocharged engine.
㉗—ASF-52 or ARF-52.
㉘—ASF-52-6 or ARF-52-6.
㉙—Calibration codes 9-2A-RO, 9-2B-RO, 1800 RPM; calibration codes 9-2C-RO & 9-2D-RO, 1600 RPM.
㉚—Except Bobcat & Pinto, 1800 RPM; Bobcat & Pinto, 1850 RPM.
㉛—Except Calif., 1800 RPM; California, 1850 RPM.
㉜—Calibration code 0-16A-R12.
㉝—If mileage on vehicle is less than 100 mi., set idle speed 100 RPM less than specified.
㉞—Calibration code 9-4A-RO, 9° BTDC; calibration codes 9-4A-R10A & 9-4A-R10N, 6° BTDC.
㉟—Models less Thermactor air pump.
㊱—Models with Thermactor air pump.
㊲—Calibration code, 9-21B-R10.
㊳—Calibration codes, 0-21A-RO & 0-21B-RO & R10.
㊴—Except calibration code 0-1H-R20, 2000 RPM; calibration code 0-1H-R20, 2150 RPM.
㊵—Manual trans., 5-7 psi.; auto. trans. models use an electric fuel pump.
㊶—Calibration code 0-15-R15, 2000 RPM; calibration code 0-15-R15, 2150 RPM.
㊷—Calibration code 0-27A-R3, 7° BTDC; calibration code 0-27A-R10, 10° BTDC.
㊸—Calibration code 0-6A-RO, 10° BTDC; calibration code 0-6A-R1, 12° BTDC.
㊹—Except calibration code 0-7P-R11, 10° BTDC; Continued

Fig. 2-6. A single table in multimake manual may cover several car makes and models. (Reproduced from *MOTOR Auto Repair Manual* Copyright © 1984 by permission of Hearst Business Publishing, a division of the Hearst Corporation.)

ing the correct spec, then, boils down to:

1. Choosing the right manual for the car you're working on.
2. Turning to the right section for information on the correct make/model, and the desired topic.
3. Choosing the correct page or table in that section.
4. Deducing the one and only correct line in that table or chart.

Before starting to work, always double check to be sure you're following the right line—of the right table—containing the true figures for your engine. Some specs do apply to all of a manufacturer's engines in a given year or all in a given displacement size. Others vary widely. Trying to set timing or adjust valves with the wrong data endangers your engine's continued good health.

NOTICE ALL THE FOOTNOTES?

Our spec tables and charts wouldn't be quite so forbidding if their figures were confined within the lines. Instead, exceptions are almost the rule in modern manuals, and especially for manuals with specs for many car makes.

GM "F" BODY

TUNE-UP SPECIFICATIONS
Firebird

Year	Engine V.I.N. Code	Engine No. of Cyl.- Displacement (Cu. In.)	Engine Manufacturer	Spark Plugs Type	Gap (in.)	Ignition Timing (deg)③④ Man Trans	Auto Trans	Intake Valve Opens (deg)⑤	Fuel Pump Pressure (psi)	Idle Speed (rpm)③④ Man Trans	Auto Trans
'84	L	6-173HO	Chev.	R-42CTS	0.045	⑰	⑰	NA	6–7½	⑰	⑰
	H	8-305	Chev.	R-45TS	0.045	⑰	⑰	NA	5.5–6.5	⑰	⑰
	7	8-305	Chev.	R-45TS⑯	0.045	⑰	⑰	NA	9–13	⑰	⑰
	S	8-305	Chev.	R-45TS	0.045	⑰	⑰	NA	9–13	⑰	⑰
	2	4-151	Pont.	R-44TSX	0.060	⑰	⑰	NA	9–13	⑰	⑰
	F	4-151	Pont.	R-44TSX	0.060	⑰	⑰	NA	5½–6½	⑰	⑰
	1	6-173	Chev.	R-43CTS	0.045	⑰	⑰	NA	5½–6½	⑰	⑰
	L	6-173	Chev.	R-42CTS	0.045	⑰	⑰	NA	6–7½	⑰	⑰
	H	8-305	Chev.	R-45TS	0.045	⑰	⑰	NA	5½–6½	⑰	⑰
	7	8-305	Chev.	R-45TS	0.045	⑰	⑰	NA	9–13	⑰	⑰
	S	8-305	Chev.	R-45TS	0.045	⑰	⑰	NA	9–13	⑰	⑰

NOTE: The underhood specifications sticker often reflects tune-up specification changes made during the production run. Sticker figures must always be used if they disagree with those in this chart. Part numbers in this chart are not recommendations by Chilton for any product by brand name.

All models use electronic ignition systems.
B Before Top Dead Center
TDC Top Dead Center
—Not applicable
NA—Not available
① Lower figure indicates idle speed with solenoid disconnected
② High altitude and California R-45TSX
③ See text for procedure
④ Figure in parentheses indicates California engine
⑤ All figures are in degrees Before Top Dead Center. Where two figures appear, the first represents timing with manual transmission, the second with automatic transmission
⑥ 31—Manual, 27—Auto
⑦ High altitude—R-45SX
⑧ 650 rpm w/AC on
⑨ Manual—21
   Auto—29
   Trans Am—16
⑩ On air conditioned models:
   550 w/AC off
   650 w/AC on
⑪ High performance—27
⑫ All M/T and low altitude A/T—R-45TS, gap 0.040
⑬ Trans Am only
⑭ With performance package
⑮ Turbocharged engine
⑯ R-44TS if a colder plug is needed
⑰ These functions are controlled by the emissions computer. In rare instances when adjustment is necessary, it should be performed by a professional technician.

Fig. 2-7. Footnotes to tables contain a variety of exceptions and special instructions. (From *Chilton's Auto Repair Manual 1984*. Reprinted with permission of the publisher, Chilton Book Company, Radnor, PA 19089.)

These exceptions are dealt with by footnotes: brief numbered (or lettered) notations at the bottom of a table or chart (Fig. 2-7). Following across the correct line for your engine, you find what should be the correct figure for ignition timing, idle rpm, or whatever. But there's a tiny number alongside the listed figure or no figure at all in the allotted space, but only that tiny number.

Numbered notes within a table point out exceptions and special instructions that apply only to that engine or car model. The figure shown in the table might apply to most engines of the type described in the left-hand column. But there could be an alternate spec for those:

☐ Sold in California, with its stringent emission standards;

☐ With automatic transmission rather than manual (or vice versa);

☐ With turbochargers or other high-performance components;

☐ With air conditioning, an air pump, or other device that wasn't installed on every engine of its type;

☐ Produced very early (or late) in the model year, with specs that differ from the others;

☐ Installed in certain models or body styles (an engine mounted in a station wagon could have specs different from the same motor in a sedan or coupe).

These and dozens of other reasons demand that a certain vehicle be set to slightly different specs than normal. So watch out for any footnotes that read "All *except* so-and-so," or "model so-and-so *only*," or any words of that sort. Be sure you know whether your vehicle is the exception or the one that's standard.

Some footnotes apply to an entire column of data. These are used to explain an abbreviation, clarify some preliminary step that's needed, and give similar general instructions.

UNRAVELING THE MAZE

At first glance, spec tables appear awesome to the uninitiated. Even number lovers can wind up with a headache. Just don't let yourself be thrown by the sight of so many figures. Patience does lead to comprehension.

The most useful tip? Use a long card or piece of paper (or a ruler) when working with any table. Position it just beneath the line pertaining to your car. You can follow along each column without picking up a wrong figure from a line above or below. No single trick will do more to ensure accurate spec work.

Practice and study help. Study any manuals you have around the house, and others that you come across. Thumb through the pages. Pay attention to chapter and system organization. Follow spec tables as you go through each chapter in this book. By the time you've finished, you'll have a terrific understanding of how they're laid out, and what data is contained within each one.

Different though they may appear, all of these manuals and charts are trying to convey the same information. Only the presentation varies. One exception is that it's hardly unheard of to come across conflicting (or missing) data. A spark-plug gap could be listed as .035 inch in one table and .040 in another. One manual might recommend setting tappets "cold" to .010 inch while another advises a "hot" (engine running) adjustment to .012.

Some inconsistencies are simple misprints (though most manuals are carefully prepared and typographical errors are not numerous). Others are based on more up-to-date information or thinking. Still others reflect a divergence of opinion.

Which is "correct?" As a rule, relying on the "factory" manual is best, but double-checking against a couple of others when in doubt is prudent. A factory manual could be published and distributed before all the facts and troubles about a new model have been investigated. A multi-make book, produced a little later, might be more reliable. There might also be a supplement to the basic factory manual that contains more up-to-date data.

One positive note is that, most of the time, finding data for a single engine is a lot easier than it sounds here. I want to prepare you for the worst, but much of your spec-study duty will go off without a hitch.

EARLY MODEL SPEC PROBLEMS

Owners of older cars face special problems in obtaining and understanding specs. The problem isn't so much for cars that are, say, 10 or 20 years old. Facts are readily available for them, and for most vehicles going back to the 1940s (even 1930s).

Both Chilton and Motor publish reprint editions of several early model manuals. Those from Chilton cover 1940-53, 1954-63 and 1964-71. Motor's manuals can be obtained with specs for cars as far back as 1935-53. The vast majority of service work can be handled using specs contained in these readily available volumes.

Certain older factory manuals are available, either in bound or microfilm form, from sources listed in the Appendix. Often, though, a better choice is dealing with one of the specialty literature dealers. They handle both factory and multi-make manuals going back to the beginning. Prices—except for certain rare or early volumes—usually aren't too bad.

A surprising number of early service manuals can be found in some public libraries. Detroit's library, not surprisingly, has an enormous collection. Quite a few manuals can be found in other cities as well, including Chicago, New York, Los Angeles, and many smaller communities. If you live in a non-urban area, some publication might be available through interlibrary loan, either free or for minimal cost.

Early model manuals contain nothing about

TUNE UP SPECIFICATIONS

Year	Model	Spark Plugs Type	Spark Plugs Gap, Inch	Breaker Gap, Inch Note A	Cam Angle, Degrees	Firing Order	Ignition Timing Mark and Location	Battery Terminal Grounded	Engine Idle Speed, R.P.M. Synchromesh Transmission	Engine Idle Speed, R.P.M. Automatic Transmission	Cylinder Head Torque, Lbs. Ft.
1935	C6	AC-46	.025	.020	35-38	153624	B	Positive	300	...	65-70
	CZ, C1	AC-46	.025	.017	27-30	16258374	B	Positive	300	...	65-70
	C2, C3	AC-46	.025	.017	27-30	16258374	C	Positive	300	...	65-70
1936	C7	AC-46	.025	.020	35-38	153624	B	Positive	300	...	65-70
	C8, C9	AC-46	.025	.017	27-30	16258374	B	Positive	300	...	65-70
	C10, C11	AC-46	.025	.017	27-30	16258374	C	Positive	300	...	65-70
1937	C16	CH-J8	.025	.020	35-38	153624	D	Positive	300	...	65-70
	C14	CH-J8	.025	.017	27-30	16258374	E	Positive	300	...	65-70
	C15, C17	CH-J8	.025	.017	27-30	16258374	C	Positive	300	...	65-70
1938	C18	CH-J8	.025	.020	35-38	153624	B	Positive	300	...	65-70
	C19	CH-J8	.025	.017	27-30	16258374	B	Positive	300	...	65-70
	C20	CH-J8	.025	.017	27-30	16258374	E	Positive	300	...	65-70
1939	C22	AL-A7	.025	.020	35-38	153624	B	Positive	300	...	65-70
	C23	AL-A7	.025	.017	27-30	16258374	B	Positive	300	...	65-70
	C24	AL-A7	.025	.017	27-30	16258374	E	Positive	300	...	65-70
1940	C25	AL-A7B	.025	.020	35-38	153624	B	Positive	300	...	65-70
	C26	AL-A7B	.025	.017	27-30	16258374	E	Positive	300	...	65-70
	C27	AL-A7B	.025	.017	27-30	16258374	E	Positive	300	...	65-70
1941-42	Six	AL-A7B	.025	.020	35-38	153624	B	Positive	425	425	65-70
	C30, C36	AL-A7B	.025	.017	27-30	16258374	B	Positive	425	425	65-70
	C33, C37	AL-A7B	.025	.017	27-30	16258374	E	Positive	425	425	65-70
1946-48	Six	AL-A5	.025	.020	35-38	153624	D	Positive	425	425	65-70
	Eight	AL-A5	.025	.017	27-30	16258374	D	Positive	425	425	65-70
1949-50	Six	AL-AR8	.035	.020	35-38	153624	B	Positive	450-500	450-500	65-70
	Eight	AL-AR8	.035	.017	27-30	16258374	B	Positive	450-500	450-500	65-70
1951-52	Six	AL-AR8	.035	.020	35-38	153624	D	Positive	450-500	450-500	65-70
	V8	AL-4S140	.035	.017	F	H	B	Positive	450-500	450-500	80-85
1953	Six	AL-AR8	.035	.020	35-38	153624	B	Positive	450-500	450-500	65-70
	V8	AL-4S140	.035	.017	F	H	J	Positive	450-500	450-500	80-85

A—Plus or minus .002".
B—"O" mark on vibration damper.
C—Fifth line after "O" mark on vibration damper.
D—Second line before "O" mark on vibration damper.
E—Third line after "O" mark on vibration damper
F—26-28 degrees (one set of points). Total dwell 32-36 degrees.
H—Cylinder numbering as viewed from rear of engine. Right bank, 2-4-6-8; left bank, 1-3-5-7. Firing order: 1-8-4-3-6-5-7-2.
J—Fourth line before "O" mark on vibration damper.

Fig. 2-8. Specifications for autos dating back to the 1930s are similar to those for later models. Reprint editions of early manuals are available. (Reproduced from *MOTOR Auto Repair Manual* Copyright © 1953 by permission of Hearst Business Publishing, a division of the Hearst Corporation.)

electronic ignitions and exhaust emissions, of course, but they contain a good many extra specs that aren't found in today's tables (Fig. 2-8). You'll need to know about breaker point gaps and dwell angles, 6-volt electrical systems, tappet clearances set hot and cold on nearly all motors, and kingpin inclination angles on cars that actually have kingpins rather than ball joints or MacPherson struts.

You might be surprised to learn, though, that most of the specs for the oldies aren't all that different than those seen today! Inside the engine, in particular, the clearances and gaps and the diameters and wear limits haven't changed much at all in at least half a century.

Real antiques, those made before the 1920s and 1930s, are another matter, of course. Specs for them are often hard to find and sometimes they are unique to boot, requiring some thoughtful interpretation. Still, once you've mastered the units and terms described in this book, you'll be prepared for anything that comes along, even if you suddenly find yourself the owner of a 1921 Star or 1911 Oldsmobile. Cars haven't changed nearly as much as many observers insist.

Identifying Your Engine

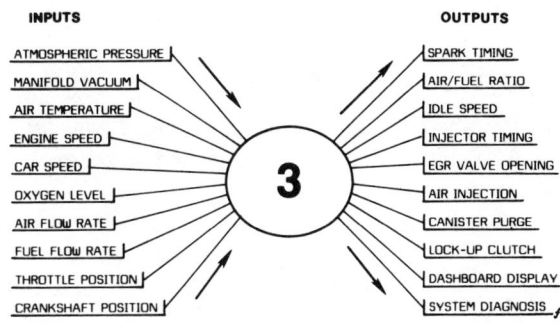

EVERY SPEC TABLE HAS ENGINE/MODEL IDENtification data in its left-hand columns (Table 3-1). Before proceeding with any sort of work, you must know exactly which engine you have in which vehicle model. That might sound obvious or even childish. Doesn't every car owner know what he or she has in the garage?

Most do. But some do not, and many others don't have the full details of how their car differs from others of its vintage. Knowing that yours is a 1985 Fiero V-6 or a 1965 Pontiac GTO V-8 might not be enough.

Observing that an engine compartment contains a four-cylinder motor of a certain make and year is sufficient for some purposes. But not always. Discovering that it's a 140-cubic-inch (2.3-liter) four with overhead camshaft, single one-barrel carburetor, rated 90 horsepower, driving an automatic transmission and 3.50:1 rear axle, mounted in a Starlite model X-24 coupe . . . Now that should be enough to satisfy every need from doing tune-up and repair work to ordering parts, talking about cars, and so forth. Best of all, you might gather most of that information by checking a single digit in the car's serial number.

Two methods are used to identify a car down to its tiniest details. Most important is its serial number. Second is observation of details—carburetor types, colors, body appearance, labels, emblems—to confirm what's learned from the identifying number.

SUCH A SELECTION!

During the first couple of decades of motoring, the number of different makes available was staggering. A car buyer in 1916 could choose not only from the familiar Model T Ford, Chevrolet, Cadillac, and other names that persist today, he could also have bought a Dart, a Hudson, a Studebaker, Packard, Case, Marmon, or dozens of other unrelated makes. Mechanics seeking data for a less-common car that pulled into the shop had a problem.

By the 1920s and 1930s, the number of separate makes had dropped off sharply. Some makes, such as Buick, produced models with several engine sizes and different specs. Most manufacturers of-

Table 3-1. Typical Engine/Model Identification Data.

Year	Model	Engine displacement cu. in./liter	VIN code
1985	Cavalier	4-112/1.8L	0
1983	Plymouth	6-225/3.7L	H
1981	Buick Regal	V6-252/4.1L	4
1981	Mercedes Diesel	5-3.0L	—
1960	Lark	6-170	—
1940	Cadillac 90	V16-431	—

fered a limited number of engine types. It was fairly easy to tell which car you had and to determine which specs had to be used.

As the horsepower race developed after World War II, the variety grew and grew. A 1947 Plymouth came with just one 6-cylinder engine. In 1957, three Plymouth V-8s and a six were available. By 1967, the total had jumped to seven, including five V-8 versions with eight different horsepower ratings from 180 to 425.

The confusion continued into the 1970s and 1980s as smaller engines became standard. Even if a manufacturer offers nothing but four-cylinder motors, they probably differ in detail when mounted in various car models. Naturally, certain specs will be identical for various motors in a given year (even through a period of years). But you don't want to miss any crucial figure that does differ; identification is the number one step.

So how do you tell the cars apart? The most important differentiator is engine size (displacement). This is explained in Chapter 4. You should also know:

☐ Compression ratio (especially for cars of the 1955-70 era, when V-8s came in a wide range of compressions).
☐ Horsepower rating.
☐ Engine style (V-8, inline four, V-6, etc.).
☐ Model year (naturally).
☐ Name of car model (Fiero, Mustang, Roadmaster, etc.).
☐ Number (and type) of carburetors.
☐ Special engine options (dual-point distributor, high-output alternator, race-ground camshaft, etc.).

MOST OF THE TIME, IT'S EASY . . .

Engine identification isn't always so difficult as it might sound here. This is especially true for modern autos. A single letter or digit in the car's identification number can tell all you need to know for using every possible spec table. Some specs are plastered right on under-hood labels. Still, the more you know about your engine and how it differs from others of the same make/model, the less chance there is of making errors when looking up data.

VEHICLE IDENTIFICATION NUMBER (VIN)

All cars manufactured in the U.S. since 1976 have a VIN. An earlier version appeared on many autos back in the late 1960s. It's in the same location on every vehicle: right atop the dashboard, and visible by peeking through the windshield on the driver's side (Fig. 3-1). The VIN might also be repeated on an identification plate elsewhere.

The VIN is a long number (17 digits since 1981; usually 13 digits or less before that). It gives plenty of information, but only two details are pertinent to the mechanic.

One of those digits or letters tells which engine is installed in the car, its number of cylinders, displacement, number of carburetors, etc. For 1981 and newer cars, that's the eighth digit (fourth digit for AMC). For models older than 1981, the engine code is usually the fifth digit.

Another digit in the VIN gives the car's model year. That's the tenth digit for recent vehicles, and the sixth for most pre-1981 cars (sometimes the first or second digit). Yet another digit, or digits, might identify the series, model or body type.

Deciphering the number is impossible unless you have a list of the codes used (Fig. 3-2). The codes can be found in the car's owner's manual or factory shop manual. An identification chart is also found in recent multi-make manuals, but not in all earlier editions (Fig. 3-3).

Some General Motors numbers are a bit confusing because the same code letter is sometimes used for engines made by different GM divisions.

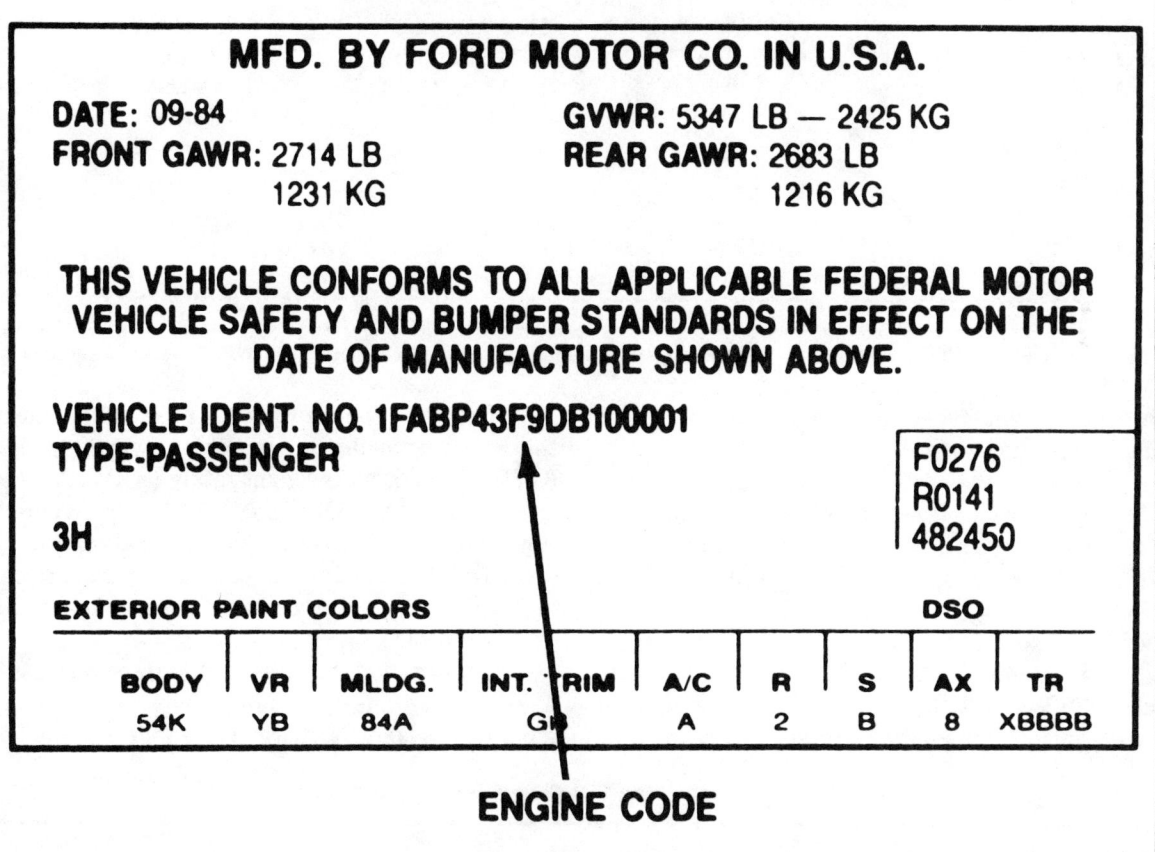

Fig. 3-1. Vehicle Identification Number (VIN) is found on the dashboard top, and often on a separate identification plate. Codes give data on the engine and many other details. (Reproduced by permission of Ford Motor Company.)

In 1976, for instance, the letter *S* was used to identify four different engines from four GM divisions.

Let's take as an example a mid-1980s Ford. Its 17-digit VIN looks something like this:

1FABP43F9FB100001

For a full translation, we look into the Ford manual, and separate the digits of the VIN into their categories. See Table 3-2.

IDENTIFICATION PLATES

Deciphering your car's VIN may be all you need to do. If you're unsure or if you want to confirm identification, additional coded data is available. For American cars made before 1976 (and some later imports) that have no VIN on the dash, all identification data will have to be found elsewhere.

An identification plate might be mounted on a driver's door hinge post, the door lock panel, the

VEHICLE IDENTIFICATION CODE CHART

1st Digit Carline	2nd Digit Series (Price Class)	3rd & 4th Digits Body Type	5th Digit Eng. Displacement (Cu. In.)—(Litres)	6th Digit Model Year	7th Digit Assembly Plant	Sequence Number
*B—Caravelle	H	22—2 Dr. Specialty Hardtop	C—225-1 BBL. (3.7) L.	A—1980	A—Lynch Road	100001
E—St. Regis	L		D—225-2 BBL. (3.7) L.		B—Hamtramck	
F—LeBaron	M	24—2 Dr. Hatchback	G—318-2 BBL. (5.2) L.		D—Belvidere	
G—Diplomat	P	29—2 Dr. Coupe	H—318-4 BBL. (5.2) L.		F—Newark	
H—Volaré	S	41—4 Dr. Sedan	K—360-2 BBL. (5.9) L.		G—St. Louis	
J—Gran Fury		42—4 Dr. Pillared Hardtop	L—360-4 BBL. (5.9) L.		R—Windsor	
N—Aspen						
S—Cordoba		44—4 Dr. Hatchback				
T—Newport/New Yorker		45—2 Seat Wagon				
X—Mirada						

* = Canada Only—(For Service refer to 'F' and 'G' carlines).

Fig. 3-2. A typical engine code chart from a factory service manual. (Reproduced by permission of Chrysler Corporation.)

firewall, or somewhere under the hood. Some are inside a front wheel well. The plate could show little more than the car's serial number (either the VIN or an earlier version) or it might contain codes for body type, transmission type, engine, paint, trim, rear axle ratio, and a host of other details. Some details are important for the mechanic and some are not.

Late-model Fords, for example, have a Vehicle Certification Label on the left-front door pillar or lock panel. In addition to the VIN, it contains information on the manufacturer, month and year the car was made, gross vehicle weight rating (GVWR), gross axle weight rating (GAWR)—plus the number of the district sales office that handled the car. More important, it includes codes for body style, trim and mouldings, axle ratio, transmission, springs, and the presence of options such as a radio or moon roof.

Even for modern cars, decoding the VIN isn't always enough. Recent Oldsmobiles, for instance, have the usual VIN character to indicate engine-

Table 3-2. VIN Categories.

IFA	B	P	43	F	9	F	B	100001
1-3	4	5	6-7	8	9	10	11	12-17

Digits:
1-3   Worldwide manufacturer identifier (that's Ford's number for U.S. passenger cars)
4   Restraint system type
5   Passenger car indicator
6-7   Line, series and body type (here, an LTD Crown Victoria 4-door sedan)
8   Engine type: in this case, a 302 cid (5-liter) V-8
9   Check digit (always a "9")
10   Model year (here, 1985)
11   Assembly plant (B = Oakville)
12-17   Production sequence number (the individual serial number)

Chevrolet & Corvette

YEAR IDENTIFICATION

1978 Corvette

1979 Corvette

ENGINE IDENTIFICATION

The engine code is the fifth digit of the Vehicle Identification Number stamped on the VIN plate on the upper left corner of the instrument panel pad, visible through the windshield.

Chevrolet

No. Cyls.	Cu. in. Displ.	Type	1972	1973	1974	1975	1976	1977	1978	1979
6	250	All	D	D	D	D	D	D	D	D
8	305	All						U	U	U
8	350	2 bbl	J	H	H	H	H			
8	350	4 bbl	K	K	L	L	L	L	L	L
8	400	2 bbl	R	R	R					
8	400	4 bbl			U	U	U			
8	454	4 bbl	W	Y	Y	Y	S			
8	454	4 bbl DE		Z	Z					

DE: Dual Exhaust

Corvette

No. Cyls.	Cu. in. Displ.	Type	1972	1973	1974	1975	1976	1977	1978	1979
8	350	200 hp	L	J	J	J	L	L	L	L
8	350	HP	L	P	P	T	X	X	4	4
8	454	All	W	Z	Z					

hp: horsepower
HP: High Performance

Fig. 3-3. Charts in multimake manuals provide identification of engine size and type. (From *Chilton's Auto Repair Manual 1979*. Reprinted with permission of the publisher, Chilton Book Company, Radnor, PA 19089.)

type—plus an enormous range of 2- and 3-character codes on the engine to differentiate between them. Code letters/numbers on the engine itself aren't necessarily the same as those used in the VIN.

Earlier-model engines can be identified by similar codes in the vehicle's serial number plate (on door post, firewall, etc.). More common is a coded engine number that is stamped or cast right on the motor block or a major component. A prefix or suffix, or a series of two to three digits within the whole number, identifies the engine size and type. Such a number could be on a tag attached to the rocker arm cover. More often it's cast or stamped on a machined pad or flange in any of several locations:

- ☐ Crankcase face.
- ☐ Between branches of exhaust manifold.
- ☐ Front of one cylinder bank, just below head.
- ☐ Distributor mounting pad.
- ☐ Alternator bracket or oil filler tube.
- ☐ Between exhaust manifold and spark plugs.
- ☐ Just about anywhere on the block itself.

Some Chrysler engines have their cubic-inch displacement spelled out directly by a series of digits on the stamped engine pad. Certain AMC motors have a displacement figure cast right into the block. Transmissions and rear axle housings have their own stampings that can be deciphered by information in the factory manual.

Locations of any identification plates, labels, or stampings should be given in both factory and multi-make manuals (Fig. 3-4). Look at the first pages for each make in the multi-make manuals or the first chapter or section in a factory book.

Let's take one example. Say we have a Ford sedan that looks like it's from the mid-1960s. It has a V-8 engine and single 4-barrel carb under its hood. As it happens, 4-barrels were offered on most V-8 sizes in that era. So that's no help.

The manual reveals that Ford's serial number plate is on the left front door pillar, and it turns out to read: 6G51Z123456. Turning to the breakdown in the manual, we learn that the first digit (6) indicates the model year (1966). The second gives the car's assembly plant. The next two digits indicate a code for the body style. Ah, but the fifth digit (actually the letter Z) reveals the engine: a 390 cubic-inch V-8 with one 4-barrel, rated 325 horsepower. The final digits are the car's individual identification number.

Sound familiar? Well, it's not much different from the VIN used on later autos. Identifying other makes or vintages, though, might require a lot more work.

Confusing? Not when you have deciphering details at hand. Problems come when you lack the proper charts and manuals.

COLOR CODES AND STICKERS

Quite a few recent engines (and some earlier ones) can be identified, at least tentatively or partially, by a quick glance. Starting back in 1963, for example, Ford began to use different colors for the air cleaner and rocker arm cover, depending on the engine's size. Of course, color codes don't help much unless you know what each color signifies.

Another modern trend is far more helpful. Since the 1960s, automakers have been mounting labels in plain sight on air cleaners or elsewhere

---

CAR SERIAL NUMBER LOCATION AND ENGINE IDENTIFICATION

ENGINE NUMBER LOCATION

1954-58—All V-8 engines. on left cylinder block between No. 1 & 7 exhaust ports.

1959-63—All V-8 engines, on left side center of left cylinder head. This number indicates detail information such as: Transmission combination, compression ratio, etc.

SERIAL NUMBER LOCATION

1954-63—On left front door hinge post. Prefixes to this number are used to identify: First, the model year. The next is a letter indicating the series on engine used.

YEAR—ENGINE IDENTIFICATION CHART

Year	Prefix	Engine cu. in.
1954-56	7, 8 or 9	V-8 324.3
1957-58	7, 8, or 9	V-8 371.
1959-60	7	V-8 371.
	8 or 9	V-8 394
1961-63	2, 5 or 8	V-8 394

Note:
1954-60—Prefix Symbol,
6—"76" series, 6 cyl.
7—"88" series
8—"Super 88"
9—"98" series
1961-63—Prefix Symbol,
2—"88" series
5—"Super 88"
8—"98" series

Fig. 3-4. Engines produced before the VIN became standard are identified by serial number and other information, using charts found in the manual. (From *Chilton's Auto Repair Manual 1963*. Reprinted with permission of the publisher, Chilton Book Company, Radnor, PA 19089.)

Fig. 3-5. Early model vehicles, like this 1936 Studebaker and 1964 Ford Falcon, aren't difficult to identify so long as you have information on decoding serial numbers. Observation of engine/chassis details may also be necessary.

under the hood. They contain not a cryptic coded number, but actual words and figures that tell the engine's size, number of carbs, and perhaps other interesting facts. For example, a label marked "300-2" lets you know you have a 300 cubic-inch motor with 2-barrel carburetor.

Recent autos have gone further yet. Printed in a small plate are various specifications needed for tune-up work. Today's manuals, in fact, advise readers to follow the instructions and specs noted on that plate rather than turn to the books. For a lot of minor tasks, then, the facts you need are right in front of you under the hood.

MODELS AND BODY STYLES

When consulting specifications for mechanical work, it doesn't always matter whether the engine is setting in a two-door or four-door body, a convertible, or a hardtop. Nor does it necessarily matter which model it is (Escort, Tempo, Lynx). Specs may well be identical for all Ford vehicles using a certain motor.

Not always though. Every bit of information you have reduces the chance of making an error. So be sure to check the body style and other codes in the VIN and the serial number plate. And for goodness sake, take a good look at the car itself. Note any emblems or details that make perfectly clear which model it is. Easy insurance.

The same engine might be used not only in several models from one manufacturer, but in different makes! A lot of those GM, Ford, and Chrysler models that are advertised as being different (better) than the rest are essentially the same as a couple of others. Same engine, same transmission, same chassis, and same specs; only the trim has changed. Even in such cases, one or two of those specs probably differ among the versions. Don't take chances.

IDENTITY PROBLEMS

You shouldn't have much trouble identifying the engine on any recent auto. Early models (Fig. 3-5) can be tougher. The serial number plate doesn't always state the model year directly. You might not have a manual that tells how to interpret information or codes that are given. The plate could be obliterated or even missing. You might not be able to find it even after careful searching all around the car. Even when you have a decipherable plate or stamped number, though, it doesn't hurt to confirm the facts with a series of observations.

First off you must know the car's "year." That's basic. The table listings refer to model year, and that might differ from the calendar year in which the car was actually manufactured and sold. Model year is usually the one-year period during which the car's appearance remains unchanged.

Most of us have no doubt about the year of our personal car(s). If you work on other people's cars, or have just purchased a "new" early model auto, determining the correct year isn't always so clear-cut as you might imagine. For certain rare or very early vintages, the answer can prove surprisingly elusive. Some owners learn to their surprise, years after buying an old car, that it isn't a 1935 as they thought all along but a 1936. Amazing but true.

Titles and registration documents aren't necessarily adequate. New models have, since the 1930s, been introduced in the fall of the preceding model year. Some models (such as the first "1964 1/2" Mustang) were brought out in mid-year. A few leftovers don't find owners, and aren't registered, until the year after they were produced.

A 1955 Dodge, then, could have been first licensed in 1954, 1955, or 1956. Its official papers might show any of those years. Not often does this happen but it happens. The likelihood varies, from state to state, with different registration procedures.

Another complication is a replacement engine of different vintage or type that might have been installed at some time. This can even be the case for recent models.

In most cases, the car's year (if not the engine's) can be determined primarily by body appearance. No surprise there. Compare yours with the grille drawings or photos in a multi-make service manual or with pictures in a book, magazine, or "spotter's guide" for older autos. Notice, too, that differences in appearance between models in two successive years have sometimes been slight. It takes an expert to tell apart a 1947 and a 1948 Dodge or a 1951 and a 1952 Plymouth, at a glance.

As for model, here too most owners know whether their garage is filled with a Mustang or a Falcon, a Firebird or a GTO, a Hudson Wasp, or a Hornet. Some spec tables list these popular names or a well-known number: 300F (1960 Chrysler), F-85 (Oldsmobile), or Series 70 (Buick "Roadmaster" of the 1950s and earlier). Others give a less-familiar factory number such as C63-1 to denote a 1954 Chrysler New Yorker.

Chrome or painted nameplates on the car might not offer the complete answer, but code letters/digits in its body serial number should. The body number might or might not be the same as the car's number. It might be on a separate plate in a different location. Information on body codes is probably available only in the factory's body service manual.

Manuals from pre-VIN days often include a list of "starting" serial numbers (the lowest number issued for each model year) or a number range for the year. Once you know the year and model, identifying the engine shouldn't be difficult. This is especially true if the manual gives details on any coding system of that day.

WHEN YOU'RE NOT SURE

Additional detective work isn't limited solely to older cars. Problems can arise in identifying more recent imports produced before standardized serial numbers or where deciphering information is unavailable. Limited-production models, and those for which full details have not yet been published, can be troublesome.

When doubt persists expert help is in order. For recent cars, that means the dealer that sold it originally. Vehicle inspection bureaus in your state should have someone available who can help with the toughies. Old-car clubs and magazine editors are often willing to offer aid. Someone out there will be able to tell you what you have (if that expert can only be found). Try the factory if nothing else works. Supply all the numbers you can find on the car.

Certain reference books help, too. The *Serial Number Book for U.S. Cars* can aid in determining an early car's model year. In case you own something really rare, the *Encyclopedia of the World's Motorcars* tells something about virtually every car ever manufactured. Back issues of *Automotive Industries* and other trade publications have information that could help.

Most of us never need more than the VIN to identify an engine and car model. It's nice to know that additional information is available, just in case.

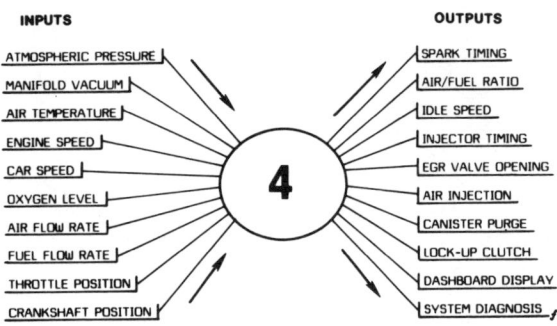

Engine Size and Style

THE FIRST IMPORTANT TABLE IN A MANUAL, or section of a manual, contains general specifications. It usually leads off the section for each make or it might be on an early page of a factory manual.

Columns at the left-hand end of our sample, Table 4-1, and of the "real" tables in the manuals identify the car and engine we're working on. Remaining columns contain basic information about the engine's size, structure, and power output. Although not needed for practical work, these general figures help compare our engine to others, and aid in looking up data from other tables. They're just plain interesting, too. Let's take a quick run through the columns, and then go on to some detailed explanations.

Year (yr.). This refers to model year (as explained in Chapter 3).

Engine CID/Liter. This column gives the number of cylinders and engine displacement (the basic indicator of engine size). 4-151 means a four-cylinder engine of 151 cubic-inch displacement (cid). That figure may be followed by an equivalent measurement in liters or cubic centimeters (cc).

Quite often the number of cylinders is preceded by a letter to show engine style: *V* for V-type, *L* for L-head or inline, *OHV* or *I* for overhead-valve. Maybe even *OC* for overhead cam, or *DOHC* identifying the less-common double overhead cam design. V8-427 is a V-8 with 427 cubic-inch displacement.

Column headings differ considerably among the manuals. You might find one headed "No. Cyl. Displacement" or "Displace. Cu. In." or "Piston Disp." Earlier manuals may have separate columns for number of cylinders (no. of cyl.) and displacement. A few have a separate column indicating valve location: in "block" for an L-head, in "head" for an overhead-valve design. There could be a "Model" column, containing either the cylinder displacement, or an actual car model name or number (C63-1, Roadmaster, etc.).

VIN Code. Recent manuals have a column giving the code letter or number in the car's VIN that indicates engine type. That's extremely helpful in determining the engine's identity, without hav-

Table 4-1. Typical General Engine Specifications.

Year	Engine no. of cyl. displace. CID/liter	Carburetor Type	Max. horsepower @ rpm	Max. Torque (lb-ft) @ rpm	Bore x stroke (in.)	Comp. ratio (to 1)
1985	4-112/1.8	E.F.I.	84 @ 5200	102 @ 2800	3.34 x 3.12	9.0
1984	V6-262/4.3	F.I.	85 @ 3600	165 @ 1600	4.05 x 3.38	22.8
1983	V6-232/3.8	2150	112 @ 4000	175 @ 2600	3.8 x 3.4	8.7
1979	4-71.8/1.2	2-bbℓ	58 @ 5800	63 @ 3800	2.95 x 2.60	9.0
1974	V8-500/8.2	4-bbℓ	210 @ 3600	380 @ 2000	4.300 x 4.304	8.25
1970	V8-426/7.0	2-4 bbℓ	425 @ 5000	490 @ 4000	4.25 x 3.75	10.25
1969	V8-427/7.0	3 carbs	435 @ 5800	460 @ 4000	4.251 x 3.76	11.00
1960	L6-170	1-bbℓ	90 @ 4000	145 @ 2000	3 x 4	8.3
1957	V8-283	F.I.	283 @ 6200	290 @ 4400	3 7/8 x 3	10.5
1948	V12-292	2-bb1	120 @ 3500	214 @ 1600	2 7/8 x 3 3/4	7.2

ing to consult other manual sections.

Carburetor Type. Number of carb barrels (and number of carburetors, if more than one): 1-bbl, two 4-bbl, 3-2 bbl, etc. There might also be a code letter for the carb's manufacturer (*C*arter, *S*tromberg, *H*olley, etc.), and a model number. This information might be given only in a detailed carburetor table that is elsewhere in the manual. For fuel injection, the abbreviation FI or EFI for electronic injection might be used.

Horsepower (hp). The advertised engine brake horsepower is discussed in Chapter 5. Through 1971, it is "gross" power of a stripped engine. Since 1972, "SAE net" horsepower has been given, with every accessory attached and operating. It's always given at a stated engine speed (rpm). Some tables have a separate column, showing hp alone, for extra engine identification.

Torque. The engine's peak turning force in pound-feet, at a stated engine speed. More on this in Chapter 5.

Bore & Stroke. Diameter of engine cylinder (bore) and length of piston travel (stroke). Traditionally, bore is listed first. Thus, a 3 1/2 x 4 cylinder has a bore of 3 1/2-inch diameter and a 4-inch stroke. Figures in earlier manuals may be given in fractional inches (3 1/4, 4 1/8, etc.). Later ones are usually decimals, to two or three places (2.99, 3.187, etc.); or in some cases, four (3.8125). A metric size is sometimes found, to tenths of a millimeter, often in parentheses following the inch measure.

Compression Ratio (Comp. Ratio, C.R., etc.). The ratio showing how much the air/fuel mixture is squeezed as the piston rises. Usually given to one decimal place (9.5:1, or 8.5 to 1, or 8.0/1).

Oil Pressure. Usually a minimum acceptable figure, in psi, that should be produced at a stated speed (either engine rpm or road mph). Not really a general specification, but it's in most tables.

Various other columns appear in one general spec table or another, showing such facts as *camshaft drive* (gear or chain), *number of main bearings*, and *valve lifter type* (mechanical or hydraulic, adjustable or solid). Some include *wheelbase*, which is nice to know, but obviously has nothing to do with the motor. Early manuals might have a column for *taxable horsepower*. This information has no purpose other than determining vehicle license fees in some localities.

ENGINE STYLES

The piston (reciprocating) engine is almost universal in cars. That's been true ever since the demise of steam and electric-powered autos. Virtually all modern engines, moreover, have overhead valves (in the cylinder head), and are of four-cycle design. Past vintages offered much more variety.

Cylinder Arrangement. Inline, V-type, and

flat engines have been produced. The inline motor has its cylinders arranged in a single row—one behind the other. It's often referred to as a "straight 8" (or 4 or 6) motor; the figure indicates the number of cylinders. A "slant 6" is an ordinary inline motor that has been redesigned to fit under a lowered hood.

V-type (vee) engines have their cylinders arranged in two banks. Modern V-8s normally have a 90-degree angle between the banks. A V-6 or earlier V-8 could have 60 degrees, or some wider angle.

A "flat" engine (also called horizontally opposed or "pancake" style) is essentially the same as a V-type, but with its cylinders 180 degrees apart, directly opposite each other. Corvair, the VW Beetle, some Subarus, and a few others have used flat engines.

Valve Structure. An "L-head" engine has both its intake and exhaust valves in the engine block (Fig. 4-1). It's called that because its combustion area cross section looks a bit like an inverted L when the piston is all the way down. It's also called a "flathead" because the cylinder head holds no valve-actuating or other devices; it's plain flat. The term "side valve" is also used because both valves are on one side of the cylinder. L-heads (both inline and V-type) used to be the most popular style, but they disappeared from American cars in the early 1960s. They're now found mainly on power mowers and such.

The overhead-valve (OHV) engine is by far the most common style used in the past couple of decades. In fact other types are rare. Also called an "I-head" (because of its cross-sectional shape) or "valve-in-head," it does indeed have both valves mounted in the cylinder head, above the piston.

The OHV is also called a "pushrod" engine because its valves are operated by pushrods rising from a camshaft farther down in the motor. Lately, the overhead-camshaft (OHC) engine has risen in popularity. This engine too has overhead valves, but with one camshaft (SOHC, single) or twin camshafts (DOHC, double) mounted directly over the valves. Valves operate directly from the camshaft lobes, with no pushrods needed.

During the performance era of the 1950s and 1960s, the "hemi" engine gained a lot of favor. Its exhaust and intake valves aren't side by side, as in the ordinary OHV. They're on opposite sides of a hemispherically shaped combustion chamber, requiring two separate camshafts. The added complexity ultimately brought about the hemi's demise.

Two other styles had their brief heyday. The T-head, popular before 1910, had valves in the block—one on each side of the cylinder. F-heads, used most by Willys in the 1940s, had one valve in the block and the other in the cylinder head. Neither design was very efficient.

Engine Cycle. Almost all modern automotive engines are of four-cycle design. Four distinct strokes make up a single complete cycle: intake, compression, power, and exhaust. An intake valve allows the air/fuel mixture to enter, and an exhaust valve opens to release the exhaust gases after burning. The crankshaft has to rotate twice, and each piston travels up-and-down twice, during one complete cycle. It's sometimes called the Otto cycle, after its originator, Nikolaus Otto, who produced an operating version in 1876.

A few auto engines have been two-cycle (two-stroke), with no valve train. The three-cylinder Saab had its fans in the 1960s, before U.S. pollution requirements did it in. Two-cycles are found today mainly in lawnmowers, motorboats, motor scooters and such. Usually they are air-cooled.

Wankel (rotary) engines, with no pistons, seemed to have a future a few years back, but soon disappeared. Diesels are common, but still limited in popularity. The diesel is structurally similar to the conventional spark-ignition engine, but uses compression ignition. Its light fuel oil is ignited by the heat of compression, not by electricity.

NUMBER OF CYLINDERS

A V-type engine might have anything from two to 16 cylinders. Inlines have been made with up to eight. Opposed engines usually have four or six.

In the modern era, four, six and eight cylinders are the most common. Years ago, however, there were various 12-cylinder engines around. Lincoln had one through 1948. Back in the 1930s, a few

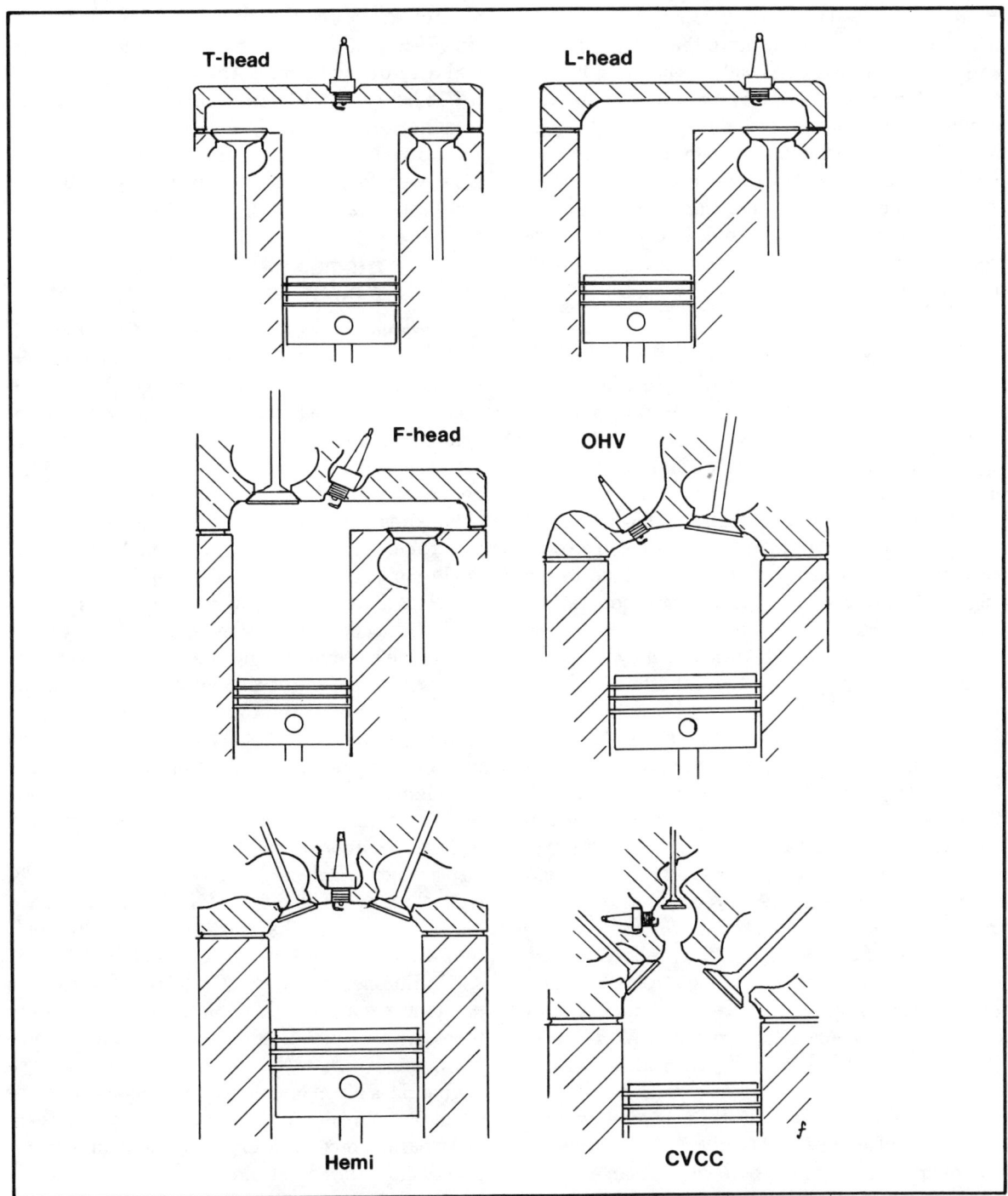

Fig. 4-1. The evolution of valve arrangements and combustion chamber shapes. Nearly all modern engines are OHV. CVCC, as used by Honda, has precombustion chamber with secondary (smaller) intake valve, giving more thorough combustion.

V-16 motors were made. Straight eights were popular in deluxe models until the Fifties. Jaguar and a couple of other specialty vehicles still offer a V-12. A handful of economy cars have come with a two-cylinder engine, including the first Crosley in 1939, and an occasional import of later vintage.

Most engines have an even number of cylinders, but there are exceptions. The two-cycle Saab had three cylinders. So does Chevrolet's recent Sprint. Mercedes diesels and some Audi models have five.

BORE AND STROKE

At car shows, in parts stores, or when describing a vehicle to a friend, we toss around a lot of numbers: Chrysler 383, 9-to-1 head, 3 1/4-inch stroke, ten-thousandths overbore, and so on. All are measures of engine size.

Before determining the total size (displacement) of any motor, we have to know its bore and stroke. *Bore* is the diameter of each cylinder hole in the engine block (Fig. 4-2). In postwar cars, bore ranges from a bit under 3 inches to almost 4 1/2 inches. The piston sliding up and down in that cylinder has an outside diameter a few thousandths of an inch smaller.

Stroke is the vertical distance traveled by each piston within its cylinder as the piston moves between top and bottom dead center (TDC and BDC), the upper and lower extremes. In smaller modern engines, that might be as little as 3 inches (even less). But stroke lengths over 4 inches are found in some big V-8s of the 1960s, and topped 5 inches in a few inline motors of earlier vintage.

Engines of the 1930s and 1940s tended to have relatively small bores, but a long stroke. The last Lincoln V-12, for instance, had a cylinder bore of only 2 7/8 inches. Hudson sixes after World War II were built with a bore of just 3 inches, but a 5-inch stroke.

Modern overhead-valve V-8s, beginning with the 1949 Oldsmobile and Cadillac, moved toward an "oversquare" design (bore larger than stroke). The larger cylinder (and piston) diameter permits greater potential power from the engine while the shorter stroke reduces friction and wear. Buick's first V-8 in 1953, for example, had a 4-inch bore and 3 13/64 inch stroke. Quite a change from the 3 7/16 bore and 4 5/16 stroke of the previous year's Roadmaster straight-eight motor.

Strokes have actually grown longer again in recent years to allow more burning time, improving combustion, and cutting emissions.

DISPLACEMENT: THE PRIME MEASUREMENT

Those familiar three-digit numbers (Chevrolet 283, Ford 352) that highlighted the big-engine era are measurements of engine *displacement*. It's the volume of air displaced (forced upward) in the cylinders as the pistons rise from the bottom to the top of their travel (Fig. 4-3). It can also be defined as the volume added to the combustion area in a cylinder as the piston moves from top to bottom of its stroke, or as the volume a piston "sweeps out" while moving up from BDC to TDC.

Note that we're talking about the total volume of air displaced. It's the amount swept away by all the engine's pistons during one complete cycle (two revolutions of the crankshaft). Each cylinder displaces 1/Nth of the total amount (N being the number of cylinders). A 240-cubic-inch, six-cylinder motor, then, displaces 40 cubic inches in each cylinder.

The figure is commonly expressed in cubic inches and abbreviated as ci or cid (cubic inch displacement). Referring to an engine's size as "283 inches" or even "283 cubes" isn't quite accurate, but this is seen and heard all the time. This could be a whole number (302) or down to tenths (302.4).

In Europe, and most of the world, displacement has long been given in cubic centimeters (cc) or liters (L). One liter is equal to 1000cc. Most modern manuals also include a metric figure. In fact, engine sizes given in liters have become almost the norm. Whichever unit is used, displacement is the most basic indicator of engine size—a direct function of its bore and stroke.

Displacement is calculated for a single cylinder, and then multiplied by the number of cylinders

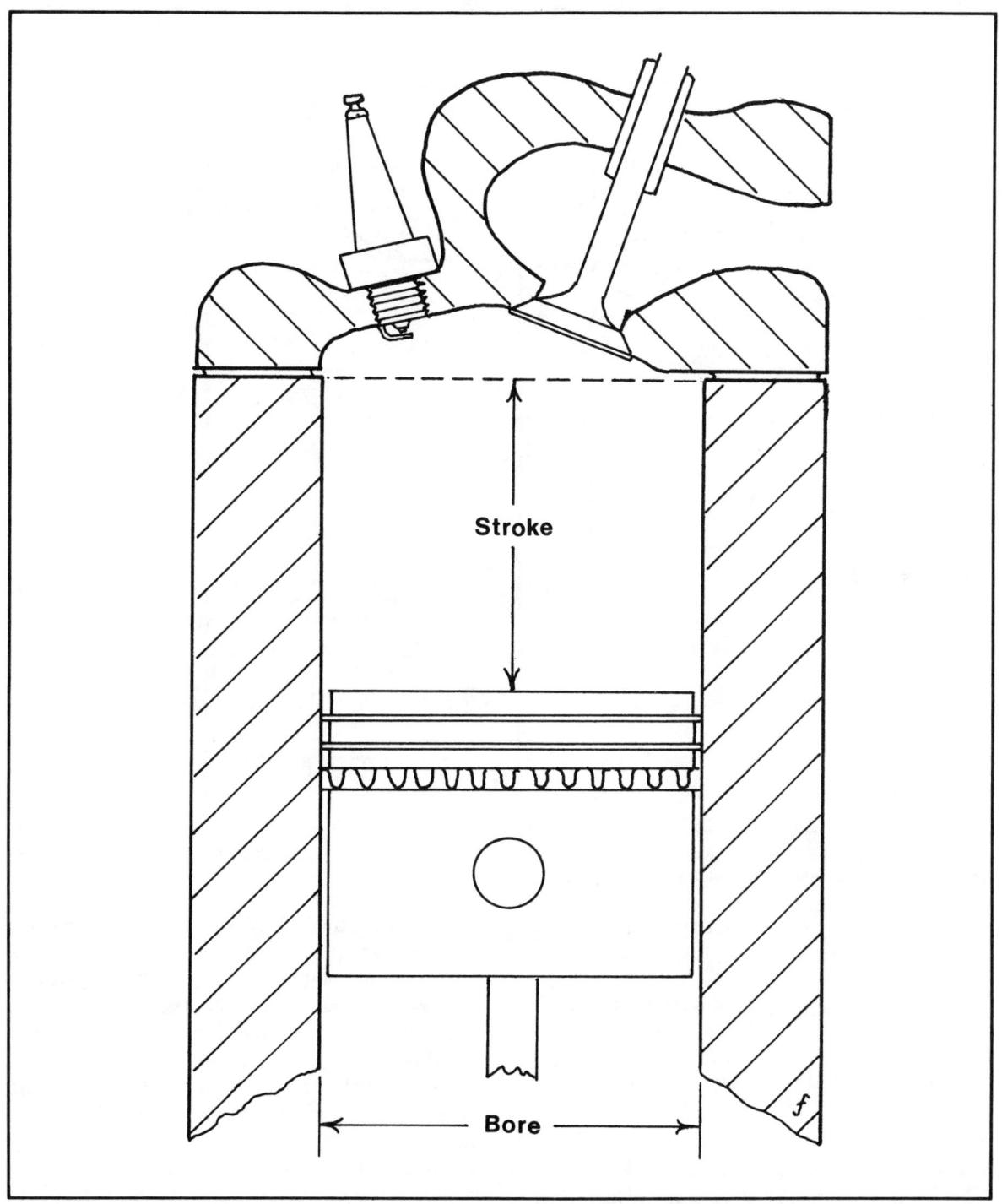

Fig. 4-2. Bore is the diameter of a cylinder. Stroke is the vertical distance traveled by the piston as the crankshaft rotates.

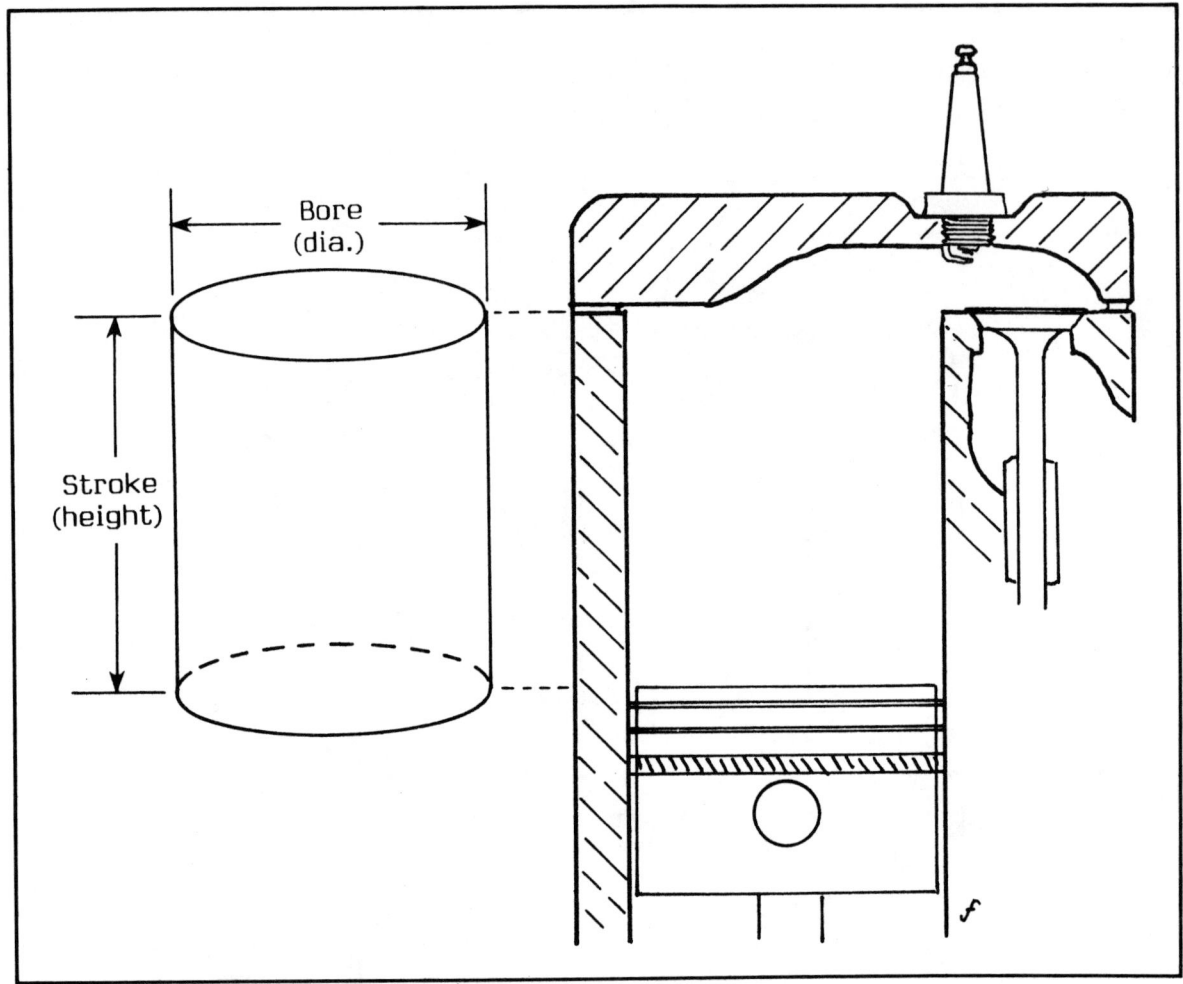

Fig. 4-3. Displacement is the volume of the imaginary cylinder formed as a piston moves from top to bottom. Old L-head engines (shown) usually had small bore, long stroke.

to determine the total for the engine. The formula may be expressed as:

$$\text{Displacement} = N \pi (B/2)^2 S$$

or

$$\frac{N \pi B^2 S}{4}$$

where N equals the number of cylinders, B the bore and S the stroke of each cylinder. Pi (π), as explained in Chapter 1, is a fixed number: approximately 3.14.

In words, then, the displacement of one cylinder is equal to pi (3.14) multiplied by the square of half the bore (that figure multiplied by itself), times the stroke length. To get the displacement of the entire engine, just multiply that total by the number of cylinders.

Thinking back to Chapter 1, it's nothing more than the standard formula for calculating the volume of any cylinder: $V = \pi r^2 h$. What we measure here is the volume of the theoretical cylinder—a cylindrical space—formed as the piston moves from top to bottom, and whose height equals the stroke length.

Let's take as an example an 8-cylinder engine with 4-inch bore and 3-inch stroke. Displacement of each cylinder comes to:

(pi) × (bore/2) × (bore/2) × (stroke)
= (3.14) × (4/2) × (4/2) × (3)
= (3.14) × (2) × (2) × (3)

which equals 37.68. Multiply that by the number of cylinders (8) and you get a total engine displacement of 301.44 cubic inches. Reduction to the nearest whole number (301), or at least the nearest tenth (301.4), is customary.

Should you ever have occasion to compute a number of displacement figures (which isn't very likely), there's a simplified version of the formula: $0.785 \, N \, B^2 \, S$. In words, the number of cylinders multiplied by the square of the bore, times the stroke, all multiplied by 0.785. That curious decimal is simply pi (3.14) divided by 4, which eliminates the step of dividing the bore in half. The multiplications in either formula, incidentally, may be performed in any sequence. The answer will be the same.

Because today's engine displacements are often shown metrically, a conversion formula will prove useful. A metric equivalent is obtained by multiplying the cubic-inch displacement by 16.387. For example, a 231 cid Buick V-6 has a metric displacement of 3785 cubic centimeters (231 × 16.387). That's about 3.8 liters, and is determined by moving the decimal point three places to the left and rounding off to the nearest tenth. Multiplying the cubic-inch amount by 16.4, or even by 16, will be close enough for most purposes.

Going in the other direction, cubic-inch displacement can be computed by dividing the metric figure (cc) by 16.387, or multiplying by .061, whichever is easier. Table 4-2 gives metric equivalents for some popular American engine sizes.

MONSTERS, MINIS, AND GUZZLERS

Engines have been shrinking since the mid-1970s when the era of the guzzler came to an end. The 500-cubic-inch Cadillac of that period is a far cry from today's Detroit offerings. Now 350 cubic inches is the maximum, and most motors are far smaller.

Big engines didn't suddenly appear during the 1950s horsepower race. They existed even in the early days of motoring. The six-cylinder Oldsmobile Limited of 1911, for example, displaced a massive 706.9 cubic inches, with a broad 5-inch bore and 6-inch stroke. The 1909 Thomas Flyer was bigger yet: a 784 cid six, with 5 1/2 × 5 1/2 dimensions. A few years earlier, Mercedes put out a four-

Table 4-2. Metric Equivalents (cc and liters) of some Popular Engine Displacements in Cubic Inches.

Cubic inches	Cubic centimeters	Liters (approx.)	Cubic inches	Cubic centimeters	Liters (approx.)
85	1394	1.4	283	4638	4.6
97	1591	1.6	289	4736	4.7
112	1827	1.8	300	4916	4.9
122	2001	2.0	318	5211	5.2
140	2296	2.3	327	5359	5.4
151	2476	2.5	350	5737	5.7
156	2558	2.6	361	5916	5.9
173	2835	2.8	368	6030	6.0
181	2968	3.0	383	6276	6.3
200	3277	3.3	401	6571	6.6
216	3542	3.5	413	6768	6.8
225	3687	3.7	427	6997	7.0
235	3851	3.9	454	7440	7.4
250	4097	4.1	460	7538	7.5
265	4343	4.3	500	8194	8.2

cylinder motor displacing 9.25 liters. That's almost 595 cubic inches (nearly 150 from each cylinder).

Displacement of postwar six-cylinder engines has been as little as 148 cubic inches in the 1949 Willys (3 × 3 1/2 inches) and up to a hefty 308 cid in the Hudson Hornet (3-13/16 × 4 1/2) of the early Fifties. Ford's economy V8-60 in the 1930s was only 136 cid (2.6 × 3.2), or 17 cubic inches per cylinder.

OHV V-8 motors range all the way from Studebaker's tiny 224 cid version of 1954 to the mammoth 500-inch Cadillac. Chrysler's hemi started life in 1951 at 331 cid. Chevrolet's trend-setting V-8 measured only 265 cubic inches in 1955. But they didn't stay small for long. The Sixties brought dozens of super-performance V-8s in the 400 to 455 cid range.

Imported cars, except for a few luxury models, have always been small. The first Volkswagens measured in at a mere 1200cc (73.2 cubic inches). They are not much different from recent Honda Civics with a 1.3-liter four-cylinder motor.

A single cylinder, then, might displace less than 25 cubic inches or as much as 62 1/2 inches on that mid-1970s Cadillac. Around 1977, though, displacements dropped abruptly. In 1976, Chevrolet still offered its 454; the next year 350 cid was tops. The mighty Pontiac 455, Chrysler 440, and Ford 460 of the muscle-car era were gone for good, never to return. Economy and efficiency are in; brute force and size are out.

ADDING INCHES

Because power output is determined in part by an engine's size, it's obvious that increasing the bore or stroke of a motor boosts its displacement—hence its horsepower rating. That's exactly what early hot rodders began to do while boring out each cylinder of their V-8s to perhaps 1/8 or 1/4 inch oversize in order to accept larger-diameter pistons. Some also installed specially made crankshafts that provided a longer stroke.

"Boring and stroking" a V-8 with original 4-inch bore and 3-inch stroke, increasing each measurement by 1/4 inch, would boost its displacement by 67 cubic inches: from 301.4 to a sizable 368.7 cid. A quarter-inch increase in bore diameter, incidentally, raises displacement somewhat more than does a stroke increase of the same amount.

Alterations have their limits. Bore expansion is limited by the thickness of the cylinder wall (Fig. 4-4). Because coolant circulates in the chambers beyond that wall, only so much metal can be removed before the structure becomes weakened, and perhaps flexing or even cracking. Some engines have quite a bit of leeway for overboring; others have rather thin walls to start with. The use of "stroker" crankshafts may also be limited by crankcase configuration.

Ordinary motorists seldom alter engine size. Neither do restorers of old cars because doing so would diminish—some say destroy—the car's authenticity. Boring/stroking is mainly the province of street rodders seeking peak performance.

At the factory, though, both methods have commonly been used to increase power output from one year to the next or to alter a basic engine into a high-performance version. For that matter, not every motor coming off some factory assembly lines necessarily has the precise advertised displacement. A certain number may have been bored slightly oversize (perhaps .005 or .010 inch) to compensate for manufacturing flaws. These nonstandard engines are generally identified by a coded stamping somewhere on the block. The difference in total displacement is minimal, but your car could conceivably have an "inch" or two more than other, supposedly equal, models.

Back in the garage, when an engine has seen a lot of miles, a modest degree of overboring often becomes necessary to restore the roundness of worn cylinder walls. Rarely is the bore increased by more than .020 or .030 inch, which would raise the displacement of our example V-8 to a maximum of 309 cubic inches—about 7 1/2 more than original.

The amount of bore increase produced by honing cylinder walls during a ring job is generally slight. It's no more than a few thousandths unless you're using the cylinder hone more aggressively than necessary. Oversize pistons shouldn't be required after honing, but become mandatory when the bore is enlarged by a significant amount.

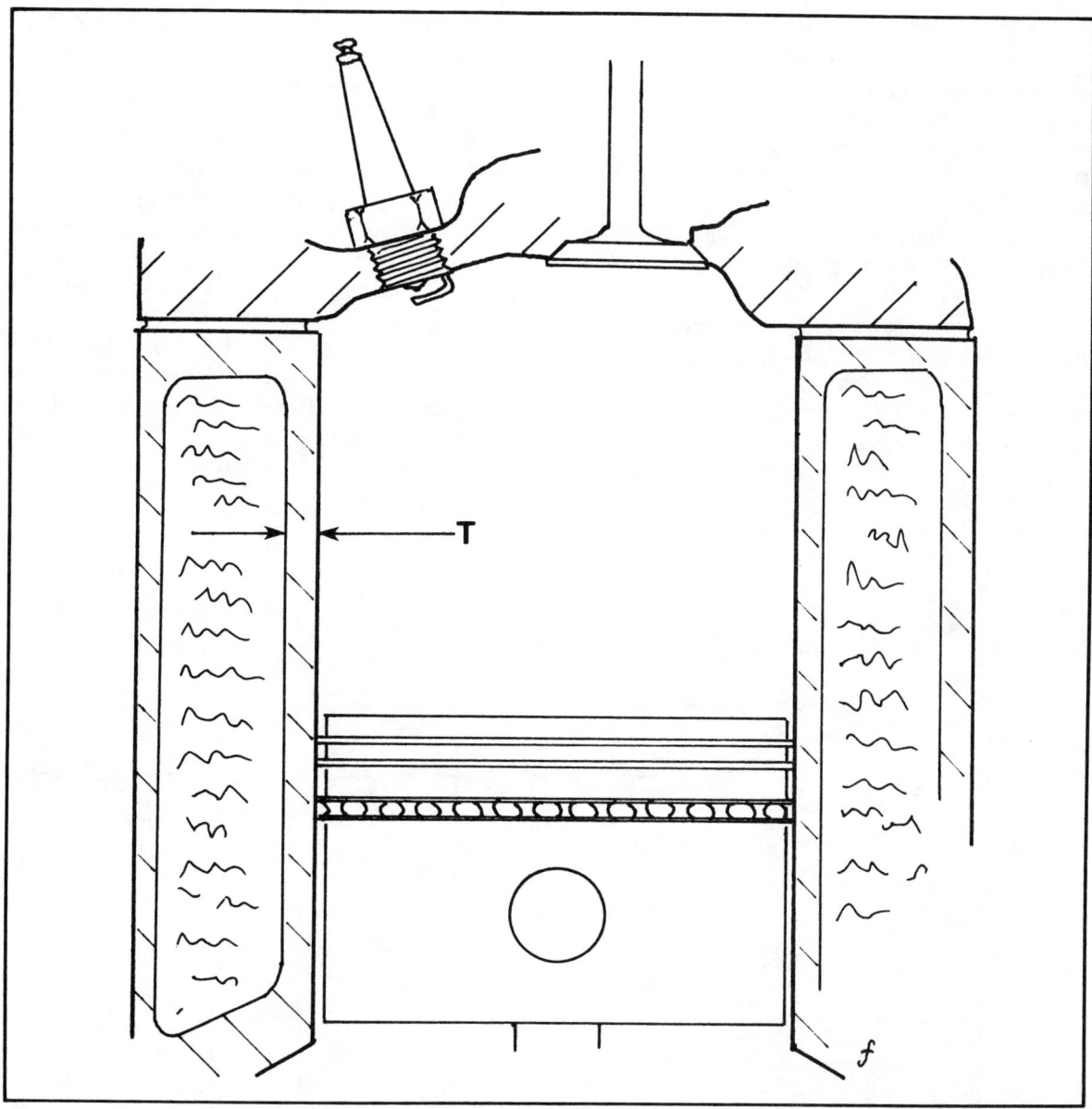

Fig. 4-4. Enlarging cylinder bore is limited by wall thickness (T) because coolant is circulating on the other side of that wall.

Grinding down a crankshaft to restore the roundness of its journals does not affect stroke length or displacement. An undersize connecting rod bearing is installed, but the piston will still be traveling its original up-and-down distance. Only by mounting a crankshaft of entirely different structure, allowing the piston to travel farther down in the cylinder, can the stroke be altered.

The manual's bore/stroke figures, then, are nominal ones. A particular engine might have been bored oversize during manufacture or rebored (even restroked) sometime during its life. This doesn't ordinarily affect the specs used for tune-ups and other minor work.

COMPRESSION RATIO

Few motorists or mechanics ever have occasion to calculate a compression ratio. Such computations are generally made only by engineers and by street rodders concerned with engine modifications. Because the figure is so crucial to a motor's power output and efficiency, we all need to know something about the factors that increase or decrease compression ratio and the potential effects of any change.

Compression ratio is the ratio comparing the total volume of space above a piston, when it's all the way down in its cylinder, to the volume when that piston is at the top of its stroke (Fig. 4-5). That is, it's the ratio between two volumes that hold the air/fuel mixture: that of the cylinder (displacement) and combustion chamber combined, and that of the combustion chamber alone (sometimes called clearance volume). We're talking here about volumes in a single cylinder, not the whole engine.

Combustion chamber volume includes the space cut into the cylinder head (containing the spark plug tip and OHV valve heads), plus the thickness of the compressed head gasket: the entire space above the top of the piston. Total volume is divided by that of the chamber alone, with the result expressed as a ratio "to one."

Let's take an example: a cylinder with displacement of 35 cubic inches, and a combustion chamber above that cylinder measuring 5 cubic inches. Compression ratio equals the total volume (35 + 5), divided by that of the combustion chamber alone

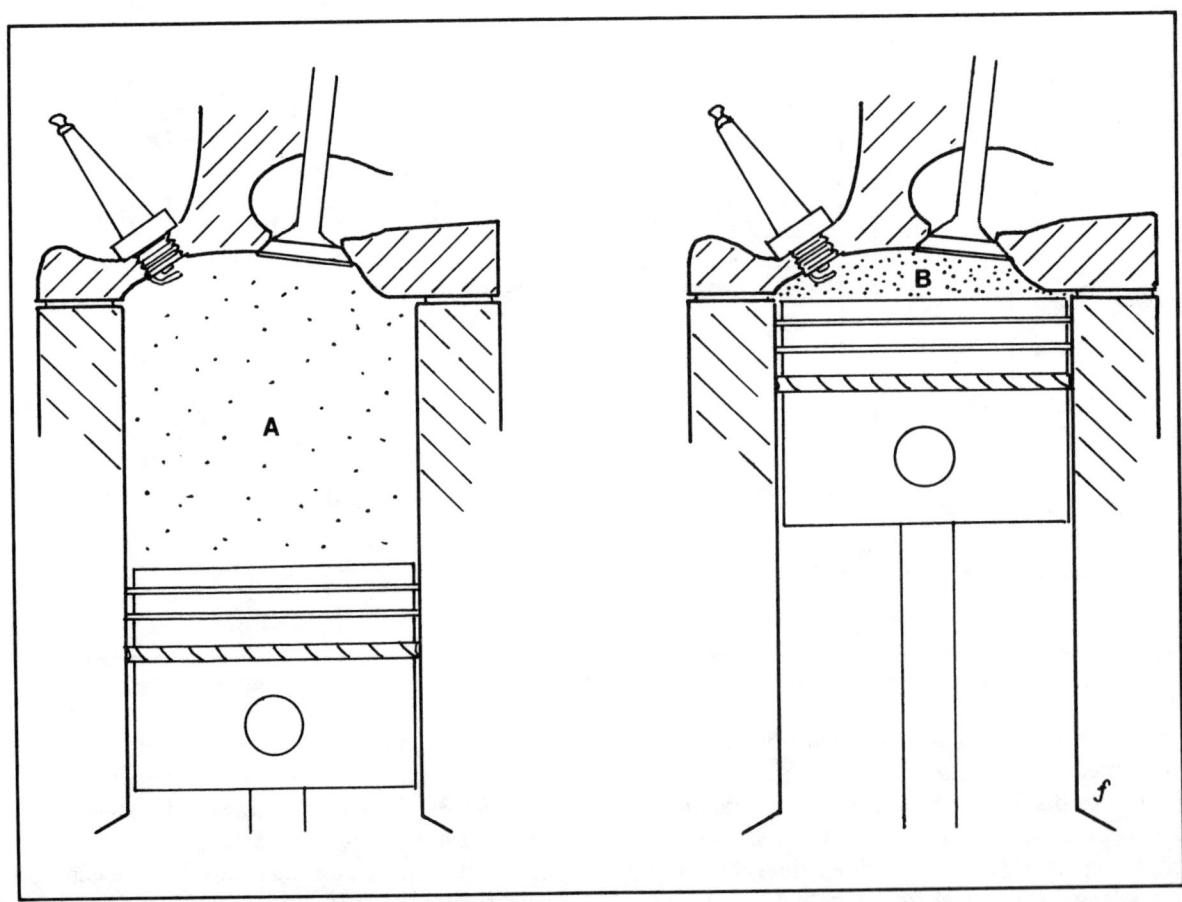

Fig. 4-5. Compression ratio is the ratio of volume A (total space above piston when it's at the bottom of its stroke) to volume B (combustion chamber only). It indicates the degree to which the air/fuel mixture is compressed as the piston rises.

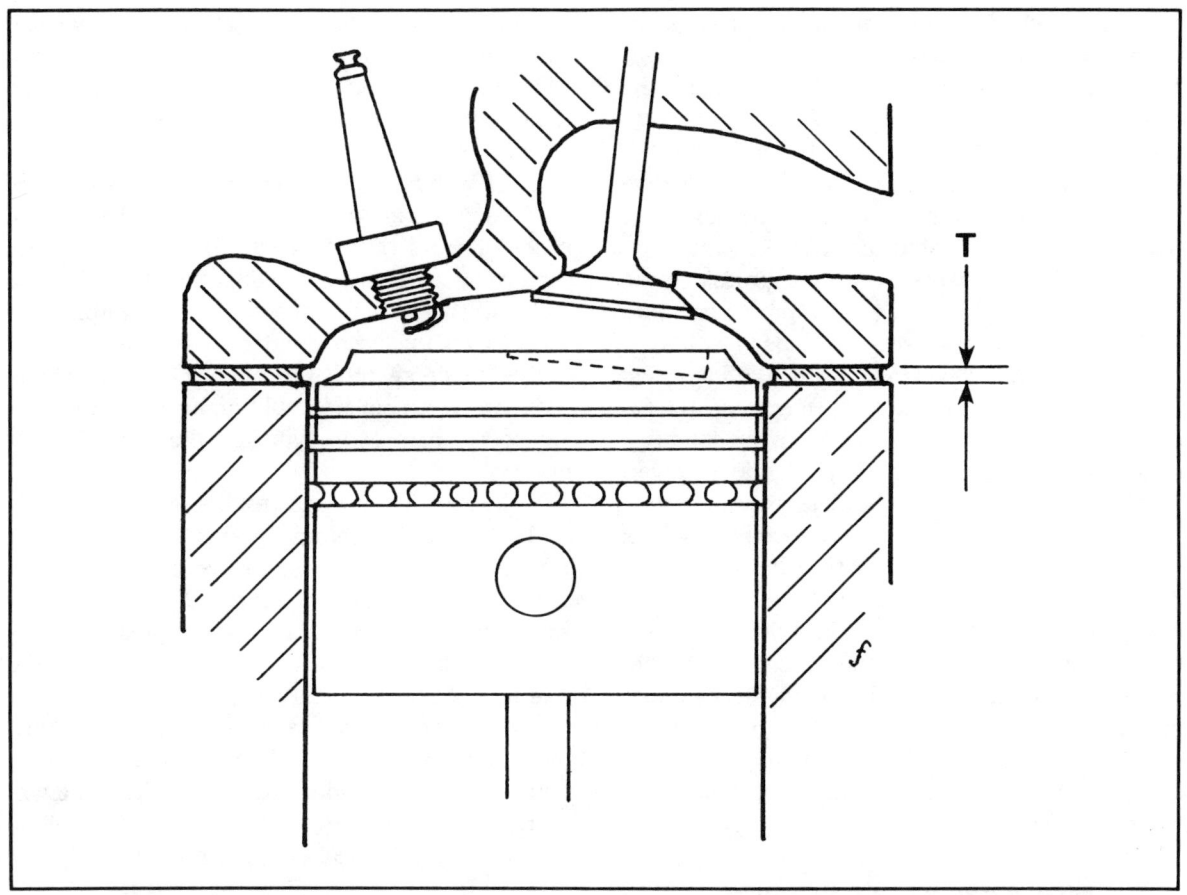

Fig. 4-6. Compression ratio can be increased by using domed piston tops (with indentations that provide clearance for valves to open) or by installing thinner head gasket (T). Both methods reduce combustion chamber volume.

(5). That comes to 40/5, which reduces to 8/1. It's generally written as 8-to-1, or 8:1.

What does this mean? Well, when the piston is at the bottom of its travel, the volume of air above it is 40 cubic inches. When it reaches the top of its compression stroke, that air (or air/fuel mixture) has been compressed into a space of only 5 cubic inches. It's been squeezed by an 8-to-1 ratio, occupying one-eighth of its original volume.

Compression ratio, then, is exactly what its name suggests: a measure of the degree to which the air/fuel mixture in the cylinder has been compressed in preparation for "firing" by the spark plug.

Cylinder displacement, as we have seen, is easy to compute when you know an engine's bore and stroke. Combustion chamber volume is not easily computed. Some very complex calculations would be needed because the combustion region is not a simple geometric surface. The space is further complicated by the presence of valve heads and spark plug. On engines where the piston tops are not flat, but have domes protruding upward into the chambers (Fig. 4-6), the calculation is even more involved.

A useful approximation can be made, however, by inverting the cylinder head and filling one of its combustion chambers with fluid. Valves must be closed tightly and a spark plug is screwed in so that the fluid doesn't leak right out. Then you pour the fluid into a calibrated container to determine its volume.

This method is common in laboratories for estimating the volume of complex structures. Remember, though, that the whole space above the piston has to be estimated. Therefore an appropriate amount must be added to allow for the thickness of the head gasket. In addition, a deduction must be made for any upward protrusion of the piston. Whew! Let's skip that one.

Several things happen when compression ratio is raised. The engine generally produces more power. Fuel economy rises too. It also demands a higher fuel octane level. Moreover, the increased combustion pressure causes more mechanical stress on piston rings and bearings. Lower the compression ratio and the opposite happens: less power, probably worse economy, but less strain on moving parts and operation with lower-octane gasoline.

Because a modest reduction in combustion chamber size has a substantial effect on compression ratio, carbon build-up in the cylinder head is a serious matter. It doesn't take much of that solid, hardened carbon deposited around the chamber surface—and on piston tops and valve heads—to reduce its volume. This could boost compression to a level that causes *detonation* (pinging) that might not otherwise occur.

Rise and Fall of Compression

Early compression ratios were quite low, on the order of 3-to-1, with plenty of space above the piston. The L-head design, in particular, was limited by the fact that its combustion area had to extend well past the cylinder edge. Both L-head and OHV motors, moreover, have to allow space for the lifting of the valves (space that adds to combustion chamber volume). Through the 1940s, and on L-head engines into the 1950s, most ratios fell somewhere between 6:1 and 7.25:1.

It wasn't merely a mechanical limit. Even if compression could have been increased by reducing combustion chamber size, early gasoline octane ratings were so low that knocking would have been horrid.

The birth of the modern overhead-valve V-8 and the Fifties horsepower race caused compression ratios to creep up steadily. Combustion chambers grew smaller, head gaskets thinner—and gasoline higher in octane. In 1948, the L-head Oldsmobile had a 6.5:1 compression ratio. The new OHV V-8 in 1949 was rated 7.25:1. By 1953, Olds offered an 8:1 ratio.

In 1955, the average compression ratio for U.S. engines was still under 8-to-1. But by the Sixties, ratios of more than 10:1 were available on high-performance engines. In 1968, Chevrolet's 427 led the pack at 12.5:1. Some modified engines exceeded even that figure, and the overall average had jumped to a potent 9.5:1 in 1969. Diesels have compression ratios considerably higher than those of gas-powered motors; typically they are 22:1 or more.

The switch to no-lead gasoline and the oil crisis of 1973 changed things forever. Following the gradual rise in compression that began in the 1950s, came an abrupt drop in the early 1970s. Chevrolets, for example, were available with compression ratios up to 11.25:1 in 1970. A year later the top rating was only 9.0:1.

Stringent pollution requirements also played a role. Compressions below 9:1 help reduce the emission of nitrogen oxides. As the Eighties began, average compression was down to just 8.2:1. The compression race was long since over.

Boosting Compression

As a rule, an engine's power (and economy) increase with a rise in compression ratio. Naturally, this phenomenon has long proved irresistible to street rodders. Any alteration that *reduces* combustion chamber volume will *increase* the compression ratio. So does increasing the displacement, but boring and stroking cost more.

Rodders have traditionally resorted to "milling" the head: machining its surface so the top of the combustion chamber sets down closer to the engine block, creating a smaller volume. Way back in the 1930s, high-compression heads were available to boost the flathead Ford V-8's ratio to an impressive 7-to-1 and Chrysler's up to 7 1/2-to-1.

When a cylinder head is planed (milled) flat to compensate for warpage, compression ratio is boosted in the same way (whether desired or not).

In many cases, a significant increase can be achieved by simply using a thinner head gasket.

The difference might appear slight, but a seemingly tiny reduction in combustion area often alters the compression ratio considerably. Moreover, a small increase in compression ratio can produce quite a boost in performance. Unfortunately, it also produces a taste for premium gasoline.

As an example, let's again take an engine with 4-inch bore and 3 1/2-inch stroke. According to our formula, it displaces about 44 cubic inches per cylinder. If combustion chamber volume is 5 cubic inches, the initial compression ratio would be 9.8:1 (44 + 5, divided by 5). Reducing the gasket thickness or milling the head surface by a mere 1/64 inch reduces that combustion chamber volume to only 4.8 cubic inches, giving a new ratio of almost 10.2:1. With a 1/32 inch change, the engine winds up with 10.6:1 compression. That is quite a substantial jump.

Like bore and stroke changes, alterations in the combustion chamber have been used by the automakers to produce performance versions of a basic engine. Studebaker's Avanti engine of 1963-64, for instance, came with a very thin head gasket compared with that of the standard 289 cid V-8. That accounted in part for the increase in compression from a sedate 8.5:1 to a sizzling 10.25:1, with a corresponding power boost.

With today's limited availability of premium fuels, a need to reduce compression ratios of older cars may become common. Some owners have done so by installing a thicker-than-normal head gasket (or even two gaskets), thereby enlarging the combustion chamber. More radical alterations, by machining, may well become essential to avoid damaging detonation in the remaining muscular engines of the guzzler decades.

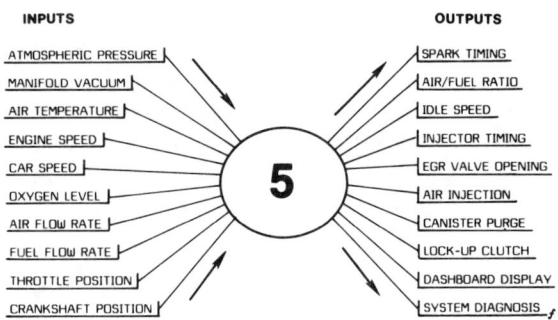

Power, Torque and Rev's

TWO COLUMNS IN MOST GENERAL ENGINE specification tables display the motor's output characteristics: one for *brake horsepower,* a second with *torque,* both at a specified engine rpm (Table 5-1). A third column showing *taxable horsepower* appears in some tables, but that figure is only for vehicle registration purposes.

Next to displacement, horsepower probably is the most discussed engine figure. Even more so in the past when horsepower ratings shot upward each year. You won't need to use horsepower or torque ratings in the course of repair/maintenance work. Both are normally computed by engineers, not mechanics, but they are important engine identifiers, and indicators of potential performance.

POWER AND WORK

Before getting into the horsepower and torque ratings given in spec tables, a few definitions are in order. We need to know about work, inertia, and power.

Any object—be it a car, a ball or a person—suffers from *inertia*: the resistance to change in speed or direction. An object that's at rest wants to remain in that blissful state. One that's already moving at a certain speed, in a certain direction, prefers to keep going precisely the same way.

Work isn't simply the stuff we do for seven or eight hours a day. It's a measure of the amount of effort (energy) needed—and used—to overcome that inertia. More specifically, work is accomplished when a certain amount of *force* moves an object (or opposing force) through a specified distance (Fig. 5-1). In formula form:

$$\text{Work} = \text{Force} \times \text{Distance}$$

Force is commonly measured in pounds and distance is measured in feet. So work is rated in foot-pounds (ft-lbs). Lifting a 100-pound weight to a height of 5 feet requires the expenditure of 500 foot-pounds of work.

One metric equivalent is the kilogram-meter (kg-m). A 100-kg weight raised 5 meters requires 500 kg-m of work. Another metric unit of work is

Table 5-1. Typical Horsepower and Torque Values.

Year	Engine displacement cu. in. (L)	Max. brake horsepower @ rpm	Max. torque (lb-ft) @ rpm	Taxable h.p.
1985	4-112(1.8)	84 @ 5200	102 @ 2800	17.8
1984	V6-231(3.8)	110 @ 3800	190 @ 1600	34.7
1979	4-71.8(1.2)	58 @ 5800	63 @ 3800	13.9
1970	V8-454(7.4)	460 @ 5600	490 @ 3000	57.8
1958	V8-370	300 @ 4600	400 @ 3000	52.8
1952	4-44.0	26.5 @ 5400	———	10.0
1940	6-216.5	85 @ 3200	170 @ 900	29.4

the Newton-meter (N·m), sometimes called a joule.

In automotive terms, *torque* (twisting force) is the most important form of work. We'll get to torque shortly.

Power goes one step further in adding the element of time. It makes a difference whether that 100-pound weight is raised to the desired height in two seconds or two hours. Power equals the amount of work accomplished in a specified time period (the *rate* at which work is done). To do work faster, more power has to be developed. As a formula:

$$\text{Power} = \frac{\text{Work}}{\text{Time}}$$

Work might be specified in ft-lbs, kg-m or joules; time in seconds or minutes.

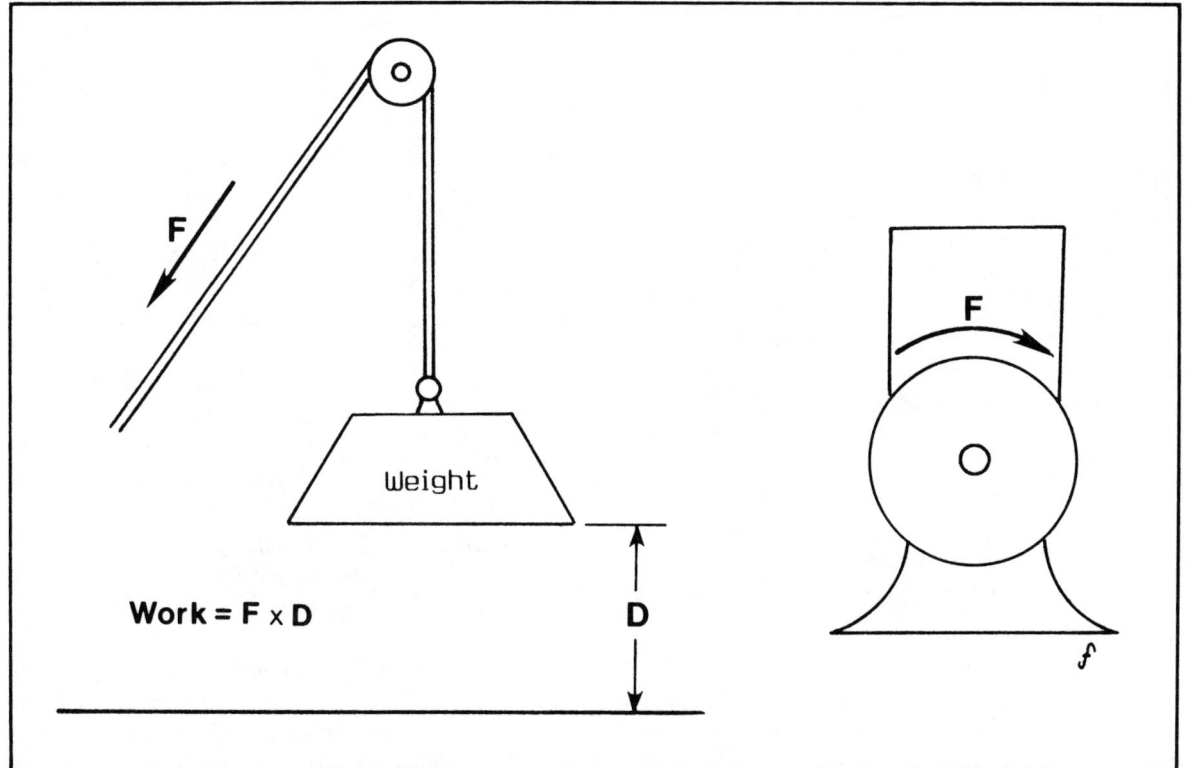

Fig. 5-1. Raising a 330-pound weight by 100 feet produces 33,000 foot-pounds of work. That amount accomplished in 1 minute equals 1 horsepower. Torque (right) is the "twisting" force applied in a rotating direction.

The most common unit of power (no surprise) is the *horsepower* in U.S. standard (SAE). One horsepower (hp) is the amount needed to perform 550 ft-lbs of work in one second; that is, to move a 550-pound weight a distance of 1 foot, in 1 second—or any equivalent. Horsepower can also be defined as producing 33,000 ft-lbs of work in one minute. Same difference. In formula form:

$$\text{Horsepower} = \frac{\text{ft-lbs per minute}}{33,000}$$

or

$$\frac{\text{ft-lbs per second}}{550}$$

As an example, let's take that 100-pound weight again. One horsepower expended will lift the weight 5 1/2 feet in one second. Keep going and it will be raised 330 feet in a minute (60 times 5 1/2). Double the horsepower and the same weight can be raised twice as fast (660 feet per minute). In other words, 200 pounds will go up the original 330-foot distance in a minute.

Does horsepower have anything at all to do with horses? Actually, yes. The unit originally was based on the presumed capability of a typical work horse. The horse could do about 33,000 ft-lbs of work per minute. So the term has stuck.

The metric equivalent is the *kilowatt* (kW). It's not seen much in spec tables or anywhere else. Motorists are so used to the term horsepower that it will probably hang on for some time, even after displacements and other measurements have turned to metrics exclusively.

Just so you know, though, 1 kilowatt is equal to about 1 1/3 horsepower. A 200-horsepower engine amounts to approximately 149 kW. How do you convert it? Just multiply the hp figure by 0.746; or multiply any kW figure by 1.341 to get horsepower.

TORQUE COMES FIRST

Horsepower receives most of the attention in talk about engines, but torque is the initial measurement, and it is at least as important. Torque is a special form of work (done by rotation, not in a straight line). It's a measurement of the engine's peak turning (twisting) force. A figure for brake horsepower is derived from the torque reading, and not the other way around.

Like other measurements of work, torque is stated in foot-pounds. To differentiate it from other readings of work and force, custom dictates that pound-feet (lb-ft) is the correct unit. That conforms to metric style (Newton-meters and kilogram-meters) in which force comes ahead of distance. In spec tables, you'll see it both ways: lb-ft and ft-lbs.

Torque is determined by the amount of force measured on a scale, and the distance that scale is away from the rotating crankshaft (Fig. 5-2). If the scale is one foot away from the flywheel or crankshaft's center, the reading in pounds of twisting force equals the torque figure in pound-feet. A reading of 200 pounds on a scale with a two-foot arm attached shows that 400 pound-feet of torque are available for doing work. Remember, work (torque) equals force multiplied by distance.

In principle, it's just like the pressure applied to a hand crank on an old-time engine. Less force is needed to produce the same twisting effect, if a longer crank is used. Thus, the distance upon which the force acts is crucial.

How can anyone measure the force of a running engine with a spring scale? The scale can't remain attached when the crankshaft keeps on turning, can it?

No, it cannot. Instead of measuring force so directly, we need to prevent the engine from rotating, but determine how much force is required to handle that job. The first device for doing so was the Prony brake. This device has a rotating drum and a brake band that clamps around its circumference. The test engine is attached to the drum and run at a constant speed, while tightening the brake band. This rising friction places an increasing load (resistance) on the engine. Speeding up the engine allows it to keep running against the increased load, but only to a certain point. At some speed, it reaches its peak and is able to handle no more.

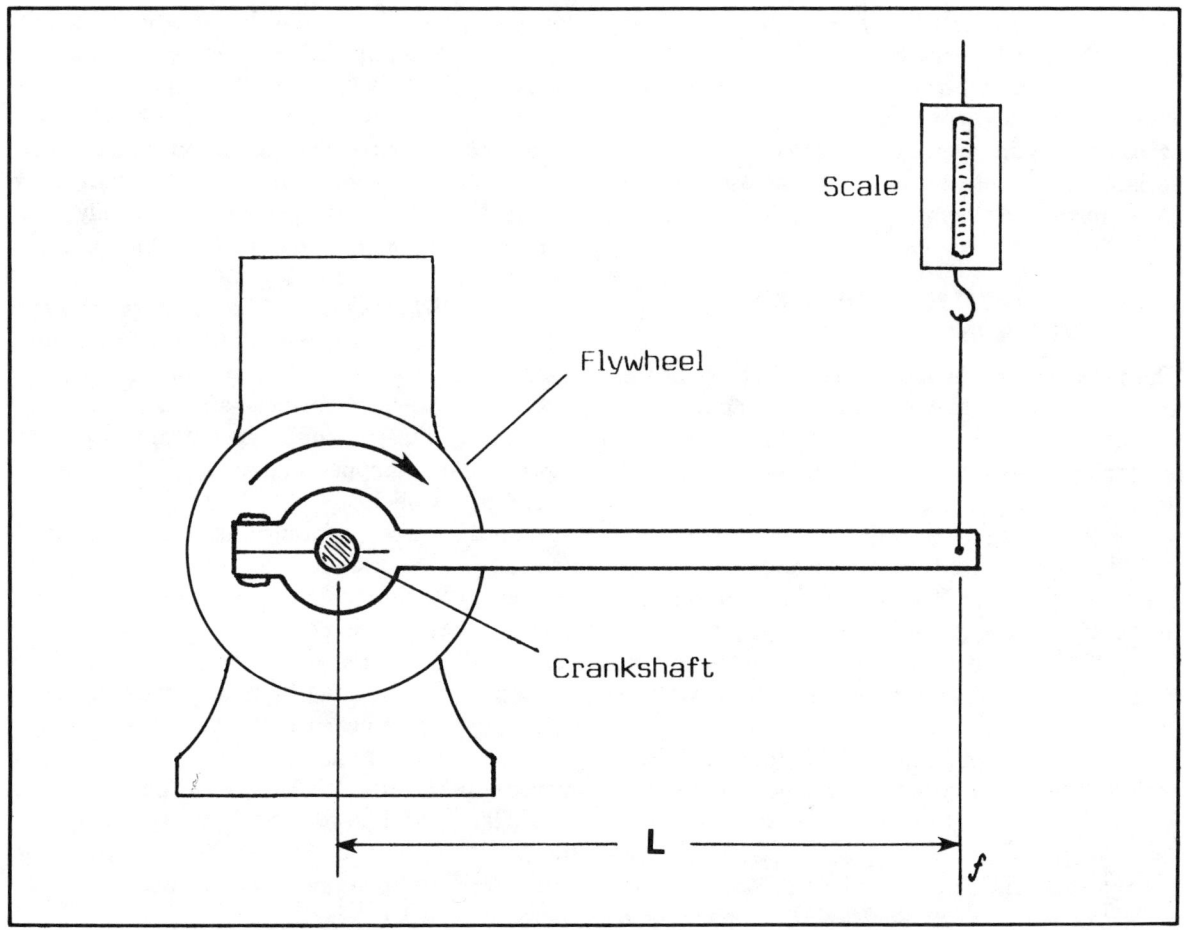

Fig. 5-2. The principle of torque measurement. Torque equals arm length (L) multiplied by force applied to arm, as shown on scale. For actual engine measurements, a braking device is used instead of a scale.

A dial scale on the Prony brake shows the amount of load. The load is the force produced by the engine to overcome the braking action. Combining with the length of the arm attached to the brake band, you get a torque figure in pound-feet (or equivalent). Brake horsepower can then be computed using a formula based on the torque reading, and the speed the engine attained before succumbing to the band's resistance. That formula is:

$$BHP = \frac{Torque \times RPM}{5252}$$

It's derived from a more complex formula that only test equipment designers really need to know.

$$BHP = \frac{2 \times pi \times R \text{ (ft)} \times S \text{ (lbs)} \times RPM}{33,000 \text{ (ft-lb/minute)}}$$

where R = arm length (radius), and S = scale reading

Today, torque and brake hp are measured with a dynamometer, driven by the flywheel of a freestanding engine. The dynamometer (or "dyno") applies a load to the engine's rotating crankshaft, and then measures how much it can handle and keep on turning. Torque and rpm are shown directly on scales. BHP may be shown on a separate scale or calculated by formula.

It's no different from the old Prony brake. Instead of friction, though, an electric generator absorbs the engine's rotational force, applying a variable load. The electrical current produced is easily measured, giving direct readings.

BRAKE HORSEPOWER: THE NUMBER ONE RATING

The figure shown in spec tables is always brake horsepower as calculated using a dynamometer or similar instrument. It's the amount of power available at the flywheel for performing useful work—actually moving the vehicle.

An engine's horsepower is directly related to both torque and speed. As torque and rpm rise, so does horsepower produced. Both horsepower and torque figures are given at a stated engine speed (rpm). They are the maximum figures obtained during testing (coupled with the engine speeds that produced these peak readings).

Torque reaches a higher value (in pound-feet) than that given for brake horsepower. Moreover, its peak arrives at a slower engine speed—sometimes less than 2000 rpm. Torque actually is the better indicator of an engine's potential performance, especially in acceleration, and the ability to climb hills without downshifting. But lb-ft ratings don't sound quite so glamorous as power figures.

If the difference between horsepower and torque is still unclear, just remember that torque is rotary force, or effort, that appears at the engine's flywheel. Power is the rate at which work is done. Torque exists regardless of an engine's speed; power depends directly on that speed. Torque does change as engine speed rises; but it may be present even when nothing is moving.

GROSS VERSUS NET HORSEPOWER

Through 1971, the published figures were for *gross* brake horsepower and torque, measured on a stripped engine. Every auxiliary part that wouldn't prevent the motor from operating was removed. Therefore, it ran against the tiniest possible load during the test. It turned little more than the fuel, oil, and water pumps (the built-in bare essentials).

Naturally, this produced the highest possible reading. Every device that an engine has to turn, from water pump to drive shaft, drains away a certain amount of power. Gross ratings were long criticized, for that reason, as being artificially high. In real life, no engine produced anything near its advertised gross figure (Fig. 5-3).

Since 1972, "SAE net" horsepower has been substituted. This is the power output with all "normal" parts attached. That includes the starter motor, air cleaner, full exhaust and cooling system, alternator, fan, and emission-control devices. In short, a fully equipped engine as it would be installed in a vehicle.

A net horsepower rating amounts to as little as two-thirds or three-fourths of the old gross measure. Whether it's really any more realistic remains open to question because specific accessories vary among "identical" models rolling off the assembly line. The ads, of course, include fine print stating that hp ratings are "for comparison only."

Torque, too, changed from gross to net measurement in 1972. Testing must be done under specified conditions: 85° F ambient air temperature, 29.38 inches (Hg) barometric pressure, and 0.38 inch water vapor pressure (humidity).

OTHER HORSEPOWER RATINGS

Although maximum brake horsepower is the only figure likely to be found in spec tables, or heard in automotive conversation, several other figures pop up now and then.

Advertised horsepower is simply another word for gross hp (or net hp in modern engines) published without an rpm figure. It's the one that appears in car advertising.

DIN net horsepower is a rating used in some countries. It's similar to SAE net, but the rating is obtained under slightly different test conditions. DIN stands for Deutsche Industrie Normen (German industry-standard).

Taxable horsepower is a figure dating back to the early days of motoring. Developed by the Royal

Fig. 5-3. High-performance V-8s of the Sixties produced gross ratings of 400 horsepower and higher.

Automobile Club of England, the formula is based solely upon an engine's bore diameter and number of cylinders. In the beginning, it gave the approximate output of an engine operating at a piston speed of 1000 feet per minute. As piston speeds rose, the formula produced an hp figure far too low to be realistic. Still, taxable hp manages to hang on while being used by some states and cities to determine the cost of a vehicle license. It appears in some tables and is occasionally called "rated" or "SAE" horsepower.

The formula for taxable horsepower is:

$$0.4 \times B^2 \times N$$

In words, this is 0.4 multiplied by the square of the engine's bore, times the number of cylinders. Stroke length and other factors contributing to actual engine power are completely overlooked. Thus, a 1947 Hudson six with 3-inch bore and 5-inch stroke (212 cid) has a taxable horsepower of 21.6. But so does a 1949 Willys with 3-inch bore and 3 1/2-inch stroke (148.5 cid). Some big-bore engines of the 1960s rate at over 60 taxable hp.

Observed horsepower is shown on a dynamometer and published in spec tables. The observed figure may need to have a correction factor applied, however, to compensate for temperature, humidity, or barometric pressure changes, and to produce a useful figure for comparative purposes.

Chassis (road) horsepower is measured on a chassis dynamometer. The car's drive wheels turn a pair of rollers that "absorb" the power. Variable braking force is applied while measuring rpm. The torque rating and speed are converted to a figure for horsepower actually available at the car's wheels.

The chassis figure is a lot lower than basic engine hp. Plenty of loss occurs through friction in the differential, wheel bearings, tires, universal joints, transmission, and clutch. Accessories like an air-conditioning compressor or power-steering pump, which might not have been installed on a test engine, absorb their share, too. An automatic transmission, in particular, soaks up an awful lot of potential power.

Other horsepower ratings are theoretical (the province of auto engineers). You'll probably never need to know how to use any of these, but let's take a quick look anyway so you can recognize them in textbooks and such.

Indicated horsepower is that developed inside the cylinders during the combustion process. It demonstrates the power actually produced by the fuel as it burns in the cylinders. The ominous-looking formula is:

$$\text{IHP} = \frac{P \times L \times A \times N \times K}{33{,}000}$$

where P = mean effective pressure (psi); L = stroke length (feet); A = cylinder area (square inches); N = power strokes per minute (rpm/2); and K = number of cylinders.

Whew! The engineers can have that one! Still, let's see what it means, just in case anyone ever brings it up.

The numerator of the fraction computes the total power developed in one minute. Divide that by 33,000 and you have the theoretical (indicated) horsepower.

Example. An 8-cylinder motor with 4-inch bore (12.56 sq. inches) and 3-inch stroke (0.25 foot), producing its peak hp at 4000 rpm (2000 power strokes per minute). Its tested cylinder pressure comes to an average of 120 psi. Substituting in the formula, we get:

$$\text{IHP} = \frac{120 \times 0.25 \times 12.56 \times 2000 \times 8}{33{,}000} = 182.7$$

You might also come across a formula with PLAN, not PLANK, in the numerator. That gives the power of a single cylinder.

Of course, the engineer needs a cylinder pressure gauge, plus another formula or two. Much more could be said about *brake mean effective pressure* (BMEP) in terms of engine efficiency. We'll just note that it's the average force exerted against a piston head through its expansion (power) stroke. The more BMEP you have the greater your engine's efficiency.

Friction horsepower is the total frictional loss in the engine (the actual amount of power needed to overcome friction). As engine speed goes up so does friction hp. It's the *difference* between indicated horsepower (derived from the above formula) and measured brake horsepower, which is always lower.

Example. If an engine delivers 180 bhp on the dynamometer, and its theoretical hp computes to 210 ihp, friction hp equals 210 - 180, or 30 fhp.

THE POWER/TORQUE RELATIONSHIP

Both horsepower and torque change with engine speed. The change is shown most clearly with curves on a graph (Fig. 5-4).

Brake horsepower is very low at idle, rising steadily as the engine speeds up. It reaches a peak at rather high speed, usually 3500 rpm or more, and then drops off sharply for the balance of the engine's rpm range. For small size or high-performance motors, maximum horsepower may not arrive until 5000 rpm or even higher.

The torque curve looks somewhat different. Torque is fairly high even at idling rpm. It rises a bit as the engine gains speed and reaches a peak at comparatively low rpm (typically around 3000, sometimes only 2000 rpm, or even less). More important, the curve is rather flat. It shows roughly the same peak torque through a wide speed range (on the order of 1000 rpm).

Drop-off is less abrupt than that of horsepower. Torque falls rapidly and steadily down to a very low level—considerably lower than that obtained at idle—while the engine remains well within its normal operating rpm range. At rapid highway speeds, then, the typical motor isn't putting out much torque at all.

Brake horsepower output is directly related to engine speed and to torque. If torque did not drop off so steadily, beginning at a comparatively low speed, horsepower would keep on rising. Torque, in turn, depends upon two factors: volumetric efficiency, and frictional horsepower.

Frictional horsepower, you'll remember, is the amount of power needed to overcome the engine's friction (to keep it going). It rises steadily as speed goes up. Brake horsepower responds to the increased difficulty of keeping going, and falls off at higher speeds.

To understand the whole story, you have to consider *volumetric efficiency*. This shows the

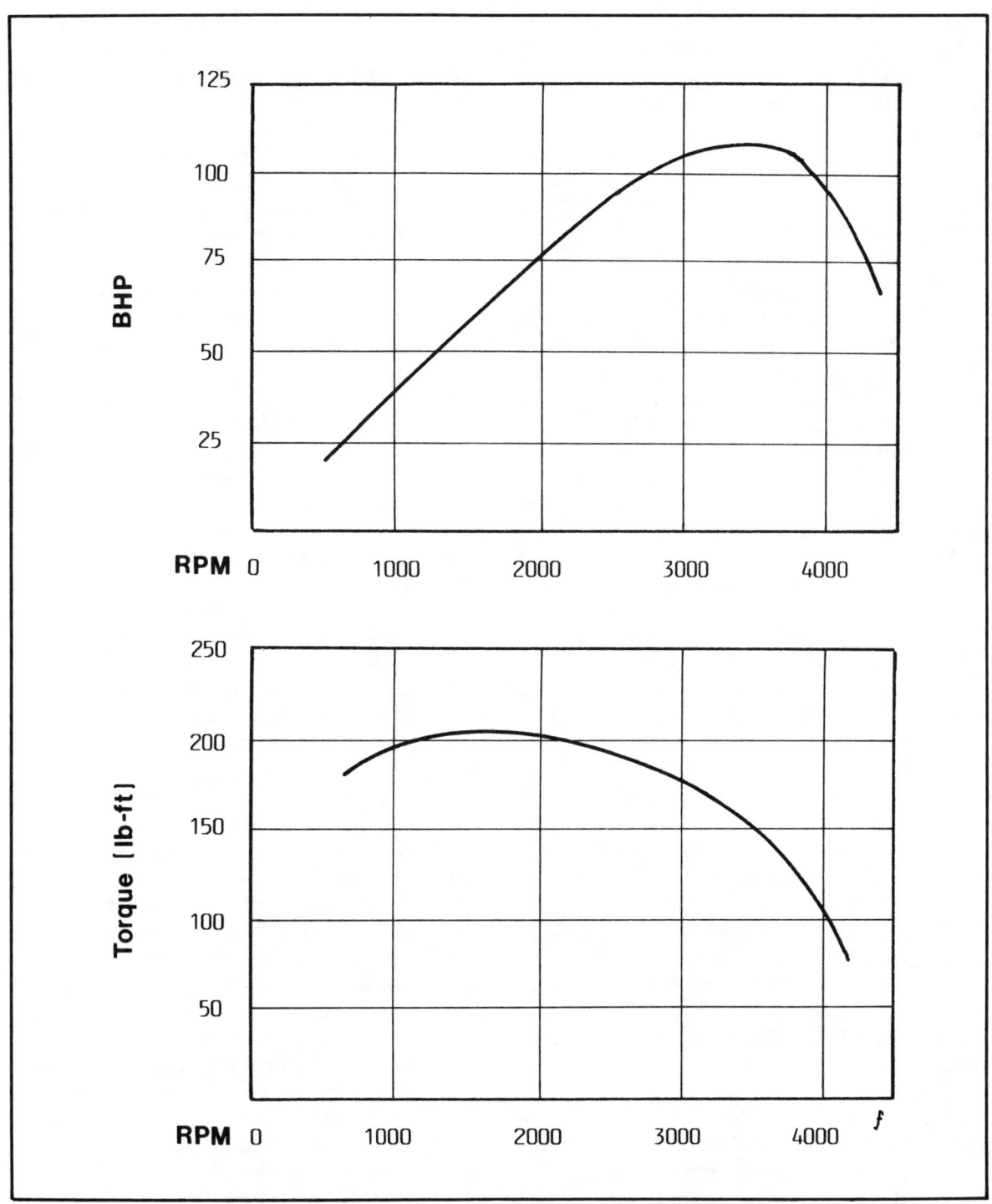

Fig. 5-4. Graphs show change in brake horsepower and torque as engine speed increases. Maximum torque is reached at a lower engine speed than peak horsepower, and remains high through a wider speed range.

amount of air/fuel mixture that actually enters a cylinder, and is consumed, compared to the amount that could enter and be used under ideal conditions. It's expressed as a percentage at a given speed. In formula form:

$$\text{Volumetric Efficiency} = \frac{\text{Total volume of air/fuel charge}}{\text{Total cylinder volume}}$$

The actual amount entering isn't easy to determine. The theoretical value (cylinder volume) is simply the amount of air displaced—the amount of space made available in the engine's cylinders—over a specified time. It's measured, by engineers, usually in cubic feet per minute.

Example: An engine draws in 200 cubic feet of air in one minute, to combine with the fuel in the carburetor. The space made available in that minute's time is 250 cubic feet. Volumetric efficiency is 200/250, or 0.80 (80 percent). For a standard engine, that would be pretty good.

Looked at another way, let's say one engine cylinder holds .040 ounce of air. Running at high speed, maybe only .030 ounce can actually make its way into the cylinder. Volumetric efficiency would be .040/.030, or 0.75 (75 percent). Again, that's not bad because high-speed efficiency could easily be as low as 50 percent. In that event, cylinders are, in effect, only half-filled, and the engine is "starving" for air.

Why such a change in volumetric efficiency? As engine speed increases, the amount of air/fuel mixture that has time to enter each cylinder must diminish. At idle, the intake stroke lasts close to 0.1 second. At high speed, it might last less than 0.01 second. That's 1/10 as much time—not enough to allow all the mixture to find its way from the carburetor, through the intake manifold, and into each cylinder.

Many factors enter into this measure of an engine's ability to "breathe" properly. These include the design of the carburetor and manifolds, valve port and combustion chamber shapes, valve sizes, and lift. Positioning the intake and exhaust manifolds on opposite sides of the cylinder, for example, improves volumetric efficiency. This allows gases to flow more freely in and out. The rating is also affected by engine speed, load, and the position of the carb's throttle valve.

Getting back to torque/horsepower, volumetric efficiency is lowest at high speeds. There's less time for the air/fuel mixture to enter each cylinder and, therefore, less fuel available to be consumed and combusted (and lower combustion pressure). The result? Torque has to drop off. And horsepower follows suit, reacting also to the steady rise in friction horsepower as rpm increases.

A look at the graph showing all four factors (Fig. 5-5) should make this relationship clear. Torque increases, along with engine rpm, only to the point where the engine is drawing in its highest (peak) air/fuel mixture. Beyond that point, torque starts to drop off. Horsepower output keeps on rising for a while, responding to increased speed, even after torque has begun to fall. (Remember, peak torque virtually always is reached at a lower speed than peak hp.)

Past a certain point, though, the lowered volumetric efficiency and increasing friction combine to soak up too much of the output, bringing torque way down. Horsepower responds with a very sharp drop. Because torque is dropping so fast, increasing speed no longer is enough to cause brake horsepower to continue rising. The engine cannot cope and power falls.

Engines differ considerably, though. A modern "oversquare" design (bore larger than stroke) tends to have a "flatter" torque curve: torque is higher at low speeds, remains at a peak through a wider rpm range, and doesn't drop off as much. How come? The larger bore and valves improve volumetric efficiency and the shorter stroke cuts down on friction loss through the pistons and rings.

The oversquare design also is likely to have higher horsepower output at medium speeds. This allows higher gear ratios in the rear end, along with slower engine rpm for a given road speed. In the 1930s, a typical engine had to turn about 50 rpm for each mile per hour of road speed. By the 1980s, engines turned much slower, typically only 35 rpm for every mph. Improved low-speed torque also

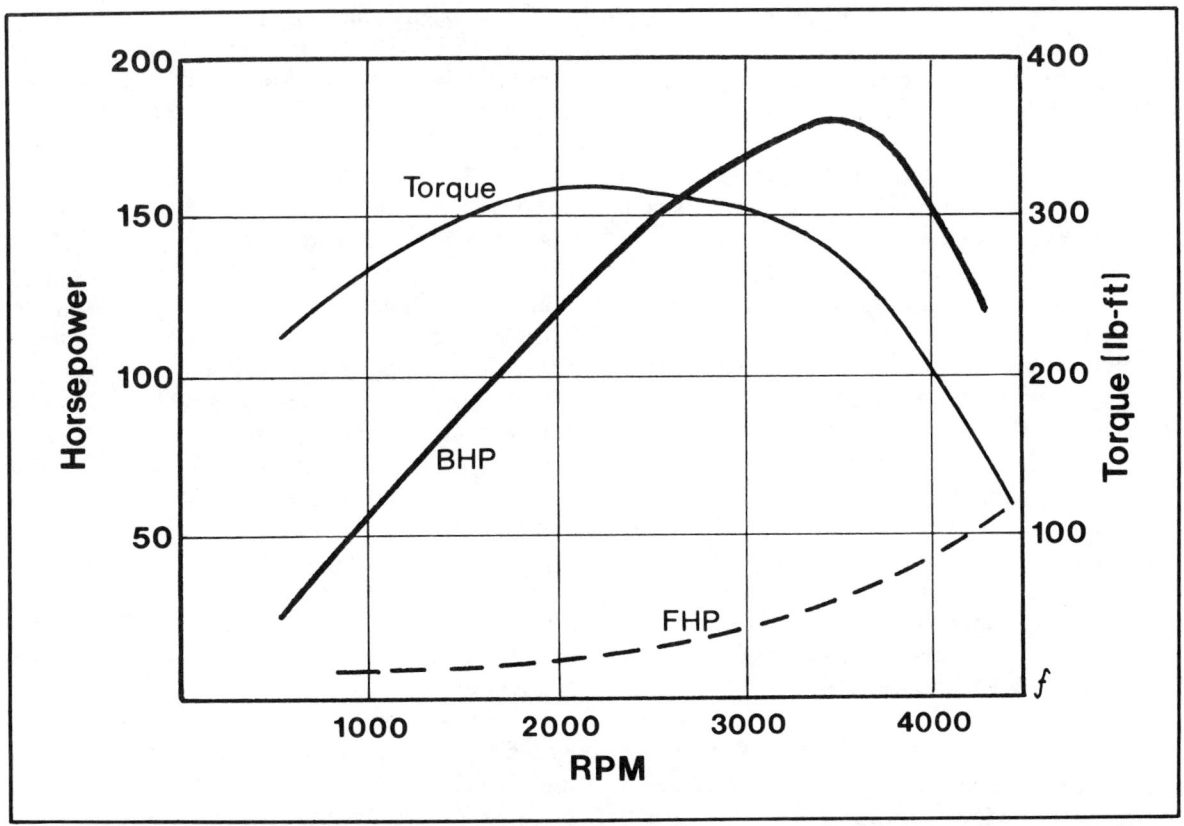

Fig. 5-5. Both torque and brake horsepower drop off as friction horsepower rises at higher engine rpm. This engine reaches peak bhp at about 3500 rpm, peak torque just above 2000 rpm.

boosts acceleration capabilities.

EFFICIENCY AND POWER LOSS

Volumetric efficiency isn't the only measurement used by engineers. They also speak of *mechanical efficiency,* which shows the portion of the output not lost to friction. It's computed by dividing the tested brake hp by the indicated (theoretical) hp. The average is about 90 percent. Like any measure of efficiency, it's actually the amount that comes out (output) divided by what goes in (input).

Want to get more complicated? There's also *thermal efficiency.* This is the relation between the power output, and the potential heat energy in the fuel that's burned to produce that output. None of us working in the garage might care much, but it's a good thing engineers can cope with formulas like:

$$\text{Brake Thermal Efficiency} = \frac{\text{BHP} \times 33{,}000}{778 \times \text{Fuel heat value (Btu/pound)} \times \text{Weight of fuel burned per minute}}$$

What's it likely to be for a typical auto? About 25 percent; three-quarters of the fuel's potential is lost somewhere along the way.

That's the whole point of considering efficiency: doing something about the losses that occur throughout the engine and driveline. In a typical motor, 30 to 35 percent of the fuel's energy is lost as heat entering the cooling system (and lubricating oil). Around 5 to 8 percent is consumed by engine friction. Another 32 to 35 percent goes straight out the exhaust. A few percent might evaporate as radiation, and perhaps 1 percent as incomplete combustion.

What's left? Only about 25 percent at the engine's rotating crankshaft. The wheels and driveline eat up another 10 percent or so. Thus, only 15 percent remains to propel the vehicle. That's thermal efficiency or, more accurately, thermal *in*efficiency.

Power loss shows up dramatically when horsepower is measured at the drive wheels, and compared to the output of the engine alone, with accessories detached. A reading of 200 hp with a bare engine could drop to perhaps 120 horsepower at the drive wheels. Losses occur in driving the fan and alternator, in exhaust heat and muffler back pressure, and in resistance of the air cleaner to easy air flow. Atmospheric conditions play a role, too. To say nothing of the transmission and rear axle, which eat up a lot of power.

THE FIFTIES HORSEPOWER RACE

In the early days, engineers had a tough time eking out more than a few horsepower from each balky cylinder. Inefficiency was the rule, and most of the fuel's potential was wasted.

Progress came steadily, however, and engines of the 1920s and 1930s grew surprisingly strong. The Duesenberg of the early 1930s boasted a mighty 320 (gross) bhp with an optional supercharger on its 420 cid Straight Eight. Ford's renowned V-8 of that era produced a more modest 85 horsepower, but became a favorite of early speed freaks because it had plenty of potential for hop-up add-ons.

Average brake horsepower in the decade prior to World War II was barely over 100, however. Massive rises didn't come until 1949 when the newly introduced Oldsmobile Rocket and Cadillac OHV V-8's ushered in the horsepower race that was to last for two decades. In 1948, average hp was only 107.9, according to *Automotive Industries*. By 1955, it jumped to about 174; in 1958, it was almost 239 (Fig. 5-6).

Thus began the age of guzzlers and muscle cars. Horsepower ratings shot upward each year in order to keep pace with presumed consumer demand for more and more power. Chrysler's "hemi" V-8 started life at 180 hp in 1951. By 1956, the Chrysler 300, with optional power pack, coaxed 355 hp from its 354 cid motor. The next year's Chevrolet, in fuel-injected dress, also achieved the magical 1 hp per cubic inch: 283 for 283. A few years later (1963), the 327-cid injected Corvette delivered a whopping 375 hp: 1.15 hp/cubic inch. Several V-8s topped 400 hp in the early Sixties.

In the midst of the horsepower race, however, a little-noticed trend trickled in: the compact car. Through the Fifties, barely visible alongside the boat-sized guzzlers, tiny imports with tiny engines steadily gained favor. As the Sixties emerged, Detroit responded to the wave with its new compacts: Ford's Falcon, Chevrolet's Corvair, Studebaker's Lark. Guzzlers still got all the glamorous attention, but the compacts were to be the forerunner of the future.

The rise in emission controls, the use of non-leaded gas, and the 1973 oil crisis combined to spell the end for muscle cars and the horsepower race. At its peak, nearly every American automaker produced a line of super-performance autos. The names form a unique backdrop on automotive history. GTO. Mustang Mach I. Buick's GS series, with 455 cid and up to 370 horsepower. Dodges and Plymouths, once modest family cars, came with engines churning out up to 425 gross horsepower.

Cadillac took the size prize at 500 cubic inches (but "only" 400 gross horsepower). The horsepower award for standard production autos goes to Chevrolet's 454, with a gross rating of 460 hp in 1970.

Published horsepower figures dropped automatically in 1972 with the shift to "net" ratings. But 1976-77 was the final season for power. Since then, horsepower has fallen steadily, and stayed down.

Nevertheless, a potent upsurge of interest in high performance arrived in the mid-1980s. Engine efficiency is the key today, and a lot of power can now be coaxed out of comparatively small motors.

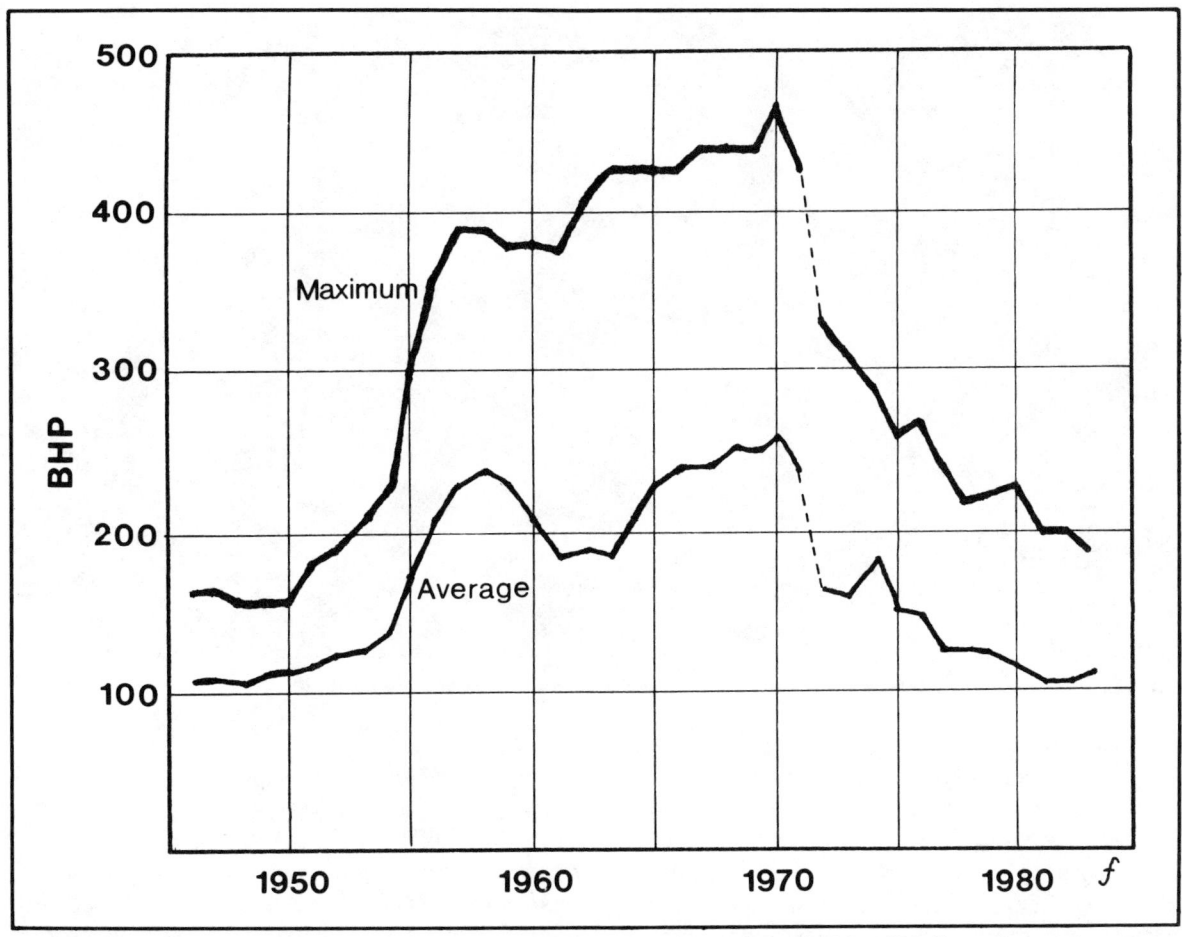

Fig. 5-6. Average and maximum brake horsepower ratings for American autos, 1946 to 1983. Note change from gross to net measurement in 1972.

ADDING HORSES IN MIDSTREAM

Whereas the horsepower race took place primarily in Detroit, among engineers and designers, adding horses began with the hot rodders (later to be called street rodders). From the early days of the automobile, a certain number of motorists, dissatisfied with the capabilities of their stock motors, have taken an interest in boosting horsepower. Many a Model T Ford found a new life as a speedster, taking advantage of a variety of bolt-on components developed by aftermarket firms.

The trend continued through the flathead Ford V-8 era of 1932-53, and into the OHV V-8 period. Street rodders are still around today. Their owners have never been satisfied with what Detroit has to offer (Fig. 5-7).

What can be done to boost horsepower? Many possibilities become apparent by noting the differences between engines in a spec table of the 1960s. The high-output versions are naturally large in displacement; brute inches do add horsepower. This is especially true when they come from raising the bore size. Compression ratios are higher because horsepower is almost directly proportional to compression.

Anything that improves engine breathing is good for an increase in power output. Larger valve

Fig. 5-7. Street rods may look old, but they usually have a powerful, modern V-8 under the hood.

heads and higher valve lift allow more mixture to enter. Improved design of passages in the intake and exhaust manifolds lets the gases flow smoothly through the engine.

Increasing the number of carburetors makes a difference. That is obvious when you note the horsepower ratings of muscular engines with 4-barrels, twin 4-barrels, or triple deuces. Installing a carb with a larger barrel diameter adds a few horses. Improved spark helps, too. Modern electronic ignitions do a far better job than the old breaker-point systems. Dual exhaust systems add several horsepower to any engine, allowing the spent gases to escape with a minimum of back pressure.

Heavier valve springs allow valves to remain tightly sealed during rigorous operation. Superchargers that force air down into the carburetor provide plenty of boost in the ratings.

Why would anyone want to add horses? The obvious answer is performance. A higher-horsepower engine gives vastly improved acceleration from a standing start or on the highway. The need for seven-second acceleration times to 60 miles an hour is arguable. There's no question, however, that good intermediate (highway) speed acceleration is a safety factor. A "reserve" of power on hand for emergencies can prove valuable one day even if it's rarely used.

Electrical Values and Measurements

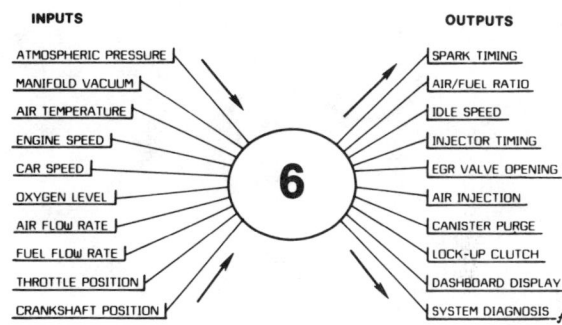

SO FAR, WE'VE CONCENTRATED ON FIGURES inherent in the engine's structure. Short of major redesign, they don't change.

Our first look at values that have to be tested, perhaps adjusted, comes in the electrical system. Specs are found in several places in a manual. There might be one table with battery data, certainly one for the starter, and another dealing with the charging system. Other electrical specs apply to the ignition system, but we'll get to those in Chapter 7. The lighting/accessory system is important, too, but fewer specs are supplied.

Before getting into actual specs, it's essential to understand something about the units involved, the electrical circuits in which those units operate, and the ways each value is measured.

Electricity is easy to overlook. Aside from an occasional glance at the ammeter, voltmeter or "idiot" light, we don't give it much thought. Only when trouble develops (or we happen to touch an exposed spark plug terminal) does the electrical system command full attention. At that time—and when planning the addition of a new accessory—a clear understanding of electrical units and their mathematical relationships becomes indispensable.

ELECTRICAL CIRCUITS

Electricity flows only in a continuous, unbroken circuit. When a wire is broken or disconnected, or a switch moves to "off" position, nothing flows at all. Current does flow in a *short circuit*, but not the way you'd like it to.

Unlike household systems that operate on alternating current (ac), in which the flow reverses direction 60 times each second, automobiles use direct current (dc). Flow is always in the same direction: out one post of the power source (battery), through the components that need power, and back into the other battery post.

Automobiles use a single-wire system (Fig. 6-1). The car frame, body, and engine block serve as one side of the circuit that is known as the "grounded" side. The other half, with electricity flowing through actual wires, is the "hot" (insulated) side.

Polarity determines the actual flow pattern.

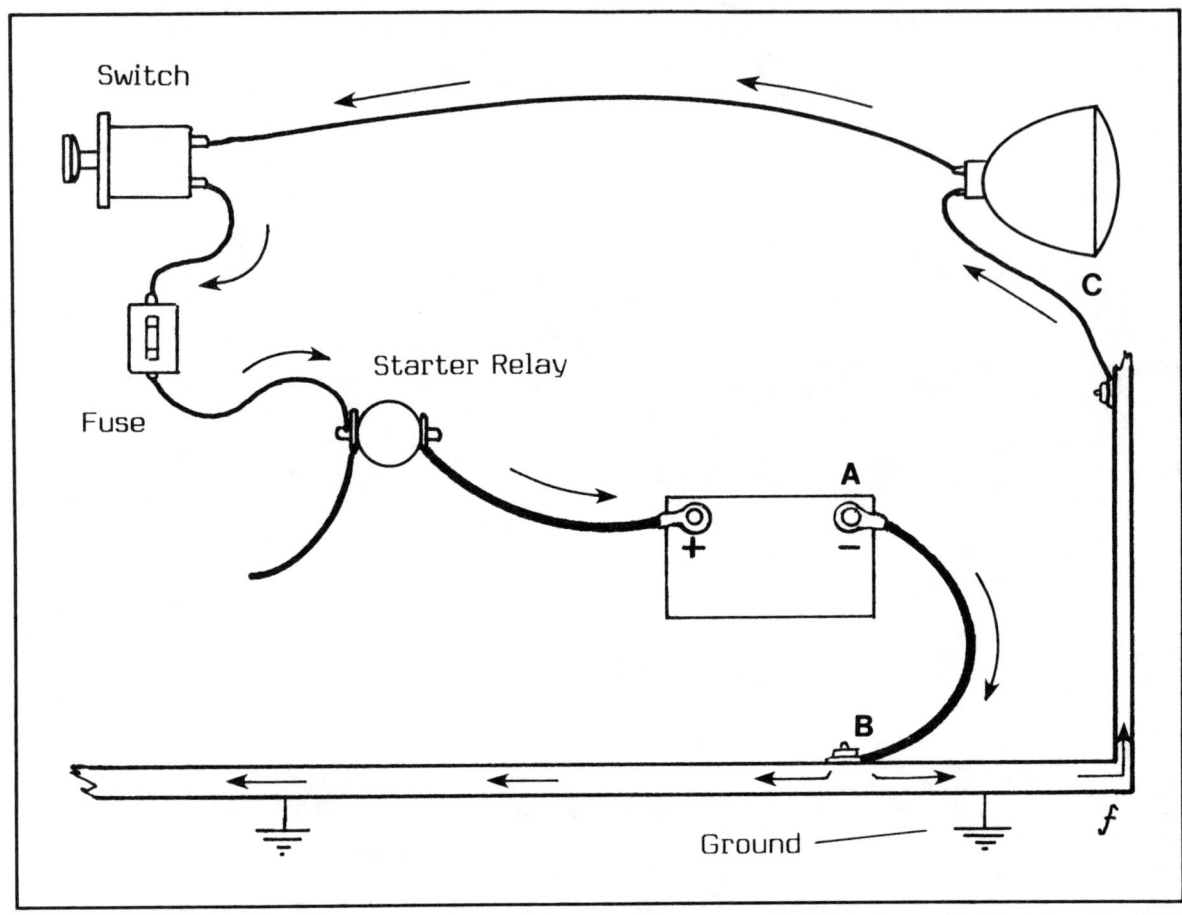

Fig. 6-1. In negative-ground system, electricity flows from negative battery post (A) into "ground" (B), enters headlight (C) and other components by way of their housings or ground connections, and then returns to battery through the "hot" wires and switches.

Many old 6-volt vehicles were positive-grounded. The positive (+) battery post connects to the car frame while the negative (−) post leads to the hot side of the circuit. Thus, electricity flows in the "obvious" way: through the wires and cables, into lights and other devices, returning to the battery via the frame.

In negative-ground systems, standard in America since the mid-1950s, flow is exactly the opposite. Electricity enters the powered components by way of their grounded connections and mountings, and then returns to the battery through the actual (hot) wires. It sounds strange, but as long as the battery is hooked up correctly the true flow direction is unimportant.

Components can be connected in *series* with the battery, requiring current to flow through each of them in turn (Fig. 6-2). A break anywhere means no current flows. *Parallel circuits* allow the current to split into several paths. This way a problem in one segment doesn't necessarily affect the others.

Automobile electrical systems consist of many separate parallel circuits, but with series circuits contained within most of them. Headlights are wired in parallel, for example, so one continues to work if its mate happens to burn out. Tail, license, and dash lamps are part of that same parallel circuit. They go on with the headlights. That combination operates independently of all the other electrical circuits. However, the fuse and switch leading to those headlights are wired in series. If the fuse "blows" or the switch hasn't been turned on, the lights do not illuminate.

VOLTS, AMPS, AND OHMS

Three basic units (quantities) act in concert in every electrical circuit: voltage, current, and resistance. Each unit is present whenever electricity is flowing.

Voltage is the unit of electrical pressure, sometimes known as electromotive force (EMF), or potential, that causes the electricity to flow. It's measured in volts (V).

Automobiles operate with two distinct levels of voltage: primary and secondary. The *primary circuit*, powered by the storage battery, produces a force, or push, of either 6 or 12 volts. The output side of the ignition coil produces a much higher voltage to "fire" the spark plugs. This *secondary* (high-tension) *circuit* provides a pressure of 5000 to 40,000 volts and is sufficient to cross the air gap between spark plug electrodes.

For convenience, secondary voltage is generally measured in kilovolts (kV), the prefix "kilo" signifying "thousand." Thus, a secondary circuit might operate at a peak of 20 kV.

Current is the actual amount of electricity flowing in a circuit. It is the quantity, or rate of flow, measured in amperes (amps, or A). Each operating electrical component—light, horn, radio, ignition coil—draws (demands) a specific amount of current. Unless that amount is available, and it's being "pushed" into the component by an adequate voltage, the device will not work correctly—if at all.

The particles that flow are called electrons. They're invisible, and awfully tiny. One ampere is defined as the amount of current flowing when *6.28 billion billion* electrons pass a given point in one second.

Starter motors are the most demanding. Some 6-volt starters require as much as 300 amps on a warm day, and 400 to 700 amps in winter when the engine is cold and reluctant. A 12-volt starter

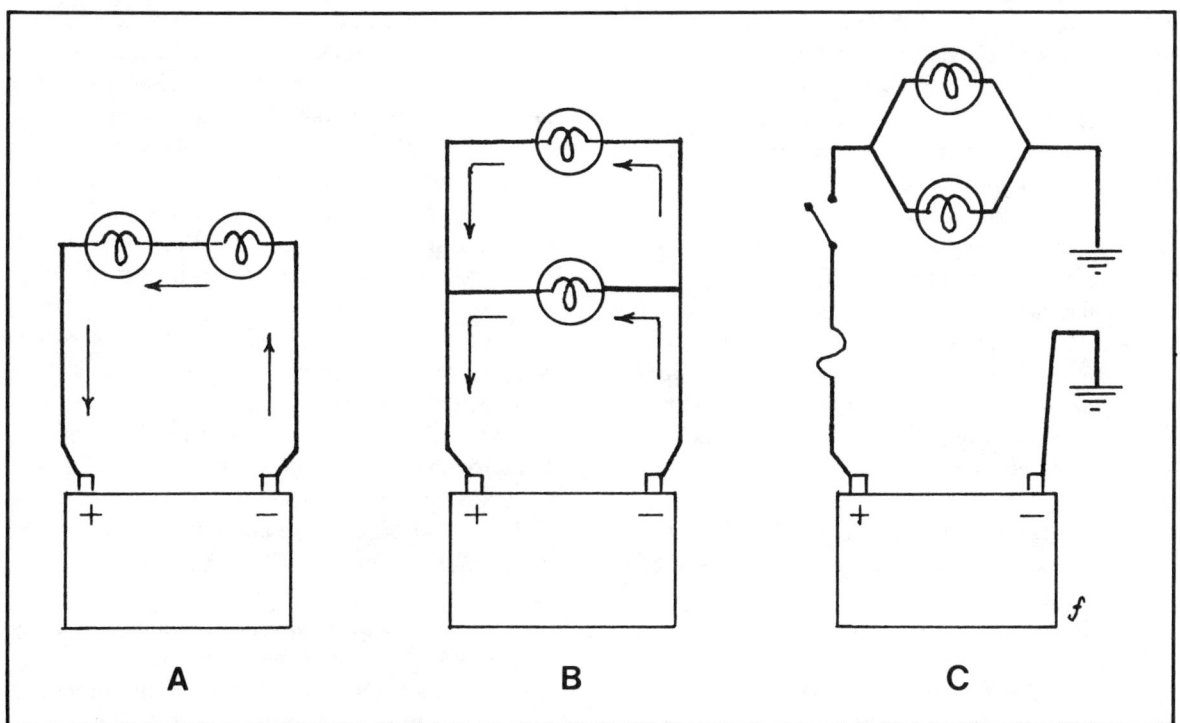

Fig. 6-2. Lights and other electrical devices may be connected in series (A) or parallel (B). Automotive circuits are often series-parallel (C); fuse and switch are in series with parallel-wired lamps.

generally draws less. Some of them, however, demand up to 500 amps in winter. Small, low-compression engines have smaller, lower-current starters.

Because a car's ammeter does not read amounts anywhere near these levels, the starter is not wired into it. Neither is the horn, and the horn will draw anything from 10 to 40 amps.

Much lower current levels flow into lights and accessories. The range is from a fraction of an amp to 10 amps or more. Six-volt units typically draw nearly twice as much as their 12-volt counterparts.

Extremely low levels, measurable in milliamps (one-thousandth of an ampere), flow in the high-tension spark-plug cables. That's why you can touch a spark plug terminal and survive, even though thousands of volts are present.

Bulbs have a candlepower rating that indicates the level of illumination they provide as well as a current rating in amps. Like most other components, they are also designed for use with a specific voltage. A 12-volt bulb used in a 6-volt system won't be harmed, and probably will light dimly; but a 6-volt bulb in the higher-voltage circuit will burn out immediately.

Resistance, the third basic unit, acts as the opposing force, or barrier, to electrical flow. It's measured in ohms (Ω, the Greek symbol "omega").

Every electrical component, from headlight bulb to starter motor windings—as well as the wires and cables, and the steel car frame—offers a certain resistance. We want the resistance in a cable to be as low as possible so that it doesn't impede the flow of current to where it's needed. Moreover, resistance creates heat, and we don't want too much of that in a wire. Same thing with switches, fuses, and connectors; the less resistance, the better.

The powered component, on the other hand, must offer some resistance to do its job properly. Were it not for the resistance in a headlamp filament, for example, current would zoom right through while doing no useful work. Most automotive devices have resistance of only a few ohms (or less). Resistance-type spark plug cables are the exception. They are rated in thousands of ohms.

Resistance in a wire depends upon its cross-sectional area and length, its material and, to an extent, temperature. Each wire or cable has a gauge number that ranges from #0 to #18 in most automotive applications. The higher the number the smaller that wire's cross section, and the higher its resistance. Doubling the cross section cuts resistance in half, but doubling length creates twice the resistance (which is good reason for keeping wires short).

Starter motor cables, intended to offer as little resistance as possible to the immense current flow, must be very thick. They are typically gauge #0, #1, or #2. Six-volt starters need the thickest cable. Main primary wires may be #12 or #14. Wires going to dash lights, carrying little current, can be thinner yet: #16 or #18. Each has a specified (SAE) maximum current-carrying capacity (25 amps for #10 wire, only 6 amps for #16, etc).

Most wires and cables use copper as the conductor because of its low resistance and moderate cost. Each gauge of copper wire offers a specified resistance per foot of length. Number 20 wire is rated at .01 ohm per foot, #10 at .001 ohm/foot, and #0 battery cable at .0001 ohm/foot. Some battery and spark-plug cables use aluminum conductors.

The engine block and chassis have at least six or seven times the resistance of the copper wires. This higher inherent resistance is offset by the large cross-sectional areas involved, and the use of large connecting devices. When all connections are clean and tight, resistance in the grounded side of an auto circuit should be negligible.

The rubber, plastic, or cloth insulator around each wire has extremely high resistance. The electricity isn't likely to escape if the wire happens to touch a metal part on the engine. Insulation must be especially heavy on the high-tension, secondary cables.

When devices are wired in series, total resistance equals the sum of the individual resistances. The total resistance of any circuit then, includes that of the powered component(s), plus all the wires, fuses, switches, auxiliary parts, and connections leading to and away from it.

For devices wired in parallel, the total resistance can only be calculated with a rather involved formula:

$$R_{total} = \cfrac{1}{\cfrac{1}{R1} + \cfrac{1}{R2} + \cfrac{1}{R3} + \ldots}$$

Parallel resistance of 2, 4, and 8 ohms would give:

$$R = \cfrac{1}{\cfrac{1}{2} + \cfrac{1}{4} + \cfrac{1}{8}} = \cfrac{1}{7/8} = 8/7 \text{ ohm.}$$

Fortunately, mechanics rarely have need to compute such values.

TEST INSTRUMENTS

Voltage is measured with a *voltmeter* connected in parallel with (across) the powered device: one test prod touching the "hot" terminal, the other going to ground. That might be the device's housing or a handy spot on engine or frame. In a negative-ground system, the negative prod goes to ground (Fig. 6-3).

Power must be reaching the component or circuit under test. When measuring starter voltage, for example, the engine has to be cranking. Voltmeters made for automotive use have two linear scales: one reading above charging voltage (0-16 volts or higher), plus a low-range scale (perhaps 0-3 volts) for evaluating voltage drop.

A dashboard *ammeter* shows not only the approximate current flow but its direction on a zero-center scale. A reading on the left side indicates the number of amperes delivered by the battery. On the right is the amount being sent into the battery by the generator. Few dash ammeters or voltmeters are accurate enough for precision testing, and cannot be "aimed" at one portion of the complex automotive circuit.

Test ammeters may have either a zero-center or zero-to-maximum scale. The latter requires attention to polarity when connected. A range of 0-600 amps or more is needed for starting circuit tests, but 0-50 amps should suffice for most other applications. Some meters require an auxiliary shunt or variable resistance.

An ammeter must be hooked up in series with the circuit. A portion of the wiring must be disconnected at a logical point, and the ammeter temporarily wired in its place. Many mechanics prefer to use an induction ammeter, which clamps around the cable being tested, producing a reading based upon the magnetic field created as current flows.

Resistance is measured with an *ohmmeter*; one prod goes to each side of the component or wire being tested. The component must be disconnected from the circuit by either electrically switching off its power or, better yet, physically (detaching its wiring or removing it completely). The ohmmeter has its own battery, and could be destroyed if connected to a circuit with power flowing. Ohmmeter scales are non-linear, and read "backwards." Zero ohms is at the right of the scale, and the lower values are spaced out more.

A volt-ohmmeter (VOM) measures all three units, as do many engine analyzers. Before connecting any instrument, be sure it's set to a scale reading comfortably higher than the largest value you expect to measure.

Special test equipment is needed for serious starter and charging-system tests. These place a variable load on the device, and measure how it performs in response.

OHM'S LAW

There is a constant, unalterable relationship between the three basic electric units. It's expressed by a simple, old formula known as Ohm's law. The law is named for the German physicist who derived

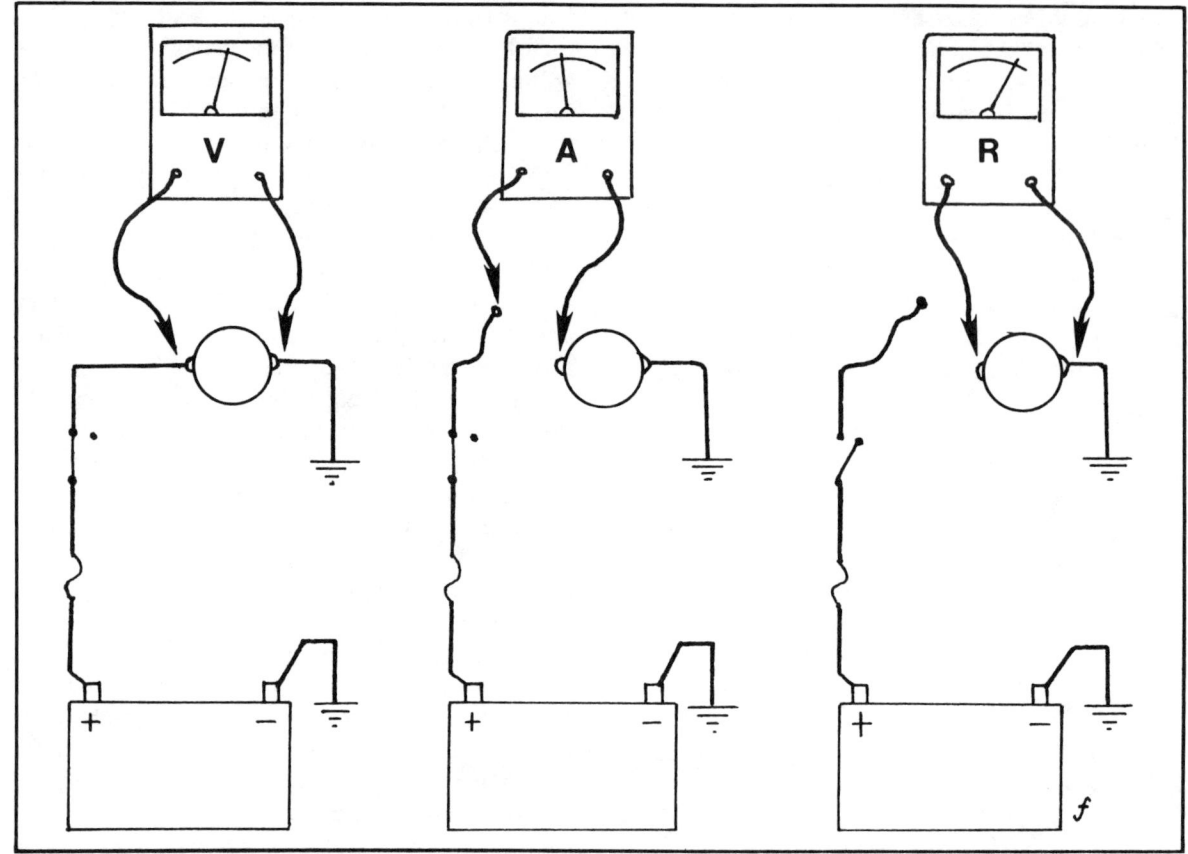

Fig. 6-3. A voltmeter (V) is connected in parallel with circuit to be measured; an ammeter (A) goes in series. Resistance (R) is measured, with an ohmmeter, with device disconnected or removed from circuit.

it. Mechanics don't often need to compute anything with the formula. When you are analyzing problems or making changes in an original electrical system, it becomes surprisingly useful.

Ohm's law states that a voltage of 1 volt, applied to a resistance of 1 ohm, causes a current level of 1 ampere to flow in the circuit. For purposes of calculation, the mathematical formula is:

$$\text{Voltage} = \text{Current} \times \text{Resistance}$$
$$\text{or Volts} = \text{Amperes} \times \text{Ohms}$$

This is often expressed using the standard symbols:

$$E = I \times R, \text{ or } V = I \times R$$

(E is electromotive force or voltage; I stands for amperage)

What does this mean? Simply that, as voltage applied to a given resistance goes up, the current flow increases correspondingly. Stated another way, if the resistance in a circuit is raised in some way, less current will flow unless the voltage propelling that current is also increased. Similarly, a greater amount of current can be forced through a given resistance only if voltage gets a boost.

Depending upon which unit you need to calculate, the Ohm's law formula can also be stated as:

$$\text{Current (amps)} = \frac{\text{Voltage (volts)}}{\text{Resist. (ohms)}}$$

or

$$\text{Resist. (ohms)} = \frac{\text{Voltage (volts)}}{\text{Current (amps)}}$$

Here are a few examples. If an ammeter shows that 2 amps of current are flowing through a bulb known to have a resistance of 3 ohms, what voltage is forcing that current through? Voltage equals the number of amps (2) multiplied by the resistance (3), or 6 volts.

If a voltmeter reveals that 12 volts are present, and the measured current flow is 3 amps, what is the circuit's resistance? It's voltage (12) divided by the number of amps (3), or 4 ohms. Note that this is the total resistance of the circuit, wires and all, and not that of a component alone.

ELECTRICAL POWER

One additional unit we need to know about is the *watt* (W), sometimes referred to as a Volt-Amp (VA). This is a measure of the power reaching a component (enabling it to do its job at the desired rate or level). One watt is the amount of power dissipation that occurs when supplied by a current of 1 ampere, pushed by 1 volt of pressure. Power, then, equals voltage multiplied by current flow:

$$\text{Watts} = \text{Volts} \times \text{Amperes}$$

$$W = E \times I, \text{ or } P \text{ (power)} = E \times I$$

For example, a 12-volt headlight bulb rated at 60 watts will draw 5 amps of current (12 volts × 5 amps = 60 watts). A dash light, needing only 3 watts to reach full illumination, would draw only 1/4 amp (12 × 1/4 = 3).

Every electrical device requires a certain amount of power—an adequate combination of current flow and voltage—to operate properly. A starter motor needs quite a lot; that dash light needs very little. Because there's a limit to the maximum voltage available, the power formula shows that current is the factor that determines whether sufficient power is at hand to do the job.

Going a step backward, Ohm's law tells us that the necessary current will flow only if the total resistance in the circuit is low enough to permit free passage. In the case of that 60-watt (5-amp) bulb, the total allowable resistance would be:

$$R = \frac{E}{I} = \frac{12 \text{ volts}}{5 \text{ amps}} = 2.4 \text{ ohms}$$

The power formula also reveals one big reason why 12-volt systems became necessary, in the 1950s, as more and more accessories were offered. Early generators needed to produce only 20 amps or so. By the end of the 6-volt era, some generator capacities had risen to around 50 amps, and increasing their physical size any further was impractical. But by jumping to 12 volts, the same amount of work could be done with just half the current flow.

An old 6-volt starter that required 3000 watts to crank a cold engine would have to draw 500 amps (6 volts × 500 amps = 3000 watts), but a 12-volt starter can do it drawing only 250 amps (12 × 250 = 3000). Both starter and generator can be less massive, the ignition coil is capable of producing the higher secondary voltage needed by higher-compression engines, and thinner (less costly) wires can be used throughout. Chevrolet's generator in 1954, for instance, could put out 45 amps at 7 1/2 volts. The following year's 12-volt version produced even greater output power by delivering only 25 amps (at 14 1/2 volts).

Well, that was the theory. As engines grew in horsepower and compression, and a huge assortment of options became available, the 12-volt generators had to keep growing, too. By the late Sixties, some of the new alternators had surpassed the current output of the biggest 6-volt generators, going beyond 60 amps.

VOLTAGE DROP

But wait. While we're on the subject of starters, there's another factor involved. As anyone testing cranking voltage has observed, the actual voltage reaching the starter motor is not the 6 or 12 volts promised by the battery. Even if the cables are adequate in size, and all connections are tight, the true voltage available is only about 4 1/2 to 5 in a 6-volt system and 9 to 10 in a 12-volt system. Voltage is even less during the first moments of cranking when current draw is greatest.

This voltage loss is perfectly normal. Such immense current flow into a heavy load overtaxes the battery's potential. Even when measured right at the battery posts, voltage is below par. Therefore, the actual current needed to produce the desired amount of work is significantly higher than it would be if voltage remained at its no-load level.

Far more important to troubleshooters is the voltage drop that occurs through wires, connections, and everywhere else in each circuit (affecting every electrical device). This happens because voltage does not remain constant throughout a circuit. It is expended, or consumed, dropping by a certain amount as it passes through each resistance in its path. Every part of the circuit—bulb, switch, terminal, wire—offers some amount of resistance, which causes a drop in voltage. The sum of all the separate voltage drops is equal to the battery voltage (Fig. 6-4).

Voltage drop takes place in the "hot" side of the circuit through every wire, switch, connector and other part between the ungrounded battery post and the powered component's terminal, and also in the grounded side. Naturally, the biggest drop of all occurs within the component itself. That amount is the actual operating voltage that causes it to light, rotate, or whatever its function is.

When all is well, this array of resistances and consequent voltage drops has minimal effect. Problems come only when connections or mountings have become loose or corroded, or a wire's strands have broken. These failures increase circuit resistance, which then reduces potential current flow. The same thing occurs when a newly installed cable or part is too small for the current load.

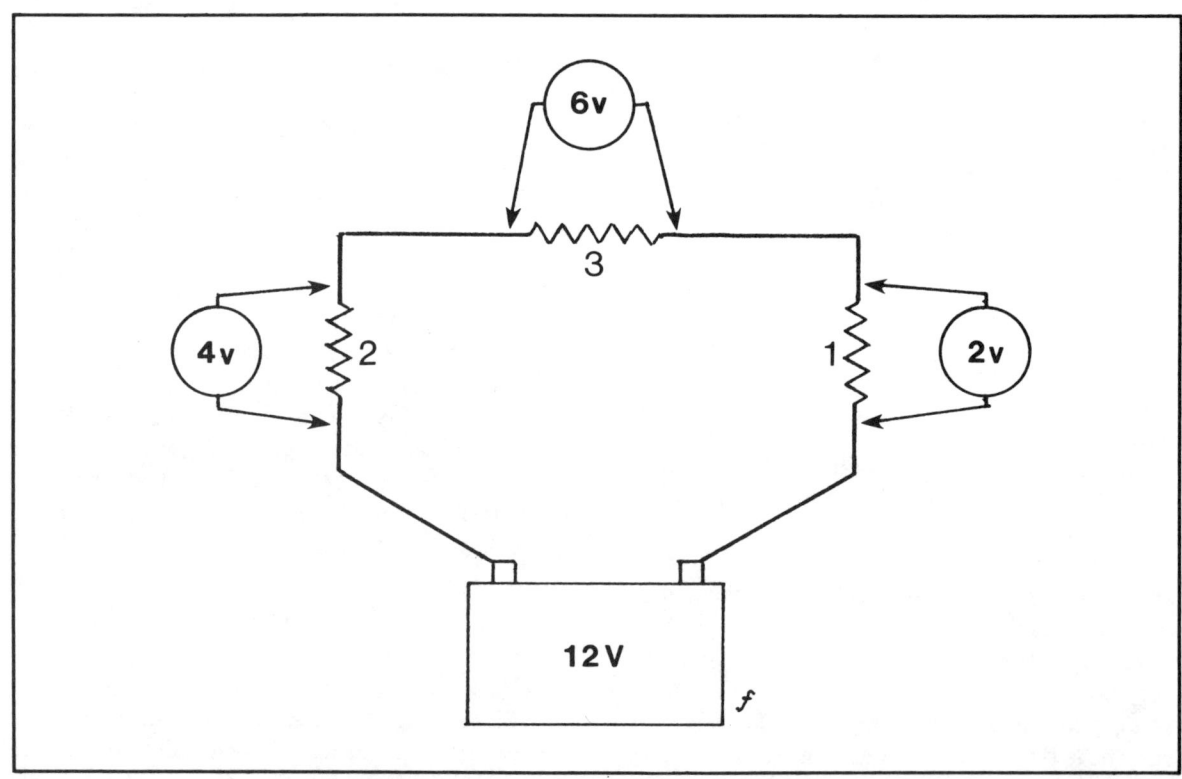

Fig. 6-4. A circuit with 12-volt battery and series resistances of 1, 2, and 3 ohms (total 6 ohms) illustrates the principles of voltage drop and Ohm's Law. Current flow is 2 amps (I = E/R = 12/6). Voltage drop across each resistance equals its number of ohms multiplied by current (E = I × R). Total of separate drops equals battery voltage (2 + 4 + 6 = 12).

70

The loss of a few tenths of a volt running to a dome light probably won't be noticed. Headlights, on the other hand, could become dangerously dim. A one-volt drop in the path toward the ignition coil results in the disappearance of several *thousand* volts at the spark plug. A fraction of a volt lost on the way to the starter could make quite a difference in cranking power on a cold morning.

VOLTAGE DROP AS A TROUBLESHOOTING TECHNIQUE

When electrical trouble appears, the first course of action is to inspect each wire and connection leading to the device that's acting up. Look for looseness at terminals, evidence of corrosion, damaged wires, and so on. Cable attachments at the battery posts and car frame (ground) are the most common culprits. Any connection or part can grow overly resistive.

If everything appears OK, drag out the voltmeter to measure the drop in each side of the circuit. A low range is needed so that you can accurately observe readings of one-tenth of a volt or less. The meter is connected in parallel with the portion of the circuit you want to evaluate. This way part of the current flows through that circuit and part through the meter.

To measure the drop through a length of cable, for example, one test prod contacts each end of that cable. One prod at each terminal of a switch reveals the drop through its internal contacts. Note the polarity of the test prods. The positive prod must go toward the positive battery post or the meter will read backward (less than zero).

What we actually measure is the resistance present in that segment of the circuit, but displayed in terms of voltage. Current must be flowing. To evaluate the starting circuit, the starter motor has to be cranking. For the headlight circuit, the light switch must be turned on. Evaluation of ignition drop requires that its switch be turned on, with distributor breaker points (if any) closed, so current flows through them.

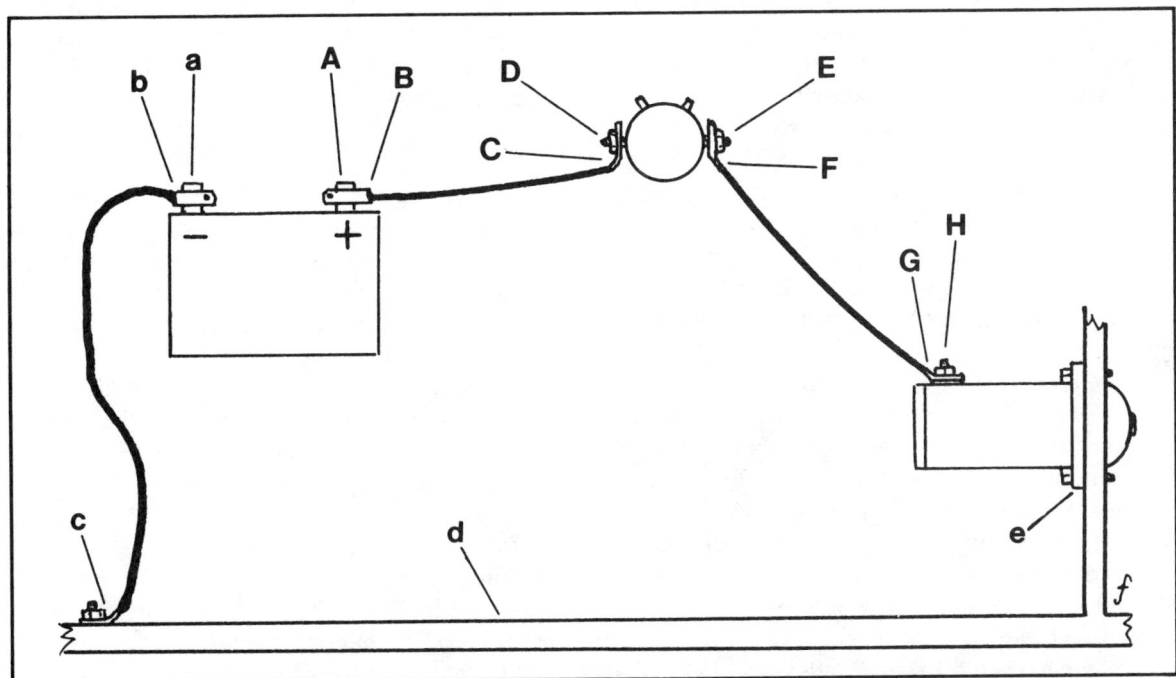

Fig. 6-5. When excessive voltage drop is found in "hot" side of starter circuit, separate voltmeter readings should be taken across each segment: (A) to (B), (B) to (C), and so forth, up to starter terminal (H). Similar readings can be taken along grounded side: (a) through (e).

Let's take the starter; it's a relatively simple circuit (Fig. 6-5). The first measurement is made on the hot side: one test prod to the ungrounded battery post, the other to the starter motor's input terminal. The meter will show full battery voltage until the starter motor is cranking. To avoid meter damage, begin with its switch in high-voltage position, and then change to low-range when the needle has fallen toward zero. Be sure to disable the ignition, by grounding the high-voltage coil cable or other recommended method, so the engine won't "fire."

A reading of 0.3 volt in the hot side of the starter circuit is generally considered excessive. Permissible voltages vary, though. Some factory manuals say 0.5 volt is acceptable. SAE standards allow 0.2 volt per 100-amp current draw. You won't find acceptable figures in any spec table, but they should be somewhere in the book. Look in the text section that deals with the part you're testing.

If the reading is high, the next step is to take separate measurements across each segment of the hot circuit: between the battery post and its clamp, between each cable end and the terminal to which it connects, across each switch, across the solenoid or relay, and so on. The reading between any terminal and its attached wire, or through a cable length, should be virtually zero (barely visible on the meter). Any reading of 0.1 volt or more is usually cause for suspicion, unless a cable is unusually long. This step-by-step procedure, evaluating the tiny drop through each separate portion of the circuit, should pinpoint the trouble spot quickly.

A similar evaluation needs to be done on the grounded side. Touch one prod to the grounded battery post and the other to the starter's metal housing (scraping away paint if need be). Permissible values are even lower than on the hot side (not over 0.2 volt, preferably less). Again, if the meter shows an excessively high drop, take separate readings through each portion: battery post to clamp, ground cable to a clean spot on the car frame, and so on. All readings should be well under one-tenth of a volt.

The procedure is virtually identical for every other circuit, but more parts and wires might be involved. Total permissible drop between the ungrounded battery post and the ignition coil should not be over 1/4 volt. For the grounded side, it should be considerably less. In the headlight circuit, a total drop of half a volt from battery to bulb is too high.

Evaluation of the charging circuit is possible only when the alternator is producing appreciable current. Turning on all the lights, plus a few accessories, should prod it into action. Total allowable drop through the insulated (hot) side, from battery to alternator, may be as much as 1/2 or 3/4 volt. It should be less on cars with a charging light rather than an ammeter.

Total drop can also be tested with one voltmeter prod touching the device's input terminal and the other connected to ground. This shows exactly how much voltage actually reaches the device. Subtract from a reading taken right at the battery to get total drop.

Note. Don't expect readings close to the "normal" 12 volts everywhere on the car. An ignition resistor might cut it down to under 10 volts at the distributor. A voltage limiter does similar duty in dashboard circuitry.

SHORTS AND FUSES

When a short circuit occurs, current flowing to a component is bypassed (shunted) away before it arrives. Electricity always takes the path of least resistance. So if a wire carrying current to a light accidentally touches ground, the electricity zips right back to the source. It never gets to the light at all. Worse yet, abnormally high current flows through this unwanted new circuit (which offers minimal resistance). That can cause the wires to heat up dangerously as well as drain the battery in a hurry.

Fuses and circuit breakers prevent that possibility. When current in excess of a fuse or breaker's rated capacity begins to flow, for whatever reason, it "blows" the fuse or "opens" the breaker, halting current flow abruptly.

Both devices are rated in amps. Any flow above that amount causes the circuit to open. A chart listing fuse ratings (and locations) is found in the owner's or shop manual. Most have a substantial safety margin that is rated higher than the anticipated current. Switches, too, have a specified amperage (current handling) capacity.

BATTERY RATINGS

Not all manuals contain battery data organized like Table 6-1. Several important ratings appear in battery catalogs or in a manual's text.

Motorists tend to buy the battery model recommended for their car without thinking much about the battery's capacity. They should. A little knowledge could reduce the risk of finding a dead battery one day.

General spec tables for early models have columns for battery voltage and polarity: 6 or 12 volts, positive or negative ground. Because virtually all modern systems are 12-volt negative ground, that information is superfluous today.

Each cell in a real-life battery actually measures about 2.1 volts. A 12-volt battery contains six cells. Tested by itself (no load), it should read 12.6 volts or more (if fully charged). Most battery figures are given for tests in a specified ambient temperature (usually 80° F).

That open-circuit voltage corresponds directly to the battery electrolyte's specific gravity. Today's maintenance-free batteries have only a self-test indicator that shows the approximate state of charge. Old-style batteries, with removable caps, can be tested with a hydrometer. A few points must be added to the hydrometer reading if electrolyte temperature is above 80° F or points must be deducted if the temperature is below that.

A fully charged battery should read between 1.260 and 1.300 specific gravity (spoken of as "twelve-sixty to thirteen-hundred"). The voltmeter should give a reading of 12.6 to 12.9 volts, open circuit. A half-discharged battery drops to around 1.225 gravity, 12 1/2 volts or less.

State-of-charge tests apply to any battery. Specific batteries have rated capacities according to standard tests. They show which battery model is acceptable for a given engine.

Ampere-Hour Capacity. The ampere-hour capacity is the ability to deliver a stated current (amps) for a specified length of time (in hours). This used to be the basic (published) measure of battery capacity. A 120 ampere-hour battery is capable of delivering 20 amps for 6 hours, 40 amps for 3 hours—any combination which, when multiplied, equals 120.

20-Hour Rating. The 20-hour rating is a more recent amp-hour rating method. It's the discharge rate (in amps) a battery can handle for 20 hours, with its no-load voltage dropping to no lower than 10.5 volts.

Reserve Capacity. The reserve capacity is the number of minutes a battery will supply current into the system if the charging system fails. A 25-amp discharge load is applied until the cells drop to 1.75 volts each (again, 10.5-volt total). This test has replaced the amp-hr and 20-hour ratings.

Cold Cranking Rating (Cold Cranking Amps—CCA). Cold cranking is the ability to function in winter. Testing at 0° F, the battery is discharged at the highest amperage rate that will maintain a 1.2-volt minimum cell reading (7.2 volts total) after 30 seconds. An additional test at −20° F, allowing 1.0 volt per cell, may be performed. The Automotive Information Council recommends that CCA rating be equal to the engine's displacement in cubic inches or 250 amps (whichever is larger). Delco batteries have an equivalent rating in watts.

The tests above are made only to derive published battery ratings. One test, commonly done in shops is *battery load* using an instrument that applies a variable current load (Fig. 6-6). A substan-

Table 6-1. Typical Battery Data.

BCI group size	Volts	Terminals	Cold cranking amps (0°F)	Reserve capacity (minutes)
24F	12	Post	500	120
24	12	SAE	325	70
71	12	Side	395	78
8D	12[1]	SAE	1000	390
1	6	Post	545	155

[1]For diesel engines.

Fig. 6-6. Test meter with variable loading control can evaluate both battery and starter motor. (Sun Electric Corp.)

tial discharge—perhaps three times published capacity—is applied to a fully charged battery for 15 seconds. Unless voltage remains at 9 1/2 volts or so, the battery is no good. Permissible readings vary with temperature: perhaps 9.9 volts at 70° F, down to 8.5 volts at zero. This test reveals whether the battery can or cannot hold a charge.

A rough, but very useful, indication of battery strength is shown by the simple cranking voltage test. Just watch the voltmeter while cranking the engine with ignition disabled so it won't start. A reading under 9 to 9 1/2 volts (4 1/2 with a 6-volt battery) means the battery needs recharging or it might be defective.

STARTER SPECS

Two of the most valuable tests of starter operation have been already described: voltage drop, and cranking voltage. Further tests are performed only when the starter responds poorly to a good battery, supplying acceptable voltage.

Data similar to that in Table 6-2 appears in most manuals (perhaps in a section devoted to the starting system). Tables often list the starter make (Delco-Remy, Bosch, etc.) and model number as well as test details.

Free Speed Test (No-Load Test). This test is done with the starter motor out of the car, and mounted in a special test instrument. The starter is allowed to turn as fast as it can, with no physical load placed upon it. Test readings markedly different from the table specs for amps, volts, and rotational speed (rpm) suggest the starter has problems. Either a range or absolute desirable figure

Table 6-2. Typical Starter Motor Specifications.

Free speed (no-load) test			Lock torque (or resistance) test			Brush spring tension	Solenoid windings (A)	
A	V	rpm	A	V	lb-ft	(oz)	Hold-in	Pull-in
91	11	5700	—	—	—	32-36	13-15	8-11
45-70[2]	9	7000-11900	—	—	—	35[1]	13-19	23-30
60	11.5	7000	Not Recommended			50-64	—	—
80	12	—	670	5	15.5	80	—	—
70-99[2]	10.6	6200-10700	300-360	3.5	—	35	—	—
48	10.0	5300	285	4.0	6.5	35	—	—
65	5.0	5000	525	3.4	12	24-28	—	—
77	5.5	2695	906	4.0	45.9	42-53	—	—

[1]Minimum. [2]Includes solenoid.

will be given for each value.

Resistance or Lock Torque Test. This test is performed on a special instrument, but with a physical load placed upon the motor to limit its rotation. The resistance test is more common in modern tables, with specs given for amperage and voltage. Specs for a lock torque test also give a recommended torque reading in pound-feet. During the test, a starter should be drawing near the specified number of amps: from about 300 to 700 or more. Recommended voltage is usually 5 V or less; torque is between 10 and 20 pound-feet. Not all of today's manuals include either spec.

Lacking the correct test equipment, you can at least test the *normal* current draw, if you have a high-range induction ammeter that clamps over the starter cable.

Brush Spring Tension. Brush spring tension is measured with a spring scale, in ounces, to determine how firmly the motor's brushes press against the commutator. In real life, this test isn't made exactly every day.

Solenoid Winding Hold-In (and Pull-In). This specification is given in some recent manuals, for certain starter models. It's a test of initial solenoid actuation and subsequent holding power, measured in amperes of current draw. This one isn't too common either, but worth knowing about if a starter solenoid doesn't seem to respond properly.

Whining or grinding sounds emanating from a starter could suggest improper clearance between the motor's drive gear and the flywheel ring gear. Proper clearance between the gear teeth ranges from about .025 to .060 inch. Shims may be added or deleted, at the starter mounting, to make any correction.

ALTERNATOR AND REGULATOR DATA

When constant or frequent readings on the discharge side of an ammeter appear or a charge light is on too much of the time, several charging system tests are possible. A basic output test can be performed "on the car." Others require removal of the alternator and special equipment.

Alternator/regulator specs (Table 6-3) might accompany other data for a given car make, or appear in a separate charging-system section. Alternator and regulator part numbers are given. There might be a color code that helps identify a particular alternator.

The initial test requires no specs at all. Simply hook up the voltmeter to the battery, and take a reading with the engine off. The reading should be around 12 1/2 volts, you'll recall. Start the motor, and the reading should rise by about 2 volts—to 14 or 15—at a fast-idle speed of 1500 to 2000 rpm. If it doesn't, the system isn't providing a charge to the battery. Either the alternator or regulator might prove defective.

Table 6-3. Typical Alternator and Regulator Specifications.

Alternator			Field Current		Regulator				
Current output					Voltage regulator			Field relay	
A	V	Engine rpm	A	V	Voltage	Contact gap (in.)	Armature air gap (in.)	Armature air gap (in.)	Closing voltage
97	13	900	2.5-5.0[1]	12	13.9-14.6	—	—	—	—
78	—	—	4-4.5	12	—	—	—	—	—
66	—	—	4.0-5.0	—	13.4-14.4	—	—	—	—
40	15	—	4	12	13.8-14.6	—	—	—	—
40	—	5000	2.5	12	13.5-14.5	.010-.018	.008-.024	.008-.018[2]	4.5-5.8
55	15	—	2.9	12	13.6-15.1	.018-.020	.042-.052	.011-.013	6.2-7.2
26	15	1250	2.38-2.75[1]	12	13.3-14.3	.012-.016	.048-.052	—	—

[1]Turning rotor shaft by hand. [2]Yoke gap.

A more reliable output test requires that the alternator be run "full-field," or wide open, with the regulator eliminated from the circuit. This permits the alternator to produce its full rated output without being held back by the regulator.

Most regulators can be bypassed temporarily by connecting a jumper wire across certain terminals (Fig. 6-7). The correct jumper connection is crucial. Be sure to check the manual's specific instructions. Doing it wrong, even for a brief test, could damage the alternator. Modern Delco alternators with built-in regulators are easier. They can be eliminated from the charging circuit by inserting a screwdriver tip through a rear hole, touching a shorting tab inside.

To perform the only truly reliable charging output test, you need an ammeter and a carbon-pile loading device, which places a variable load on the alternator. Output current is just as important as voltage. A battery-post adapter, with built-in ammeter shunt, makes it easy to hook up the meters.

Current output should be within about 5 amps of the rated figure. Some engines with electronic ignitions allow more leeway—closer to 10 amps. If a current reading is appreciably lower, or voltage isn't close to 14 volts, the alternator isn't performing. Newer Delco alternators, though, will be OK with a reading as low as 13.2 volts, when putting out the full rated current. Always check the car's manual.

All output tests require some precautions. In addition to correct jumper connections, don't let the alternator run wide open for more than a few seconds. Limit engine speed to about 2000 rpm. Wiring in some recent systems should never be disconnected or altered for test purposes.

Note. Unless the battery needs it, even a perfect system probably won't produce the rated voltage or current. Switch on the lights, and an accessory or two, for a minute or crank the engine for 10 seconds in order to drain the battery a bit. Then try again. No accessories should be on during most serious testing, though, as their current draw distorts the output figures.

Now, let's look at the actual alternator specs.

Current Output. (Hot Output, Rated Output, Current Rating, Ampere Rating). Current output is the published capacity of an alternator, in amps. The spec table may show an ampere rating alone or one in combination with a recommended voltage reading. Perhaps an engine rpm figure, too. If so, the engine should be run at the suggested speed, noting its current and voltage output. Some tables give voltage and current ratings for more than one speed: perhaps 2000 and 5000 rpm.

Operating Voltage (Voltage Output, Running Voltage). Operating voltage is acceptable voltage at a specified engine speed, or at a stated current output. Some tables give an acceptable voltage range at a certain test temperature. It may be a separate table listing or part of the output current columns. Essentially, it's the same test as that for current output.

Alternator Field Current (Field Coil Draw, Field Current Draw). The alternator field current is a rating in amps (usually less than 5 or 6 A), showing the current drawn by the field coil as it creates a magnetic field. The current spec may be accompanied by a voltage or temperature requirement. You connect an ammeter into the field circuit, and then switch on the ignition. The alternator may have to be rotated by hand while watching the ammeter scale. The test isn't ordinarily made unless the alternator fails to produce full output voltage and current.

When an alternator checks out OK, but the system still provides little or no charging, similar output tests are needed with the regulator in action (no jumper wires). Unless voltage and current fall within the spec range, the regulator may be faulty. Don't forget the simple voltage drop tests in order to be sure wiring and connections are solid.

Regulator Voltage. Regulator voltage is

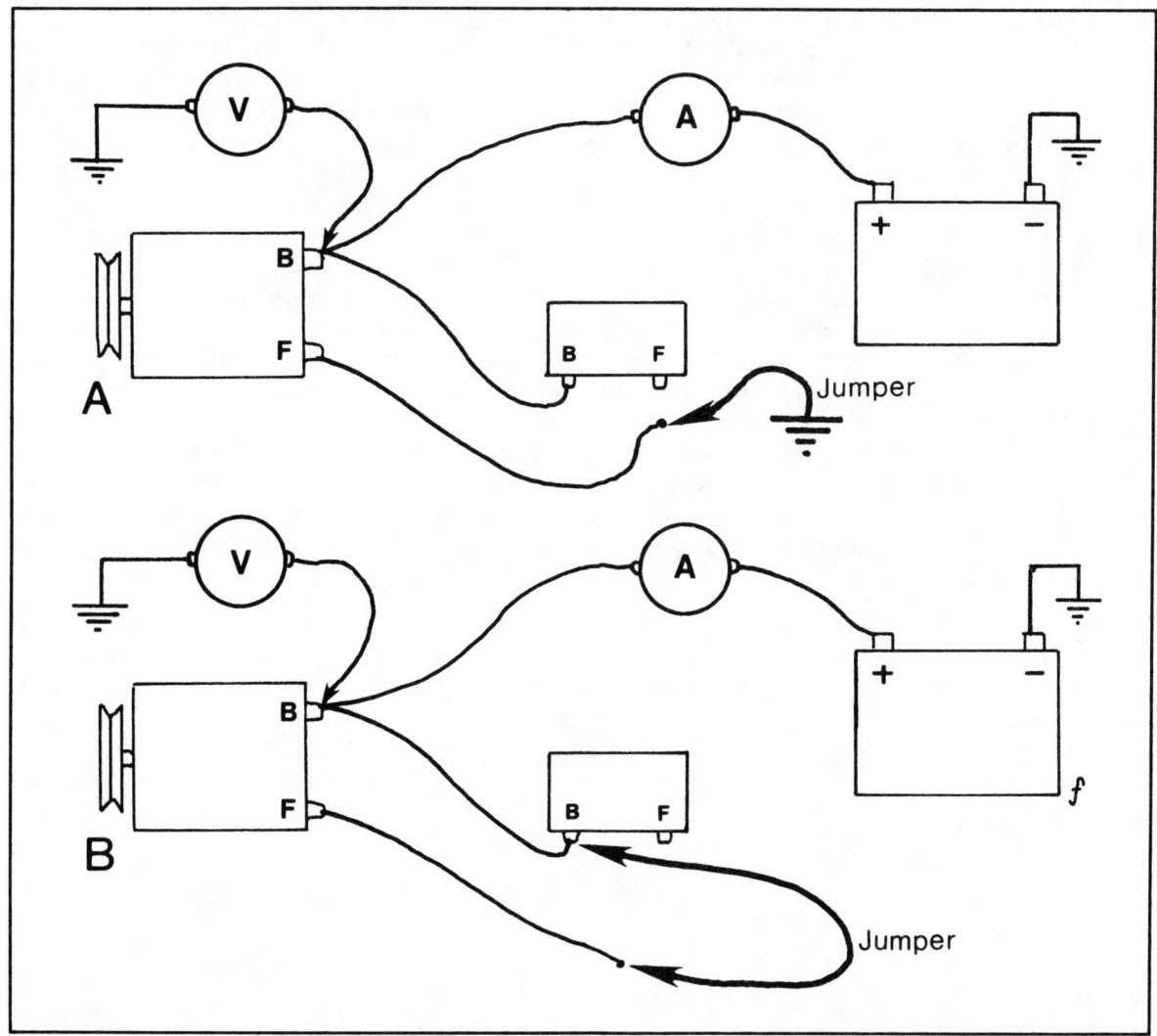

Fig. 6-7. Typical jumper connections for testing full voltage and current output of an alternator with an externally grounded field (A) or an internally grounded field (B). The actual jumper hookup might be made at alternator or regulator, depending on vehicle.

similar to the alternator output voltage spec, usually given as a range, to tenths of a volt. Current load and engine rpm can be given (or a test temperature). Whatever the details, it's an output test with the regulator in the circuit. Acceptable readings run from barely over 13 to almost 16 volts.

Field Relay Closing Voltage. This is the voltage at which the relay's points first make contact, allowing the alternator to deliver current. This is a much lower reading than previous tests (often only 2 to 3 volts or less), and is usually given as a range (to tenths of a volt). The test applies only to mechanical regulators and is given when they fail to provide adequate output readings.

Mechanical regulators also have several physical measurements that can be checked. Many are adjustable. Figures are given in thousandths of an inch (usually a range). Gaps are measured with a feeler gauge (while the ignition is shut off).

Voltage Regulator Air Gap (Armature Air Gap). This is the distance between the movable contact armature and the iron core which, when magnetized, pulls the armature downward.

Field Relay Air Gap (Armature Air Gap). Same as above, but at the field relay section of the regulator.

Voltage Regulator Point Gap (Contact Gap). The distance between the actual contact points, when not energized (open). If not actually adjustable, some can be bent.

Field Relay Point Gap. Same thing, but at the other section of regulator.

Nearly all regulators made since 1980 are electronic (solid-state) and nonadjustable. Some mount inside the alternator. A few do have adjustments, though, to be made when voltage or current readings don't come up to par. Certain Ford regulators, for instance, have a voltage adjustor screw.

DC GENERATORS

An alternator is actually an ac (alternating current) generator. Specs and tests for old dc (direct current) generators, used on American cars until the 1960s, are similar to those for alternator systems. When problems show up, however, repairs are often easier and less expensive.

Output and field current tests are virtually identical to alternator tests, but the method of "jumping" terminals at the regulator varies. Be sure to check the manual. It's nice to know, though, that as a rule less damage will occur even if you do it wrong. A dc generator can be hooked to a battery and run as a motor in order to check current draw.

If a dc generator isn't performing, it could be something as simple as weak brush tension. A spec like that described for starter brushes is given in the manual. The dc regulators are mechanical, often in three sections, with adjustable points.

Ignition Tune-Up Specifications

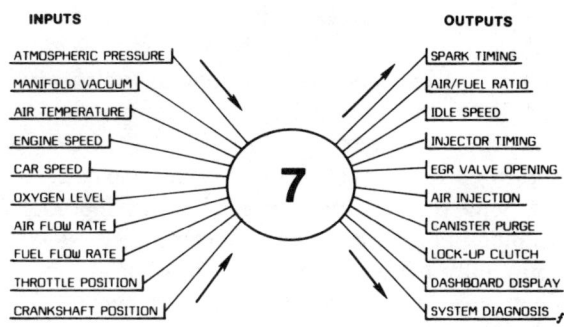

TUNE-UPS AIN'T WHAT THEY USED TO BE. BEfore the advent of electronic ignitions and computer-controlled functions, a session of tune-up duties was a favorite activity for do-it-yourselfers. It was also a major source of income for professional repair shops.

Specifications were numerous, but generally well understood. Saturday-morning mechanics who knew little or nothing about engines could at least set spark plug and point gaps.

Some of the old-time tasks still need to be done, but quite a few have disappeared from the automotive lexicon—never to return. No longer are there any distributor points to replace. Spark plugs last thousands of miles without attention. Few valve clearances need to be adjusted.

Nevertheless, data is more important than ever in what remains of a tune-up. And for owners of earlier-model autos, nothing has changed at all.

The typical tune-up spec table is split between data on the ignition system and other tune-up duties. So are these chapters. Additional information on the distributor is generally found in a separate table, elsewhere in the manual.

Modern cars, of course, have an "emissions control" label under their hoods that contains some, perhaps all, of the data needed for an ordinary tune-up. Information in a manual's tables or charts should be used only if the label is missing or its data incomplete.

THE IGNITION SYSTEM

Every ignition system, whether of modern or early vintage, consists of two separate circuits: the *primary* (low-voltage) and *secondary* (high-voltage). Its sole function is to allow an electrical impulse of sufficient voltage to build up, and send it to the correct spark plug at the best possible moment for firing the fuel charge.

The primary circuit consists of the battery, the breaker points (earlier models), ignition switch, ballast resistor, and primary winding of the ignition coil. The secondary circuit includes the coil's high-tension windings, the distributor cap and rotor, spark-plug cables, and the plugs themselves. Electronic ignition systems, as found on American autos since the mid-1970s, changed some of the components, but the job done remains similar.

The ignition portion (Table 7-1) of our sample tune-up table includes data on the spark plugs, breaker points (if any), firing order, and ignition timing. The remaining steps that make up a full tune-up, including carburetor and valve adjustments, will be dealt with in the next chapter.

Engine identification data, as usual, are found in the left-hand columns of the tune-up tables, often in abbreviated form: only the number of cylinders and displacement (6-235, V8-318, etc.). A horsepower rating or other detail may also be listed.

Some tune-up tables are loaded with footnotes, spelling out alterations in data or procedures that apply only to certain versions of a basic engine. Footnotes are especially numerous for engines that deviate from "normal" by having performance options or air-conditioning, meeting California emission standards, and so forth.

Watch carefully for references to diagrams of firing order, timing mark location and style, and other facts, found on another page in the manual. Not every detail can be incorporated in a table. Comprehensive instructions for setting idle speed or adjusting timing might appear in the text.

SPARK PLUGS: TYPE AND GAP

One column under the "spark plug" heading gives the part number of the plug that was originally installed at the factory. An abbreviation for the manufacturer's name (CH—Champion, AC, AL—Auto-Lite, etc.) may be included. If not, the brand is easily deduced from the style of the part number.

Naturally, your motor might have plugs from a different manufacturer. Whenever plug numbers don't match that shown in a spec table, it's worth checking an interchangeability chart, just to be sure they are an acceptable equivalent. Various plugs have been discontinued over the years, and they have been replaced by different (equivalent) numbers. So finding a "wrong" plug in an earlier-model car isn't necessarily cause for alarm.

A different plug number could have been installed for a reason, however. At times, a spark plug in a hotter (or colder) heat range is installed. Heavy city driving, for example, may demand a hotter plug than normal in order to prevent fouling. Too hot a plug, though, can cause *preignition* (firing too early, due to the plug's own heat). In severe cases, *detonation* could even occur (with possible engine damage). Only in rare cases should a plug be more

Table 7-1. Typical Ignition Tune-Up Specifications.

Year	Engine	Spark plug		Distributor		Firing order	Ignition timing		
		Type	Gap (in.)	Dwell angle (deg.)	Point gap (in.)		Mark location	Degrees	
								MT	AT
1985	4-112	R44XLS	.035	Electronic		1342	—	—	—
1985	V6-231	R44TS8	.080	Electronic		165432	Controlled		
1984	V6-232	AWSF-52	.044	—	—	15426378	Damper	12B	10B
1980	V8-350	R46SX	.080	—	—	18436572	Pulley	—	18[2,4]
1979	V8-403	R46S2	.060	—	—	18436572	Damper	—	20[2]
1979	4-121	N-8L	.035	47	.018	1342	Damper	12	12
1976	4-121	N8Y	.026	62	.016	1342	Flywheel	Ball[3]	
1971	V8-307	R45TS	.035	29-31	.019[1]	18436572	Damper	4B	8B
1969	6-199	N14Y	.035	31-34	.016	153624	Damper	TDC	5A
1963	6-230	44N	.035	32	.019	153624	Pulley	3-5B	
1953	8-263	AC-46X	.025	21-30	.016	16258374	Flywheel	ADV	
1953	V8-239	CH-H10	.030	28	.015	15486372	Pulley	Groove	

[1]Used points .016 (turn adjusting screw in until misfire, then back off 1/2 turn). [2]At 1100 rpm. [3]At 1600 rpm. [4]Toronado, 16 degrees.

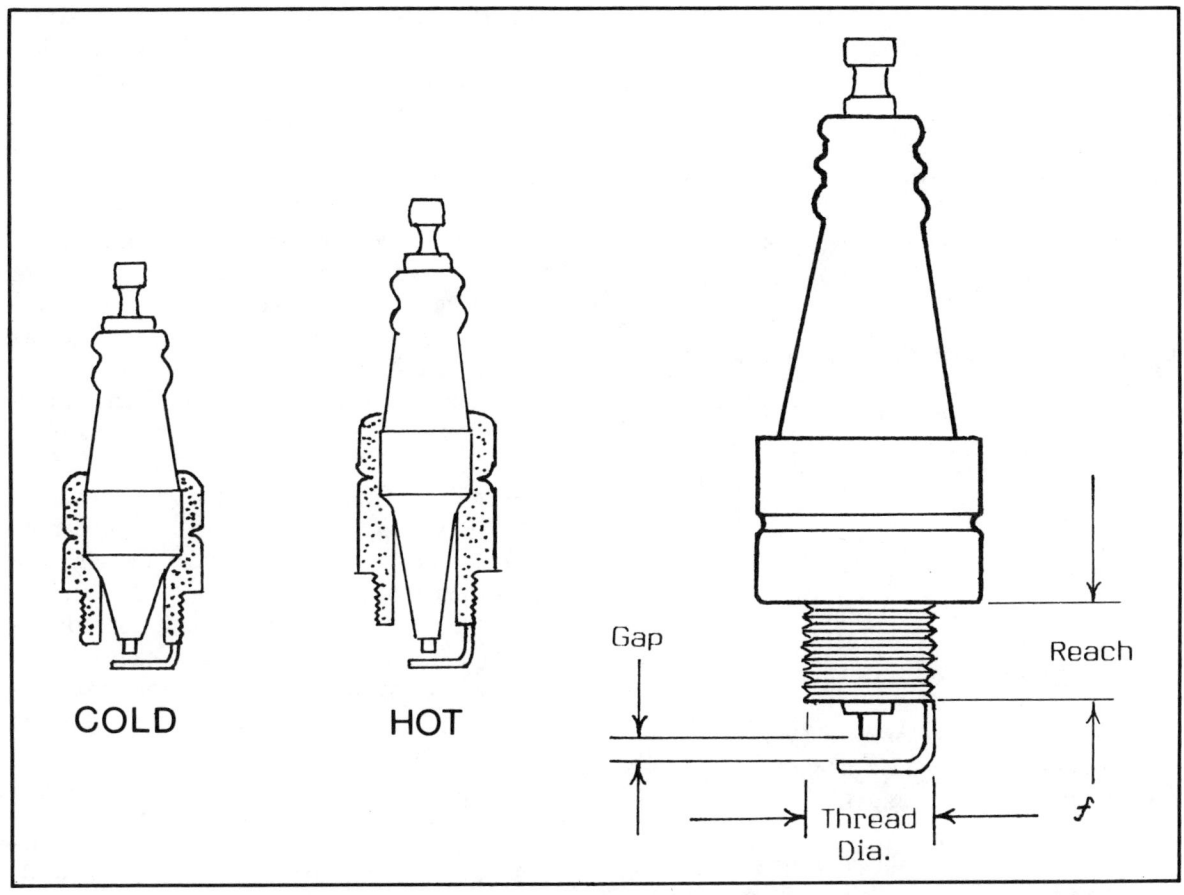

Fig. 7-1. Spark plugs come in heat ranges colder or hotter than normal (left), determined by insulator size and shape. Important plug dimensions include electrode gap, thread diameter, and reach.

than one unit of heat range away from the recommended part number.

Heat range is determined by the insulator's diameter and length. A hot-running plug has a long, thin insulator tip (Fig. 7-1). A short, heavy insulator allows quicker heat transfer for cooler operation.

The other spec column gives the "gap" setting. This is the recommended distance between spark plug electrodes, in thousandths of an inch. Even motorists who rarely peek under the hood usually know that one.

A single figure for gap is generally given (occasionally an acceptable range). Engines of the 1950s and earlier had plug gaps as small as .025 inch; others range up to .035 or .040 inch. Some high-energy electronic ignitions use plugs with a much wider gap (.060 to .080 inch) to create a stronger, high-voltage spark. As a rule, a spark plug's gap widens by one-thousandth with every 1000 to 2000 miles of driving.

Measure with a wire gauge for accurate results. Adjust the outer electrode so the gauge of desired thickness just fits into the space, with a slight "drag." It shouldn't slip in too easily, but neither should any real force be required—certainly not enough to bend the electrode outward as the gauge enters.

Except under unusual running conditions, setting a gap narrower or wider than recommended is unwise. Be sure electrode edges are flat; a rounded edge has a great effect on the plug's firing voltage.

81

You need to know a spark plug's hex size (13/16, 7/8, etc.), to determine which wrench to use for installation/removal. Plugs also vary by thread size. Thread diameters range from 10mm to 18mm. A few oldies are larger (up to 7/8 in. or more). Thread reach varies from 1/4 to 3/4 inch.

DISTRIBUTOR POINT GAP AND DWELL ANGLE

Tables covering American cars made after 1974 have nothing in the distributor point gap and dwell angle space, except perhaps the word "electronic." But for earlier models with mechanical breaker points inside the distributor, this data is crucial; it is the heart of the tune-up. AMC kept breaker points in its smallest engine right up to 1980. Various foreign models kept them even later. For the vast majority, electronic ignition has long since taken the place of the primitive breaker-point method of producing a spark.

Whenever you adjust a set of points, you're actually setting the dwell angle. That's the period of a distributor cam's rotation during which the points are closed—their electrodes making contact, passing primary voltage along to the ignition coil (Fig. 7-2).

Correct dwell angle allows sufficient high voltage to build up in the coil's secondary windings. That voltage is then released as soon as the breaker points cease contact. If the points aren't closed for a long enough time before each firing, secondary voltage might not be adequate. If the time is too long, the system might not have time to recover before firing the next cylinder in sequence.

Data can be taken either from the "gap" or "dwell" column of a spec table. Either one does the job, but the use of a dwell meter gives greater accuracy.

Point gap (breaker gap, breaker point opening) is the distance between the contacts when they're farthest apart. The movable contact is forced all the way outward by any lobe on the distributor shaft's cam. It's measured with a metal feeler gauge. Each gap spec is in thousandths of an inch (either a single figure or, occasionally, a range). The average gap figure is around .020 inch, but they do range from about .014 to .025 inch. In some cases, one figure is given for new points and a narrower one for a used set. Gap narrows as new points wear in due to erosion of the rubbing block.

Dwell angle (point dwell, cam angle) is given in degrees of distributor rotation—either a single figure or an acceptable range. The average is 30-35 degrees, but some are under 30 and others are more than 50 degrees. An engine with fewer cylinders generally has a higher dwell reading. For a six-cylinder engine, 30-degree dwell means the points are closed half of the time—open for 30, then closed for 30—for each cylinder in turn. Higher dwell would mean the points were closed more than half the time.

A dwell reading rises as new points wear in, and the point gap narrows. For that reason, some mechanics set dwell slightly on the low side of a range rather than dead center.

A dwell meter shows the angle directly, in degrees, on a calibrated scale. Test leads connect to the input terminal of the distributor or the distributor terminal of the ignition coil (whichever is more convenient).

Adjustment usually is made by loosening a screw, and then moving the stationary point contact inward or outward as needed. Check the new gap with a feeler leaf or watch the dwell reading while cranking the motor with the starter.

GM distributors, starting in the 1950s, are even easier to adjust (with the cap in place and engine running). All you do is insert a small hex wrench through a sliding window in the cap, and then turn it to move the contact.

Dual-point distributors take a bit more time. As a rule, one contact set is blocked open with a scrap of cardboard. Take a dwell reading of the operating set while cranking the motor. Then block that one open while testing the other. You should find a dwell spec for each separate contact set as well as a figure for total dwell (both working normally).

HIGH TENSION: THE IGNITION COIL

Not all spec tables contain figures for either primary or secondary voltages or data on the ignition coil. Important values may be found somewhere in a ser-

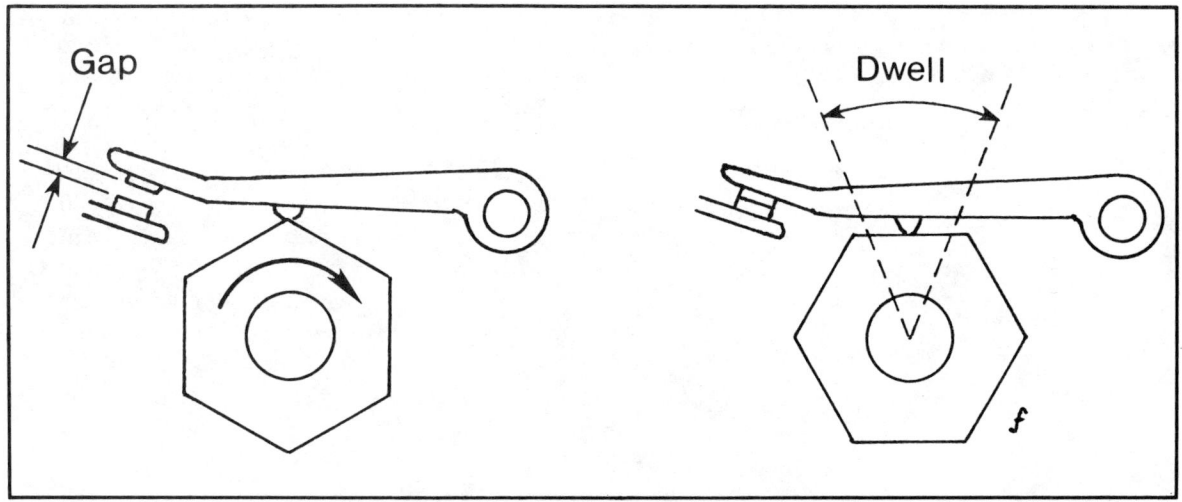

Fig. 7-2. Breaker point gap is the distance the contacts are apart when forced all the way outward by a rotating cam lobe. The dwell angle is the number of degrees of cam rotation during which the points remain closed.

vice manual, however.

Primary voltage is nominally 12 volts (6 volts for cars prior to the mid-1950s, and a few later foreign makes). That doesn't mean a voltage test along the ignition circuit always shows that amount. When 12-volt systems came in, it soon became evident that this was too much for breaker points to handle without burning up mighty fast. So a ballast resistor was added, and this lowers the voltage to between 9 and 10 1/2 volts.

Electronic ignitions can survive higher voltage, but ballast resistances are still around. Some engines use a separate resistor unit while others use a wire segment. Many are temperature-sensitive, delivering less voltage at lower speeds. During cranking, the resistance normally is bypassed to give maximum voltage for firing. Once in a while, it might be necessary to measure one with an ohmmeter.

When ignition problems occur, and the primary circuit is suspect, a voltage drop test (as described in Chapter 6) is step one. A drop test across breaker points is especially useful. This tells how much *point resistance* there is. For brand-new points, a drop of 0.1 volt is permissible; for used points, a higher reading—perhaps 0.25 volt—might be fine.

Secondary voltage (high-tension) comes from the output windings of the ignition coil, as the magnetic field across primary and secondary windings collapses. The coil is capable of providing 20,000 to 40,000 volts to the spark plugs (perhaps 50-60 kV in electronic systems). That output isn't measured with a voltmeter, but does appear on oscilloscope ('scope) screens used in professional shops and by some amateur mechanics (Fig. 7-3).

A coil doesn't always produce its maximum voltage. It delivers only the amount demanded by each of the spark plugs (which could be 10,000 volts or less). A narrow spark plug gap requires less voltage, as does lower pressure within the cylinder, and a rich fuel mixture. Voltage reaches a peak during low-speed acceleration with the throttle partly open. Too high a voltage at any plug means something is wrong.

Induced voltage is something you might hear about now and then. It's the voltage that appears at breaker points—as much as 200 volts—after the full secondary voltage has been sent to the spark plug. Sort of a backlash voltage that nobody wants because it produces arcing across the point contacts. We don't have to measure this one.

Measuring a coil's *current draw* with an ammeter is occasionally useful. In pre-electronic days, a typical coil drew 4 to 5 amps. That's quite a bit for points to carry (which is why they were prone to burning). Today's coils draw less.

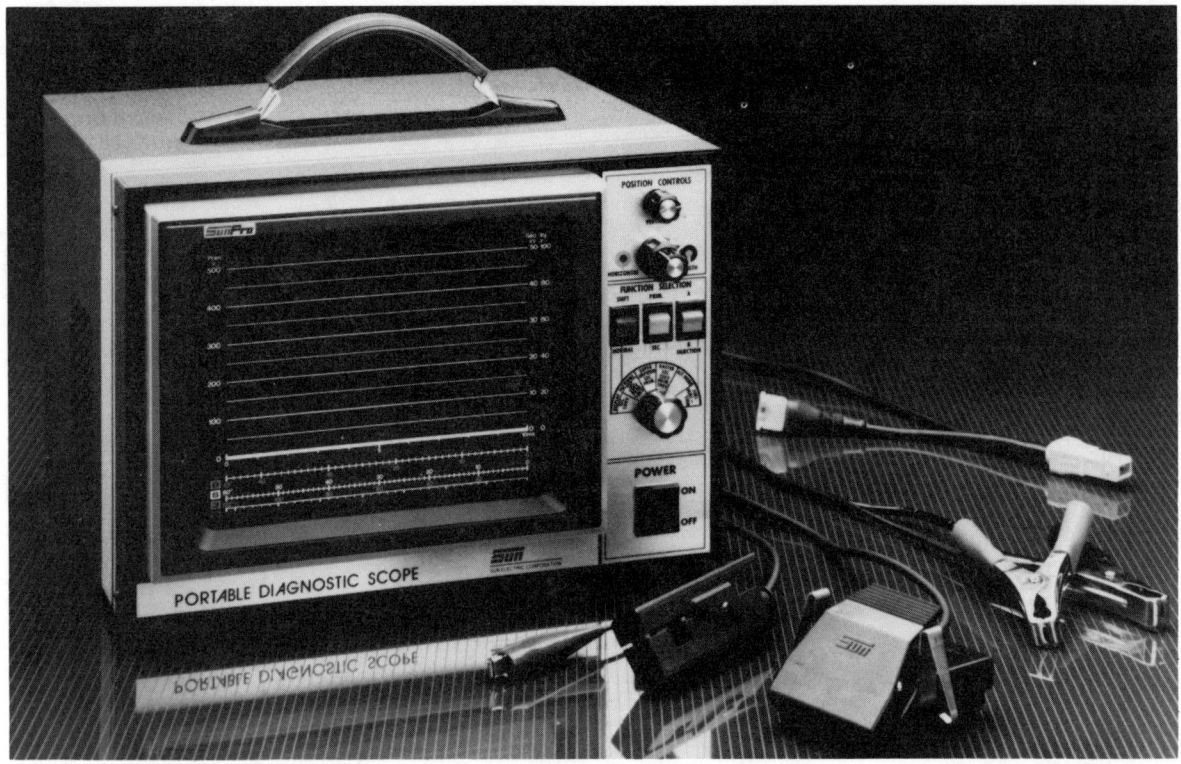
Fig. 7-3. Oscilloscopes show ignition waveform and important specs as patterns on CRT screen. (Sun Electric Corp.)

Coil resistance figures are valuable when the coil is suspect. Measured with an ohmmeter, resistance across the primary windings should be around 1 to 2 ohms; it's a little less for some electronic systems. Secondary windings read much higher (as much as 30,000 ohms).

Polarity is crucial to coils. Installed backwards, the coil might function all right, but doesn't put out its full-scale voltage. Most of the time you can tell from the connections whether it's wired in correctly. An old-time test still comes in handy. All you do is hold (carefully!) one of the spark plug cables near the engine block (ground), with an ordinary lead pencil's point between the terminal end and the engine. Have someone crank the engine. Watch the spark that appears. If the electric "flare" seems to travel from the pencil to the engine block, polarity is OK. But if it appears to go in the other direction, the coil probably is wired in backward. This isn't so likely with modern coils that are installed right inside the distributor.

Cable resistance is our last test of the high-tension circuit. Years ago, spark plug cables, being made of ordinary copper, had minimal resistance. The copper interfered with radio reception, so the resistance cable came along. A typical cable measures up to 25,000 ohms (even 50k if it's a long one). Excess resistance cuts available voltage at the plug's gap.

FIRING ORDER

Getting back to our ignition tune-up table, firing order is the sequence in which the cylinders are fired during one complete cycle. In other words, the order in which they receive their jolt of high voltage to the spark plugs as the distributor rotor turns. You don't really have a burning need to know it unless the distributor cap is coming off, and you must later reconnect it without having drawn a diagram of the original wiring.

You must at least know which plug is number 1 for timing purposes, however. Also, you need to know which cylinder is halfway removed in the firing order, for valve adjustments. That's the one with its piston at the top, completing its *exhaust* stroke, when No. 1 is at its point of firing (TDC) on *compression* stroke. For six-cylinder engines, it's the fourth cylinder in the order (1-5-3-*6*-2-4); for eights, the fifth (1-8-4-3-*6*-5-7-2).

Some tune-up tables show the actual firing order. More often, there's a reference to a set of diagrams that applies to the motor in question (Fig.

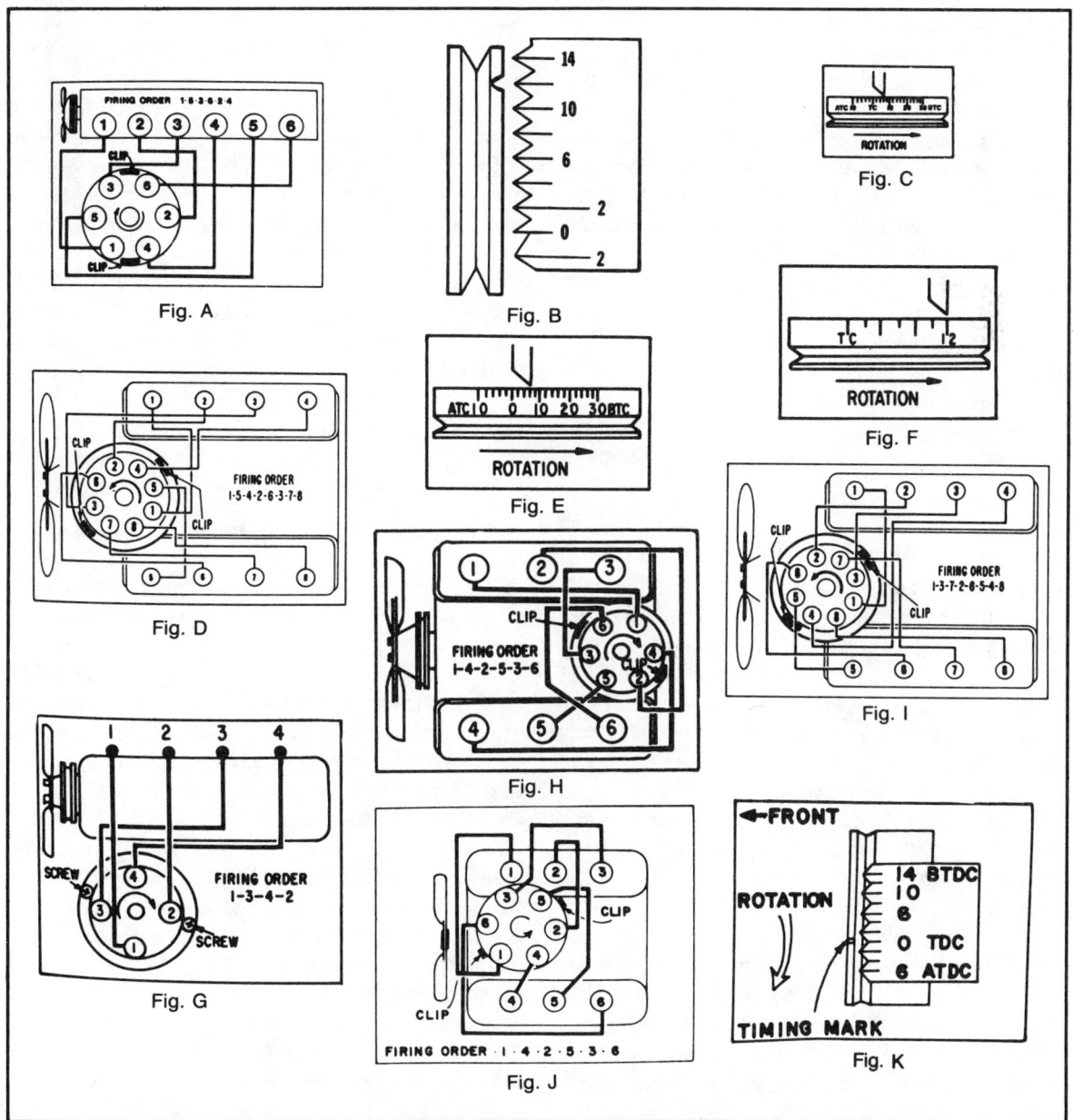

Fig. 7-4. A typical manual page showing firing orders and ignition timing mark diagrams. (Reproduced from *MOTOR Auto Repair Manual* Copyright © 1984 by permission of Hearst Business Publishing, a division of the Hearst Corporation.)

7-4). Firing order is cast right into the manifold of some engines. There is no excuse not to know those.

Learning an engine's firing order also tells you about the numbering of its cylinders. Surprisingly, this is not standardized. Number 1 cylinder is nearly always the one at the front, next to the fan, except for a few European makes of earlier vintage. Inline engines, then, are numbered from front to back: 1 through 6 (or whatever).

V-type engines have No. 1 at the front, too. But it might be on either side. Number 2 could be right in back of it or at the front of the opposite bank.

Four-cylinder inline motors have a firing order of either 1-3-4-2 or 1-2-4-3. Inline sixes are nearly all 1-5-3-6-2-4, except for a few oldies with 1-4-2-6-3-5 orders. GM V-6s fire in 1-2-3-4-5-6 or 1-6-5-4-3-2 sequence; Fords in 1-4-2-5-3-6. V-8 motors have several possibilities: 1-5-4-2-6-3-7-8 or 1-3-7-2-6-5-4-8 for Fords, 1-8-4-3-6-5-7-2 for most others.

Confusing? All you need to know is the one in front of you.

IGNITION TIMING

Timing the ignition is another time-honored, Saturday-morning chore. It's also another one that is disappearing from the ordinary tune-up because of the microcomputers inside today's electrical systems.

By setting the ignition timing, we're *synchronizing* the ignition to the mechanical motion of the crankshaft, pistons, and valves (Fig. 7-5). We want the high-voltage surge to burst at the spark plug's electrode gap, at just the right time, to ignite the air/fuel mixture that's entered the cylinder. Not too soon and not too late.

What does this mean? Picture the piston rising within its cylinder on compression stroke, squeezing the air/fuel mixture. That volatile mixture has to be ignited shortly before the piston reaches the top of its stroke. How long before? That depends on the particular engine, and on its speed and load. In a few engines, the mixture should be ignited slightly *after* the piston reaches top dead center (TDC). For peak performance, in any case, the mixture should *finish* burning by the time the crankshaft reaches 15 to 25 degrees after top dead center (ATDC). And we want that whether the engine is loafing or lugging or running fast or slow.

Timing, then, is based on the number of degrees of crankshaft rotation, before or after the piston reaches the top of its travel. It can't be expressed in *distance* from the top because there's no easy way of measuring that. You can watch the crankshaft pulley with a strobe light and find out exactly how far along the piston is at the moment of firing. At a few degrees BTDC, the piston is very close to the top of its stroke.

Specifications refer to *initial* (basic) timing, usually set while the engine runs at idle speed. As the engine speeds up, or the vacuum level in the intake manifold changes, one or two *advance* units (described below) may alter the basic distributor setting. Tables usually contain two columns: one tells the location of the timing mark, and another gives the actual spec.

On Your Mark . . .

Basic timing is set with a timing light connected to a power source, and to the No. 1 spark plug. As the engine runs at idle speed, shining the light at the timing mark gives the illusion that it's standing still. It isn't, of course, but this helpful phenomenon lets us determine precisely when that plug is firing. Each time the light flashes it "freezes" the timing mark. By inspecting the scale, you know how close the piston is to TDC when the spark plug receives its jolt of electricity.

Where is that timing mark? That's what the "location" column in the table tells you. Early manuals generally say so directly: on the vibration damper (harmonic balancer) at the front of the engine; on the crankshaft pulley that holds the damper; or on the flywheel at the engine's rear, visible through an inspection hole in its housing. Modern manuals generally refer you to a diagram that shows what the mark looks like. It's often combined with the firing-order diagrams mentioned earlier. Nearly all recent engines have their timing marks on the vibration damper.

Timing marks vary quite a bit, though. Many

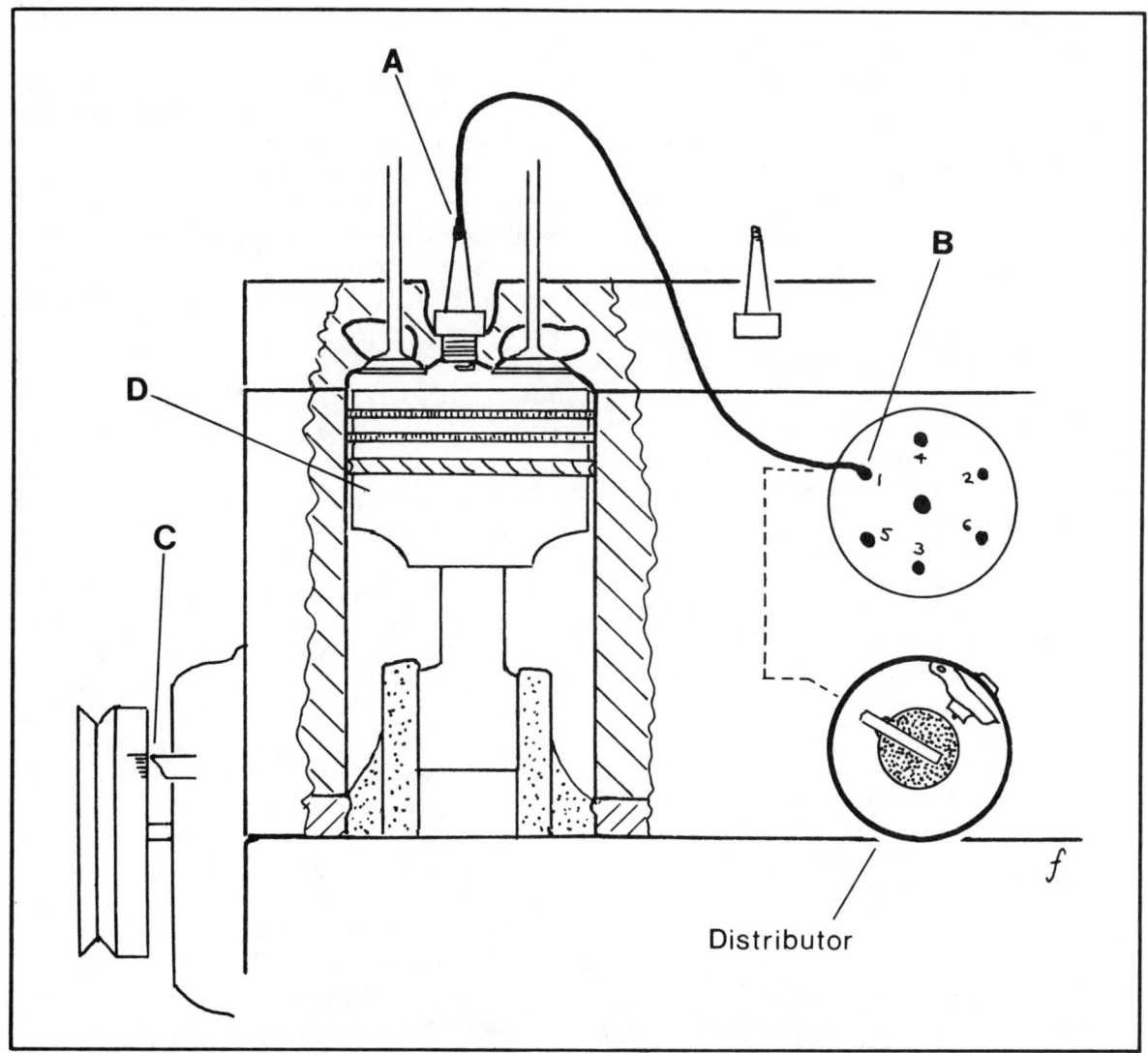

Fig. 7-5. When the ignition is correctly timed, the spark plug for the No. 1 cylinder (A) receives a high-voltage surge from distributor cap terminal (B) just as timing marks at the vibration damper (C) come into alignment. This shows the piston (D) has risen to optimum height on its compression stroke (both valves closed).

engines have a calibrated scale on the timing gear cover that is used to mate with a notched mark on the damper. Others have a scale or marking on the pulley or damper that aligns with an engine-mounted pointer.

Timing Specs

Once you've determined what the mark and scale are supposed to look like, and found them on the actual engine, what does the specification in the other table column mean? Like the mark layouts, the data appear in various forms. Most typically, it's a figure in degrees (8° BTDC, 2° ATDC, or perhaps "zero"). This means timing is correct when the pointer or other indicator aligns with the stated figure on a calibrated scale—either before (B) top dead center (TDC) of crankshaft rotation or, less commonly, after (A). Such a scale has inscribed lines that correspond to a range of degrees, with TDC denoted by "zero." A few scales have no figures inscribed; you must refer to the manual's diagram to determine how many degrees each mark on the scale signifies. Timing specs range from 20 or more degrees BTDC to a few degrees after.

Instructions for some early engines give no actual figure. Instead, they specify that the pointer or indicator be set to match a *groove* in the damper, a *notch* in the pulley, or perhaps a steel *ball* in the flywheel rim. Or it might have to mate with a single mark on pulley or flywheel, identified by the inscription "IGN," "ADV," "5," or some other cryptic notation. These motors have no calibrated scale, but usually have another marking on the pulley/damper/flywheel to show when the engine is precisely at TDC for No. 1 piston.

Sounds complicated, but the timing mark diagram should make the arrangement clear. The spec table may have a notation stating whether the vacuum line has to be disconnected from the distributor and plugged, before checking timing. If not, assume that it should be so that no advance comes into play.

There may be a separate data column for cars with automatic transmissions. Also, the same basic engine could have several different timing specs, depending on its performance options, high-altitude operation, California emissions standards, and other variants.

Using the Timing Light

Older timing lights hooked directly to the No. 1 spark plug's terminal with a special adapter. Most lights sold today are the inductive type, with a clamp that wraps around the cable. Not only is it quicker and easier to use, it's essential to avoid damage to electronic ignition systems.

Unless the table specifies otherwise, timing is checked with the engine idling. A few performance engines have to be checked at much higher rpm. In either case, connect a tachometer first to be sure running speed is within specifications.

All you do, then, is point the light toward the timing mark. If the appropriate marks appear to be aligned, timing is OK. If not, the distributor has to be loosened and rotated slightly one way or the other, until they do align.

Recent electronic ignitions have provision for checking timing with a magnetic pickup rather than an ordinary timing light. That's fine if you have such an instrument, but there may also be a provision for using the ordinary light. Many current electronic ignitions, in fact, have no timing specs at all. The whole thing, including advance, is controlled electronically. Before long, timing will be a forgotten task.

CENTRIFUGAL ADVANCE

Data on advance mechanisms are often found in a separate table of distributor specifications (Table 7-2). Advance is needed so the spark will be applied at a different time when the engine is running faster or under load. Some engines have a centrifugal advance and some a vacuum advance; most earlier models have both. New ones? Probably neither.

Centrifugal advance changes the spark in relation to engine speed (Fig. 7-6). The specification gives the number of degrees of advance that should be produced at a stated rpm. The data usually include a figure for the speed at which advance begins, and another indicating maximum advance.

Example. "0-2 @ 1000; 24 @ 3500" means advance should begin at around 1000 rpm, reaching a maximum of 24 degrees at 3500 rpm.

Degree figures usually are given in terms of rotational speed of the distributor shaft, rather than the crankshaft. Remember, the distributor turns at one-half crankshaft speed.

How does it work? A set of weights moves outward by centrifugal force as engine speed increases. This rotates the distributor's breaker plate (or equivalent component in a breakerless ignition) slightly, causing the spark to be delivered to each plug a bit earlier than usual. It has to be earlier as engine speed increases so that there's enough time for combustion to be completed by the time each piston gets 15 to 25 degrees past TDC. That's when the pressure of the burning air/fuel mixture reaches its peak.

Some tables have one or two additional columns to show intermediate advance. They give

Table 7-2. Typical Distributor Specifications.

Year	Centrifugal advance, degrees @ distributor rpm			Vacuum advance		Max. retard, distrib. degrees @ vacuum
	Advance starts	Intermediate	Full advance	Inches vacuum to start plunger	Max. adv. distrib. degrees @ vacuum	
84		Electronic spark timing				
82	0-1.6 @ 600	0-2 @ 900	4.5 @ 2500	4	12 @ 11	—
80	1 @ 600	3 @ 1200	7.5 @ 1800	4.5	12 @ 9.5	—
72	1-5 @ 650	8-10 @ 900	14 @ 2000	10.5	10.5 @ 15.5	—
72	1/2 - 2 1/2 @ 500	2-4 @ 750	12 @ 2000	5	13.5 @ 20	4 @ 20
63	1 @ 750	—	12.2 @ 2175	None		—
62		None		1 @ 0.5	13 @ 6.5	—
53	1 @ 365	—	10 @ 1200	1 @ 10	5 @ 12	—

spark timing for speeds between the starting point of the advance and its peak. A separate "total advance" figure occasionally is given, for testing when the vacuum hose is connected—both centrifugal and vacuum advances working.

But wait a minute. How can you tell how much advance is supplied at a certain speed? Nearly all testing of advance mechanisms is done with the distributor out of the car, mounted in a special instrument. A scale shows the exact amount of advance at any speed. Nothing to it, provided you have such an instrument.

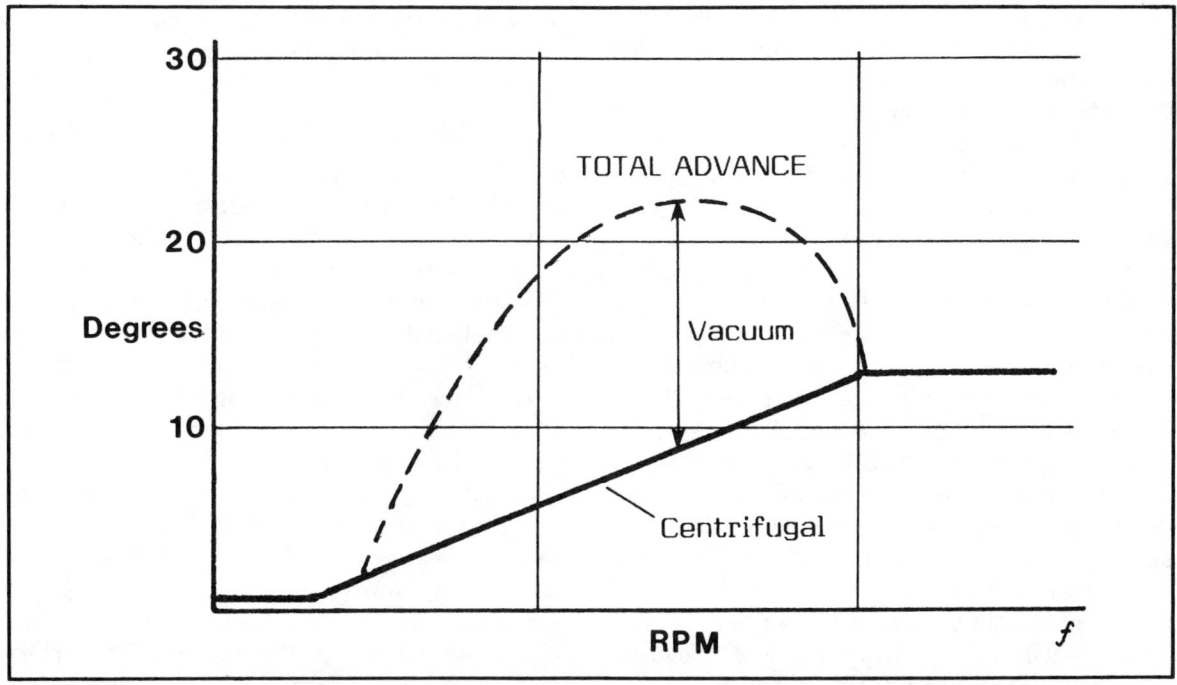

Fig. 7-6. Total advance, in degrees of distributor rotation, includes both vacuum and centrifugal advances (on engines that have both). Centrifugal advance depends solely on engine speed. Vacuum depends on level of manifold vacuum at any given moment. Peak total advance is reached when the car is cruising at road speed (throttle partly open).

A few deluxe timing lights also include a scale for testing advance. With an ordinary timing light, you can at least get a rough estimate. Just watch the position of the timing mark as the engine is speeded up. Try it with the vacuum hose connected (both advances working), and again with the hose detached, for checking centrifugal advance alone.

VACUUM ADVANCE

Until recent years, most distributors also had a vacuum advance unit mounted on the side of the housing. A hose connects the vacuum advance to a port fitting on the carburetor base, above the throttle valve. As the amount of manifold vacuum changes, in response to load variation, diaphragm action moves the distributor's breaker plate back and forth to alter the timing.

Vacuum is highest at part throttle. A smaller amount of mixture enters, and it burns slower. Without more advance, it might not burn completely before the piston gets far past TDC.

At idle, no advance is needed and none is supplied because pressure at the port, just above the closed throttle valve, is near atmospheric. Then, as the throttle opens a bit, it exposes the port connection to the high vacuum in the manifold below. During hard acceleration or full-throttle operation, vacuum drops very low so no advance is applied.

Vacuum, not surprisingly, is measured with a vacuum gauge (Chapter 10). Specifications are given in "inches of mercury," which is the standard measure of vacuum. One column gives the number of "inches to start plunger" or other words meaning the same thing. That's the vacuum reading at which advance begins. A second column shows maximum advance, in degrees of distributor rotation, at a specified vacuum level.

Example. Six inches in the first column, 10° @ 12 inches in the second, means the breaker plate should begin to be affected by the advance's plunger when vacuum at the carb port reaches 6 inches of mercury. Maximum advance of 10 degrees should occur with a vacuum of 12 inches.

A few modern engines have a similar spec for *distributor retard*, affecting emission control. Spark is retarded (occurring later than normal) whenever the throttle is closed. This is accomplished either with a solenoid or a second diaphragm connected directly to the intake manifold.

Needless to say, many amateur mechanics omit investigation of advance readings during an ordinary tune-up. They're easy to check in a big distributor tester, but a lot tougher "on the car."

MORE DISTRIBUTOR DATA

That separate distributor spec table may include a few other bits of information.

Rotation shows whether the distributor rotates clockwise (CW) or counterclockwise (CCW). A handy fact that's easy to forget.

Breaker arm spring tension is a reading in ounces that would be obtained when pulling the movable breaker point outward with a spring scale. Often overlooked, but a weak spring can make contacts hesitate to return to closed position, causing high-speed running problems.

Condenser capacity is a rating in microfarads (mfd, or μF), which has little real use. Condensers are seldom measured; they are only tested for shorts and replaced when questionable.

ELECTRONIC IGNITION: WHAT'S NEW?

Electronic ignitions first appeared in the 1960s, as an option, and became standard on most American engines by the mid-1970s. The first electronic systems weren't so much different from normal. Transistors were used to augment the operation of a conventional breaker-point type distributor. This allowed higher current levels to flow, which permitted higher and more reliable voltage to develop in the coil. But the full current didn't have to go through the point contacts.

Eventually, the breaker points themselves disappeared, and electronic methods controlled the flow of primary current into the coil. Most important to note, however, is that nothing really new was being done. All that changed was the method of interrupting current flow to the coil's primary windings, which causes its magnetic field to collapse and produce high voltage. The coil doesn't care how current gets there. Electronics replaced what was actually a very primitive system that served engines well for many decades.

The components that make up modern ignition systems have different names and appearances, but perform a task surprisingly similar to the past. Most still have the equivalent of a coil and distributor, even if the coil is mounted deep inside.

Instead of a breaker plate and contact points, there's a sensing device, perhaps called a "magnetic pickup" or "pickup coil." This responds to rotation of a trigger wheel, also known as a "reluctor," an "armature," a "timer core" or something else, depending on the system's manufacturer and vintage. As each blade passes the sensing unit, a signal is sent to an electronic control module that amplifies the signal and triggers the ignition coil. What happens then? The coil sends out high voltage to the distributor cap and rotor, and then out to each plug in turn, just as it always did.

There's no physical contact between parts inside the distributor, nothing to wear out or erode, and no settings in the usual sense. Few, if any, parts are replaceable or repairable. When trouble develops, a whole unit probably has to be replaced.

There are, however, a few tests specified in service manuals (Fig. 7-7). They fall into three categories:

1. Measurements of air gap between components, such as the trigger wheel and magnetic pickup.
2. Resistance or continuity checks between various parts, using an ohmmeter.
3. Voltage tests at specified points in the primary circuit, including the pickup, control module

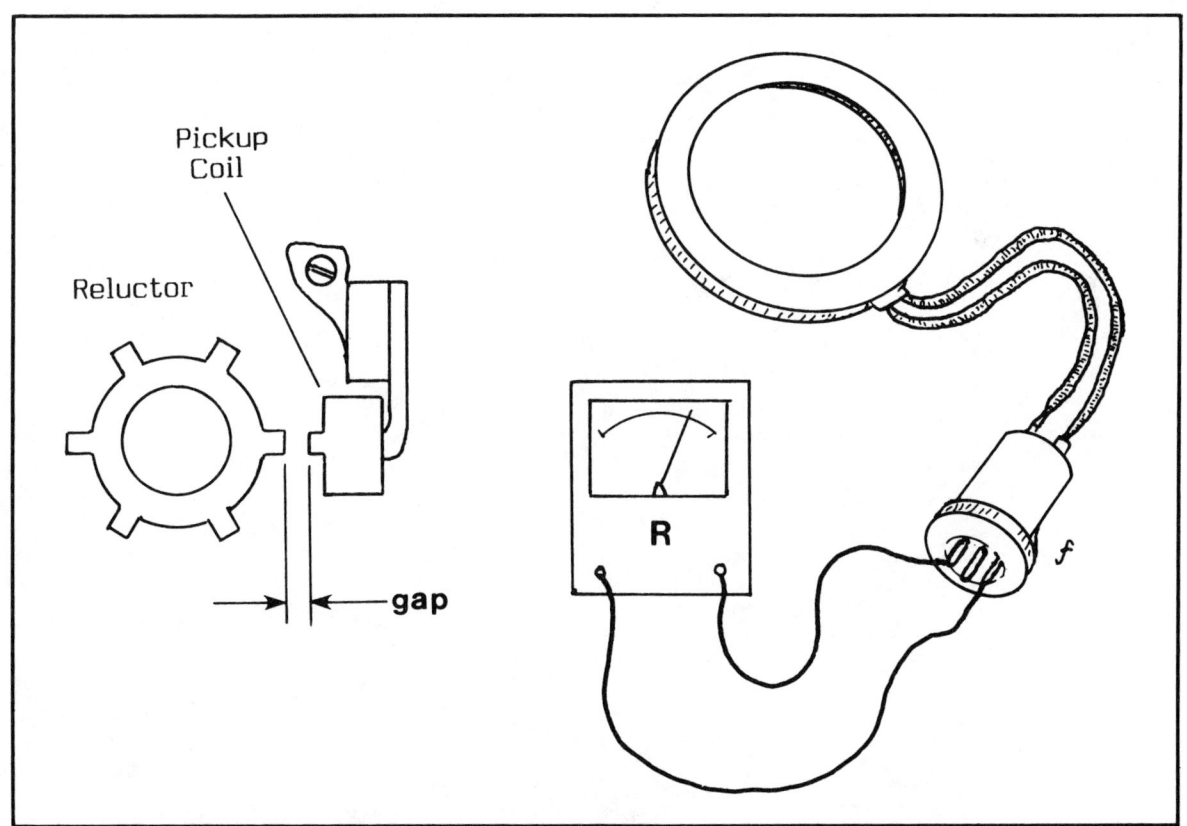

Fig. 7-7. Typical electronic ignition measurements include air gap sizes, such as those between reluctor and pickup coil (left), and component resistance (right).

and coil; often done by disconnecting harness plugs.

Specs are not ordinarily given in any tune-up table, but they're in the factory service manual—along with details on how each has to be measured.

Follow the instructions exactly. Electronic systems can be permanently damaged by incorrect test procedures. Use a non-magnetic (brass) feeler gauge to measure air gaps; don't use a steel gauge. If the manual says ignition must be off during certain resistance or voltage checks, be sure it is off and stays off. For safety's sake, it pays to consider the engine as "running" whenever its ignition is turned on.

An even bigger change in modern motors has to do with timing. Chrysler's Lean Burn, Ford's Electronic Engine Control (EEC) series, and other systems have no mechanical advance controls. They use sensors to alter the amount of advance. Spark timing responds directly to changes in engine temperature, manifold vacuum, speed, air flow, and other conditions. More on computer control is given in Chapter 11.

Future systems will use electronics to an even greater extent until the working of the ignition system may be incomprehensible to an old-time mechanic (if it isn't already). Its primary purpose—supplying a spark to ignite the air/fuel mixture in the cylinder at just the right time—has not yet changed. Only in ways of measuring that right time, responding to shifting demands of the engine, has electronics come into full-scale prominence under the hood. Even the disappearance of the distributor, occurring first on the 1984 Buick, hasn't eliminated the need for the job it has performed all these many decades.

Finishing the Tune-Up

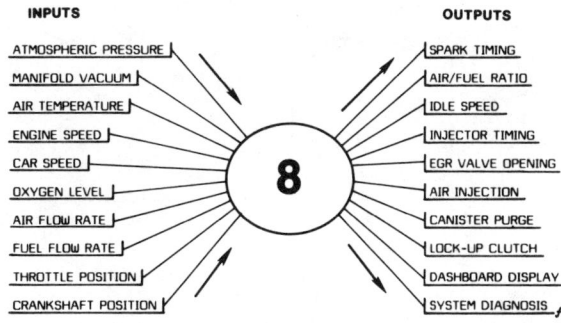

IGNITION WORK IS ONLY HALF OF A TUNE-UP. Recent engines may have virtually nothing to be done for the ignition. Our typical tune-up spec table, then, also contains data on idle speeds, compression and fuel pump pressure, and valve adjustments (Table 8-1).

IDLE SPEEDS

At least one idle speed specification is given for nearly all cars, regardless of vintage. Most have two or more.

Curb idle speed (engine idle speed, idle speed, hot idle speed) is the basic setting. It's measured in rpm using a tachometer, with engine fully warmed up and idling. Tables often give separate specs for manual transmission (MT, Std. Trans., or Synchromesh) as opposed to automatic transmission-equipped cars (AT).

A letter *N* following the rpm figure indicates that an automatic transmission should be in neutral; letter *D*, in Drive range. Naturally, you will have the car's wheels blocked during "Drive" testing, and hand brake set so it cannot possibly roll forward.

Specifications may take the form of a single figure or an acceptable range (examples: 700 rpm or 600-800 rpm). Most modern idle speeds run in the 500 to 900 rpm neighborhood. Earlier ones could be 400 rpm or less; high-performance motors could be over 1000. Specs may differ for cars sold in California, for those intended for operation at high altitudes, and so forth.

Many modern spec tables give two separate rpm figures. They are often separated by a slash mark (600/700 rpm). The lower figure is generally intended for measurement with the throttle solenoid disconnected; the higher is for use with the solenoid energized. In some cases, it means the air conditioner must be shut off. Always check the manual when two figures are given in order to be sure which device is referred to, and how it should be made inoperative.

Idle adjustment is generally made at the throttle linkage or a solenoid alongside the carburetor (Fig. 8-1). Occasionally it is somewhere on the carb

Table 8-1. Typical Non-Ignition Tune-up Specifications.

Engine	Curb idle speed (rpm)		Fast idle speed (rpm)		Fuel pump pressure (psi)	Valve clearance (inches)	
	MT	AT	MT	AT		Intake	Exhaust
4-112	800	700	—	—	—	Hydraulic	
V6-232	—	500-600D	—	—	40-45[1]	—	—
4-156	See sticker		—	—	4.6-6.0	.006	.010
V6-231	Controlled		—	2200	4 1/4 - 5 3/4	Hydraulic	
4-1.3L	650-750	—	3000	—	—	.006C	.008C
V8-403	—	500/600D[2]	—	1000	5 1/2 - 6 1/2	—	—
6-225	750	750N	2000	1900	—	—	—
V8-332	600	—	—	—	5.5	.026H	.026H
8-327	400	400	—	—	—	Zero	Zero
8-323	300	—	—	—	—	.008H	.010H

[1]Frame mounted pump. [2]Higher figure with solenoid energized.

body. For relatively new cars, stick to the recommended figure. On oldies, however, there are times when the stated speed is a hair too slow to prevent stalling. In fact, a few specs show a "minimum" idle speed. Overly fast idle, though, wastes fuel and can boost emissions.

Many tables give a separate listing for *fast idle speed*. This is theoretically measured with the engine cold. The throttle control rests on the high spot (kickdown) of the carburetor linkage's fast-idle cam. An automatic transmission should be in neutral. As a practical matter, the engine need not be cold. Just move the linkage "step" to the position it would be in if the engine *were* cold, with the automatic choke almost closed. Naturally, the rpm figure shown is considerably higher than that for hot idling (as much as 2000 rpm or even more).

Some tables also include details on automatic choke adjustment. Mainly, they show how the alignment marks on the choke housing must be positioned for "normal" operation. It should also tell how far (and in what direction) the housing can be rotated to get a richer or leaner mixture.

IDLE MIXTURE

Modern engines have no provision whatever for adjusting the idle mixture, and certainly no specs for doing so. Beginning by 1972, idle limiter caps were installed on all carburetor mixture adjusting screws. This prevented unauthorized changes that could result in dramatically increased pollutant emissions. Adjustment was possible only within a narrow range. Only factory-authorized mechanics were permitted to remove a cap and alter the setting any further.

Early models do have full mixture adjustment potential, and it's an important part of their tune-up. Some tables give a nominal setting (starting point) for the mixture screw: loosened one turn from full inward position, 3/4 turn, etc. In the old days, screws were adjusted to deliver maximum rpm, shown on a tachometer. But to keep emission levels down, mixture changes should be made only with the aid of emission-test instruments.

FUEL PUMP PRESSURE

Nearly every tune-up table includes this figure, yet it's not measured all that often. Not unless the fuel pump is acting up. Pressure can have quite an effect on high-speed performance, however.

Pressure is measured with an ordinary vacuum gauge hooked into the fuel line between pump and carburetor. The auxiliary scale is marked in pounds per square inch (psi) to show pressure.

Specs are typically given as a range (sometimes a minimum). Permissible readings vary from under

3 psi to 8 psi or more in hungry high-performance engines. Electric fuel pumps have much higher readings of 30 psi or more.

COMPRESSION TESTING

A popular saying among mechanics is that you can't tune an engine with poor compression. Thus, a compression test should be part of any serious tune-up. It tells whether the piston rings and valves are sealing tightly, preventing combustion and exhaust gases from escaping into the wrong channels. Compression pressures are also covered in the next chapter, but concentrate here on the cranking-pressure test itself (the basic indicator of engine condition).

What you are measuring is the amount of pressure that builds up in each cylinder as its piston rises on compression stroke. A compression gauge is screwed into, or held against, a spark plug hole. Then, the engine is cranked with the starter through several compression strokes.

Few tune-up tables since the 1960s have included a specific compression reading. Instead, they insist that only a comparison between cylinders is crucial. So long as the readings for each cylinder are within, say 10-15 psi of each other, or none is more than 25 percent below the highest reading, all is well. The absolute figures are considered unimportant.

Not so for earlier cars and the earlier manuals. One column in those tables gives a specific compression reading (in psi) to shoot for. It could be a range or single figure somewhere between 100 psi for early low-compression motors to about 200

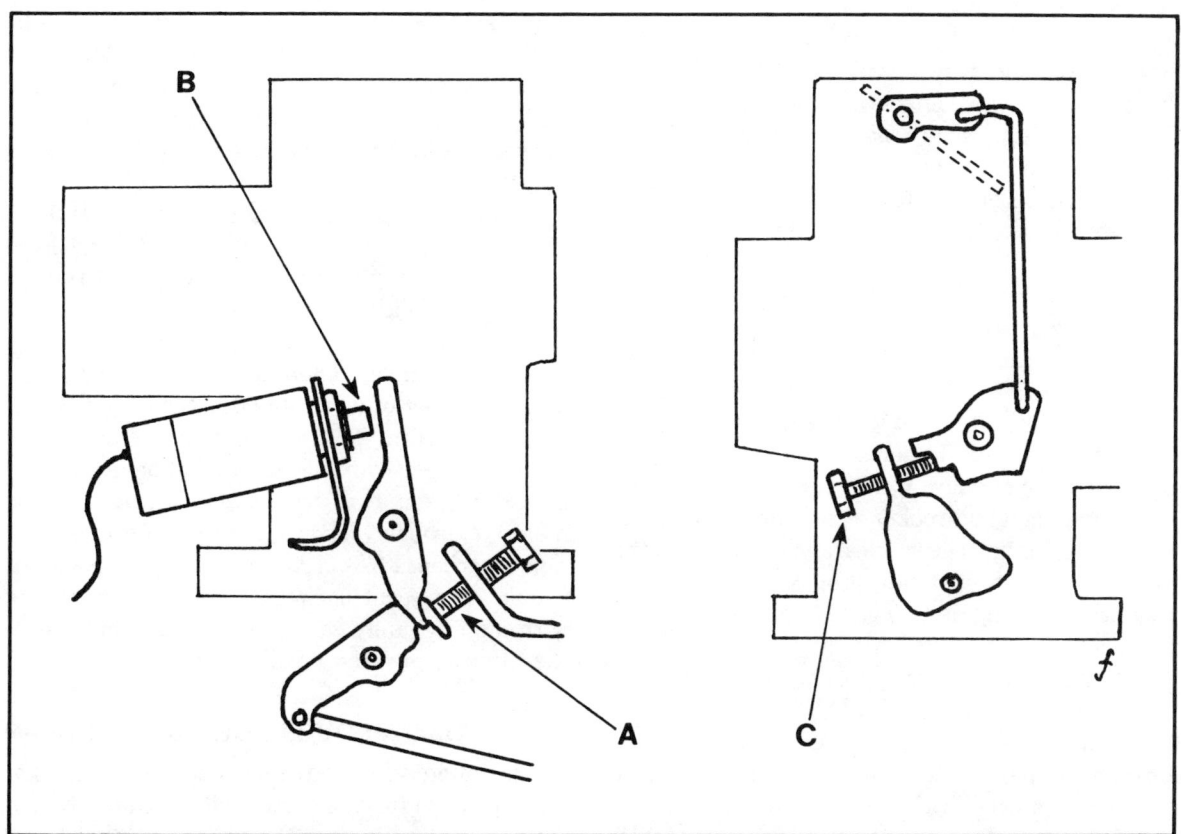

Fig. 8-1. The basic idle speed setting is commonly made by turning throttle stop screw (A). Adjustment of solenoid plunger position (B) is also needed on modern carburetors. Many carbs have a fast-idle, speed-adjusting screw (C) that contacts stepped cam in choke linkage.

psi for later models with super-high compression ratios. Compression pressure is closely related to compression ratio.

Any significantly low reading suggests leakage somewhere in the cylinder. The compressed air/fuel mixture is either exiting prematurely from one of the valves or making its way down past the ngs into the crankcase.

One or two manuals also give a recommended *engine vacuum* reading. Most omit it because vacuum fluctuates for so many reasons.

VALVE CLEARANCE

Valve lash (tappet clearance) data often appear in a separate table with stem diameter, face angle, and other valve details (Chapter 12). But they're frequently part of the tune-up table, and certainly part of many major tune-ups.

Many engines from the past couple of decades have no specification for valve lash because they have hydraulic valve lifters that cannot be adjusted. Earlier models usually have solid (mechanical) lifters, with a lash specification in thousandths of an inch. So do quite a few modern engines. This is especially true for imports and high-performance models.

The valve clearance specification indicates the desirable gap between the valve stem end and the part that pushes the valve open. It's measured with a feeler gauge leaf inserted into the space (gap), when the valve lifter is at its lowest point of travel, allowing maximum looseness.

Tappet clearance is measured between the valve stem end and rocker arm of an OHV motor (Fig. 8-2). For an L-head, clearance is between the stem and the tappet adjusting screw. With an overhead-cam engine, any gap is right at each camshaft lobe.

Adjustment is made by turning an adjuster nut with a wrench or screwdriver. A few OHC motors use small shims, added or deleted as necessary, to change the gap. Others have an adjusting screw acting on an eccentric.

A narrow range may be given in the spec table: .006-.008, .013-.015, etc. More often, it's a single figure such as .024 inch. Recommended clearances vary from .005, in tiny old Crosleys, up to .030 inch or so in more contemporary motors.

A figure followed by the letter *H* (or noted as such in the column heading) indicates that clearance must be measured with the engine hot or perhaps running. Letter *C* means the motor should be cold. Clearance changes considerably as an engine warms up.

Specifications for intake (I) and exhaust (E) valves are occasionally identical. Most often the exhausts need wider clearance because they are more subject to damage from the extremely high temperatures of the exhaust gases.

In case of doubt or when severe operation is anticipated, it's generally best to set clearances a trifle on the wide side. All the more so for exhaust valves. Tight valves are prone to *burning*. The rim of the valve face, where it contacts the seat, actually burns away, causing horrid leakage.

Remember, too, that whenever a feeler leaf of given thickness can enter the gap it reveals that clearance is at least that wide. It could be wider if the camshaft lobe isn't quite in the correct position to put the lifter at its bottom-most point.

Valve trains with hydraulic lifters and individual rocker arms—as used on GM and Ford engines for many years—have a different type of adjustment. With the engine running, you tighten the adjusting nut to "zero" position (no clickety sound discernible). Then tighten, past that point, by the number of turns stated in the spec table. It might be 1 turn, 2 1/2 turns, or possibly "zero."

Even those hydraulic lifters that have no possible adjustment may have a specification in the table. It probably shows a very wide clearance range: perhaps .078-.178 inch. This is the space that should be present between stem and rocker arm with the lifter fully collapsed. Outside that range, the lifter or pushrod needs to be replaced.

VALVE TIMING: DURATION AND OVERLAP

Valve timing refers to the sequence of events that takes place in the valve train with each rotation of the crankshaft. Because the camshaft turns at one-half crankshaft speed, each intake valve opens and closes once—as does each exhaust valve—with

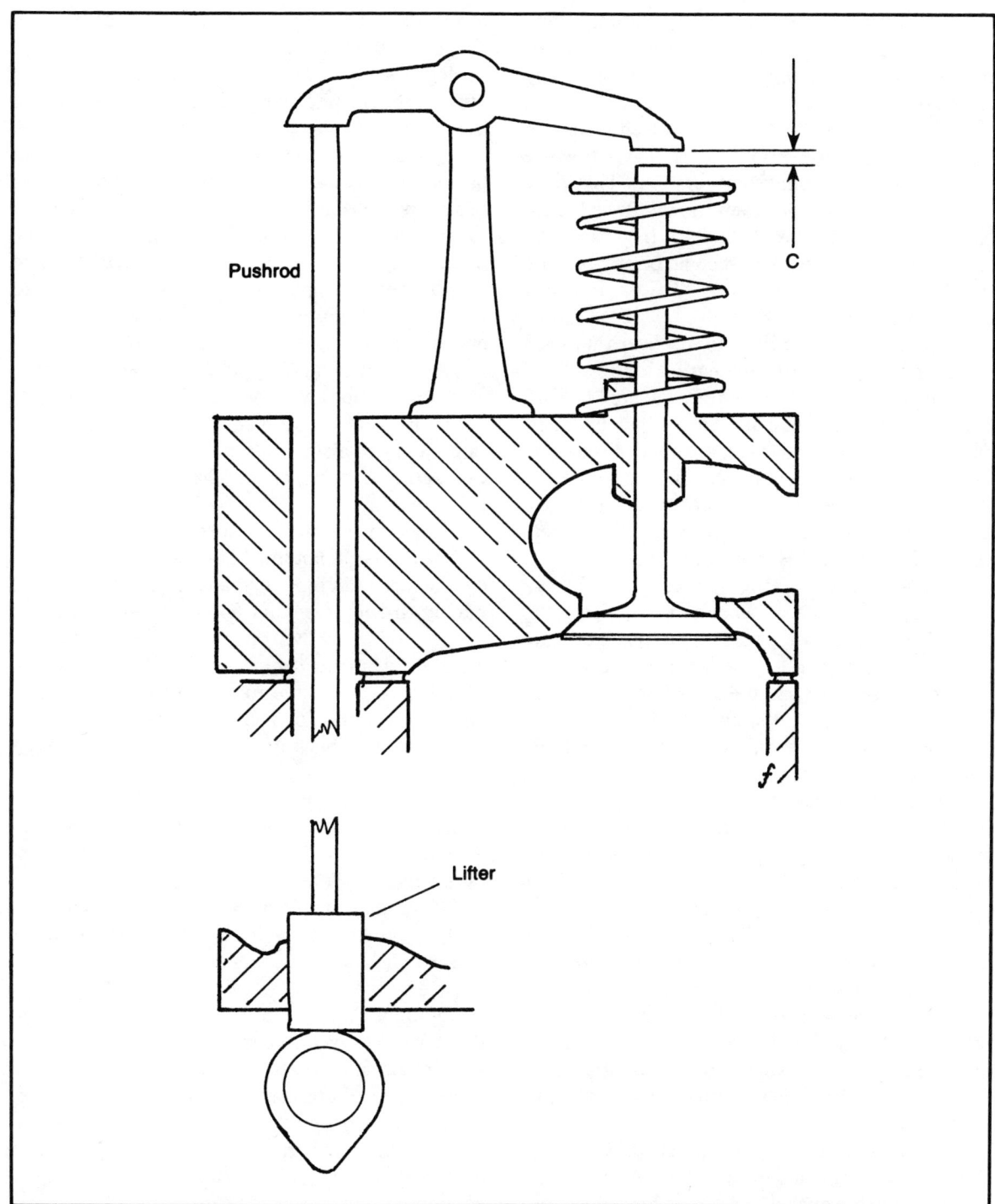

Fig. 8-2. Valve clearance (C) of the OHV engine is measured between the rocker arm and valve stem end. The valve must be fully closed. The lifter rests on heel of cam lobe, making clearance as wide as possible.

every two turns of the crankshaft. Timing, then, indicates the position of the crankshaft when a particular valve first begins to open, and when it is fully closed.

Many tune-up tables include a specification for *intake valve opening* in number of degrees before top dead center (of crankshaft rotation). This gives the crankshaft position when the intake valve for No. 1 cylinder just begins to open (as the piston gets ready for its intake stroke). It could be anything up to 50 or more degrees before TDC or, in a few cases, slightly after TDC.

You might be surprised to discover that each valve isn't open for just 180 degrees (one stroke of the crankshaft). And even more bewildered to learn that the intake and exhaust valves of a cylinder, during part of each full cycle, are open at the same time. New air/fuel mixture coming in before the burnt gases have left the cylinder? An exhaust valve opening before the piston has reached the bottom of its power stroke? How can that be?

It's necessary so changing pressure in the cylinder helps force the gases in and out, aiding the normal flow. This way, enough mixture gets into the cylinder, and the exhaust gases are fully scavenged (sent out) with each stroke.

An intake valve might open 15 degrees before the piston reaches the top, and stay open until 50 degrees past the piston's bottom position, well into the compression stroke (a total of 245 degrees). Cylinder pressure is still low as that next compression stroke begins. Keeping the valve open actually helps the mixture enter smoothly. The exhaust is open for a similarly long period.

The period during which a given valve is open, either totally or partially, is called *valve duration*. The period when both valves are open, around the end of an exhaust stroke and the start of the next intake stroke, is *valve overlap*. During that period, low pressure in the exhaust port (past the valve) helps draw in the needed air/fuel mixture for the next "firing."

A typical valve timing diagram (Fig. 8-3) shows the sequence of events for one cylinder. Note that the intake valve opens 15 degrees before the piston reaches TDC on the previous exhaust stroke. The exhaust valve is still open, and remains so until 20 degrees after TDC—well into the intake stroke, during which a fresh air/fuel mixture is drawn into the cylinder as the piston moves downward.

Before the piston is anywhere near the bottom (45 degrees before BDC), the exhaust valve has begun to open again. Intake and exhaust are open together now for a total of 100 degrees (until the intake finally closes at 55 degrees after BDC). The exhaust remains open, allowing the spent gases to exit, until 35 degrees (15 + 20) after the intake opens again for the next stroke. And on and on.

An engine running at high speed for considerable periods will benefit from longer valve duration. This allows it to "breathe" better, getting plenty of air/fuel mixture into each cylinder. Competition (racing) engines have markedly higher valve overlap.

What does all this mean to the working mechanic? Well, not much. Specs for duration and overlap aren't in tune-up tables, and are of interest mainly to engineers and hop-up enthusiasts.

Even the "valve opening" spec isn't often needed. Unless timing gears have become misaligned, often due to a slipped timing chain, valve timing shouldn't change.

You can check valve timing by placing a calibrated *degree wheel* around the circumference of the crankshaft pulley. Rotating the crankshaft by hand, you can then determine how many degrees in advance of TDC you are at the moment the intake valve for Number 1 begins to lift.

How can you tell? With a solid-lifter engine, it's fairly easy. After temporarily adjusting the tappet to zero clearance, just mount a dial indicator to show exactly when the valve begins to move.

Nothing can be done about valve timing, even if it's found to be out of spec, except for removing the timing case to see that the gear marks mate properly. Furthermore, if the intake valve for No. 1 cylinder is correctly timed, all the others have to be too. The camshaft is rigid after all. There's an absolutely fixed relationship between all the cylinders.

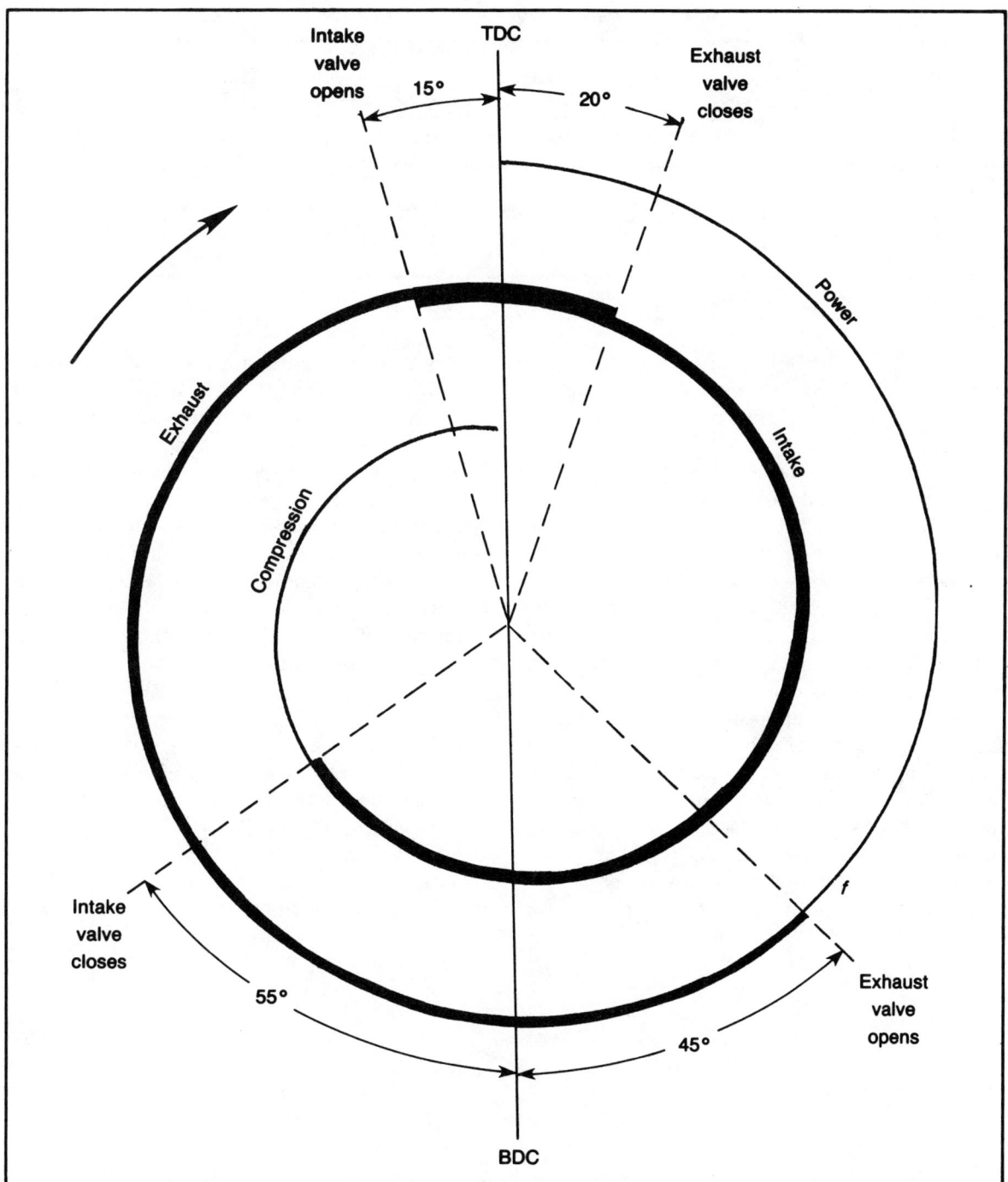

Fig. 8-3. A typical valve timing diagram. Intake and exhaust valves are open at the same time (valve overlap) through 35 degrees, before and after Top Dead Center (TDC).

99

Table 8-2. Typical Diesel Tune-up Specifications.

Engine disp.	Warm valve clearance (inches)		Injection pump setting (deg)	Injection nozzle Pressure (psi)		Idle Speed (rpm)	Compression Pressure (psi)
	Intake	Exhaust		New	Used		
8-350	- - -	- - -	4A[1]	- - -	- - -	600D	- - -
4-1.6L	.008-.012	.016-.020	Align marks	1885	1740	770-870	398-483
2404	.004	.016	24B	1564[2]	1422[2]	750-800	284-327
8-350	- - -	- - -	4 1/2[1]	- - -	- - -	750/600	275 min.

[1]Use diesel timing meter. [2]Maximum, 1706 psi.

DIESEL DATA

Tune-up data for diesel engines (Table 8-2) differs somewhat from spark-ignition motors. First off, there are no ignition specs. Diesels are known as compression-ignition engines. The fuel charge is ignited by heat of compression instead of by a spark.

Their 22:1 or 23:1 compression ratio causes the air to reach 1000° F or so, easily igniting the fuel as it enters the cylinder. Therefore, a spark plug and its need for firing at a precise moment is irrelevant. Diesel combustion chambers have glow plugs to aid in cold starting, but their purpose is merely to warm up the fuel not ignite it.

Some diesel tune-up specs are identical to those for gas engines. Valve lash (clearance) specs may be indistinguishable from the usual ones, with hot or cold settings to a specified number of thousandths of an inch. Idle speed data are similar, but adjustment is made at the fuel injection pump housing by turning a screw or linkage part.

Compression testing is just as important for diesels, too. The figures are a lot higher—typically 400 to 500 psi—because of the much higher compression ratio in diesel engines. Thus, a higher-reading gauge is needed.

A few additional specs may be given that are entirely different. Pressure data for the fuel injection pump is an example. There may be a specified setting for *injection timing* to ensure that fuel arrives at the right moment. It may be nothing more than a recommendation to align a pair of marks on the crankshaft pulley. This is much like setting ignition timing on a gas engine.

Nozzle pressure testing requires special high-pressure gauges. In many cases, pressures approach 2000 psi, and an ordinary gauge would be useless. Two recommended pressures might be given: one for a new pump, another for one that's been in use for a while. As with gas engines, the wise mechanic looks for descriptions of test procedures in the manual's text, rather than relying on the spec tables alone.

Engine Pressures and Temperatures

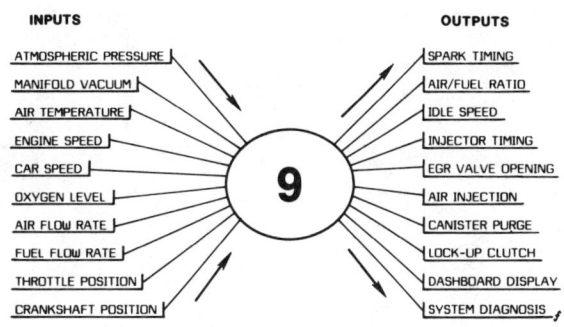

THE INTERNAL COMBUSTION ENGINE IS A mass of varying pressures and heats. Depending on where a measurement is made, there are slight pressures, moderate pressures, and amazingly high pressures. They're changing all the time as the engine runs. The same thing happens with engine heat; it varies from moderately warm to sizzling hot.

Most of these pressures and temperatures are not listed in any spec table, but anyone working on engines should be familiar with them. Table 9-1 shows only those which need to be measured: coolant pressure and temperature, as found in a cooling system table; plus oil pressure, which is part of general engine specifications.

ATMOSPHERIC PRESSURE

All the pressures within the engine are expressed with reference to the pressure in the atmosphere all around us. It's in the air, everywhere—actually, the weight of all that air. Although atmospheric pressure is exerted in every direction—up, down, sideways—its earthward force is easiest to imagine (Fig. 9-1).

Pressure, as anyone who has pumped up a tire or tested engine compression knows, is commonly measured in pounds per square inch (psi). A figure in pounds alone tells us next to nothing. We must know the surface area against which a given force is pushing. And because the square inch is the standard reference in the non-metric system, psi is the customary measure. In metrics it's kilograms per square centimeter (kg/cm^2). Same idea just different measurement units.

Example. A 100-pound weight, setting atop a pillar with an area of one square inch, exerts a downward pressure of precisely 100 psi. 100 pounds, 1 square inch, get it? But put that same weight on a pillar with 5-square-inch area, and its pressure downward becomes 20 psi (100 divided by 5). On a one-half square-inch pillar? That would be 200 psi. Pressure exerted by every step of a woman's spike heel gets into *thousands* of psi, because of the small surface area.

Atmospheric pressure can be thought of, in the

Table 9-1. Typical Engine Pressure and Temperature Data.

	Cooling system data		General specs
Engine CID/Liter	Radiator Cap Relief Pressure (lbs)	Thermostat Opening Temperature (degrees F)	Oil Pressure (psi)
V8-302/5.0	16	195	40-60
V6-173	15	195	50-65
V8-350	15	180	35-45
6-170	12-15	190	35-60

same way, as the weight of all the air above a one-square-inch area of the earth's surface. You can visualize it as an air column many miles tall, and you're weighing the whole thing. Measured at sea level, this pressure (or weight) amounts to approximately 14.7 psi. To be more exact, it's 14.696 (sometimes called "one atmosphere").

As air expands and contracts in response to temperature and weather changes, its pressure fluctuates slightly. Altitude has an even greater effect. With each 1000-foot rise in elevation, atmospheric pressure drops by about 1/2 psi. It is down to around 14.2 psi at 1000 feet and nearly 12 psi in mile-high Denver. Chugging up Pike's Peak,

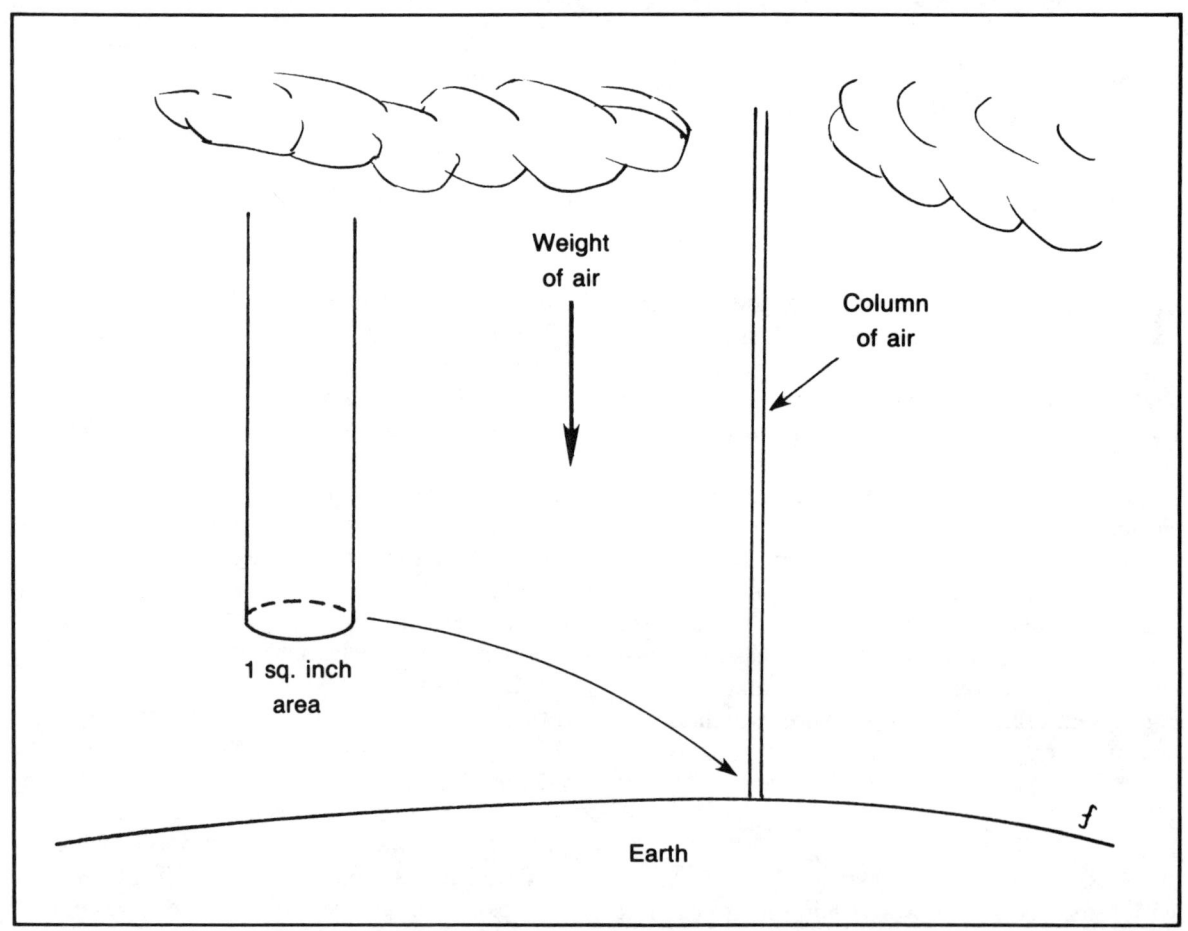

Fig. 9-1. Atmospheric pressure can be thought of as the weight of a column of air 1 square inch in area, extending from the ground all the way up to the top of the earth's atmosphere. At higher altitudes, pressure is lower because there isn't as much air above the ground.

pressure gradually approaches half that at sea level. The air is actually "thinner" at high altitudes, occupying more space for a given weight, thereby exerting less pressure. As mountain residents have learned the hard way, this makes quite a difference in engine operation, often demanding internal carburetor changes and a new look at cooling system specifications.

Scientists generally deal with absolute pressure: the total pressure evident at a point, including that produced by the atmosphere. Pressures measured in automobiles, on the other hand, are gauge pressures—the quantity above that of the air alone. Any reading amounts to the difference between the total pressure and the atmospheric pressure. When a tire gauge shows 20 psi, the total pressure is almost 35 psi. The 14.7 psi atmospheric pressure is there even as the tire sets flat, and each stroke of the pump adds to that starting point.

Most postwar engines have at least four distinct pressures inside; that is, four pressures greater than atmospheric. These are found acting upon liquids in the cooling, lubrication, and fuel systems—and as compression/combustion pressure of the air/fuel mixture in each cylinder. That last one is the pressure that matters most (getting the old crankshaft to turn).

COMPRESSION AND COMBUSTION

Some of the highest pressures are right in the combustion chamber where the compressed air/fuel mixture is ignited and burns. As each piston rises

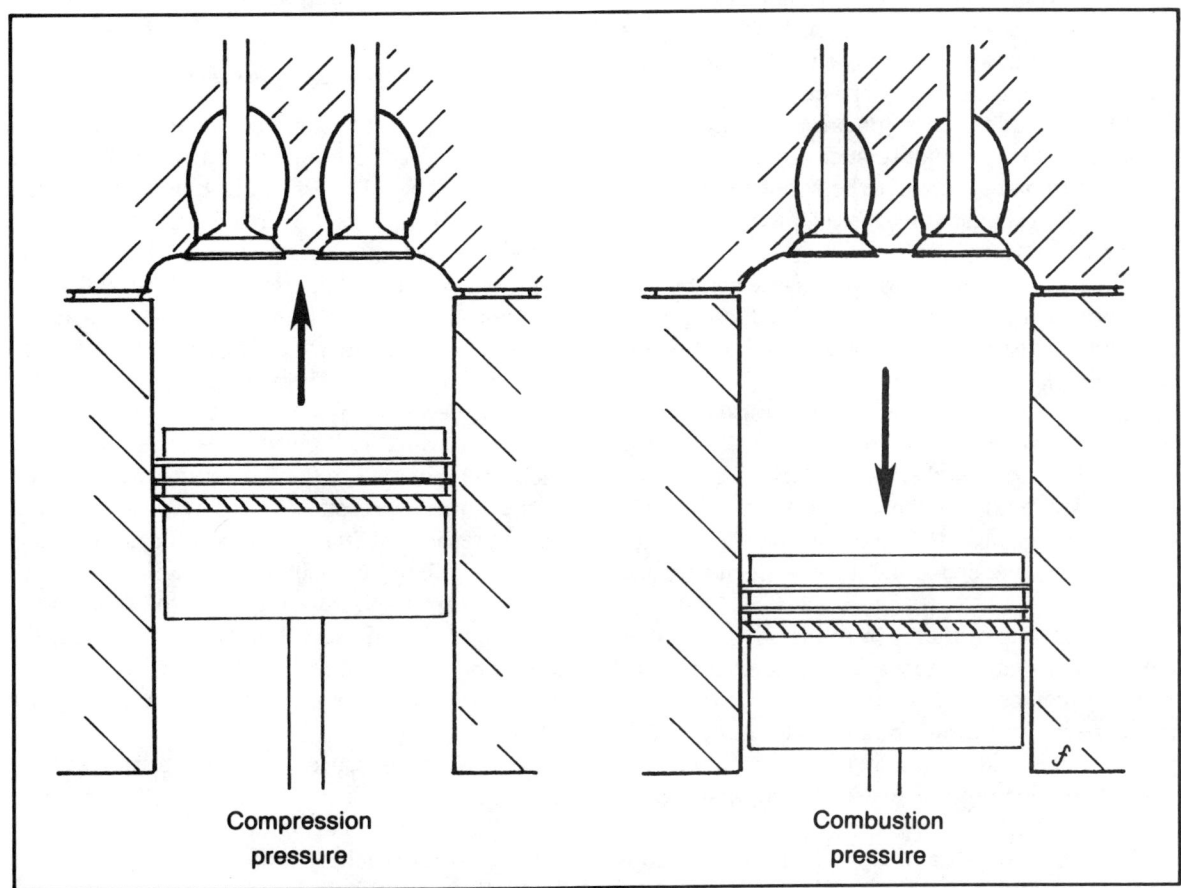

Fig. 9-2. Compression pressure builds up as the air/fuel mixture is squeezed by the rising piston. Combustion pressure, which forces the piston downward on power stroke, is much higher.

on its compression stroke, with both valves tightly closed (we hope), compression pressure between 100 and 200 psi builds up in the small combustion chamber above the cylinder (Fig. 9-2).

Engines with higher compression ratios (smaller chambers) produce higher pressure. Actual compression pressure varies with engine speed, dropping to as little as 35 psi at idle.

After a spark plug fires, the burning mixture expands fast, forcing the piston downward. This combustion pressure within the cylinder can reach 600 psi (even 1000 psi in some motors). That is about four times the compression pressure. Its peak comes with the throttle wide open (just after the piston begins its downward "push").

That's an awful lot of force acting against the piston head and against the crankshaft journals down below. A 4-inch-diameter piston with 600 psi hammering it down is carrying a total force of some 7500 pounds on its head surface. Looked at that way, it's a wonder that engines last as long as they do while having to endure such treatment. Some pressure remains, to eject the spent mixture out through the exhaust valve, as the piston then rises on exhaust stroke.

We don't have occasion to measure combustion pressure. That's for engineers. But testing compression pressure is part of any major tune-up (Chapter 8).

In general, a higher compression ratio produces higher compression pressure. How come? Because the engine with a higher compression ratio has a smaller space above the piston, into which the air/fuel mixture has to be compressed. Force any gas into a smaller space and its developed pressure has to go up.

An old rule-of-thumb formula gives a rough idea of what can be expected. Just multiply the engine's compression ratio by the atmospheric pressure in your area, then add the atmospheric pressure, and add the number 5 to that total. That is, compression pressure = (c.r. × a.p.) + a.p. + 5. Not precise but interesting.

As we've seen, atmospheric pressure drops from about 14 1/2 psi near sea level and down to around 11.8 psi at 5000 feet. Using that old formula, an engine with 8:1 compression should give a reading in the neighborhood of 135 psi at low altitude, but perhaps only 110 psi in Denver.

A compression pressure reading lower than specified by the factory (or deduced from the formula) does not, of course, suggest that the engine's compression ratio has been lowered. Rather, it's normally due to leakage past worn rings or valves, preventing full build-up of pressure with each piston stroke.

Compression readings higher than normal, on the other hand, may well result from an increase in compression ratio. Rather than suspecting the car's previous owner of surreptitiously altering the engine, though, look to an accumulation of carbon as the more likely culprit. When carbon takes up part of the space, compression ratio goes up.

OIL PRESSURE

Down in the crankcase, the oil pump produces pressure to drive the lubricant around the engine to parts that need it. Pressure builds up because of the small spaces through which the fluid is forced: the clearances between crankshaft and camshaft journals and their surrounding bearings. For this reason, running pressure diminishes as an engine grows old and its bearing clearances enlarge. Oil then flows too freely, with pressure dwindling to a risky level.

Oil pressure is highest when the oil is cold, thick, and reluctant to flow. After warmup, it drops to the normal pressure at highway speeds. For years, pressure of 30 to 45 psi was the norm. Many specs are still in that neighborhood. Some engines, however, operate at pressures up to 75 psi or so. A few, like the old "stovebolt" Chevrolet six of the 1950s and earlier, are content with a mere 14 psi. At idle speed, acceptable pressure may be only a few psi.

Specified pressure could be a range or a minimum figure. Usually it is at a certain running speed (in either rpm or mph). A relief valve keeps pressure from reaching a dangerously high level. It may be adjustable in case the pressure becomes unusually high. Unfortunately, no adjustment can boost pressure in a tired engine with overgrown clearances.

COOLANT PRESSURE

Early cooling systems were unpressurized and vented to the atmosphere (the outside air). The higher-compression, hotter-running engines of the late 1940s and 1950s created a need for pressure.

Why? Because each psi of pressure in the coolant—whether plain water or anti-freeze—raises its boiling point by about 3 degrees Fahrenheit. Water that ordinarily boils at 212° F will remain stable until about 225° with a 4-pound pressure cap, as used on some of the first pressurized systems. With the 12 to 15 psi radiator cap that became typical by the late 1950s, the boiling point reaches 250° to 257°.

Beyond that, the water pump works more efficiently in a sealed system. The *relief pressure* (system pressure) rating in a cooling system data table may be a single figure, such as 15 psi, or a range like 14 to 18 psi. When pressure reaches the rated level, a relief valve in the cap opens, to release any additional buildup.

A pressure gauge that fits the radiator cap opening is used to test a system for leaks by applying pressure equal to that normally supplied by the cap. Otherwise, coolant pressure is assumed to be OK so long as the cap is of the correct pressure rating and in good condition.

FUEL AND OTHER PRESSURES

Gasoline in Henry Ford's Model T reached the carburetor by force of gravity. Other autos of early vintage used a vacuum tank that stored up "force" to propel the fuel toward the engine. Nearly all cars since the 1930s have used a fuel pump (either mechanical or electrical).

Fuel pressure specs, as we've seen in Chapter 8, are found in tune-up tables of most manuals. A fuel pump in good condition puts out somewhere between 2 1/2 and 7 psi. In a few high-performance engines, it could be as high as 9 psi. Fuel pressure is actually highest at idle (when flow is slowest) and weaker as engine speed increases.

In most engines, modern or old, air enters the carburetor or injection system under atmospheric pressure. In motors with superchargers or turbochargers, it's given a substantial boost that is as much as 10 psi over the usual pressure. That forces the mixture into the cylinders with much greater enthusiasm than usual. More on blowers in Chapter 10.

Other pressures exist elsewhere in the car. There are high levels of hydraulic pressure in brake and power steering systems, pressures in automatic transmission segments, and so on. As a rule, they're measured with a gauge only when a problem is suspected. Specs may be in a manual's text, but not in the ordinary tables.

ENGINE TEMPERATURES: A MASS OF HEAT

When we think of heat in an engine, the figure that comes to mind is coolant temperature (the 200 or so degrees that we try to maintain in the antifreeze). Any engine, though, is a mass of miscellaneous temperatures ranging from that of the coolant to more than a thousand degrees.

Combustion gases can reach a temperature of up to 4500 degrees (F) at their peak. All of this heat has to be dissipated (passed along) to adjoining engine parts. Some goes into the valve seats, a little into the valve guides, more to the piston head and cylinder walls.

The whole idea of cooling an engine is to take advantage of the principle of heat dissipation. Coolant circulating through water jackets in surrounding regions helps heat to diminish in a hurry from parts and surfaces that reach extreme temperatures. At least, that's what we hope will happen—and it usually does.

Valves are the hot spot. An exhaust valve's head can reach 1300—even 1600—degrees. Its stem may be only a hundred degrees cooler. Intake valves, subjected to less of the intense heat of the burned fuel mixture, run a bit cooler.

Heat in the cylinder wall ranges up to 700 degrees at the top (some motors run considerably cooler). Farther down the cylinder it is perhaps 300 degrees. The combustion chamber surface might measure 500 degrees. A piston head also may get

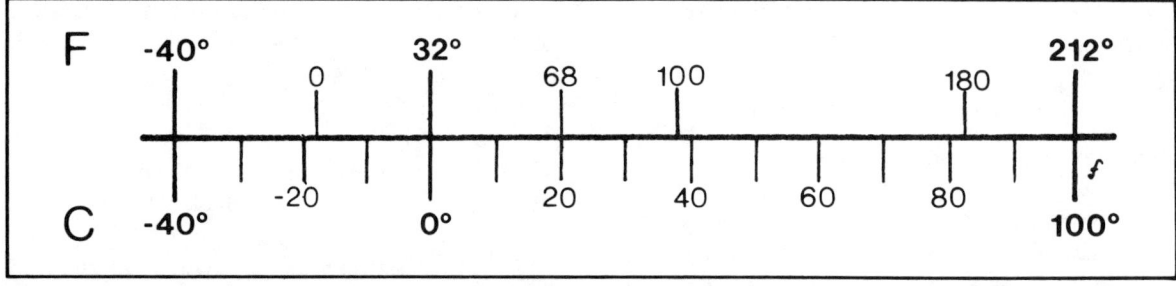

Fig. 9-3. Relationship of Fahrenheit (F) and Celsius (C) temperature scales.

to 500, its top ring a bit less, and its skirt only half that heat. Spark plug electrodes? Some reach 1500 degrees and others half that figure. Except for watching the dashboard temperature gauge, we don't ordinarily measure any of this internal heat.

OVERHEATING:
CURSE OF THE OLDER AUTO

We don't see nearly as many boiling, overheated engines on the highways as we did a couple of decades back. Before cooling systems reached their present efficiency, geysers of steam erupting from car radiators were a common sight on any Sunday afternoon drive. Rush hour traffic was worse yet.

Today's engines run quite a bit hotter than the old ones, but their designs are unquestionably better able to cope with the increase. As we've seen, pressure in the cooling system adds to the boiling point, cutting the risk of serious overheating. Using antifreeze instead of water raises the boiling point even further. The customary 50/50 mixture of ethylene glycol antifreeze and water boils at a temperature about 11° higher than water alone, and around 268° with a 15-psi cap (making boilover an unlikely event indeed).

It's also important to note that the boiling point is reduced at higher elevations: about 2°F for every 1000-foot rise in altitude, down to just 185° or so at 15,000 feet.

A coolant's freezing point is no less important. Plain water can freeze solid at just 32 degrees. On a frigid morning, that could spell the end for a radiator—and perhaps a motor. Selecting an appropriate mixture of ethylene glycol and water produces the desired (lower) freeze point. Oddly enough, antifreeze alone—or in an overly strong mixture—freezes at a higher temperature than that nice 50/50 combination.

Coolant temperature is controlled by the thermostat, which opens and closes to allow more or less fluid to flow into the motor's water jackets. Thermostat opening temperature, in degrees Fahrenheit, is part of cooling system specs. Most of today's 'stats are rated at 195 degrees. A second figure may show the temperature at which it should be fully open (perhaps 218 degrees).

Earlier thermostats opened at 180 or 160 degrees. It used to be common practice to install a hotter (180°) unit in winter and to switch to a 160° in summer to minimize the risk of boilover. Nowadays, it's unwise to deviate from the recommended rating.

Automotive temperatures are usually given in degrees Fahrenheit, but readings in centigrade (Celsius) are growing (Fig. 9-3). Converting one to the other isn't too difficult if a table isn't at hand. In formula form:

$$C = \frac{5}{9}(F - 32)$$

$$F = (\frac{9}{5}C) + 32$$

Example. A reading of 180° F. Subtract 32 from 180, which leaves 148; then multiply that amount by 5, and divide by 9. The answer is 82.2 degrees C.

Vacuum, Carburetion and Emissions

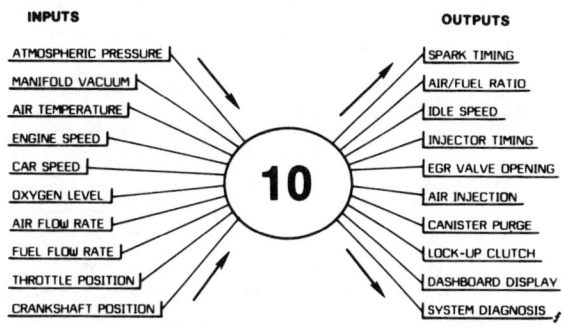

LET'S START THIS CHAPTER WITH A SEEMingly easy question. What makes the engine run? Is it gasoline? Air? A mixture of both? The starter motor? Good fortune?

It's all of the above, of course, but only when one crucial factor is present. That factor is pressure accompanied by its intimate relative, vacuum. Specifically, it's the principle of pressure differential (Fig. 10-1) that permits an engine—any engine—to operate.

Were it not for the inevitable attempts by both gases and fluids to equalize any pressure differential—to move obediently among spaces containing varying pressure—the engine as we know it couldn't exist. All the Herculean efforts of Nikolaus Otto, the Duryea brothers, Ransom Olds, and their brethren motoring pioneers would have proved futile. Air flowing into an engine compartment would never bother to enter the carburetor. Gasoline would wait patiently in the carb's float bowl (or in the gas tank) forever. Vacuum and pressure, then, not only allow air and fuel to enter the motor's cylinders; they permit the principles of carburetion to come into play on gasoline engines.

VACUUM: IT LETS THE ENGINE RUN

Pistons are often said to suck, or draw, the air/fuel mixture down from the carburetor and into the cylinders. It seems logical, but it's not quite accurate. Because of the vacuum created in each cylinder, in sequence, air is actually pushed down the carburetor barrel by atmospheric pressure (Fig. 10-2).

Vacuum itself is frequently described as the absence of pressure or absence of air. As zero pressure? Not quite. A perfect vacuum is rare indeed. Even an old-fashioned electronic vacuum tube, commonly thought to be devoid of air, still contains a bit of pressure. A light bulb, too. All the vacuums we find in daily life are partial, most accurately referred to as a *vacuum pressure* or any pressure that's lower than atmospheric.

When any space contains such a partial vacuum, gases in surrounding areas—acted upon

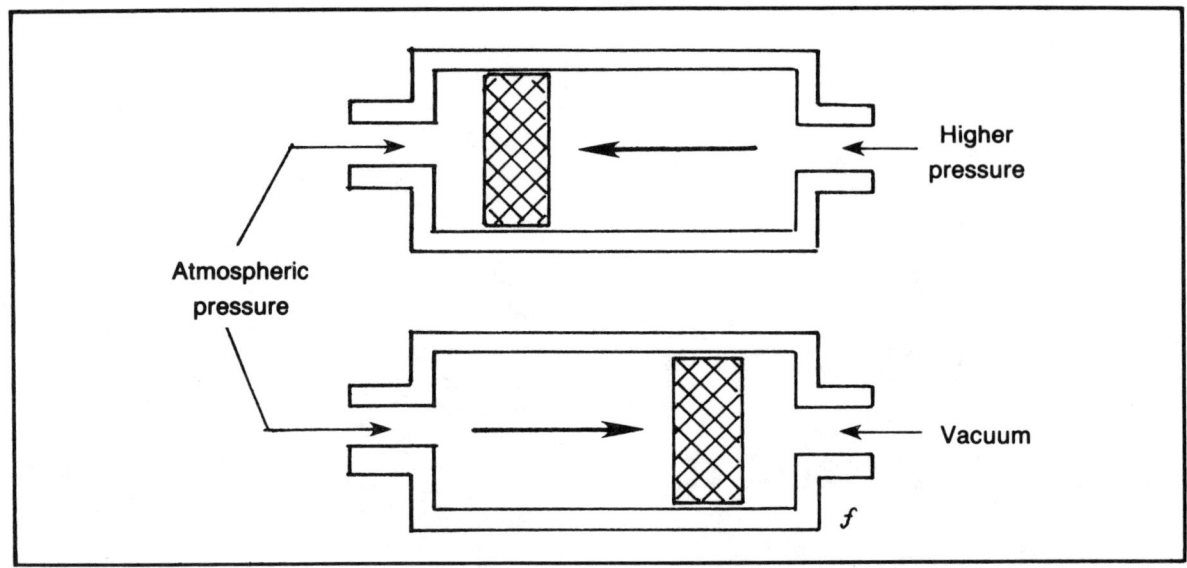

Fig. 10-1. When one port of a fuel pump or other device is open to atmosphere and the other to a higher pressure (top), the pressure differential causes the piston or diaphragm to force air or fluid toward the a.p. side. When exposed to a vacuum (bottom), movement is in opposite direction.

by atmospheric pressure—will be forced into the lower-pressure region. They can't resist. They're compelled to try and "fill up" any partial vacuum they can get to. It might help to think of vacuum as "negative pressure." Then the areas with positive pressure constantly try to equalize with the negatives.

Each piston creates such a low-pressure space at the top of its cylinder, as it moves downward on the intake stroke. Pressure has to drop because the space available for air has enlarged. The reduced pressure extends into the intake manifold, and up through the carburetor barrel. This upward-creeping partial vacuum must be filled by air that enters the engine in an attempt to equalize the pressures, occupying the space vacated by the piston.

Vacuum Readings: Inches of Mercury

You've probably used a vacuum gauge to check engine condition, so you know there's vacuum in the intake manifold. That's where the gauge connects for testing. But wait—that gauge isn't calibrated in psi, the unit of pressure.

Absolutely true. It's calibrated in "inches of mercury" or in metrics (millimeters of mercury). These are the conventional ways of describing any pressure lower than atmospheric. The measure refers to the height of a vertical column of mercury that would be supported when acted upon by a stated pressure (Fig. 10-3). Weathermen talk about barometric pressure, in terms of inches, and that figure is always around 30. In fact, the "normal" 14.7 psi atmospheric pressure is equivalent to 29.92 inches of mercury (Hg). One psi is equal to 2.036 inches.

Engine vacuum measurements are just the opposite: the *difference* between atmospheric and manifold pressures. A reading of zero on the vacuum gauge means no vacuum is present. That is the pressure is *equal* to atmospheric. The higher the scale reading the greater the vacuum (and the lower the actual pressure).

A perfect vacuum would reach 30 inches on the scale (far greater than we'll ever see). An 18-inch reading equals pressure of about 11.9 inches (29.9 minus 18). Table 10-1 illustrates the relationship.

Vacuum gauges, incidentally, contain no mercury. The reading is simply equivalent to that which would be obtained by measuring the vacuum with

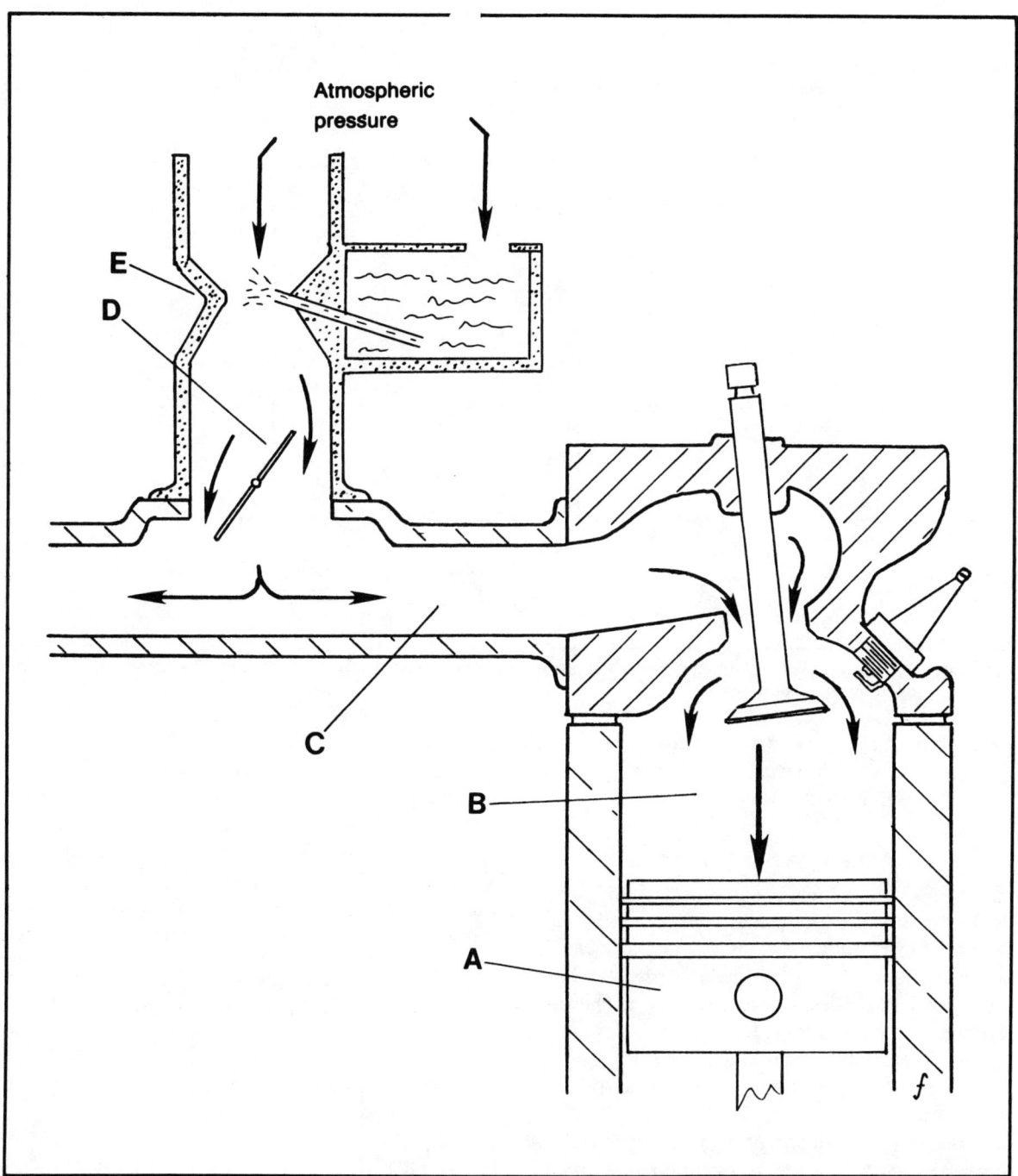

Fig. 10-2. As piston (A) moves downward on intake stroke, a partial vacuum is created in cylinder (B) above, spreading into intake manifold (C). Whenever the carburetor's throttle valve (D) is open, air flows down the barrel, forced by atmospheric pressure, in an attempt to equalize the pressures. As air passes the carb's venturi (E), the vacuum becomes stronger, causing fuel—pushed down by atmospheric pressure—to emerge from the main discharge nozzle, mixing with the air.

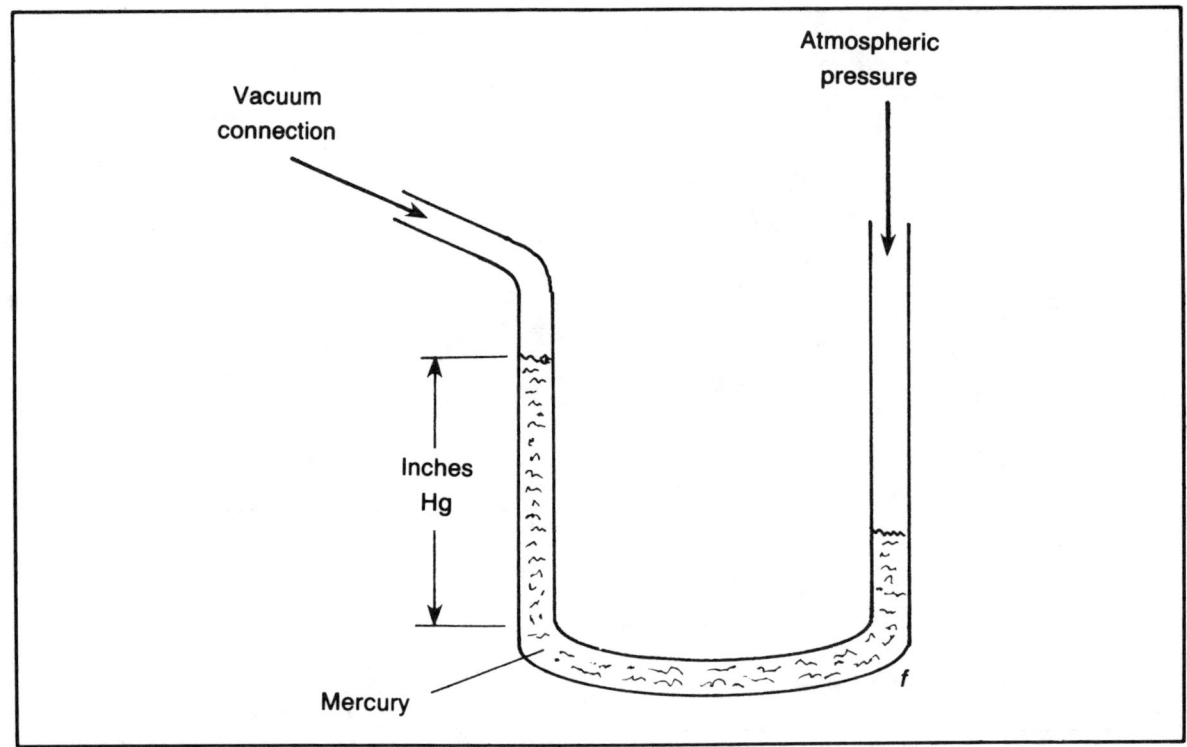

Fig. 10-3. When one end of a U-tube is connected to vacuum, and the other end is exposed to atmospheric pressure, mercury rises to show vacuum level.

a column of mercury, as in a barometer. Most gauges also have a scale calibrated in psi (above atmospheric) to measure fuel pressure.

Normal and Abnormal Vacuum

At idle speed, manifold vacuum between 17 and 22 inches is considered normal for most engines: toward the high end for 8-cylinder motors, lower for sixes and fours. As the gas pedal is pressed down, manifold vacuum drops. It actually approaches zero during hard acceleration. The highest reading ever achieved is about 25 inches (momentarily) when the motor is gunned. Then the pedal is released abruptly.

Because of reduced atmospheric pressure at higher elevations, a vacuum gauge reads about 1 inch Hg lower for each rise of 1000 feet in altitude above sea level. At 5000 feet, a 13-inch reading might be perfectly normal.

What's considered normal also depends on the particular engine. A few spec tables include a recommended reading, but most do not. High-performance engines with extensive valve overlap produce somewhat erratic gauge readings. Emission controls may lower the expected figure.

Manifold vacuum changes continually with engine load and the position of the carb's throttle valve. It is also affected by various engine defects

Table 10-1. Equivalent Readings of Pressure and Vacuum.

Pressure (psi)	Pressure (inches Hg)	Vacuum (inches Hg)
14.7	29.9	0
12 1/2	25	5
10	20	10
7 1/2	15	15
5	10	20
2 1/2	5	25
0	0	30

such as worn intake valve guides, leaking piston rings, and anything else that might let unwanted air into the intake manifold or connecting passages. When that happens, there's less vacuum (pressure is closer to atmospheric), and performance suffers.

For that reason, the vacuum gauge has always been a good indicator of engine condition. Most manuals include a chart of vacuum readings and fluctuations that suggest a variety of internal maladies.

Only a few dashboards have come with a built-in vacuum gauge, but it's a popular accessory item. Regular glances at the gauge show how much of your driving is done with vacuum at an efficient level.

Vacuum Inside the Carburetor

As the air moving down the carburetor barrel toward the intake manifold passes the main discharge nozzle, tiny particles of fuel enter the stream. How come? Because liquids respond to pressure changes, too. Atmospheric pressure constantly pushes down against the gasoline in the float bowl, through a vent, at normal 14.7 psi force. As pressure within the carb's throat drops lower, fuel is forced out of the nozzle in the form of a spray mist. Passing through the intake manifold, this "atomized" air/fuel mixture approaches its boiling point, and turns into vapor that soon will be exploded.

The downward air flow occurs whenever the carb's throttle valve is open, exposing the barrel(s) to the lower pressure in the manifold below. But the vacuum level farther up the barrel, at the nozzle itself, may not be strong enough to attract sufficient fuel at all times. The action is dramatically enhanced, though, by a constriction (*venturi*) formed in every carb's throat. Because of the "venturi effect," the air becomes lowest in pressure right at the discharge nozzle.

The degree of venturi vacuum depends upon air speed, which is controlled by the throttle valve. The faster the air's velocity, the stronger the vacuum. This means more (and better-atomized) fuel will be added.

Why? Because when air moves faster it becomes thinner or "stretches," reducing its pressure. Air speeds up whenever it's forced through a narrow space such as a venturi. In fact, most carbs have one or two booster (secondary) venturis—little cylinders near the fuel nozzle—in series with the integral main constriction. These increase air flow and drop the pressure even more. Such a boost is most needed at slower engine speeds when air flow is most sluggish.

Vacuum is always strongest right at the venturi, except at idle, when the throttle is closed so little air flows (Fig. 10-4). Between the venturi and throttle valve, vacuum is less (closer to that in the manifold).

As the throttle opens wider, vacuum becomes more nearly equal from venturi down into manifold, and air flow is at its peak. When the choke valve at the top is closed, cutting off air from the outside, vacuum is high throughout the barrel. This produces the richer mixture (higher proportion of fuel) needed for starting.

Uses of Engine Vacuum

In addition to allowing the engine to run, vacuum serves several useful functions. In pre-electronic days, it controlled the distributor's vacuum advance. Vacuum actuates a piston in some automatic chokes, overriding the choke valve to prevent stalling or cut emissions during warm-up. It draws crankcase vapors through some positive crankcase ventilation (PCV) systems. It makes power brakes possible.

Vacuum has a purpose in operating heated air systems at the air cleaner, in fuel vapor emission control systems, and in exhaust gas recirculation systems. Old Tri-Power Pontiacs used vacuum to cut in the two end carburetors at the most opportune time. Before electric windshield wipers became standard, vacuum was used to power them as well. Handy stuff that vacuum.

FUEL SUPPLY

Fuel pressure is discussed in Chapter 9. Fuel pump volume is no less important. Adequate pressure does little good unless it delivers a sufficient quantity of fuel.

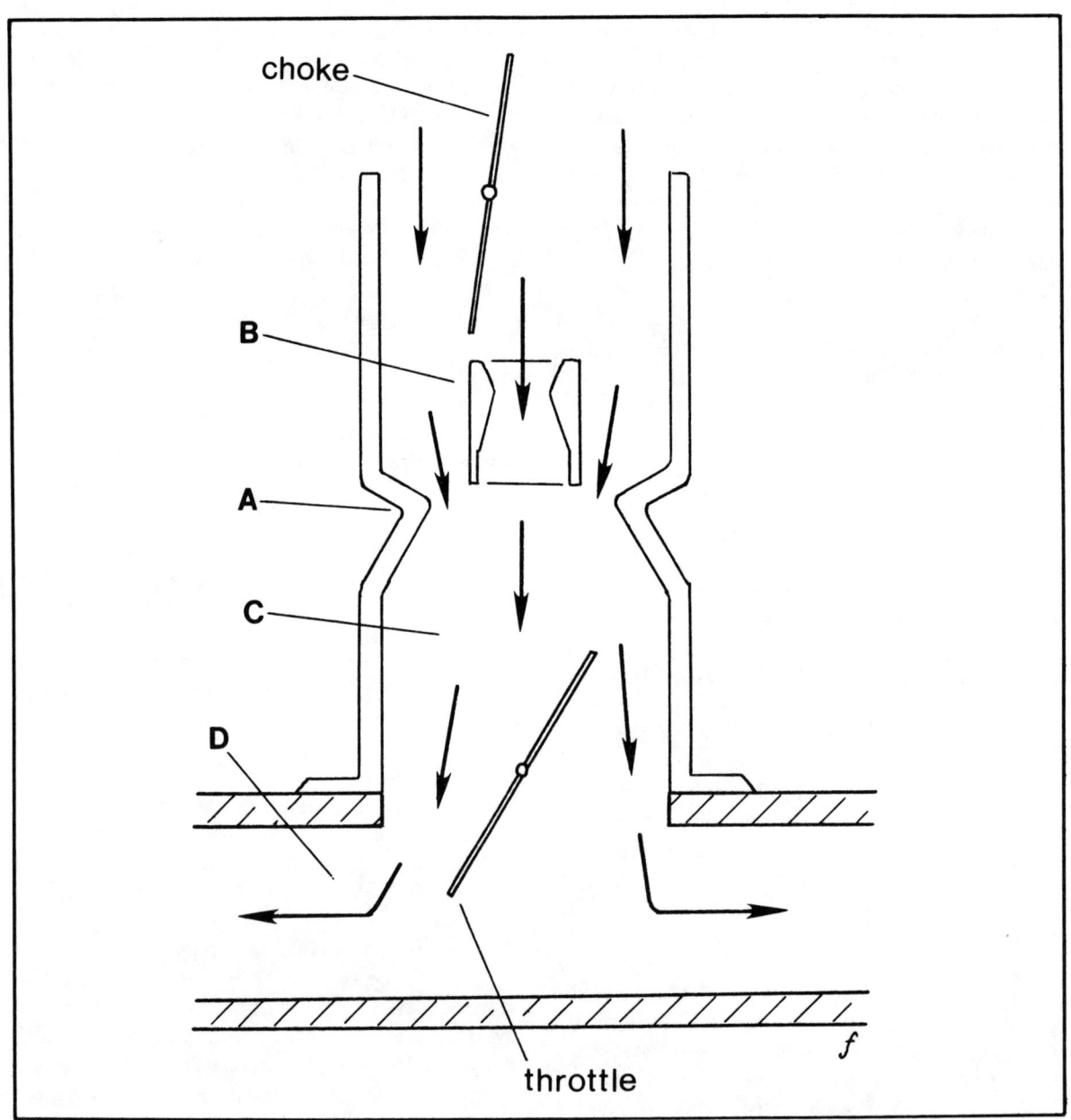

Fig. 10-4. Vacuum within a carburetor is strongest at main (A) and booster (B) venturis, and less in the ported section (C) and intake manifold (D).

Specs vary, but a mechanical pump should deliver about a pint of fuel in half a minute or less. Output can be tested by disconnecting the fuel line at the carb, and then cranking the engine while you time the fuel flow into a jar of appropriate size. Volume requirements for electrical pumps may differ.

CARBURETOR CAPACITIES

To reach an engine's peak capability, you want as much air to flow into the cylinders as you can get.

That's why the multibarrel was developed.

Early engines used a single-barrel carb. So do some smaller motors today. Two-barrel carbs appeared on larger engines before World War II. The four-barrel, introduced on the 1952 Oldsmobile and Cadillac, boosted potential even more, and contributed much to the horsepower race.

If an extra barrel helps, how about a whole extra carb? Not a bad idea. Back in 1941, for example, Buick offered dual carburetors (called "Compound Carburetion") that boosted horsepower from 150 to 165. Hot rodders of early vintage enjoyed adding a carb or two to their bored-out, stroked Ford V-8s. Maybe with bigger-than-normal barrels, too.

During the performance era, from 1955 to 1975, twin 4-barrels delivered the height of fuel flow. "Three deuces" (three 2-barrels) appeared on several Fifties models, but never achieved quite the same popularity. Performance enthusiasts grew almost as ecstatic about the names and models of certain carburetors, like Carter's AFB, as they did about the cars they were mounted in. Few motorists worried too much about economy. Fewer still cared about emissions.

Besides, it was possible to drive economically with a big carb or two. Extra carbs cut in only when needed. That's what happens with a 4-barrel, too. During ordinary operation, only the two primary (smaller) barrels have their throttle valves open. But as soon as the gas pedal goes down hard, the larger secondary plates open to let the big blast in.

Somewhere in the general spec table, you'll probably find a column listing the number of carb barrels, and perhaps the barrel size, as well as the model number. You won't find many specs for airflow capacity, but it's an important factor. This is a rating in cubic feet per minute (cfm) that shows how much air the carburetor is capable of handling each minute. For performance, the higher the better.

Increasing the number or size of carburetors, then, does a lot for performance. Conversely, a gas-guzzling motor should improve in economy by taking away a carburetor or installing a more miserly (smaller) one. That doesn't happen often, however.

Americans have seldom been too enthusiastic about cutting performance. In addition, care must be taken to be sure you're not starving the engine, risking internal harm.

For many years, most carburetors have had a rigid venturi, but variable venturis make for more efficient running. A few European engines have used them, and quite a few experiments have been done with them. So far they're still uncommon.

BOOSTING THE AIR SUPPLY

While manifold vacuum, booster venturis, and multiple carburetor barrels deliver enough air and fuel for most purposes, high-performance motors might demand more. Speeding up the incoming air would help produce that stronger mixture for the cylinders when they're most greedy. During hard acceleration, let's say. How to do it? Add a supercharger or turbocharger (Fig. 10-5).

We hear a lot about turbos today, but the principle is the same for both. The supercharger, or blower, is a rotary air pump that raises the pressure of air entering the engine to a level higher than atmospheric. This augments the normal vacuum action. The faster-moving air draws a hefty shot of fuel, and delivers a super-compressed charge of air/fuel mixture to each cylinder.

Blower force can jack up rated power by up to 40 percent. In fact, horsepower rises almost proportionately with any increase in actual manifold pressure. Therefore, every "inch" of reduction in vacuum down there makes a big difference in power output.

Mechanically driven, high-speed superchargers, generally run by a belt from the crankshaft pulley, were offered on several early American engines. The centrifugal unit used on the 1934-41 Graham, running at 5 1/2 times engine speed, was mounted between the carburetor and intake manifold. It gave a 35-horsepower boost along with a lean mixture for good fuel economy. Other blowers were above the carb, "pushing" high-pressured air down its barrels.

The 1954 Kaiser Manhattan came with a McCulloch blower that produced a modest 1 1/2 psi boost. By stomping on the gas, the solenoid-

Fig. 10-5. Turbocharger uses exhaust gases to spin turbine that boosts incoming air flow, adding power to modern high-performance motors.

activated unit reached 5 psi, helping to coax 140 hp out of its basically 118-hp, six-cylinder engine. A few 1957 Thunderbirds can still be found with the rare Paxton blower option on their 312 cid engines.

Studebaker was the postwar leader in supercharging. A variable-rate McCulloch was standard on the 1957-58 Golden Hawk and all Packards. Its 5-psi boost caused the 289-cid V-8 to churn out a mighty 275 hp (65 more than standard). In 1963-64, a Paxton blower was installed on the Avanti R-2 engines.

Mechanical drives were troublesome, though, and consumed quite a bit of engine power themselves. So beginning with performance Corvairs and Olds F-85 Jetfires, the turbocharger assumed the role of driving in a mightier mixture. Same idea but driven by exhaust gases. That's what we find on today's performance motors. Turbocharging can raise horsepower by 25 percent or even 40 percent. The dual-level unit on the 1985 Chrysler LeBaron GTS, for instance, delivers up to 9 psi boost.

Chrysler from 1958-61 used a different method to improve the mixture flow through the manifold of its 300-series engines. Ram Induction produced a "natural" supercharging effect. The system consisted of eight 30-inch tuned tubes carrying mixture from twin 4-barrels. Looking like a nest of chubby pythons, they smoothed out the usual pulsations that occur as valves open and close, delivering a more even flow into the cylinders.

AIR/FUEL RATIO

The composition of the mixture of air and gasoline changes considerably, depending on engine speed, load, and temperature. For economy and efficiency, the ratio between the two is crucial and for emission control it is mandatory.

The ideal ratio is called the *stoichiometric fuel mixture*. It's about 14.7:1. That's 14.7 parts air (by weight, not volume) to one part fuel. In theory, this ratio should produce complete burning of the fuel's carbon and hydrogen, leaving nothing but carbon dioxide and water to go out the exhaust.

It's not that simple, of course. No engine operates under optimum conditions at all times. Fuel burns with mixture ratios between about 7 1/2 and 20 to 1. Sometimes a richer mixture, with proportionately more fuel, is needed and sometimes you need a leaner ratio. During ordinary cruising, you might come close to the ideal figure, consuming perhaps 15 (even 17) pounds of air to each pound of fuel. Any ratio greater than about 15:1 is a lean mixture.

Step on the gas, though, and you've created a richer mixture (around 13:1). At idle, the ratio might be 12:1. For cold starting, the richest mixture is mandatory (only 8:1 or 9:1). The best ratio for economy is around 16:1; for power, it is about 12:1. Diesels have a much higher air/fuel ratio (in the neighborhood of 100:1).

A few modern tune-up tables give a specification for air/fuel ratio under test conditions. It's presumed that if the ratio is close to ideal during the test, it will stay good during harder conditions. Maybe but maybe not. An air/fuel ratio check should be part of emissions testing. Any fuel that goes unburned is going to wind up in the exhaust as nasty hydrocarbons.

None of us has a gauge mounted on the dash to show the present ratio or a method of changing it. Computerized control, however, can keep tabs on the mixture and compensate accordingly. If it senses too much oxygen in the exhaust, it signals the carb to richen the mixture.

The ratio is based on weight, but how much is that really? At the ideal 15:1 air/fuel ratio, it's 9000 gallons of air for every gallon of gas. Looked at another way, the engine draws in 9300 cubic feet of air to each cubic foot of gasoline. In smaller terms, that is half a teaspoon of gas for each cubic foot of air. How come? Because a cubic foot of air weighs only 1 1/4 ounces. The same amount of gasoline weighs a whopping 775 ounces (48 1/2 pounds).

GASOLINE OCTANE

Octane is not a measure of the fuel's actual quality or power capability. It shows nothing more than the level of resistance to detonation. That's the tendency of a fuel to explode spontaneously (prematurely) in the cylinder, before the spark plug fires, causing engine "knock." The lower a gasoline's octane figure the less resistant it is to knocking.

Two different octane ratings have been used in the past: a Research Octane Number (RON), which comes from low-speed tests with wide-open throttle, and a Motor Octane Number (MON) derived from full- and part-throttle tests, at low and high speed. RON tends to produce a figure about eight numbers higher. Nowadays, the figure seen on a gas pump is the Road Octane Number or Posted Octane. It's an average of the Research and Motor amounts.

Since 1923, octane has been boosted by adding certain knock-resistant hydrocarbons or additives—notably tetraethyl lead. That's why high-octane gas used to be called "Ethyl." More recently, the serious danger produced by lead in auto exhausts has caused leaded fuel to dwindle in availability. Cars since 1975 have been designed to operate on unleaded fuel, which has a lower octane rating.

Many older cars still need leaded fuel. Why? Because they had higher compression ratios. The higher the compression ratio the greater the need for higher octane fuel. Those super-performers of the Sixties, with compression ratios of 10:1 and up, are in big trouble today.

Back in the 1930s, octanes were low (often 80 or less). By the late 1950s, regular-grade gas rated around 91, premium rated 99, and super-premium fuels rated a bit over 100 in Research octane were available.

In the 1980s, leaded premium gas might reach a posted (average) octane of about 96 (leaded regular about 90). Unleaded regular might be only 87 octane, but that's enough for many engines. In higher altitudes, lower octane may suffice.

Diesel fuel has a similar figure for cetane. That figure indicates how easily the fuel will ignite. The higher the cetane number the lower its ignition temperature.

CARBURETOR ADJUSTMENTS

Your handy service manual probably has a separate set of tables for carburetor settings in addition to the basic idle-speed adjustments described in Chapter 8. Because carburetors come in so many styles, their spec tables look pretty frightening with numbers all over the place and with strange column headings. Table 10-2 shows a few. You might also find figures for any of the following:

- ☐ Fuel level.
- ☐ Float drop.
- ☐ Dashpot (throttle modulator) plunger-to-throttle-arm gap.
- ☐ Secondary throttle linkage.
- ☐ Vacuum break: throttle level or choke side.
- ☐ Fast idle cam clearance.
- ☐ Idle vent or internal vent opening (throttle closed).
- ☐ Control vacuum regulator.
- ☐ Various choke settings.

The thing to remember is that nearly all the figures are nothing more than clearances between one part and another, or the distance a part should travel (Fig. 10-6). Specs are usually in thousandths of an inch and are measured with a leaf-type feeler gauge, a drill bit of specified size, or some special scale or tool. Some are measured with the parts in normal position. Others are measured with one of them shifted a certain way. The only trick is determining (1) which parts a spec refers to, and (2) how each of them has to be maneuvered before any measurement or test can be valid.

Because carburetors vary so much, and some part names differ between makes/models, diagrams showing each clearance and measurement are invaluable. Nearly all manuals have them.

Most measurements you might have to make are external. You will have to adjust screws or other devices right on the carburetor body or, more often, you will have to connect linkages and mechanisms. If acceleration is sluggish, you might be interested in checking the accelerator pump adjustment. Idling problems suggest improper settings of a throttle-positioner solenoid that helps control emis-

Table 10-2. Typical Carburetor Specifications.

Carb Model	Float level (in.)	Secondary Air valve Opening (in.)	Secondary Air valve Spring (no. of turns)	Accelerator pump travel (in.)	Bowl vent clearance (in.)	Choke unloader (in.)	Choke vacuum kick (or break)
Carter TQ	29/32	1/2	1 1/4	33/64	---	0.310	0.100
Carter BBD	1/4	---	---	0.500	0.080	0.280	0.150
Roch. 2MC	5/16	---	---	Fixed	---	0.220	27°/.157"
Roch. 4-bbl	7/16	1[1]	1/2	Fixed	---	0.220	27°/.157"
Carter BBD	1/4	---	---	15/32	0.080	0.280	0.130
Holley	0.69	---	---	Hole #2	---	0.095[2]	0.150[3]

[1]Highest step. [2]Pulldown. [3]Dechoke.

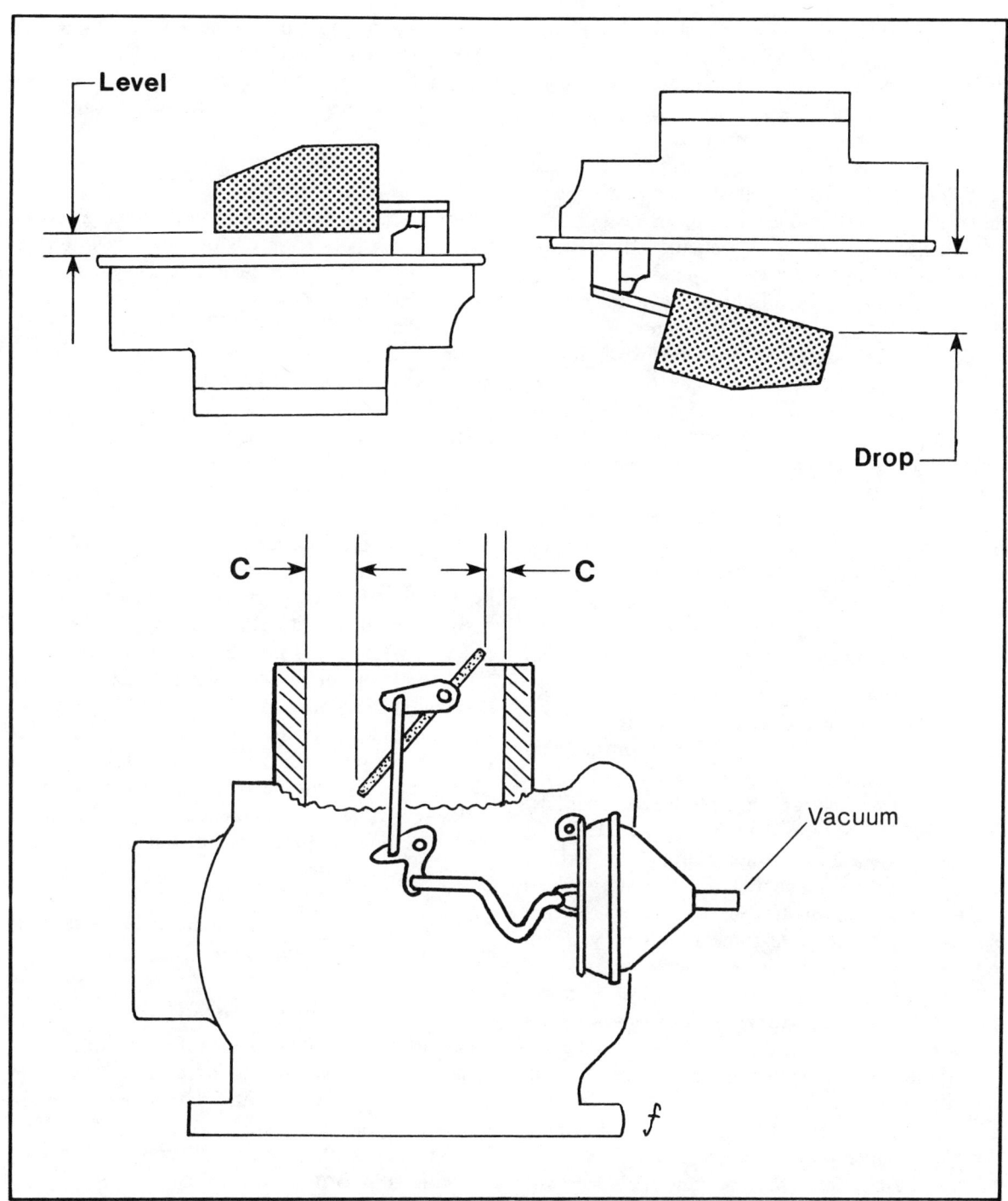

Fig. 10-6. Common carburetor adjustments. Float level is checked with the air horn inverted. Float drop is checked with the air horn in the normal position. Clearances between the choke valve and air horn (C) may have to be measured with vacuum applied (pull-off), throttle wide open (unloader), and/or linkage in specified position (vacuum break).

sions or a dashpot that prevents stalling. Vacuum and electrically activated devices may have to be adjusted with the engine running, shut off, or both ways. Mechanical ones don't ordinarily care whether the ignition is on or not.

Many adjustments, then, aren't made to the carb itself, but to some accessory—often related to emission control—that mounts on or near it. Examples are exhaust gas recirculation devices, or heated-air systems that warm up air entering the carburetor. Some recent linkages have an angular measurement (made with a protractor).

When a carburetor needs serious work, it also has a large number of internal specifications. Not all are found in the carburetor spec tables. Look for exploded diagrams that name and show each internal part so that you can tell where each adjustment and measurement has to be made.

A few voltage settings also may be given, such as *throttle position sensor voltage,* for electronically controlled carburetors. Note whether the device has to be energized.

CHOKE SETTINGS

Manual chokes on early model engines were easy. Either the choke plate shut all the way with the knob pulled out, and opened fully when the knob was pushed in after warmup, or it didn't.

Automatic choke adjustments are more serious. Somewhere in the tune-up or carb spec table should be a bit of data on the choke. Often, it's nothing more than a recommendation that two marks—one on the choke housing, another on the rotating cover—be placed in alignment. When you experience hard starting or erratic warm-up, you might be advised to richen or lean out the mixture. Shift the setting by one or more notches away from the zero (index) position.

Modern chokes have a crucial pull-off (or pull-down) setting to make sure the choke isn't creating an overly rich mixture during warmup. The initial clearance figure between valve and air horn may have to be checked with vacuum applied to the choke's diaphragm. A clearance spec might be called *vacuum break* or *vacuum kick.* Even if the choke works properly during cranking, and is all the way open when the engine is hot, it might be improperly positioned in between. Other choke specs include *intermediate choke rod position* and *unloader,* the latter with throttle wide open.

FUEL INJECTION

After remaining remarkably unchanged in basic operation for half a century or more, carburetors finally face a new electronic future. They may even face extinction.

Mechanical fuel injection systems have been around since the 1930s on European autos. Injection was an option on 1957 Chevrolet and Pontiac V-8s; it was even available on the Rambler Rebel. It helped give that '57 Chevrolet a horsepower rating of one hp per cubic inch: 283 for 283.

Injectors spray fuel into the intake manifold or cylinder through a nozzle. There, the fuel joins with air to create the combustible mixture, just before it's needed. Gasoline-powered engines usually have indirect injection, with nozzles positioned in the intake manifold, near the intake valve for each cylinder. Fuel pressure may be as low as 10 psi.

Diesels prefer direct injection (right into the combustion chamber). For obvious reasons, fuel must be under very high pressure (1000-3000 psi or more) to cope with the pressure built up as the piston rises into the 20:1 or tighter compression ratio. Injection may be constant, or intermittent, with a computer-controlled pulse time.

Not many specs are given for fuel-injected motors because they have few moving parts. Any settings may be no more complicated than placing a pair of marks in alignment.

EMISSIONS CONTROL

Years ago, few people seemed to care how many hydrocarbons and noxious oxides escaped from auto exhausts. Not until 1955 did the first federally sponsored pollution research program begin. The Environmental Protection Agency (EPA) started operations in 1970.

Positive Crankcase Ventilation (PCV) systems were the first form of emission control device. Before they became mandatory on cars sold in

California in 1961 (and nationally two years later), crankcase fumes entered directly into the atmosphere. The PCV valve directed them, instead, back into the carburetor to be burned with the newly arriving fuel.

Control of unburned hydrocarbons (HC) and carbon monoxide (CO) started in California, in 1966, and became nationwide in 1968. National concern for nitrogen oxides (NOx) came in 1973.

Air pumps, exhaust gas recirculation (EGR) systems, and countless other mechanical devices (and internal engine alterations) appeared in the 1960s and 1970s. Some were effective at reducing emissions and others were less so. Catalytic converters became standard on almost all cars in 1975. Three-way converters reduce all three pollutants.

The Clean Air Act of 1970 set standards for new cars through 1976. It's been amended several times since to stiffen the requirements. By 1985, California and Federal standards were to be identical.

Few specs apply to the devices themselves (only to the actual emission outputs form the vehicle). Certain spec tables give maximum levels for the major pollutants. Even if they don't, there's a rigorous standard for each model year. HC and NOx were first measured in parts per million (doesn't take much to cause trouble), carbon monoxide level as a percentage. Later standards are given in grams per mile.

Few do-it-yourselfers possess instruments for measuring pollutants. Even the large professional instruments usually test only HC and CO. Nitrogen oxide testers are more often found in laboratories.

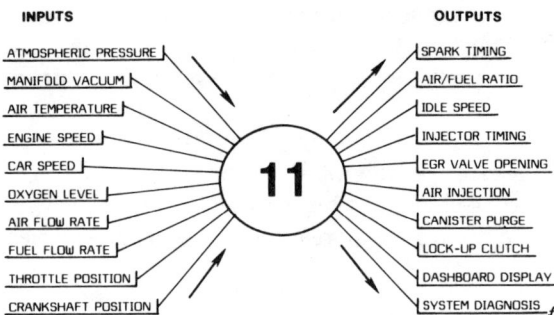

Computer Control and Testing

IT'S HARDLY NEWS TO SAY THAT THE COMPUter has taken over much of modern life. That includes the region under the hood of today's automobiles. Each year the number of computer-controlled functions rises. Few experts dare to predict what might appear there a few years down the line.

The microprocessor (the works of a microcomputer) plays an equally large role in auto servicing. The meters in a do-it-yourselfer's garage aren't computer-controlled. Not quite yet. Professional shops need the latest equipment if they want to service the high-efficiency engines of the Eighties and beyond.

COMPUTERS UNDER THE HOOD

We don't see them. Most of us are barely aware they exist. But electronic controls are all around, working steadily, every time we turn on the ignition key. In one form or another, they have been around since the mid-1970s.

Electronic ignition came first. While the first systems didn't involve computers in the real sense, they paved the way for eventual introduction of silicon-chip devices.

As discussed in Chapter 7, electronic ignition took the place of the old breaker points, producing a more potent, precisely controlled spark. Keep in mind that its ultimate purpose was essentially the same as the mechanical system it replaced. Electronics did the job more efficiently, but it was the same job.

The situation is similar for many of the electronic controls that have appeared since (beginning with Chrysler's Lean Burn engines of 1976). They perform functions that either were accomplished by mechanical or electrical means or could have been (at least in theory).

An electronic control that alters spark advance in response to changing engine vacuum, for example, is doing the same job as the primitive vacuum advance unit with its diaphragm action. Carburetor mixtures weren't ever controlled by external means, but they conceivably could have been. Automatic-transmission shift points have been controlled by throttle position, among other factors, for decades. Engine vacuum could have done more in affecting crucial engine functions.

In principle, then, electronics isn't really doing so much that's new or different. One very large exception is that microcomputer-controlled engines can respond to several, even dozens, of constantly changing factors at once. The main point of the computer is that it can:

☐ Take in information from a number of sources;

☐ Weigh all that data in accordance with rules programmed into its electronic circuits; then

☐ Cause physical actions to take place as a result of its near-instantaneous computations.

In no way could ordinary mechanical or electrical controls do so much or do it fast enough to make a difference.

Each engine of the Eighties has a different set of computer controls. A typical version, even early in the decade, could monitor over a dozen different conditions in and around the engine, and use those measurements to control almost as many different systems. Besides that, today's engines contain more and more diagnostic capabilities. Their dashboard indicators reveal a host of malfunctions as they develop.

Like all computer systems, automotive controllers have both input and output connections. Pertinent information is fed into the computer from the engine (input). The microprocessor circuitry in a control module analyzes and manipulates that data, and then sends out control signals (output) that cause the engine's operation to change in certain ways (Fig. 11-1).

Inputs arrive from sensors placed on and around the engine. These sensors monitor a variety of operating conditions, or physical quantities, including:

☐ Pressure in intake manifold (manifold absolute pressure).

☐ Atmospheric (outside) air pressure.

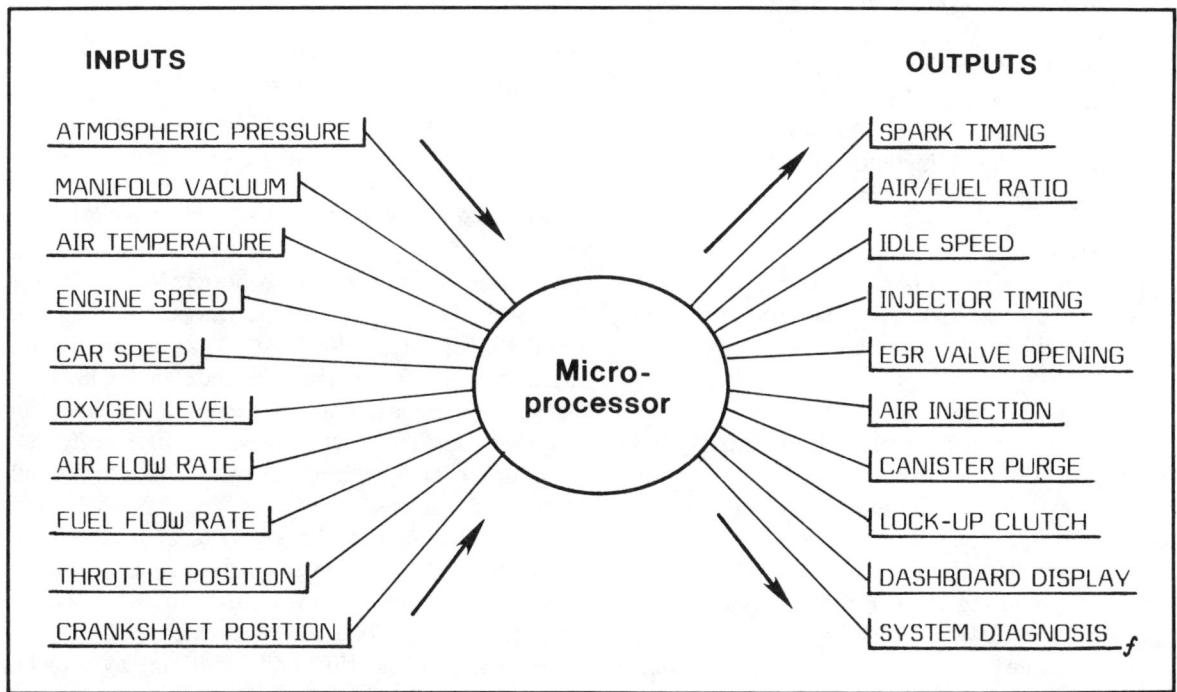

Fig. 11-1. The microprocessor in a computer-controlled engine receives inputs from various sensors, and sends output signals to components that need adjustment.

- ☐ Coolant temperature.
- ☐ Intake (outside) air temperature.
- ☐ Intake air humidity.
- ☐ Throttle valve position.
- ☐ Crankshaft position (angular).
- ☐ Ignition pulses.
- ☐ Engine speed (rpm).
- ☐ Vehicle speed (mph).
- ☐ Air intake rate.
- ☐ Fuel flow rate and temperature.
- ☐ Exhaust gas recirculation (EGR) valve position.
- ☐ Oxygen content of exhaust gas.
- ☐ Tendency of engine to "knock."

Dozens (even hundreds) of times every second, each sensor transmits an electrical signal to the computer. At every instant, then, the computer "knows" how fast the car is moving, the engine rpm, load (manifold vacuum), important temperatures and pressures, and so forth. Working at startling speed, it weighs each factor, calculating which (if any) operating conditions need to be altered to keep efficiency, economy and emissions at their most desirable levels.

New control signals then go out to the operating components. Solenoid-controlled valves and switches, vacuum-activated diaphragms, and other devices act almost instantaneously to produce needed changes in such functions as:

- ☐ Ignition spark timing.
- ☐ Fuel mixture (air/fuel ratio), altered by movable metering rods or variable venturi size.
- ☐ Fuel-injection timing or pulse width.
- ☐ Idle speed.
- ☐ Cruise control speed.
- ☐ Exhaust gas recirculation (EGR) valve opening.
- ☐ Early fuel evaporation valve opening.
- ☐ Air injection to catalytic converter, exhaust ports, or air cleaner.
- ☐ Eliminating two or more cylinders from operation (V-8/6/4).
- ☐ Torque converter clutch (in automatic transmission).

At the same time, recent systems provide dashboard displays of engine condition—plus a series of diagnostic checks!

Control takes place in two ways: proportionally or in terms of limits. In the first, the microcomputer responds to a constantly changing voltage supplied by the sensor that is directly proportional to physical changes as they occur. Other inputs send a control signal only when the factor being monitored goes above or below some preset limit.

Does the engine actually run any better than its noncomputer predecessors? Well, that's not so easy to answer. It definitely produces a lot fewer pollutants, and burns up a lot less fuel. Without electronic controls, most experts agree that emission standards of the mid-1980s and beyond would be impossible to meet. So they're here to stay.

In the near future, control systems should become even more efficient as engineers develop techniques for monitoring important engine conditions that have, in the past, been too difficult or too expensive. These include:

- ☐ Engine torque output.
- ☐ Cylinder pressure at various piston/valve positions.
- ☐ Air flow into individual cylinders.
- ☐ Valve opening/closing rate.
- ☐ Just about any parameter that can be measured and converted to an electrical signal.

Microcomputers are finding increased use beyond the engine compartment, too. In the mid-1980s, Mercedes and Continental, among others, first offered computerized antilock braking. Microprocessors in each wheel compensate for icy and wet surfaces (even operating differently during turns). They cut the risk of brake lockup or failure enormously.

Applications in the steering and suspension systems have been slower in arriving, but may work wonders for future comfort and stability. Sensors will monitor road surfaces and traction, producing the best possible ride and handling, by altering spring and shock absorber action.

ON-BOARD COMPUTER DIAGNOSTICS

Spark advance and air/fuel ratio might be changing dozens of times every second, but you'd never know it. Modern under-hood computers offer one additional feature that will indeed be noticed: the ability to analyze and diagnose malfunctions. As far back as 1974, Toyota had a dashboard sensor panel that showed whether a light bulb was burned out, fluid levels were too low, brake linings worn dangerously thin, and other safety considerations.

Diagnostic systems have appeared on most autos since then, but some of them still deal with rather simple messages. Knowing that a headlight is out is important, but the electronic warning isn't exactly a technological thrill. A few automakers have gone further, and significant diagnostics are sure to become the rule.

Lincoln's Mark VII, for example, gave a warning to check the air suspension. BMW's oil-change warning indicator not only checks the oil level and odometer mileage, but keeps track of the *type* of driving its owner does. Drive it hard and it tells you to change oil a lot sooner.

Of particular interest are the 3C diagnostic systems introduced by GM in 1981, and their descendants and relatives on other makes. In addition to switching on a warning light when something goes wrong, these systems allow the mechanic to derive a more detailed diagnosis. Sometimes, this is done by using jumper wires to produce readings of various quantities stored in the computer. Hand-held testers (Fig. 11-2) are available that tap into the on-board diagnostic system and display necessary readings on a digital scale.

Such diagnostic systems haven't replaced the working mechanic, and aren't likely to, but they do help him or her in troubleshooting the electronically controlled functions. Service manuals give details on these diagnostic checks, spelling out the terminals that have to be "jumped" or hooked to a test instrument, and telling how to interpret readings.

FUTURE DASHBOARDS

For many years, science fiction writers have pic-

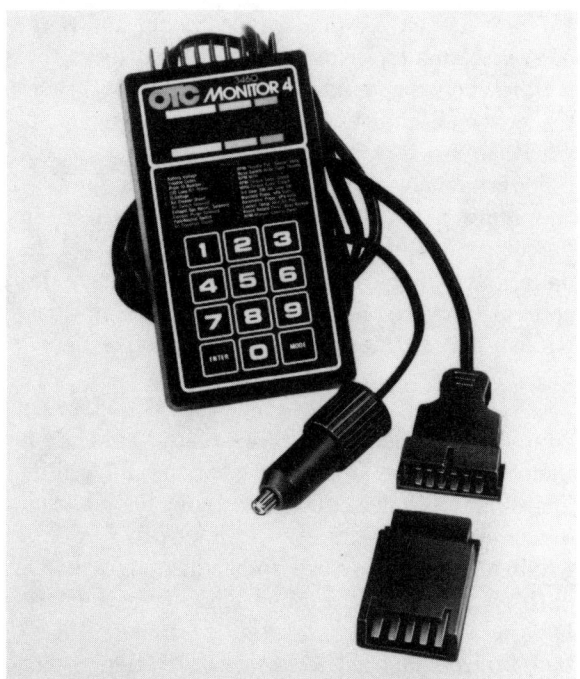

Fig. 11-2. A hand-held diagnostic analyzer connects to under-dash computer output terminals, giving useful information on malfunctions. (OTC Tools & Equipment.)

tured the car of the future as one that is, for all practical purposes, driven automatically. Sensors in the highway keep the car in the middle of the lane. Radar and sonar maintain a safe distance from cars ahead. All the futuristic driver would have to do is sit back and relax. And when something broke down, the car might even fix itself or, at least, tell the mechanic what the trouble is.

Quite a few of the fantastic possibilities are within the reach of technology. Some could be put into use at any time if cost were less of a factor. So far, however, many of the present and projected uses of the computer as a motoring aid are a bit on the frivolous side. They do not really take advantage of technology's potential.

Without a doubt, cars will have touch-screen dashboards that eliminate the ordinary knobs and controls. Handy perhaps but they would not be doing anything truly new. Talking computers, using speech synthesis techniques, appeared early in the

1980s. They have a limited vocabulary and range of subject matter. Not everyone likes them, but they're likely to remain anyway. Maybe they'll start saying something that cannot be shown just as easily on a dial or screen.

Or maybe not. Detroit has often been guilty of supplying a surplus of glitter and fluff in its vehicles. The future is likely to hold even weirder dashboard surprises. Perhaps a latter-day equivalent of the tail fins of the Fifties. How about windshield wipers that turn on when a sensor detects water?

Not a bad idea. Convertible tops that closed at a raindrop's notice were around many years before the computer age. Computerized door and ignition locks that recognize only the car's owner should cut down on stolen autos. Tamper-proof digital odometers might dissuade some villainous used-car entrepreneurs. On the other hand, thieves always have been resourceful. Steering-wheel ignition locks were supposed to put a halt to theft, too.

We already have dashboards that show both instant and average fuel economy, and tell how far we can go on the remaining gas. Dashes also show data on elapsed trip time, estimated time of arrival, and other travel trivia. Before long, cars may offer full navigational aid by perhaps using the NAVSTAR satellite system. Touch the screen and detailed maps show exactly where you are, how to get to your destination, conditions en route, and goodness knows what else (Fig. 11-3).

Automatic comfort settings that adjust the mirrors, seat, steering wheel and pedals as you climb in can be pleasant. Dashboards that listen to the motorist's oral commands to switch on accessories are interesting gadgets. Navigational aids could change the whole concept of long-distance motoring.

Still, some of the most valuable future electronic aids will be the diagnostic systems. Sensors that reveal useful details about malfunctions, tell which systems need servicing, and even predict which parts are close to failure are a good deal more valuable than automatically raising radio antennas or even automatically adjusted suspension systems

Fig. 11-3. The futuristic dashboard of the experimental Mazda MX-02 offers navigational data and many more facts that aren't yet available on other automobile dashes.

that change from soft to firm ride. A light that tells not only that the engine is overheating, but exactly where the hot spot is located—perhaps why it's happening—can be a lifesaver.

Other intriguing possibilities lie with the transmission. The automatic transmission hasn't changed nearly as much during the past half century as many motorists believe. On the whole, it's a primitive device, basically hydraulic/pneumatic/mechanical, even when electronic sensors control the shift points. A true computerized transmission, eliminating the whole concept of shifting, could simplify operation and servicing and boost performance/economy at the same time. Electronics might finally bring about the true infinite-ratio transmission that's been sought for many decades.

COMPUTERS IN THE SHOP

One thing for sure is that more electronics under the hood means fewer specs needed by the repair person. An exception is someone expert enough to deal with failures in the electronic modules.

During recent decades, auto repair has become largely a matter of removing and replacing parts rather than repairing and adjusting, as in the old days. With electronics, it cannot help but be more of the same—and worse. Try taking an electronic clock or transistor radio into a shop, and you get a hint of what's bound to happen with auto service. Everything is less expensive and easier to replace rather than test out and repair. Besides, there's often no real way to adjust or service an internal component. Either the whole unit works or it doesn't.

What does the mechanic need to do to combat this insidious menace, the computer? Learn to use it of course. For mechanics working in professional shops or having access to professional equipment (perhaps in an auto repair class), that's easy enough to do. An enormous number of new test instruments not only test computer-equipped autos, but incorporate computers in their own internal circuits. The professional shop that tries to get by with yesterday's instruments cannot long survive in this age of electronics.

Much of today's test equipment has evolved from the oscilloscope. Every apprentice mechanic for the past couple of decades has had to learn to connect, observe, and interpret the patterns on a 'scope screen.

What came to be known as an engine analyzer consisted of a 'scope along with several other instruments: an accurate vacuum gauge, cylinder leakage tester, dwell-tachometer, ammeter, voltmeter, and eventually a set of emission test meters. At first glance, today's "intelligent" engine analyzers don't look that much different. Some of them aren't. They've simply substituted digital readouts and CRT displays for the old-fashioned meters, but perform essentially the same tests as before.

Other computerized analyzers for shop use are very much different (Fig. 11-4). More than a collection of separate testers, they operate automatically, using decision-tree logic to trace the path of a fault until its source is located and analyzed. These programmed analyzers can recognize a reading or condition that's out of spec, pinpoint the component at fault, and determine what adjustment or repair will provide the remedy. Many go a step further by producing a printout of the diagnosis. Not only is that beneficial to the car's owner, it helps the mechanic follow the logic and determine what has been done.

In some cases, today's mechanic can perform a thorough diagnosis and tune-up in a matter of minutes. He may do little more than enter an identifier number for the vehicle to be tested and hook up the few cables. The machine's memory holds specifications for all current car models, and compares test results with each one to make its determinations. Nothing is overlooked. Every test is the same: quick, accurate, automatic, complete.

Furthermore, the automated tune-up or diagnostic test sequence can be performed nearly as easily by a brand-new apprentice as by an old hand. The on-screen, step-by-step explanations actually help the new mechanic learn the procedure as he goes along.

Therein lies the rub. If it's all so easy, what do you need an experienced mechanic for? Sure, the computerized test centers often have provision for

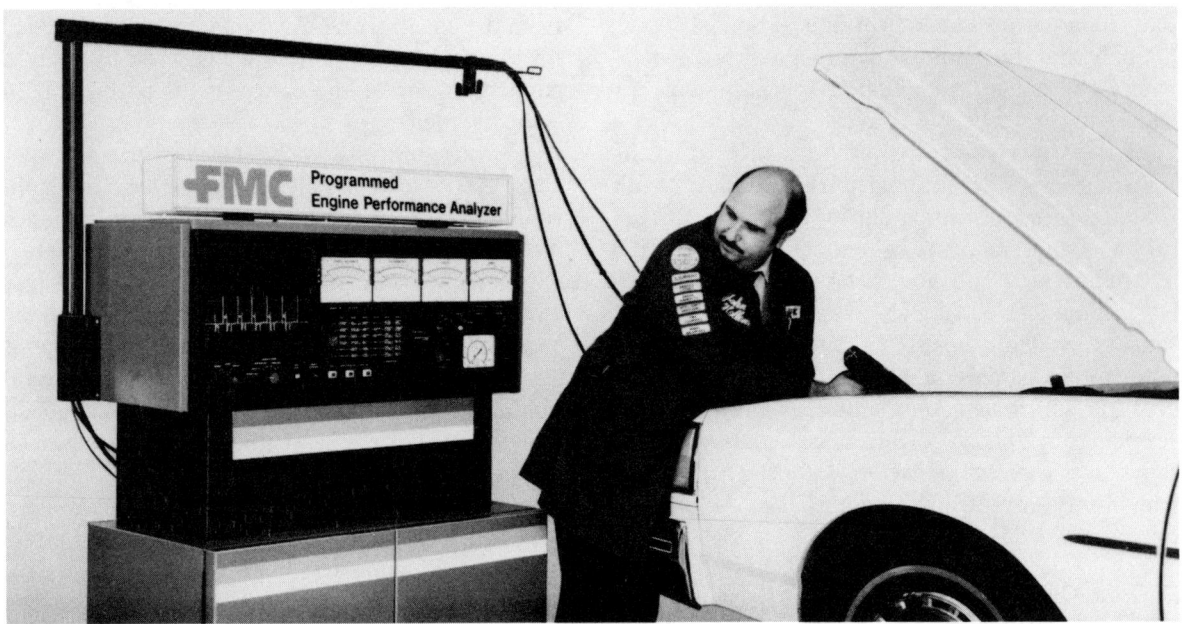

Fig. 11-4. Modern computerized engine analyzers not only perform familiar tests, but follow a programmed test procedure (FMC Corp.)

manual (nonautomatic) operation, which produces a more detailed analysis. There might be an old-fashioned oscilloscope showing the ignition waveform, but the important functions are shown on an easy-to-read bar graph or CRT display that makes some sense even to a total automotive neophyte. No meters to peer at and no knobs to be adjusted with a steady hand and eye.

Obviously, the mechanic comes in most handy after the testing is completed. There may come a time, as one GM vice president has predicted, when cars no longer will need tune-ups or overhauls. For a while, however, real human mechanics have to continue getting their hands dirty. Computerized robots have not yet learned to remove and replace spark plugs, clean carburetors, and measure component clearances.

What does all this mean for the amateur mechanic? For the most part, he or she will have to struggle along with noncomputerized gear. Most of it is simply too costly for the do-it-yourselfer's garage. More and more low-cost test instruments incorporate digital displays and microcomputer circuitry. Before too long, all of us may be tracking down engine data with a CRT display or even a home printout.

Engine analyzers are just one form of instrument that uses the computer. Exhaust emission analyzers have changed in a similar way. Many deliver a neat printout showing levels of HC, CO, and other such nastiness. Computerized gear also is used for modern wheel alignment and balancing.

Here is the big question. Does computerized testing do a better job than traditional equipment? Well, yes and no. That wheel balancer, for one, does nothing new or different. It just works faster and more accurately with less effort and thought. Some of the engine analyzers do tricks that wouldn't be possible without the microprocessor. They can dissect and analyze automotive functions that weren't even measurable by anyone other than engineers a few years back. They can combine measurements and specs internally in ways far beyond those available to flesh-and-blood diagnosticians. As time goes by, they'll do even more, and all of us who work on cars will have to learn more to keep pace.

Inside the Engine

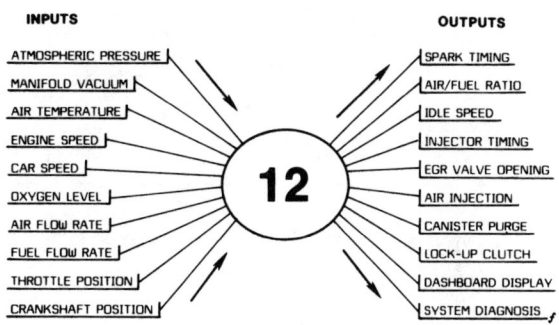

WE'VE ALREADY DISCUSSED A COUPLE OF clearances (small measured distances between moving parts) such as valve lash on engines with adjustable lifters. Pull off a cylinder head, though, and what do you find down below? A mass of small clearances, gaps, and close fits between components.

Spec tables provide data on the valve train (Table 12-1), and on the bottom end (big end): the pistons and bearings. Valve specs are needed whenever the valves have to be ground to ensure a tight seal between a valve and its seat. Bottom-end data becomes important for a serious overhaul. We'll get to those a bit later.

Clearances are needed for two reasons:

☐ To allow space for oil to flow between moving parts and cut friction, which leads to excessive heat and wear.

☐ To allow for thermal expansion, which could cause a moving part to "seize" against a surrounding component if it grows too large.

One interesting fact is that the specs for internal clearances haven't changed much in the past half a century. Glance at a tune-up table from 1948 and it looks a lot different from the modern version. Valve or bearing specs don't. Oh, the allowable clearances might be slightly tighter nowadays, but when you pull off all the electronic and emission devices from a contemporary motor, it doesn't look (or measure) a whole lot different from one of its ancestors.

Nearly all clearances are measured in thousandths of an inch or, in some cases, ten-thousandths. Figures given in a table may take the form of an acceptable range or a specific clearance to shoot for. We also need to measure various diameters (both inside and outside).

A few situations allow for no clearance at all. Parts are designed to come together with a *press-fit* (no "play" between them) or even a *shrink-fit*, whereby one part has to be heated and expanded in order to fit over or around another. Those parts are really tight when they cool off.

Table 12-1. Typical Valve Specifications.

Valve Angles (degrees)		Valve Spring Installed Height (in.)	Valve Spring Test Pressure (lbs @ in.)	Stem-to-guide clearance (inches)		Stem diameter (inches)	
Seat	Face			Intake	Exhaust	Intake	Exhaust
46	45	1-23/32	200 @ 1.25	.0010-.0027	.0010-.0027	.3410-.3417	.3410-.3420
30I	29I[4]	1.786	1951 @ .411	.001-.003	.001-.003	.3715-.3725	.3715-.3725
45	45[1]	1-11/16	144 @ 1-5/16	.001-.003	.002-.004	.372-.373	.371-.372
45	45	1-1/4	42 @ 1.263	.0008-.0027	.0017-.0036	.3098-.3105	.3089-.3096
46[2]	45	1.88	312 @ 1.38	.001-.0025	.0012-.0027	.3715-.3722	.3713-.3722
45	45[3]	---	100 @ 1-55/64	.002	.003	.37	.37
	30I/45E	---	99 @ 1-53/64	.0017	.0035	.3715	.3697
45	45	---	26 @ 2	.0015-.0035	.0025-.0045	.2790	.2790

[1]Exhaust 43. [2]Aluminum heads 45. [3]Exhaust 47. [4]Exhaust 44-1/2 seat, 45 face.

VALVE TRAINS: RUNNING AT HALF SPEED

In all 4-cycle engines, the camshaft that controls valve rise and fall rotates at half the crankshaft speed. The crankshaft has to make two full revolutions while a given valve goes through its complete cycle of opening and closing. How is that done? It's simple. The gear or sprocket mounted at the front of the camshaft has twice as many teeth as the crankshaft gear. That's true whether it's an overhead-valve, overhead-cam or L-head design or driven by gear, chain, or belt.

Even so the valves see a lot of action (and heat). At highway speed, a valve may be rising and falling against the pressure of its spring 2000 times per mile.

Before doing any valve work, you have to know which valves are the intakes and which are the exhausts. A diagram or figure should be in the manual. An inline 4-cylinder engine, for example, might have an arrangement like: E-I-I-E-E-I-I-E. That means an exhaust valve is at the very front, followed by a pair of intake valves, a pair of exhausts, and so on.

When the cylinder head is mounted, it's not always easy to tell the valves apart. With the head off, you can easily see which valves feed into the intake manifold and which feed into the exhaust. Besides, the exhaust valves are nearly always smaller in diameter. The intakes need to draw in as much air/fuel mixture as possible; so they're big.

High-performance engines need the biggest ones that fit. A spec table might or might not give the actual valve head diameters.

Valve Face and Seat Angles

Most modern valves are ground to a 45-degree angle (Fig. 12-1). Some intakes are designed with a 30-degree angle, relative to the cylinder head surface, in an attempt to induce the air/fuel mixture to flow most smoothly into the cylinder.

When grinding valves, you use a machine—or the traditional hand "lapping" method—to smooth the surface of both the valve face, and the valve seat in the cylinder head. In an old L-head motor, the valve seat is in the engine block.

Not all valve faces are ground to the same angle as their seats. The modern trend has been to grind at an *interference angle*. Valve seats might be ground to 45 degrees, but the mating valve faces to 44 degrees. That degree or two difference causes the valve to make contact only along a thin line around its circumference.

At first glance, this would seem to produce inferior sealing, but the interference angle helps a valve settle into position after grinding. Before long, the mating faces take on the same angle anyway, making solid contact.

Valve Spring Height and Pressure

Do-it-yourselfers don't always pay much attention

to the valve springs. Their strength plays a vital role in valve seating, though. All the more so for higher-performance engines, that use stiff springs to make sure the valves close rapidly and tightly.

Installed height is the distance between the machined surface of the cylinder head at the base of the spring, and the underside of the retainer that mounts above the spring. Actually, it's often measured with the spring removed. Specs run between 1 and 2 inches (either a fraction or decimal).

Spring height measurement is especially important after valve grinding. If it is too large, shims can be installed below the spring. A reading of .060 in. over spec, though, suggests something very wrong with the valve's length. Maybe it's stretched. In any case, the spring isn't the culprit.

Test pressure evaluates the spring itself. It doesn't hurt to check whenever valve springs are removed. Specs are given in pounds of force needed to compress the spring to a stated height (in inches). A special mechanical test device is needed. Its gauge shows how much downward force is being exerted, and a ruler scale displays the spring height as a result of that force.

Typical force to be applied is about 200 pounds, but specifications range from well under a hundred to more than 300. Even with such high levels of force, most springs should maintain a test height between 1 1/4 and 1 3/4 inches. Heavy-duty engines that use dual springs have separate specs for the inner and outer.

If the recommended force pushes it substantially lower than the spec suggests, the spring is weak. You're not likely to find one too strong.

Valve Stem-To-Guide Clearance

Clearance between the valve stem and its guide allows the desired amount of oil film to develop and flow between the two surfaces. But we don't want the clearance so large that oil passes into the combustion chamber. It's most crucial with intake valves because engine vacuum tends to suck up any loose oil and mist from the guide whenever the valve is open. Any oil that enters the combustion

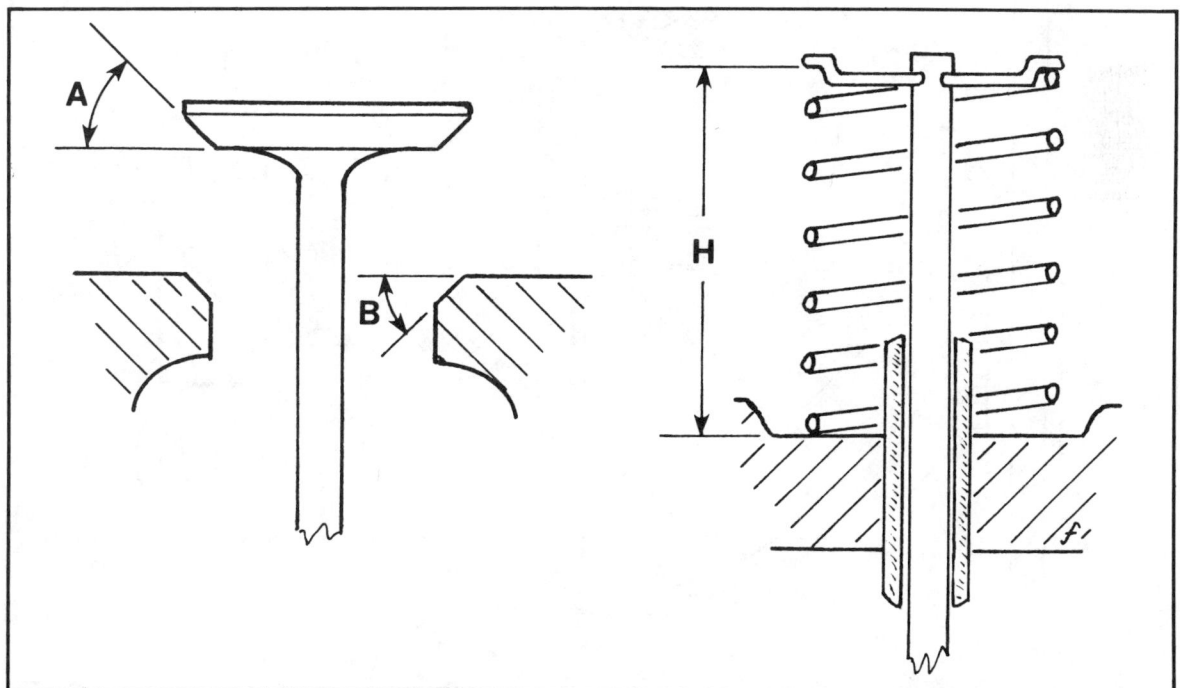

Fig. 12-1. Valve face (A) and seat (B) angles could be identical, but are often ground to a degree or two difference. Installed spring height (H) is measured to underside of valve retainer.

area is going to find its way out the exhaust. Loose exhaust valve guides pass oil too, but not to the same degree.

Excessive stem-to-guide clearance (Fig. 12-2) also adversely affects valve seating. The valve tends to approach at an angle, hesitating slightly as it has to slide sideways into position. Tight valve stems want to bind in their guides. Thus the valve might not close rapidly enough and seal firmly.

Recommended stem-to-guide clearances run between .001 and .004 in. Some permissible sizes are tight as .0005. A range is usually given, either in thousandths of an inch or (often) ten-thousandths.

In a few cases, a larger clearance figure is given for the hot (head) end of the valve stem. Specs may be identical for intake and exhaust valves, but the exhaust is often slightly looser because it's hotter and less prone to passing oil.

Spec tables also give figures for *valve stem diameter* in thousandths or ten-thousandths of an inch. It's usually a range, but allowing no more than .001 variation. Intake and exhaust valves might differ, but nearly all stems measure between .340 and .380 (around 3/8 inch). You need to measure stems when clearance is too large, but you don't know whether the valve or its guide is the culprit.

Valve Lifters

We've already discussed adjusting valve lash on engines with solid lifters (tappets). This affects valve timing slightly. When too small, the valve may begin to open a little too soon and close a trifle late.

The main purpose of tappet clearance, though, is to make sure the valve returns all the way down onto its seat as it closes. Without that clearance, the valve might hesitate and tend to remain slightly open, allowing a little of the combustion mixture

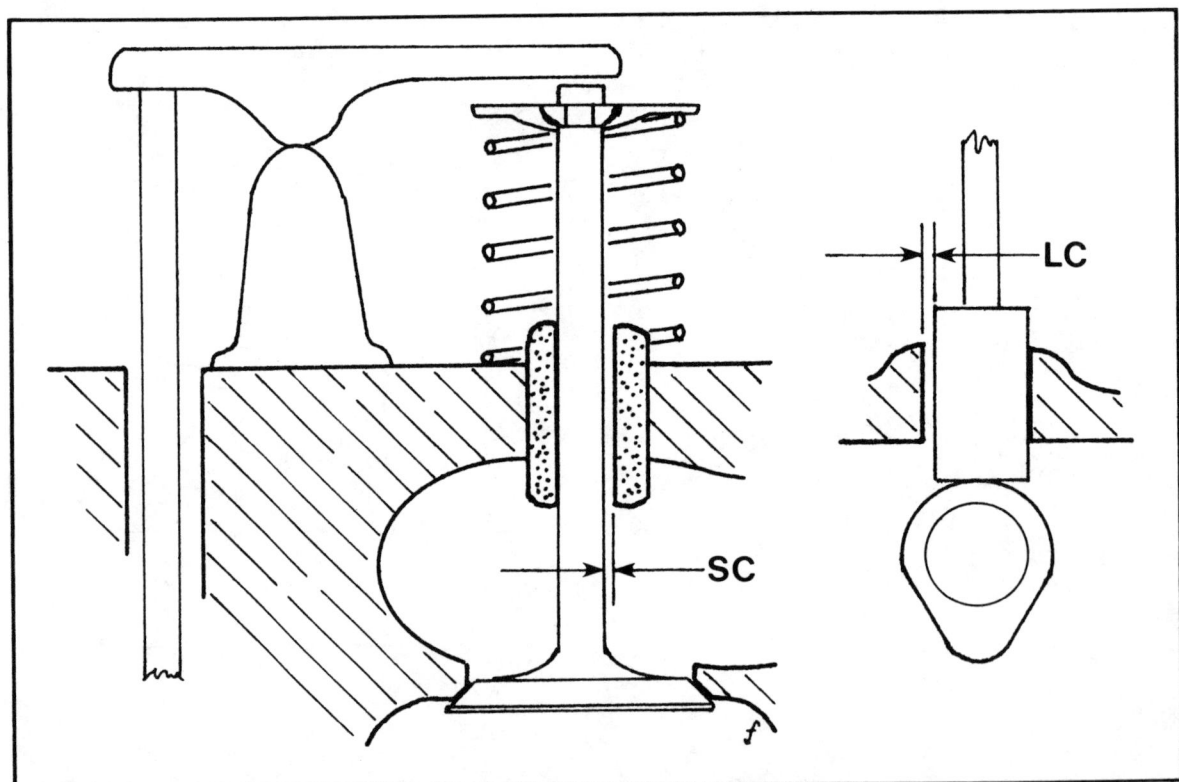

Fig. 12-2. Valve stem-to-guide clearance (SC) is crucial for keeping oil out of the combustion chamber, especially at intake valves. Lifter-to-guide clearance (LC) on OHV engines isn't quite so serious.

or exhaust gas to escape. Before long, the rim of the valve head and its seat would become pitted and, eventually, "burn" so it would leak with every cycle.

Why do we need more than a couple of thousandths of an inch? Partly this is to be absolutely certain the valve seats itself firmly, but also because of—what else—thermal expansion. The valve must seat tightly when cold, during warm-up, and also when the valve stem has expanded to its maximum length. Clearance varies a lot (usually shrinking as the engine heats up). At one point, valve lash might be a few thousandths larger than when it was cold, but later in the warm-up period, it could be .010 inch tighter. Thermal expansion is also the reason some specifications call for clearances to be adjusted with the engine cold and others hot.

Insufficient tappet clearance plays an added role in terms of heat transfer. A valve cools somewhat while it is seated. If clearance is too small and the valve stays open longer than it's supposed to, that cooling is impaired. This is especially important with exhaust valves that run at extremely high temperatures.

Excessive valve lash isn't much better. The valve might cool properly and seat tightly, but operation will be noisy and harsh. The valve head hits its seat with a jarring blow, and the (OHV) rocker arm bangs hard against the valve stem. The strain could lead to damaged parts.

As a rule, valve lash tends to grow larger due to the incessant pounding action upon the valve stem end. Stretching of the stem could reduce the clearance.

Another kind of clearance is important to the valve lifters, whether solid (adjustable) or hydraulic. Clearance between a lifter and its guide is especially important on old L-head engines. Excessive wear causes the lifter to rock slightly as it is driven upward by the camshaft lobe, contacting the valve stem at an angle. This can add to noise and increase wear of the valve guide above. Fortunately, wear tends to be gradual and slow because lifters receive plenty of oil. Clearance isn't quite so crucial for OHV engines. Any cocking as the lifter rises is compensated for by the pushrod, before the action is transmitted to the rocker arm and valve.

Typical lifter-to-guide clearances run around .001 to .002 inch. Specifications aren't given in every valve table.

Camshaft Lobes and Valve Lift

Valve lift is the distance a valve rises above its seat in response to the size and shape of the rotating camshaft lobe. A spec appears in some valve data tables. More likely, it's buried in the text of a manual. Most are between 0.25 and 0.5 inch; often it is higher for exhaust valves.

A high-lift cam, with lobes designed to raise the valve lifters more than the customary amount, is used in many high-performance engines. Each valve opens wider to allow more air/fuel mixture into the cylinder. That is exactly what you want for top performance. Lobe shape (*ramp angles*) affects not only "breathing" efficiency, but valve opening and closing time (as described in Chapter 8). Lift measurement is most useful for determining camshaft lobe wear.

On an old L-head motor, lift is easy to measure with the cylinder head removed. Just adjust clearance to zero (temporarily). Then crank the engine by hand and measure how far each valve rises. Use a dial indicator for greatest accuracy. With an OHV engine, you might try to measure pushrod movement. Accurate measurement, though, may be possible only by using a micrometer right on the camshaft's lobes. It is easy with an OHC engine, but it requires that the camshaft be pulled out of the others.

Measured at the lobe, lift is the difference between the distance from the nose (pointed end) to the center of rotation, and the distance from the heel to the center (Fig. 12-3). That gives the total travel of the lifter—and, with allowance for lash, the L-head or OHC valve itself—from fully closed to all-the-way open position.

OHV motors are a little different. Each valve doesn't rise the same distance as the lifter that causes it to operate. The rocker arms act as levers so actual valve lift is somewhat more than the lift produced by the cam lobe. The lobe may cause a

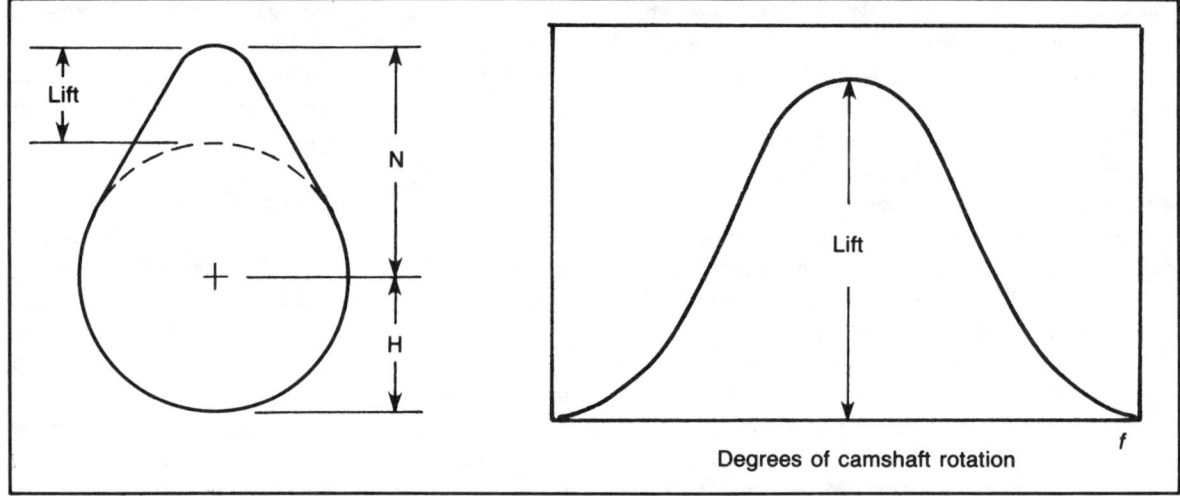

Fig. 12-3. Valve lift is the difference between the distances from the center of the camshaft lobe to its nose (N) and to its heel (H). Lobe shape controls not only lift, but time and rate of valve opening/closing (as shown on graph).

pushrod to rise by, say, .300 inch. If the rocker arm has a 1 1/2:1 ratio, the valve itself should move 1 1/2 times as far, or .450 inch.

Somewhere in a manual, you'll also find additional specs related to the camshaft: journal diameter, clearance, and end play. The diameter of each journal may not need to be measured, but clearance is far more important than many mechanics realize. Some of us take great pains in measuring valve and crankshaft bearing clearances and give not a moment's thought to the camshaft. Oil flows too readily, losing plenty of pressure, when clearance has grown much above the original .001 or .002 inch.

Perhaps it's understandable that the camshaft is neglected because specs aren't generally found alongside those for the other bottom-end clearances. You have to search for them. Camshaft bearings wear at about half the rate of those at the crankshaft.

End play is the degree of front-to-back looseness in the camshaft. It's similar to the same measure we'll make at the crankshaft shortly.

PISTONS AND RINGS

Many do-it-yourselfers rarely, or never, get below the valves and cylinder head in the course of their garage work. Neither do a lot of working mechanics. Instead, they send engines out to a machinist for most serious overhaul duties.

Still, all of us should know about piston fit (Table 12-2) and crankshaft data. Even if the pistons, rings, and bearings are seldom seen, some awareness of their clearances—and what happens when they grow too large—just might prove useful when diagnosing engine problems.

Pistons rub against their cylinder walls at a fantastic rate. At highway speeds, a piston may move up-and-down 50 times each second, traveling 3 to 4 inches with every stroke. That's a lot of motion: perhaps 2000 feet per minute of (theoretical) metal-to-metal contact. So it's hardly surprising that cylinder walls gradually wear down, growing larger in diameter.

Clearance that allows oil to flow, and heat to be absorbed through the cylinder wall and into the coolant passages, is mandatory. Nevertheless, we don't want too much. Looseness would not only cause noisy operation, but might let oil seep into the combustion chamber, and combustion gases work their way downward to the crankcase.

Piston Clearances

Logically enough the outside diameter (O.D.) of a

piston is slightly smaller than the inside diameter (I.D.) of the cylinder in which it slides. That clearance between piston circumference and cylinder wall allows a thin oil film to form.

Because the piston gets hotter and expands faster than the bore surrounding it, clearance also provides space for the piston to grow. Aluminum pistons expand more rapidly than those made of cast iron. Some have a slot in the skirt to allow for expansion without risking excessive growth in diameter.

The piston top (head) enlarges much more than the bottom portion (skirt), which runs a lot cooler. For that reason, the head and the *lands* (segments between each ring groove) are supposed to be about .030 in. smaller in diameter than the piston skirt. Ring groove wear sometimes causes the lands to grow considerably, approaching cylinder diameter when hot. Needless to say that could bring major problems.

Precise figures for cylinder bore and piston skirt diameter aren't always given in piston spec tables. Furthermore, the pistons in many modern engines are not round at all, as in the old days, but *cam-ground* (oval-shaped). The skirt diameter across the thrust face, perpendicular to the piston pin, is .002 to .009 in. larger (Fig. 12-4). This allows the piston to fit itself to the cylinder wall as the engine warms up, becoming virtually round when fully heated.

Clearance between the two diameters is the important factor. A figure for piston clearance (skirt clearance, piston-to-bore clearance) is given in thousandths of an inch, often ten-thousandths. It's normally a range.

Typical clearances run from about .001 to .004 inch. In some engines, a clearance as small as .0002 or as wide as .007 might be permissible. It should be measured at the top of the piston skirt, and sometimes with the piston setting in a particular position in its cylinder. Clearance of a cam-ground piston is based upon the larger of the two diameters.

Piston Pin Fit

A piston pin (wrist pin) holds the piston onto the upper end of the connecting rod. Pins come in three basic styles:

☐ Locked to the piston, rotating freely in the upper end of the rod.

☐ Snugly press-fit in the rod, but free-floating in the piston bushing.

☐ Locked to neither part.

There may be a specified clearance between its bushing in the piston or its bushing in the connecting rod.

Pin clearances are on the tight side, with just enough slack to allow free rotation in a bushing. Typical specifications run from essentially zero up

Table 12-2. Typical Piston and Ring Specifications.

Piston Clearance (inches)	Ring End Gap (inches)			Ring Side Clearance (inches)		
	Compression			Compression		
	Top	Bottom	Oil	Top	Bottom	Oil
.0007-.0017	.010	.010	.015	- - -	- - -	- - -
.0008-.0018	.010	.010	.015	.002-.004	.002-.004	.005-.011
.0025-.0033	.010-.022	.010-.028	.015-.055	.0030	.0030	.0000
.0018-.0026	.010	.010	.015	.002-.004	.002-.004	Snug
.001-.002	.010	.010	.015	.003-.005	.003-.005	.000-.0035
.0003-.0013	.013 min.	.013 min.	.015 min.	.0015-.0030	.0015-.0030	.000-.005
.0005-.0015	.010-.020	.010-.020	.015-.055	.0012-.0027	.0012-.0032	.000-.005
.002 shim[1]	.015	.015	.015	.001-.0025	.001-.0025	.001-.0025
.002 shim[2]	.005	.005	.005	.0015-.003	.0015-.003	.002-.0035

[1]5-12 pound pull. [2]Light pull on shim.

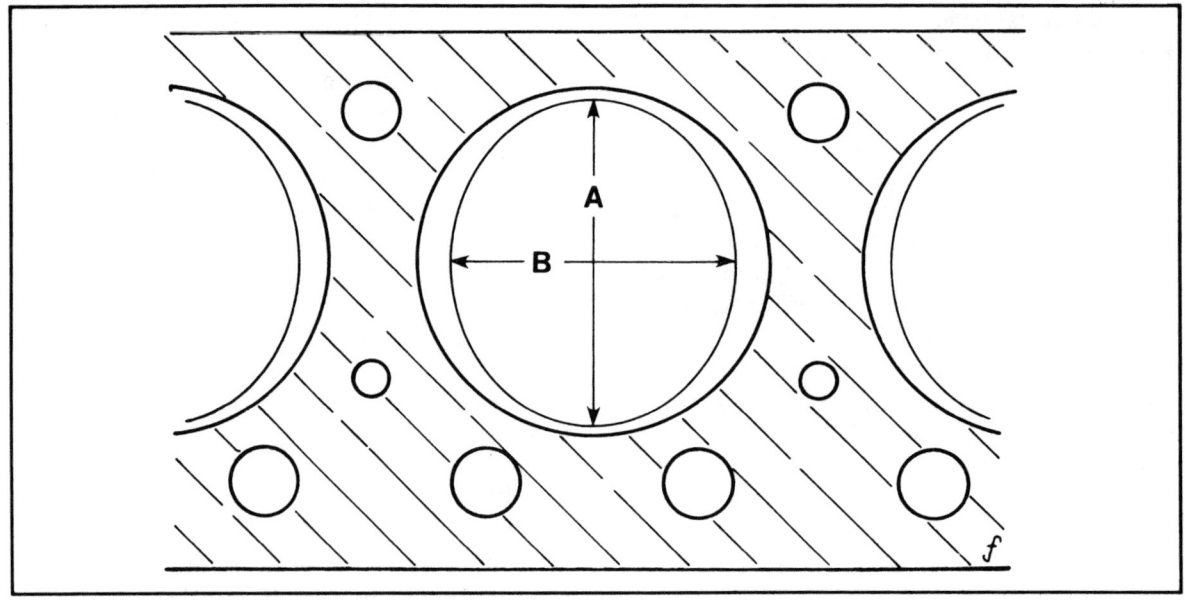

Fig. 12-4. The cam-ground piston is oval-shaped (elliptical), and is several thousandths of an inch larger in diameter when measured perpendicular to engine length (A) than parallel (B).

to .0004 (seldom more than .001 inch). The tight ones are often referred to as a press or interference fit; sometimes they are called a slip fit. As a practical matter, any "play" that can be felt means clearance is excessive.

Piston pin diameter is often specified in a table column. Measurement is most needed to evaluate pin wear. Check the difference between its center and ends.

Piston Ring Gaps and Clearances

No piston alone would provide a very effective seal between the combustion chamber and crankcase. The enormous pressure built up on each compression stroke could easily squeeze through. Sealing is the job of the piston rings.

Most pistons have two compression rings that press snugly against the cylinder wall to form a seal that prevents "blowby." That's the passage of combustion gases down into the crankcase where they don't belong. They also have one, sometimes two, oil-control rings. These scrape oil off the cylinder wall on each downward piston stroke, sending it back to the oil pan through slots inside the piston ring groove.

Rings also help dissipate piston heat because the piston itself should not contact the cylinder wall. Diesels can have five or more rings.

We're all familiar with worn rings as a prime cause of oil smoking out the exhaust and low engine compression. Actually, wear in the cylinder wall, rather than at the outer contacting edges of the rings, is the principal culprit. Rings have a remarkable capacity to flex and accommodate themselves to changes in cylinder surface and size. To a point anyway.

Two important ring measurements appear in spec tables: *side clearance* and *end gap* (Fig. 12-5). A small side clearance is needed so the ring is free to move up and down slightly, sealing tightly against both the cylinder wall and the top or bottom of the piston groove. In fact, some rings are designed to twist a bit in their grooves.

Tight rings cannot mate with the cylinder wall and piston groove as best they might. Excessive side clearance has an even less pleasant effect; it allows the ring to move too far up-and-down. In effect, it "pumps" a bit of residual oil up into the combustion area with each piston stroke. Not what we want at all.

A typical new piston has about .0015 or .002 in. clearance above each ring (sometimes a bit less for oil rings). Clearance of essentially zero, or as much as .010 in., might be acceptable on a given engine. Some spec tables give exact clearance figures; they can differ for each ring. A range is the usual style.

Not all manuals include side clearance data. A figure for groove depth is even harder to find, but no less important. The ring must be free to move inward and outward to follow the contour of the cylinder wall. This is especially important when that wall no longer is perfectly round and vertical.

End gap specifications are always in the tables. That's the distance between the ends of a cold ring as it sets down inside the empty cylinder, near the top. End gap allows the ring to expand with increasing engine temperature. If it's too small, the ends could meet and butt against each other, causing the ring to break. A piston could even bind or "seize" in its cylinder. Bad news.

Naturally, end gap grows wider as the rings and cylinders wear down. Even when new, a tiny gap remains when the engine is at operating temperature. A small amount of "blowby" gas does pass through the gap, but not enough to be concerned about until the gap has grown substantially.

Far better to have a trifle too much expansion space than too little.

The gap must be checked whenever new rings are installed or old ones are evaluated. Spec tables nearly always have separate columns for the compression and oil rings; sometimes a third column is provided for the lower compression ring. It's usually a single figure, sometimes a minimum, in thousandths of an inch.

Compression rings usually require an end gap between .010 and .020 inch. Typically, it is about .003 to .004 inch of gap per inch of cylinder diameter. Oil rings may need as much as .035.

CRANKSHAFT DATA

Moving down to the bottom end, we come to the crankshaft journals and their bearings. Three or more main bearings hold the crankshaft in place and permit it to rotate freely. Connecting rod bearings allow vertical movement of each rod and attached piston, as the crankshaft turns.

Some engines have a main bearing between every cylinder, and at the front and rear. Most have fewer mains than cylinders. The exact number might be given in the general engine spec table.

A connecting rod's larger (bottom) end contains a bearing that rotates around the rod journal

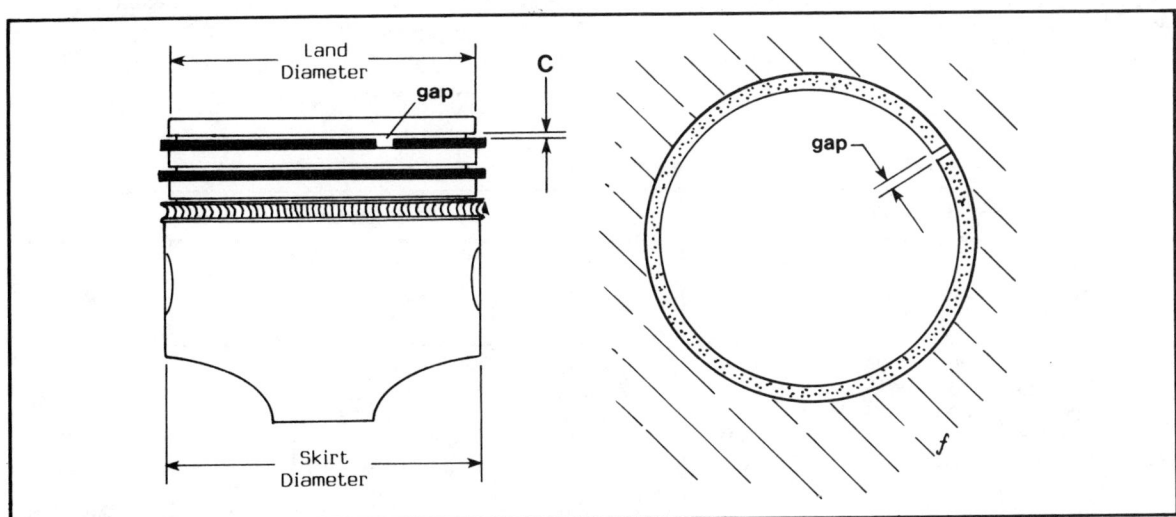

Fig. 12-5. Piston ring's end gap closes as the engine warms up and the ring expands. Side clearance (C) is measured with ring mounted in piston; gap when ring alone is inserted into engine cylinder (right). Piston land diameter is smaller than skirt diameter.

(crankpin). Each time the crankshaft makes a complete revolution, every rod journal has turned in a complete circle. Its piston travels from top to bottom and back to the top again.

For several decades, engines have used precision (insert) bearings. That wasn't always the case. Years ago, babbitted bearings were the rule. Soft metal was poured in the rod's saddle bore, and then ground carefully to proper size and roundness. Insert bearings may simply be replaced when worn. It's much easier.

Bearing Clearances

Table 12-3 includes specifications for outside diameter (shaft diameter) of both the main and rod journals. During overhaul, they might actually have to be measured.

Both are given in thousandths or ten-thousandths, and either as a single figure or a narrow range—typically within .001 inch. Main bearing journals are larger in diameter, but not always by much. The majority of both main and rod journals fall in the 2-to-3-inch category.

Oil clearance, as usual, is the more important measurement (Fig. 12-6). When new, journals are perfectly round, and have a very smooth, hard surface. The bearing inserts surrounding them are coated with a much softer material. Naturally, that wears down a lot faster. Clearance between journal and bearing allows the familiar thin oil film to flow.

If clearance in a main bearing is too small, the crankshaft won't turn freely, and that journal receives insufficient lubrication. Overheating might then occur and harm both the bearing surface and the journal. In short, big troubles.

Excessive main bearing clearance produces a distinctive knocking sound (actually a dull "thud" or "thump"). It's the kind of noise that, once heard (or more accurately, felt), is never forgotten. Unless that looseness is dealt with quickly, the engine's days are numbered.

A loose main bearing can also cause the engine's oil pressure to drop to an unsafe level at idling speed. Oil flows too freely, too easily, through the enlarged space. Its pressure diminishes and impedes flow to other parts of the motor.

The effect of tight rod-bearing clearance is similar to that of tight mains: restricted rotation and lubrication, followed by overheating. Moreover, other parts—including cylinder walls, pistons and tappets—that depend on oil thrown off the sides of the bearing as the crankshaft spins may "starve" for oil, and be in danger of running dry.

A loose rod bearing is no better. The surplus space allows the bearing surface to bang against the journal as the rod ends its stroke, producing a metallic "rap." It also causes surplus oil throw-off, sending too much onto the cylinder walls and other areas. In modern full-pressure systems, a loose rod bearing can also cause a drop in oil pressure.

A knocking or overheated bearing, not receiv-

Table 12-3. Typical Crankshaft and Connecting Rod Specifications.

Rod Bearings			Main Bearings			
Shaft (journal) dia. (in.)	Oil clearance (in.)	Side clearance (end play)	Shaft (journal) dia. (in.)	Oil clearance (in.)	Thrust on no.	Shaft end play (in.)
2.2487-2.2495	.0005-.0026	- - -	2.4995	.0003-.0018	2	.006-.015
2.1865-2.1875	.0010-.0025	- - -	2.7495-2.7505	.0010-.0025	3	.0035-.0095
2.000	.0005-.0026	- - -	2.9998	.0005-.0022	5	.0035-.0085
1.9670-1.9675	.0009-.0026	.0079-.0118	2.1631-2.1636	.0008-.0026	Ctr	.002-.007
2.0934-2.0955	.001-.003	.002-.007	2.4986-2.5001	.001-.003	3	.0015-.0065
2.199-2.200	.0009-.0025	.015-.021	2.7490	.0013-.0025[1]	5	.006-.010
2.298	.0014	.006	2.4984	.0015	3	.006
1.5990	.0015-.0035	.006-.014	1.9990	.000-.003	- - -	.002-.006

[1]No. 5: .0024-.0070 inch.

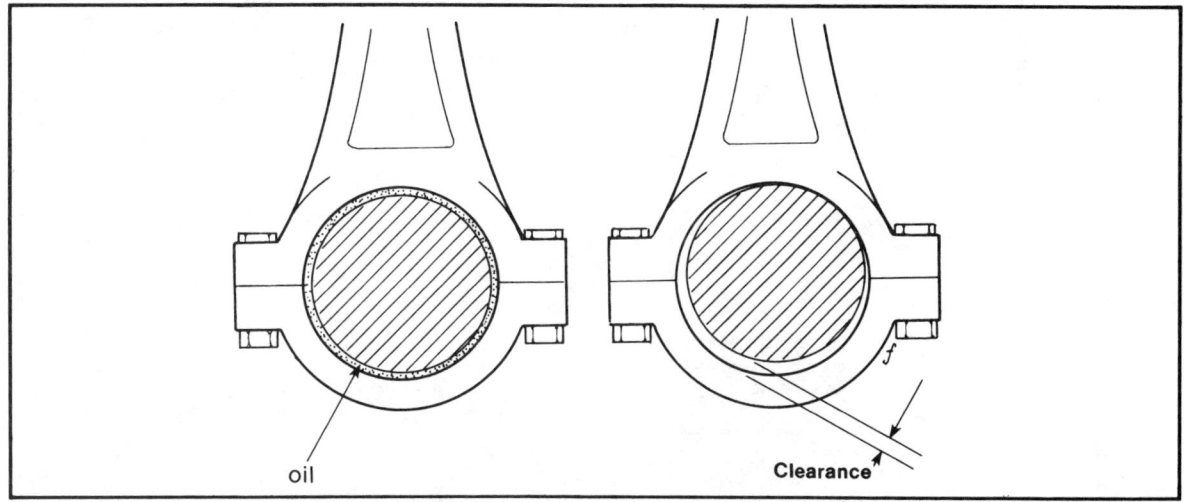

Fig. 12-6. Crankshaft journals are supposed to ride in a surrounding cushion of oil, never touching the surrounding bearing (lift). Clearance, however, is measured with the inner part pressed against the outer; it's the difference between the two diameters.

ing its share of lubricant, could "spin," attaching itself to the journal and rotating inside the saddle bore of the connecting rod. Bad news indeed. Most drastic of all is the "thrown" rod. A thrown rod has bonded itself to the journal in response to gross overheating, broken along its length, and slammed right into the side of the cylinder or crankcase. It means the end of one engine.

Clearance specs usually take the form of an acceptable range, given in thousandths or "tenths." Typical clearances for both rod and main bearings run between .001 and .003 inch. As little as .0001 (that's mighty little) is permissible in a handful of engines. There could be a different clearance spec for certain main bearings or all may be identical.

Side and End Play

Two other clearance specs are found in some crankshaft data tables. Frequently ignored, connecting rod side clearance and crankshaft end play should be checked during any overhaul.

Rod side clearance (end play) is the distance between each connecting rod and its adjoining crankshaft throw. It must be loose enough so the rod doesn't bind, but not so loose that it flops around on the journal. Specs vary quite a bit from around .004 to as much as .018 inch.

One column in the spec tables gives information on main bearing thrust. It might say "Thrust on Bearing No. 4" or "End Play Held by No. 3." That tells you which main bearing has to be measured to determine the crankshaft's end play—its forward/backward (lengthwise or axial) movement. Looseness, in short.

This is done by measuring the tiny space between the special thrust surface on the crankshaft and the smoothly ground flange of the stated bearing cap (when the crankshaft is pried all the way forward or back). End play specs run between .002 and .009 in. (generally given as a range).

ELSEWHERE IN THE ENGINE

A few other important clearances exist in the engine's innards. Examples are between the oil pump impeller and its housing, where the camshaft contacts the oil pump's drive gear, between the teeth on a timing gear, at a distributor's drive gear, and clearances within the water pump.

Not all have a spec in the usual tables, but figures can nearly always be found in a factory shop manual. Once you've developed a "feel" for the major clearances, and an awareness of their significance, the others come easy.

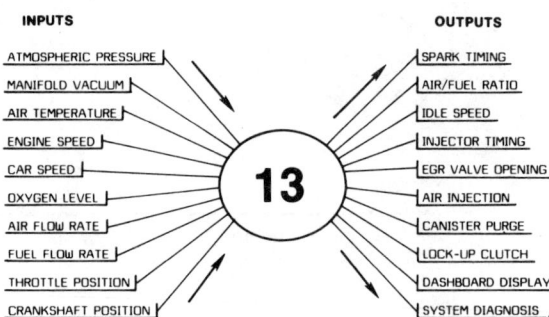

How Worn Is Worn?

NO MATTER HOW CAREFULLY AN ENGINE IS maintained, a certain amount of wear occurs in all moving parts. Sometimes more than car owners realize.

It's not unheard of for a crankshaft bearing, for example, to wear down by five thousandths after just 30,000 miles of driving. With poor maintenance, the rate of wear goes up even more dramatically. When the odometer approaches six figures without an engine overhaul, some of those internal clearances, that once were tiny, probably have become gaping holes. Friction can be minimized by proper design and cut down even more with proper care, but never eliminated.

Ordinary running, then, causes the surfaces of mating parts to erode—little by little. The bulk of that wear takes place during warm-up periods. That's why we hear all those warnings not to race engines when they're cold. Test motors run continuously at normal operating temperature (never allowed to cool) show amazingly little wear even after lengthy sessions.

As a rule, one part is designed to wear down faster than its mate. Bearing inserts, for example, are much softer than the crankshaft journals they encircle. Therefore most of the wear takes place in the bearing surface. It's a lot less expensive and easier to replace a bearing than to renew a crankshaft.

As clearance grows, oil flow becomes less efficient. The excessive slack adds to engine noise. Piston rings that used to return oil to the pan with every downstroke begin to let a little bit, then more and more, creep up into the combustion chamber. Valves with worn guides no longer seat themselves quickly. And on and on.

Furthermore, even the ordinary wear that erodes parts gradually tends to produce changes in the metallic surfaces (scuffing, scoring, etc.). The degenerative process speeds up rapidly when lubrication is inadequate or the oil becomes loaded with contaminants and dirt. Even if clearances remain tolerable, the parts are steadily suffering damage.

Does a measurement over the recommended size or clearance always mean major work is needed? Is the engine on its last legs? Well, not necessarily. The amount of wear we might tolerate depends on a lot of factors, including the car's age and value, the type of driving it gets, the particular part, and so forth. A clunker bought for a couple of hundred dollars, driven only a few miles each week, might survive a bit more laxity of specs than a late-model vehicle that sees heavy, constant use.

In short, there are no absolutes when it comes to evaluating wear. Still, we can suggest a few guidelines. So let's take a quick run through the engine's internal parts, trying to separate normal from abnormal wear, and see how bad wear has to be before we have to take action.

VALVE TRAIN WEAR

Valve Faces. The angles of the faces and seats aren't going to change as the miles pile up, but the mating surfaces are almost sure to grow pitted and rough. That's the sign that a valve grind is in order.

After appropriate grinding, the valve head's margin (Fig. 13-1) should be at least 1/32 in.; better yet, 1/16. If not, the valve has to go because a sharp rim is prone to overheating.

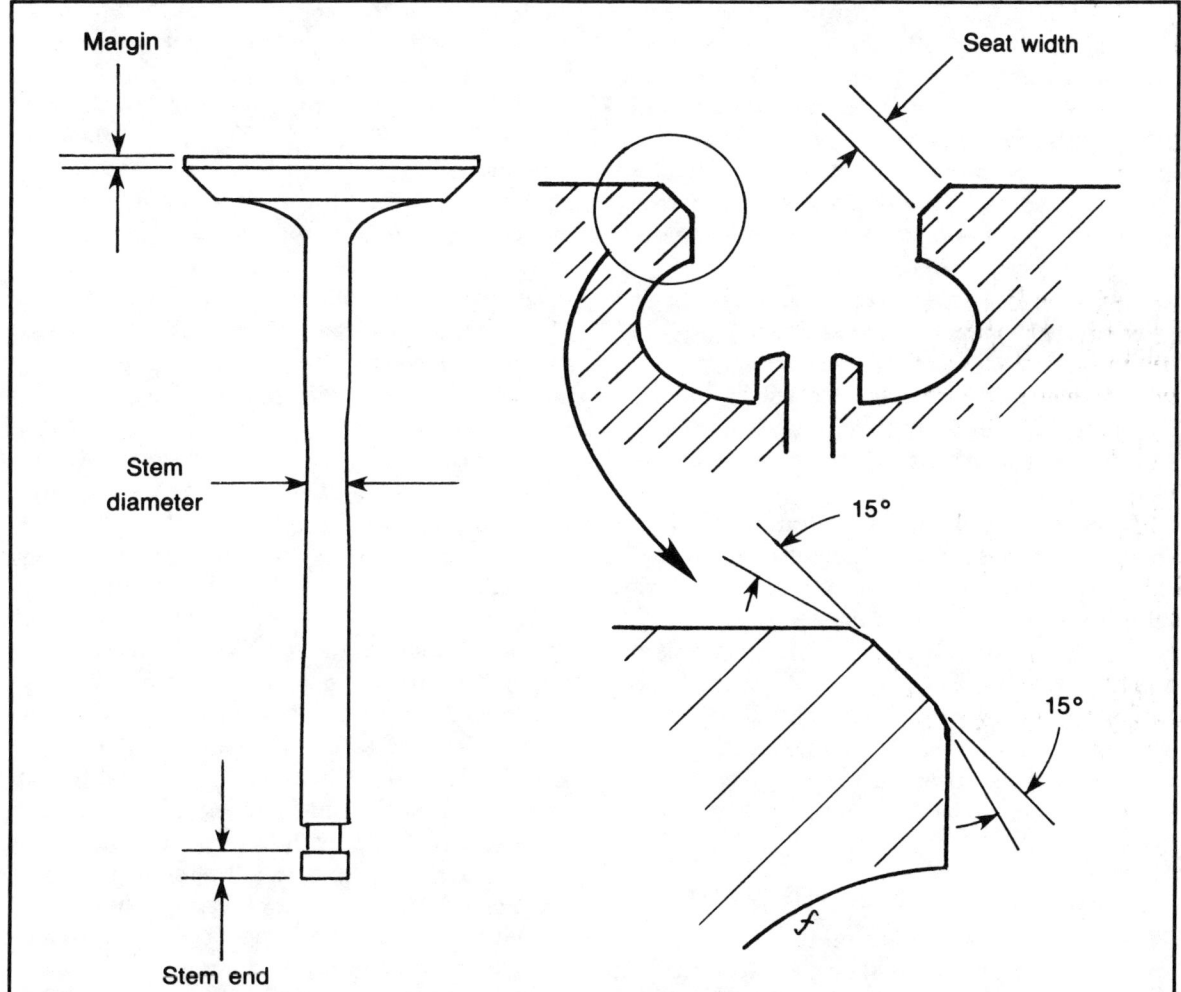

Fig. 13-1. Valves need to be checked for minimum margin size, wear along stem diameter, and worn stem ends. An overly large seat width may be corrected by "step grinding" (right).

Valve Seat Width. About 3/32 inch is the maximum safe limit for exhaust valves (maybe 1/16 for intakes). Greater than that the seat should be step-ground.

Valve Seat Concentricity (Runout). This means the valve sets right in the center of its seat. Runout, as measured with a dial indicator, shouldn't be over .002 or .003 inch. Excessive runout is probably caused by a misaligned valve guide.

Valve Stem-to-Guide Clearance. More than .002 or .003 in. above the maximum book figure means either a new guide or new valve is needed. Maybe both. When working on an old, tired engine, don't be surprised to find a few guides showing looseness of .006 or more. Sometimes a lot more. Guides generally wear much more rapidly than valve stems, and often unevenly (larger at the ends than in the center).

Measure the actual valve stem diameters, too. This is not only to determine if they're undersize, but to check for uneven wear—smaller in the middle than at the ends. About .001 in. undersize is OK and .002 might be acceptable, but marked variance, or a noticeable "step," tells you a new valve is wise.

Worn guides in many older engines are replaceable. Modern guides are usually integral (part of the head). They have to be reamed oversize to accept an oversize valve stem or knurled to an undersize diameter.

Valve Lifter-to-Guide Clearance. When looseness reaches five thousandths or so, it's time for a new (oversize) lifter. Its guide, integral with the engine block, must be reamed to fit.

Valve Spring Pressure. A few manuals demand tolerance within 1 pound of the book figure. For big V-8s it is perhaps 5 pounds. Realistically, 10 percent pressure loss is hardly a disaster. The spring should also measure within 1/16 inch of vertical as it stands alone; spring squareness is important.

PISTON AND CYLINDER WEAR

When an engine block came off the assembly line, its cylinder bores were almost perfectly round (equal in diameter from top to bottom). They don't stay that way forever. Cylinders do not wear evenly, either. Because of the side thrust of the piston as it goes downward on the power stroke, wear is greatest crosswise (perpendicular to the length of the engine). Thus, the cylinder becomes oval-shaped or out-of round.

But that's not all. The pressure of the piston rings against the cylinder wall causes greater wear in the top portion of the cylinder. Therefore, the wall becomes tapered with virtually no wear at the very top, above the rings. There is plenty of wear below the ridge that forms on the wall at the upper limit of ring travel and there is tapering down the lower portion of the cylinder, where very little wear occurs (Fig. 13-2). The primary measure of cylinder wear, then, is its taper: the difference between the largest and smallest diameters.

The piston skirt may also wear down or even collapse (shrinking considerably). Whenever clearance has grown too large, the piston rocks back and forth as it travels downward (especially on its power stroke), producing a noise known as "piston slap." Moreover, the thicker oil film no longer can be controlled effectively by the oil ring.

Insufficient clearance is hardly likely to develop as a result of wear, but can occur when pistons are not fitted properly during an overhaul.

In general, a cylinder that reveals a taper of more than about .012 in., or is out-of-round by much more than .005, needs to be rebored, with new oversize pistons fitted. Even .007 in. taper can be too much. In high-mileage engines, it's not unusual to find .020 clearances, with pistons rocking madly.

For light duty operation, you might get by with honing the unworn (bottom) section to match the top, and install oversize rings. Standard piston rings can generally accommodate themselves to a cylinder with modest taper (say, less than .006 in.) or slightly out-of-round without allowing oil to pass into the combustion chamber. Marginal tapers can sometimes be dealt with by installing oil control rings of heavier-than-normal pressure.

Piston Pin. In most cases, any "play" that can be felt means a new (oversize) pin is needed, and its bushing must be reamed to fit.

Piston Ring Side Clearance. About .004 in. clearance is considered marginal for most engines,

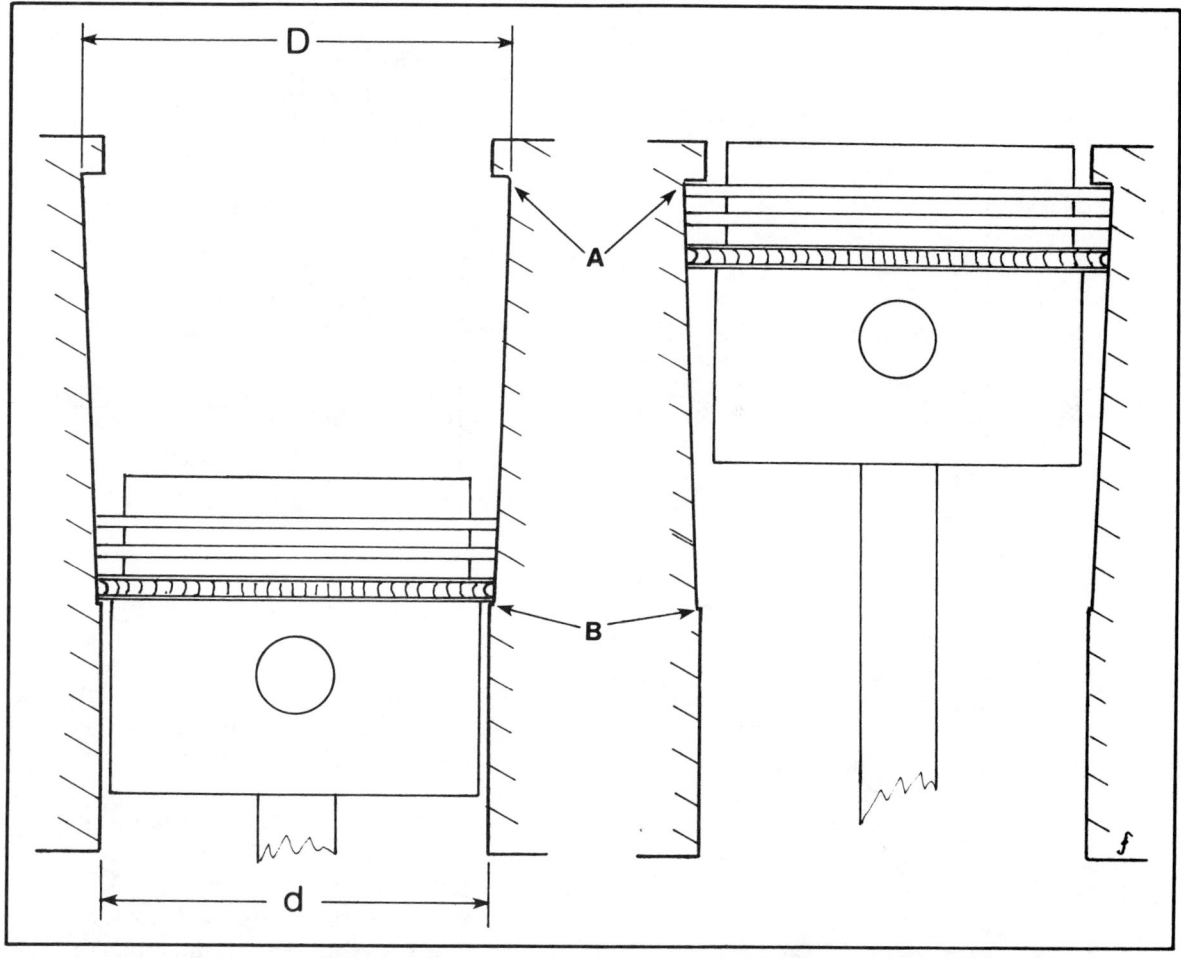

Fig. 13-2. Cylinder wall taper is the difference between the largest (D) and smallest (d) diameters. High-mileage engines reveal a very discernible ledge just above the highest point of ring travel (A), and a slight ledge at the lowest point (B).

and .006 is too much for proper sealing of the gases. The top compression ring groove usually wears the most, and unevenly to boot.

Ring End Gap. When the gap has doubled in size, new piston rings may be needed. Measurement isn't made to evaluate the need for new rings, though. It's part of the assembly process when fitting rings during an overhaul. Actually, the minimum gap is more important in order to prevent binding.

CRANKSHAFT AND CAMSHAFT JOURNAL WEAR

Main or rod-bearing clearance of four thousandths over the specified figure is almost certain to lower the engine's oil pressure. Doubling the suggested clearance multiplies a rod bearing's oil throw-off about five times. Quadruple the clearance and throw-off is boosted 25 times. Thus, when clearance approaches twice the recommended size, bearing work is mandatory—before a knock begins.

Because a bearing surface wears more rapidly than the hardened journal it surrounds, a new bearing would seem to take care of the looseness. Unfortunately, journals wear down too. And not always evenly. They often become "flat" (out-of-round). They may also be tapered, unequal in diameter at each end (Fig. 13-3).

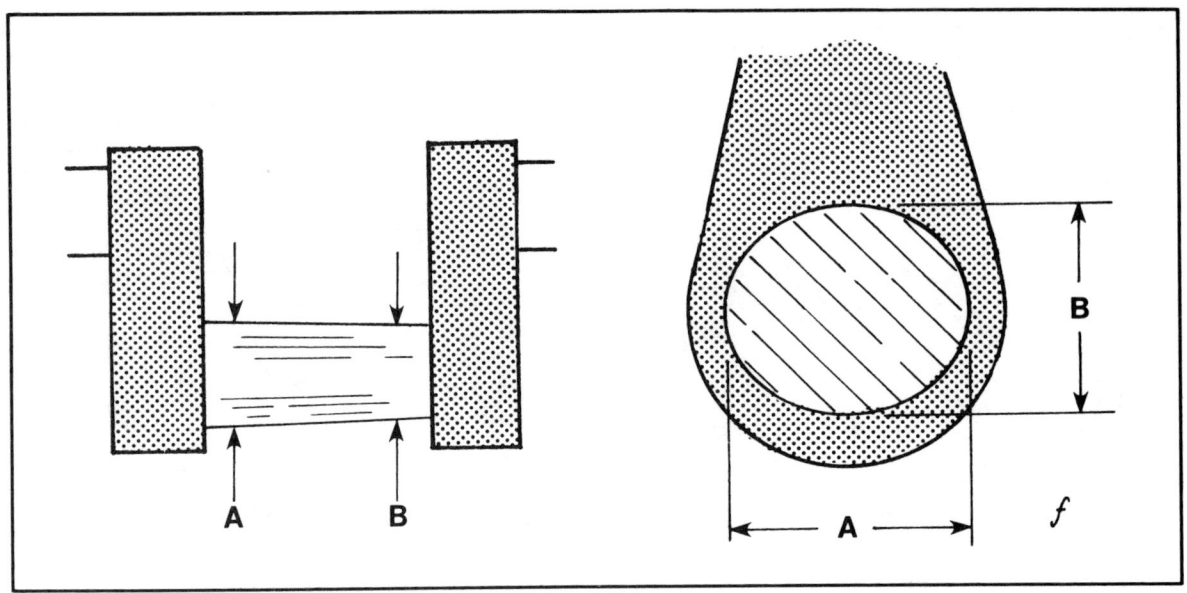

Fig. 13-3. The taper (left) and out-of-roundness (right) of crankshaft journal are evaluated separately by subtracting smaller diameter (B) from larger (A).

No new bearing, even undersize, is likely to provide an effective oil film—or to last long—if the journal is out-of-round by more than .0015 in. or tapered by over .001. Such a crankshaft has to be reground (which is major surgery).

Occasionally, the saddle bore of a connecting rod becomes out-of-round. Installing a new bearing insert will do little good.

Camshaft bearings need attention when clearance reaches .005 in. or so. Maybe sooner. A camshaft that's no longer straight—more than .001 or .002 in. runout—needs to be replaced.

How about the camshaft lobes? Even a .005-inch loss of valve lift can threaten performance. Most important the lobes should be virtually equal. A reground camshaft may be the only answer.

WEAR ELSEWHERE IN THE ENGINE

Oil Pump. Clearance between the oil pump's teeth and its housing should be less than about .006 inch. Between the teeth of the oil pump drive gear and the camshaft gear, .010-inch looseness might signal trouble.

Timing Gears. On motors with contacting gears rather than chains, clearance between the mating teeth shouldn't be much over .008 in. As with all gears, too little clearance (backlash) is just as bad. Check it at several meshing points.

Distributor Shaft. A modest amount of "play" (say .006 in.) can make an enormous difference in breaker-point dwell stability.

Some important measurements have no specification. Water pump looseness, for instance, is normally checked by "feel."

One note of warning is that whenever a book figure is available it's wise to stick to it. Only when an engine expects to see light duty, or is mounted in a worn-out body, should the suggested limits be exceeded to any significant degree.

Precision Tools and Measurements

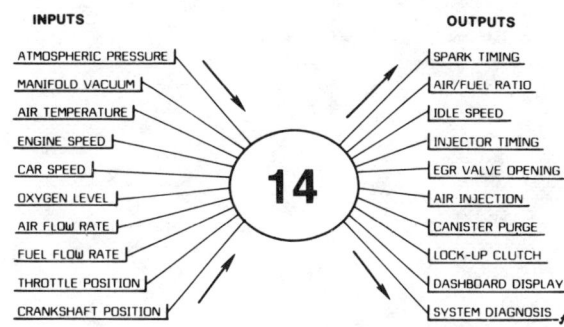

WHENEVER THE ENGINE HAS TO COME apart for an overhaul, precision measurements become inevitable. To replace rings, check valve wear, inspect crankshaft journals (Fig. 14-1) or handle any other serious work inside the motor, you'll need a couple of precision instruments.

Furthermore, you need to know how to use them. You must be able to take readings accurate within a thousandth of an inch—even an occasional ten-thousandth.

Two types of measurements are made on engine parts: actual size and clearance. Comparing the current diameter of a crankshaft journal to its original specification reveals the amount of wear it's suffered.

As a rule, clearance around a moving part is more important than its exact dimensions. The way two parts fit together, or move against each other, determines how well lubricant flows between the surfaces. A measurement that shows surplus clearance doesn't always tell which part is the culprit, but it demonstrates that there's a problem.

Clearance between two flat surfaces (rocker arm to valve stem end, piston ring end gap, etc.,) is easily measured with a flat feeler gauge. But we are more concerned with the clearances between round parts and the surfaces against which they slide or rotate (a piston in its bore, a rod bearing around its journal). Excessive clearance shows that one or both contacting parts are worn beyond usability. If it's within spec, measuring the actual sizes of each part might not even be necessary.

These cylindrical clearances can be determined in two ways. You might measure the outside diameter of the inner part and subtract that figure from the inside diameter of the "hole" in which it rides. Often, that's the best approach. For other parts, though, it's permissible—even desirable—to measure the degree of "looseness" or "play" directly. With the inner part setting in position, you use a dial indicator or other device to determine how much space exists around its circumference.

THE "FEEL" OF A THOUSANDTH

Measuring to the nearest thousandth with a

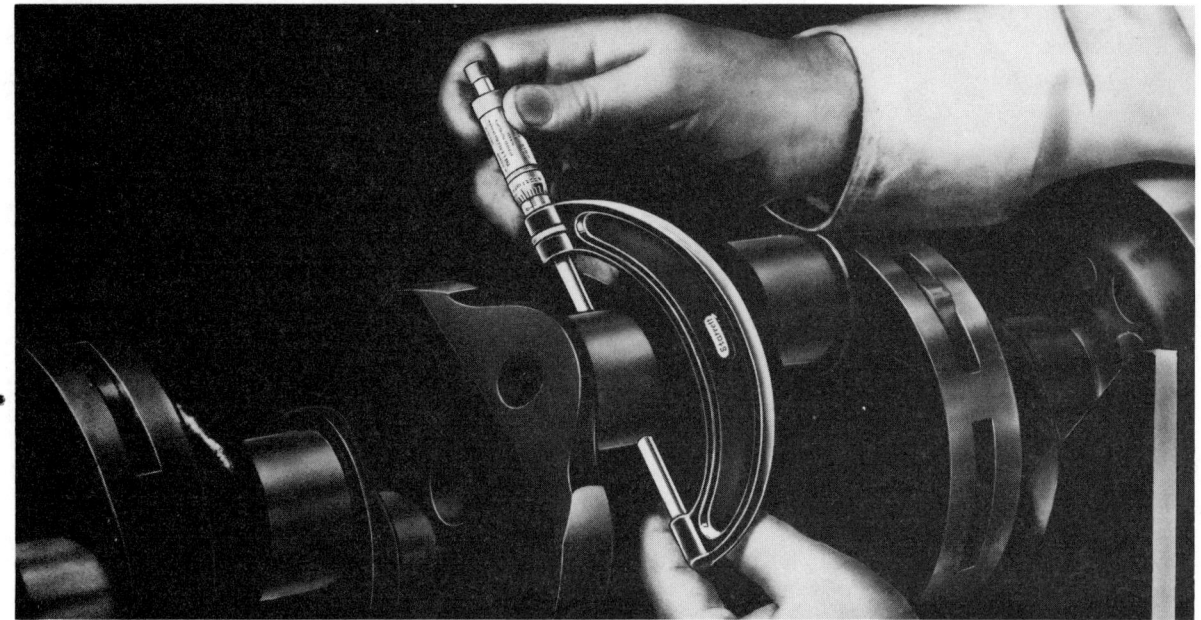

Fig. 14-1. Measuring crankshaft journal diameter with outside micrometer. (Courtesy of The L.S. Starrett Co.)

micrometer or other instrument isn't always so easy. To the nearest ten-thousandth is tougher yet.

As one fellow quickly discovered during a brief "career" as a lathe operator, there's quite a knack to using instruments correctly. Some people learn easily. Others never quite get the hang of it.

His foreman could slip a metal gauge around a newly turned part in an instant to determine whether its O.D. was acceptable. Our novice machinist, try as he might, couldn't get that gauge to fit around the product of his labors at all—even though it was smaller in diameter than the test gauge. Needless to say, he soon turned to another occupation, doubtless to the relief of his foreman.

Similarly, the inexperienced auto machinist can measure a piston or valve stem and declare it a thousandth or two different from its actual size. Why? Because he or she doesn't know just how tight it should feel against the micrometer.

Without a doubt, the best way to learn about "feel" and "fit" is to take a quick class in machine shop techniques. You might not want or need to learn to use all the machinery, but some practice with the measuring tools will prove invaluable. Learning on your own isn't impossible, but you can never quite be sure you're not always just a hair off. You need to compare your impression of snugness with that of an experienced machinist.

Let's describe the common instruments, then, along with a few tips on their use. We'll begin with those measuring outside diameter (O.D.) and other external dimensions.

OUTSIDE MICROMETERS

The outside micrometer (micrometer caliper) is surely the number one tool in the auto machinist's kit. Although it easily measures objects with flat surfaces, it's most often used to check the O.D. of crankshaft journals, valve stems, pistons, pins, valve lifters, and many other round parts.

All micrometers are direct-reading in thousandths of an inch (.001). Some have an additional vernier scale graduated for accuracy to ten-thousandths (.0001). "Mikes" have a range of just 1 inch. A single one might cover 0-1 inch, 3-4 inches, or some other range. Some have interchangeable anvils to cover an extended range. The tool is adjusted to fit around the part by rotating a thimble. Size is interpreted from graduations on the thimble and sleeve (Fig. 14-2).

A good 0-1 inch micrometer costs $40 and up. A 0-4 inch interchangeable-anvil model runs around $120. You also need a standard—a precision-made metal gauge block—for periodic checking of the mike's accuracy.

When using a micrometer or any other precision tool, never rely upon a single measurement. Check the part at several points along the surface to determine uneven wear, and compare worn to unworn segments. Where appropriate, measure both vertically and horizontally to evaluate out-of-roundness. While the smallest outside measurement of the contacting surface shows total wear, its largest diameter is generally used to determine clearance (subtracting from the I.D. of the surrounding component). Substantial differences between the various diameters suggest the need for a new or resurfaced part even if clearance is OK.

A valve stem, for example, should be measured at several spots along the section that contacts the valve guide, and compared with unworn portions at top and bottom. The most significant measure of a piston—used to determine clearance within its cylinder bore—is its O.D. at the skirt top, perpendicular to the piston pin. It should also be miked parallel to the pin, and at the skirt bottom and ring lands.

The horizontal diameter of a connecting rod journal is usually larger. It's compared with specifications to show actual wear. Subtracting vertical diameter gives a reading of flatness. Measurements at front and rear evaluate taper.

READING A MICROMETER

The basic outside "mike" has two scales: one along the horizontal sleeve, another around the thimble's beveled edge. Both are needed to derive a reading in thousandths of an inch.

Reading the instrument is quite logical once you see the basic principle. It's all based on the fact that the spindle screw's *pitch* is 1/40. That is it has 40

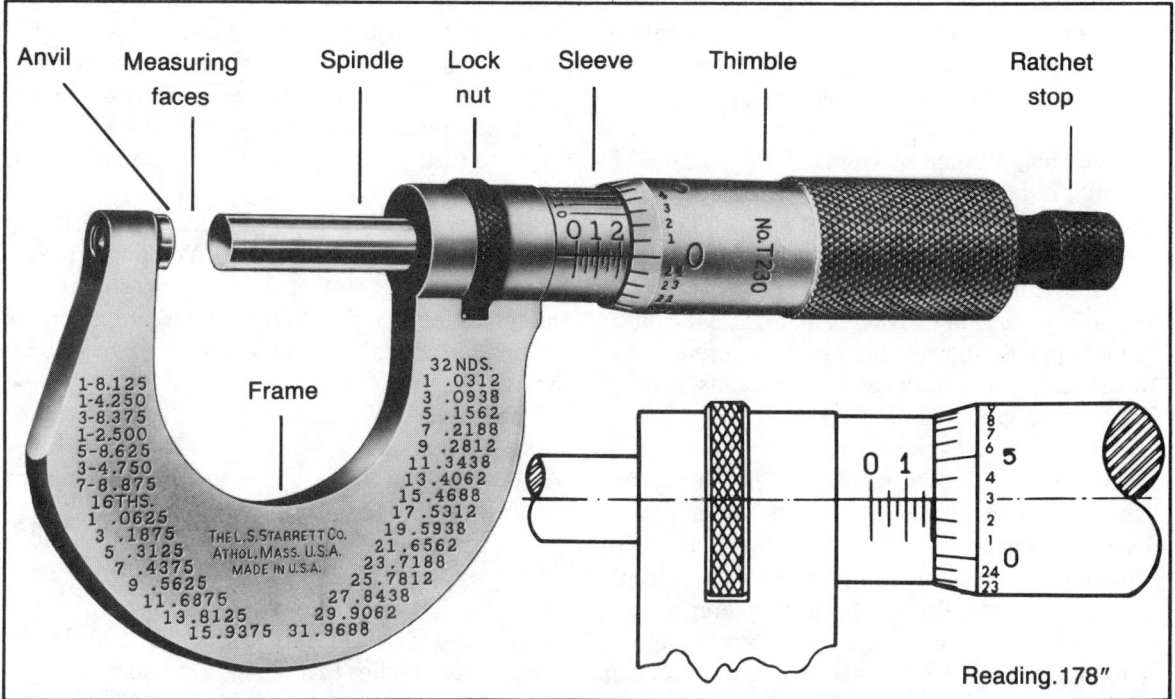

Fig. 14-2. Micrometer reading is the sum of: 1) number of long vertical sleeve divisions, multiplied by .100 inch; 2) additional shorter sleeve divisions, multiplied by .025; and 3) the numbered thimble graduation that aligns with sleeve line, multiplied by .001. Total reading shown is .100 + .075 + .003 = 0.178 inch. (Courtesy of The L.S. Starrett Co.)

145

threads per inch, and the tool's measuring range is exactly 1 inch.

The sleeve reading line, too, is 1 inch long. To coincide with the screw threads, it is divided into 40 equal segments—each 1/40 inch or 25 thousandths (.025) wide—represented by vertical lines. For ease in reading, every fourth division has a longer vertical line (numbered 1, 2, 3, etc.). Each of these wider divisions represents 1/10 inch or 100 thousandths (.100). Finally, the thimble edge has 25 numbered graduations, each equivalent to *one* thousandth (.001).

In the closed position, only the zero division on the reading line is visible (barely) and the zero on the thimble aligns with the reading line. Moving the thimble from zero to the first graduation separates the spindle and anvil faces by just .001 inch. Each full rotation of the thimble moves the spindle exactly .025 inch away from the anvil face, revealing one division on the reading line. (The line may not quite be visible, but lies right under the thimble edge.) With every fourth rotation, a longer (numbered) division appears, showing a separation of .100. After 40 rotations, all divisions are visible, and the micrometer has opened by its full 1-inch range.

A reading it taken by counting the number of vertical graduations visible on the sleeve and multiplying by .025 (the width of each). Then add the number of thousandths; this is indicated by the numbered thimble graduation that now aligns with the reading line. For convenience, this can be done by adding three figures: the sizes represented by .100 divisions, by additional .025 divisions, and by .001 thimble graduations.

It's not unlike counting change from a $10 bill (which consists of 1000 pennies). The numbered sleeve divisions are equivalent to dollars, the shorter divisions to quarters, and the thimble graduations to cents—with a decimal point in front of the result. Naturally, if your micrometer has an anvil larger than 1-inch capacity, a digit denoting its minimum range goes ahead of the decimal (2.178, for a 2-3 inch mike).

Some micrometers have an additional set of horizontal vernier graduations on the sleeve, providing accuracy to one ten-thousandth (.0001). The number of thousandths is first determined as above. Then you note which of the 10 horizontal lines aligns precisely with one of the graduations on the thimble edge. That's the number of "tenths" to be added to the basic reading: the final fourth digit. Why? Because those 10 vernier divisions occupy the same space as nine thimble divisions. Thus the difference in their widths is precisely one-tenth of a thimble division, or one ten-thousandth.

Too tedious? Well, outside mikes with a digital readout showing thousandths directly are available at higher cost. They too have a vernier scale for the extra "tenths" reading. Metric micrometers work on the very same principle.

Before measuring anything, see that the zero graduation on the thimble aligns with the sleeve's reading line when the mike is closed (anvil and spindle faces just touching). To measure a round object, rotate the thimble until the faces are far enough apart to fit around easily. Hold the anvil against the part as you pivot the micrometer slowly up and down, while rotating the thimble inward. As the spindle face makes contact, shorten the swing, searching for the true (largest) diameter. Use light pressure with only your thumb and index finger to turn the thimble. The instrument should fit snugly around the part.

How snug? If you have a standard mike, that's what requires skill and practice. You might prefer one with a ratchet stop; it cannot be overtightened. Others have a friction thimble to create a similar limit. As practice, you might try measuring some unworn feeler-gauge leaves.

For greatest accuracy, read the micrometer without removing it from the part. If you must withdraw it to see the scale, use the lock nut to secure the thimble in position.

INSIDE MICROMETERS

To determine clearance, you must also know the inside diameter of the surrounding part. An inside micrometer handles that job for a cylinder, connecting rod bore, or any part with a relatively large "hole." Inside mikes have a range of either 1/2 inch or 1 inch. By using interchangeable extension rods, they can measure any I.D. from 1 1/2 or 2 inches (depending on head size) up to 8 inches or more. Each has a scale similar to that of an outside mike, with graduations on thimble and sleeve.

A complete set, graduated for .001-inch accuracy, costs at least $60. Before each use, test the instrument against an outside mike to be sure the rod is attached properly. Be sure to add the length of the head and rod in order to get total size.

Using an inside micrometer demands patience and practice because it must be precisely perpendicular to the cylindrical surface. Measuring a cylinder bore is like a juggling act. One contact is held against the cylinder wall, while the other must be "rocked" up and down—and back and forth—as you rotate the thimble to expand the contacts across the true diameter. Cocked just a hair, the reading will be far off the mark.

CALIPERS

Although micrometers are preferred for most precision work, the *vernier caliper* does an acceptable job on many O.D. and other external dimensions. It's like a high-accuracy ruler, but offers the bonus of inside and depth measurements.

Range is 6 inches or more, but the jaw lengths restrict O.D. and I.D. capabilities to a smaller limit. Most vernier calipers are graduated for accuracy to thousandths. Reading the scale is slightly tricky, but no tougher than a mike. In fact, some machinists prefer calipers to micrometers for regular use.

Vernier calipers have a sliding jaw on a beam rule graduated in .025-inch units. A total reading comes from adding:

- ☐ Whole inches;
- ☐ Tenths of an inch;
- ☐ The .025 graduations; and
- ☐ Thousandths, determined by noting the highest number on the vernier scale that lines up exactly.

Reading the number of thousandths on a vernier caliper is similar to deducing ten-thousandths on the high-accuracy micrometer. The vernier scale has 25 divisions, occupying the same space as 24 bar divisions (each of which is .025 in.). The difference between the division widths, then, is .001 inch.

A good vernier unit costs nearly as much as micrometer. Those with an easier-to-read dial scale are even more expensive. Cheapies are limited to fractional sizes (no closer than 1/128 in.).

Ordinary *calipers* come in either inside or outside style. Either is adjusted to fit around or within a part, and then withdrawn and measured against a ruler. Accuracy to 1/64 inch is about the best you can hope for.

A good ruler, incidentally, should be in every garage. Preferably you should have one made of steel, with 1/64-inch graduations.

HOLE GAUGES

If you don't have an inside micrometer or need to measure smaller holes, other instruments are available.

Small-hole gauges (Fig. 14-3) show I.D. of holes up to 1/2-inch diameter, such as valve guides and shaft bushings. They also measure groove widths. The gauges are not direct-reading. You turn the adjusting knob until the split ball contacts expand out against the surface, extract the tool, and measure its O.D. with an outside mike. Applied at various depths, the gauge can check guide bell-mouthing and other uneven wear (but not out-of-roundness). A set of four, covering 1/8 to 1/2 inch, costs around $40.

Telescoping gauges (Fig. 14-4) are similar, but measure the I.D. of larger holes: lifter guides, piston pin bushings, even cylinder bores. The contact points are under spring tension. When inserted into the hole, they expand to the part's diameter. The tool can then be locked, removed, and measured with an outside mike. As with the inside mike, keeping the gauge straight to get a true diameter can be touchy. Used carefully, it can evaluate out-of-roundness with some accuracy. A set of six, measuring 5/16 to 6-inch holes, would set you back about $70.

Another possibility for small I.D. tests is the nonadjustable *Go/No-Go plug gauge* (Fig. 14-5). Its

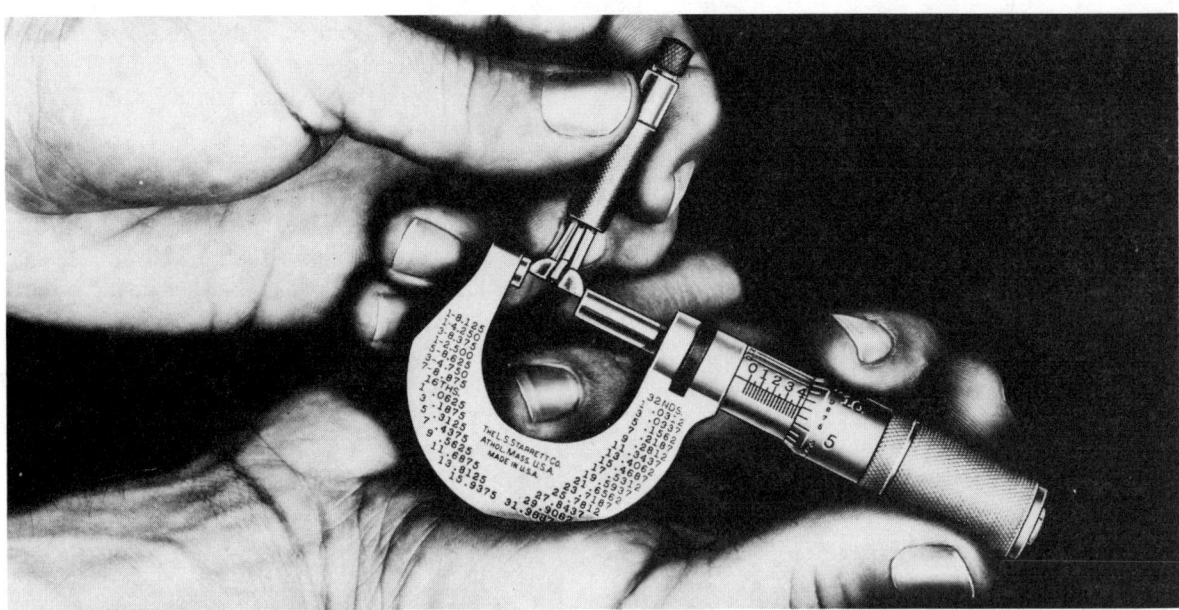

Fig. 14-3. Small-hole gauge's contacts must be measured with a micrometer after withdrawing it from the part being checked. (Courtesy of The L.S. Starrett Co.)

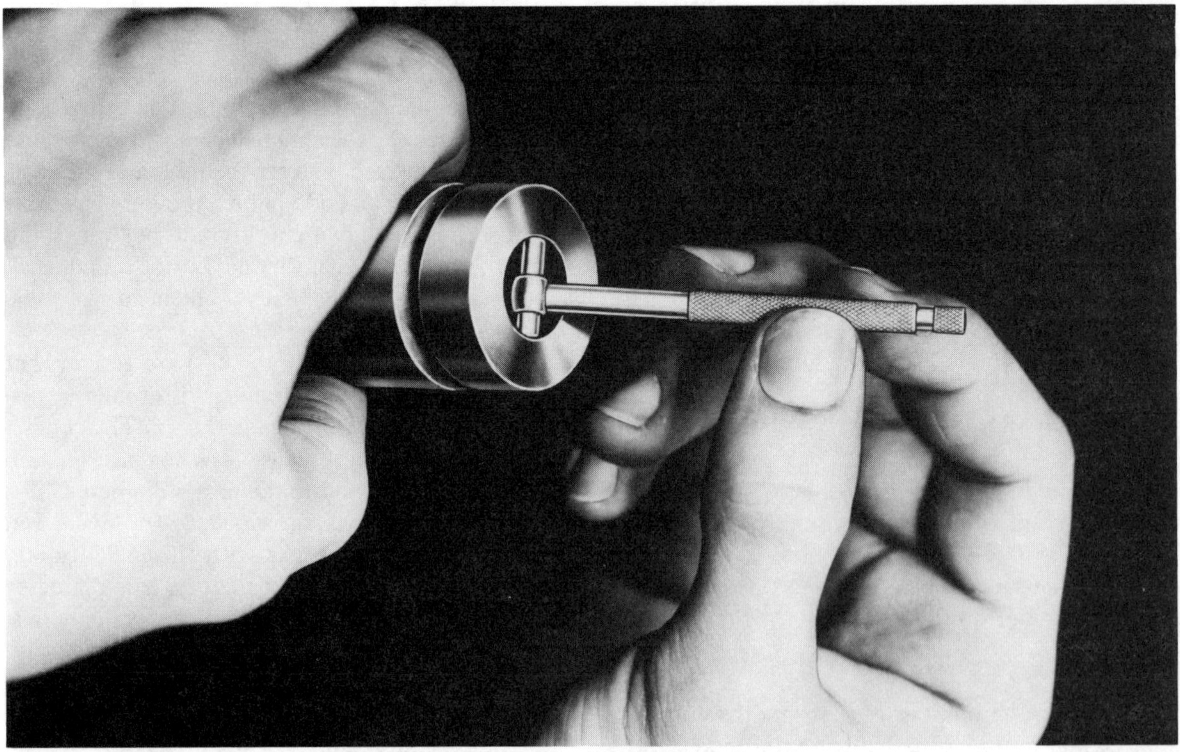

Fig. 14-4. A telescoping gauge has contacts under spring tension; they can be locked and measured with a micrometer. (Courtesy of The L.S. Starrett Co.)

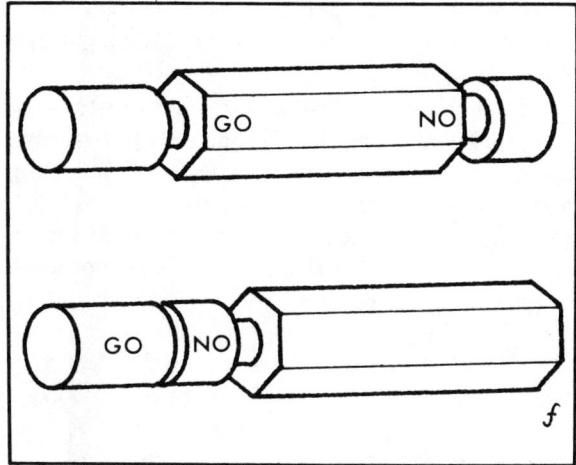

Fig. 14-5. Go/No-Go plug gauges come in double-ended (top) or stepped form, with twin solid plugs of slightly different diameter.

handle holds two solid gauges, a few thousandths apart in diameter. If one segment will enter a hole, but the larger will not, the true diameter is somewhere between the two. They're handy, but cannot evaluate uneven wear or reach into deep holes.

DIAL INDICATORS

Dial indicators have many applications around the engine. They don't measure size, but display clearance directly. The indicator must be positioned so its contact point touches the moving part to be tested (Fig. 14-6). As you wiggle the part toward and away from the instrument, its "play" (clearance) is shown by needle movement around the indicator's scale.

Indicators for automotive use are generally

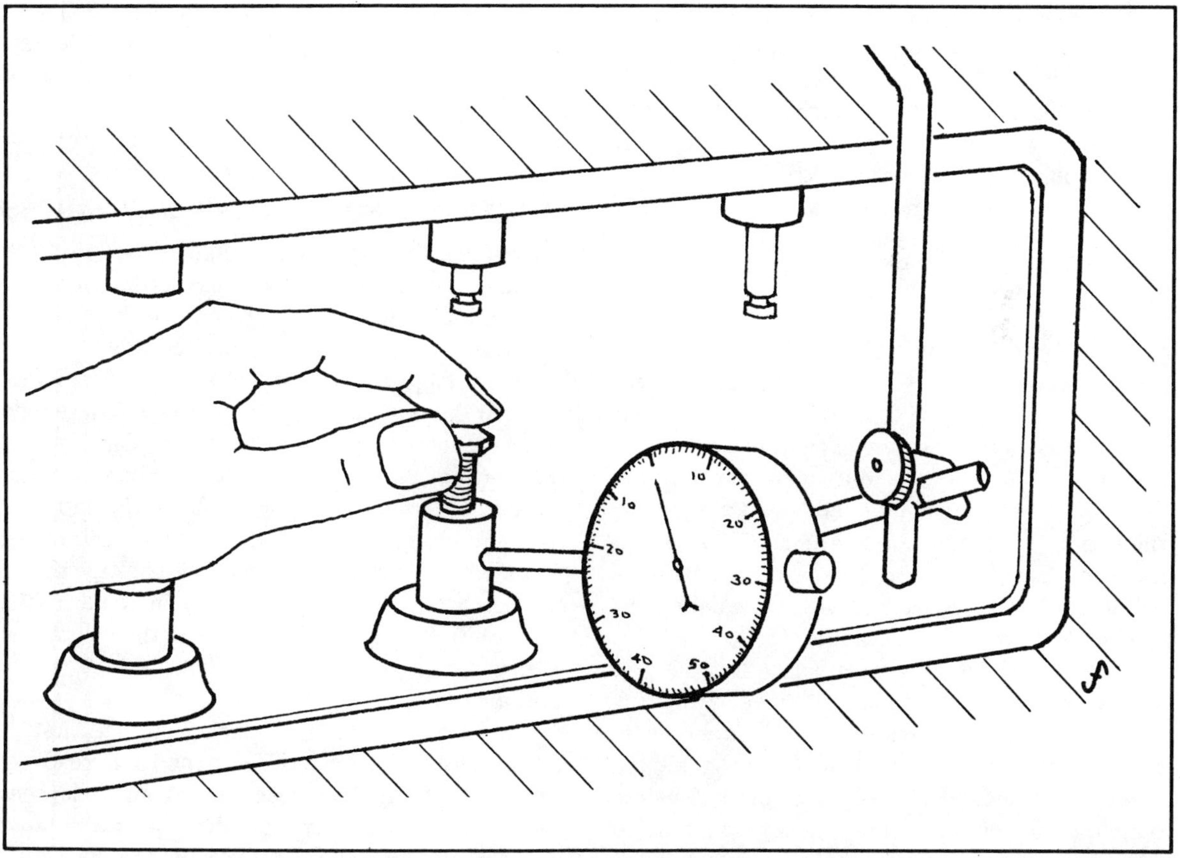

Fig. 14-6. A dial indicator can be used to check valve lifter-to-guide clearance. Wiggling the lifter back and forth causes the needle to move through several graduations, showing clearance directly in thousandths.

graduated in thousandths, and occasionally in ten-thousandths. Each full rotation of the needle may cover .050 or .100 inch, and the indicator is usable through a total range of several times that distance. (Its needle rotates repeatedly.)

A good-quality dial indicator can be found for as little as $40. It's useless without a mounting device that clamps or attaches magnetically to the engine.

Valve stem-to-guide clearance is measured by mounting the indicator so its contact point touches the side of the valve stem, as the valve sets in its guide. Reading is most accurate when contact is as close as possible to the guide's end. If the needle moves through three .001-inch graduations, as you wiggle the valve stem, clearance is .003 inch. Couldn't be simpler.

Dial indicators can also show runout (out-of-roundness or misalignment) of a rotating part as it's turned slowly by hand. Mounted below a connecting rod cap or adjacent to a camshaft, it can display bearing clearance as you move the rod or shaft up and down. Mount it at the front of the engine to get end play of the camshaft or crankshaft, as you pry the shaft forward and back. There are lots of possibilities for measuring movement and looseness.

FEELER GAUGES AND SHIMS

Leaf-type *feeler gauges* (thickness gauges) measure distance between two flat, parallel surfaces: point contact gap, tappet clearance, piston ring end gap, and so on. Nearly every do-it-yourselfer has used one. A full set with flat metal leaves of every thickness, in thousandths from .0015 (1 1/2 thousandths) up to .035 inch or so, costs only a few dollars. When a needed size is not available, two thinner leaves can be stacked.

If one leaf enters a given space but the next largest will not, clearance is between the two figures. It's easy enough except when one of the parts moves as you insert the leaf. You should feel moderate resistance, a slightly loose drag, as though a leaf one-thousandth thicker would almost fit.

For tappet clearances, many mechanics prefer a Go/No-Go leaf gauge that has two close thicknesses on a single stepped leaf. It's faster but no more accurate.

Leaf gauges are also used to check piston ring end gap by inserting the ring squarely into the cylinder bore with the aid of an inverted piston. Ring groove side clearance is measured above each piston ring; a leaf of the suggested size should not enter the groove more than 1/16 in. Groove depth checks require a tapered gauge measured against a micrometer.

Camshaft end play can be checked by inserting a leaf between the shaft's backing plate and gear; crankshaft end play, alongside a specified bearing cap, while prying the shaft to one end.

Separate feeler leaves, or *shims,* made of thin, flexible metal are sometimes used to evaluate clearance between round parts. Some manuals give a specification for piston-to-cylinder clearance based on testing with a shim of given thickness. You need a spring scale to show how much pressure is required to pull the leaf upward. The shim should be inserted perpendicular to the piston's pin.

PLASTIGAGE FOR BEARING CLEARANCES

Brass shim stock was once commonly used to check bearing clearances. The machinist noted how freely the crankshaft would turn by hand, with a shim inserted and the bearing cap torqued down.

Plastigage is a safer method that is not likely to harm the bearing or journal surface. All you do is place a short strip of this thin, round plastic across the bearing surface—near the center, but not over the oil hole. Install and torque down the cap, and then remove it to see how much the plastic has been flattened. A comparison scale on the package shows the equivalent clearance directly in thousandths (Fig. 14-7). Plastigage is available in three common sizes to reveal .001-.003, .002-.006 or .004-.009 inch clearances.

Wipe any oil off the bearing surface first; it would dissolve the plastic. For the basic reading, a rod journal should be positioned about 30 degrees away from vertical. Repeat with the journal rotated 90 degrees to calculate out-of-roundness.

When testing a main bearing, it's important to

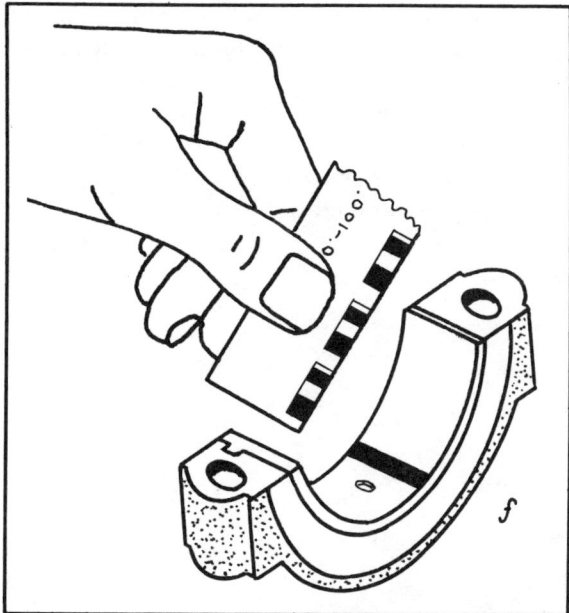

Fig. 14-7. A Plastigage strip is compressed and flattened by torquing down the bearing cap. It is then measured against the width scale on the package to determine bearing clearance in thousandths of an inch.

take weight off the crankshaft (perhaps by jacking it up slightly or inserting paper shims in the other main caps). If Plastigage shows excessive clearance or suggests uneven wear, measuring the journal with a micrometer is the next step.

SPECIAL MEASURING TOOLS

Are your pockets overflowing with dollars? Then all sorts of test instruments are available that make precision measurements quicker, easier, or more accurate—perhaps all three. Amateur mechanics aren't likely to own all the instruments already discussed (much less the specialty tools). If you're in the business, or planning to enter it, you need to know what tools could be purchased that might speed up your work.

A cylinder bore indicator, for example, does the same job as an inside micrometer or telescoping gauge. But it's far, far easier to use. Accurate, too.

TIPS AND TECHNIQUES

The most important guide to keep in mind is that you aren't checking merely for wear (for measurements outside the book figures). You're looking for wear that's uneven. At the same time, you'll be inspecting part condition. A cylinder bore must be checked for waviness, pockets, and scoring. A piston skirt may be scuffed. Crankshaft journals could be scored or pitted. The list is nearly endless.

No measurement can be valid unless the part or surface is clean. Wipe away all grease and dirt, scrape off carbon, and use wire brushes and chemical cleaners to get down to sparkling metal.

Don't stop with the figures in the spec tables. Manuals give many specific instructions for measuring certain parts. Tension may have to be released from one part. Another may have to be moved to one side to get a proper reading. Some require certain measuring instruments, and using the wrong one—even if it seems reasonable—could produce false readings.

How accurate must your measurements be? Obviously, when you're replacing a single, noisy rod bearing or renewing valves in a tired old engine whose other parts are barely holding together, tolerances within a thousandth or two may be more than sufficient. When overhauling a valuable engine, the "book" figures should be duplicated with greater care.

When a range is given (bearing clearance of .0003-.0029 in., say, or .002-.003), a reading close to the middle is generally best. With a single figure some judgment is needed. Clearance a hair tight, to allow for initial wearing-in of a new part, is sometimes desirable. In certain cases (tappet clearances, for one), a slightly loose setting is wiser.

CAN YOU MEASURE IT YOURSELF?

The better question might be: Should you measure it yourself? Or should you turn over the precision measurements to a local machine shop?

The answer depends not only on your skill and tool kit, but on the type of repair that might be needed if trouble is located. If you don't expect to take on a re-ring job or bearing replacement yourself, there's probably little value in measuring the parts on your own.

Another problem arises when you've taken the engine apart, but don't have all the "proper" measuring tools at hand. Well, sometimes you're in luck.

Some measurements that are best taken with a dial indicator, for example, can be done with a plain feeler gauge. Whenever you lack the ideal instrument, take a good look at the situation. What is it that has to be measured? A linear space? Maybe a feeler gauge will fit in there. A cylindrical clearance? If the manual recommends a small-hole gauge and you have none, a dial indicator might do.

Improvisation is a skill in itself. Still, there's no substitute for the right instruments in the hands of a patient, careful craftsperson.

Hardware

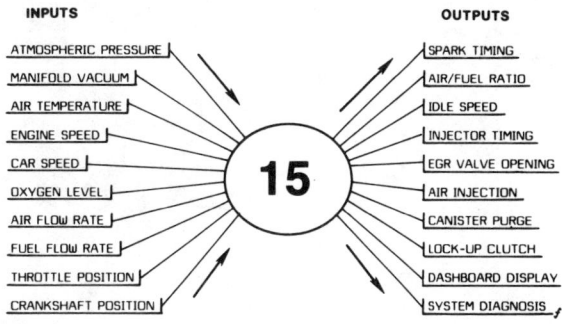

THREADED FASTENERS HAVE BEEN WITH US since ancient times—long before the automobile was even a glimmer in its inventors' fertile brains. We use threaded hardware constantly in auto repair work, in the workshop, and around the home, yet it's surprising how little some of us know about these indispensable objects.

We tend to take hardware for granted, concentrating instead on the more "glamorous" automotive parts. A 4-barrel carburetor is more fascinating than a cap screw, and a camshaft's function is more intriguing than a lockwasher's.

So let's take a look at the basics of threads and the types of fasteners used in automobiles. Then we'll consider tensile strength and, in the following chapter, learn how to tighten all the hardware properly. That way, we can minimize the woes of broken-off bolts and studs that plague many a repairperson.

SCREW AND BOLT SIZES

Threaded fasteners are designated by three measurements:

☐ Outside, or shank, diameter of the "male" bolt or screw.
☐ Shank length.
☐ Thread pattern—either pitch (distance between threads) or number of threads per inch.

A *male* fastener is any bolt, screw or stud with outside threads; a *female* has inside threads (a nut or threads formed in a "hole" in some part).

Outside diameter is given as a fractional figure (5/16, 1/2, etc.) for bolt sizes of 1/4-inch and larger. For smaller fasteners, a single number is used: from #0 (a tiny .06 inch diameter) through #12, which measures .216 in. This outside measurement is often called the major diameter, and is distinguished from the minor diameter, which is the inside (smallest) measure of the cut or forged thread (Fig. 15-1).

Bolt or screw length is always given in fractional inches (1 1/2, 3/4, etc.). It refers to the entire length of the shank (from the base of the head to the tip of the thread). It doesn't matter whether the bolt is threaded full-length or only part way; its

153

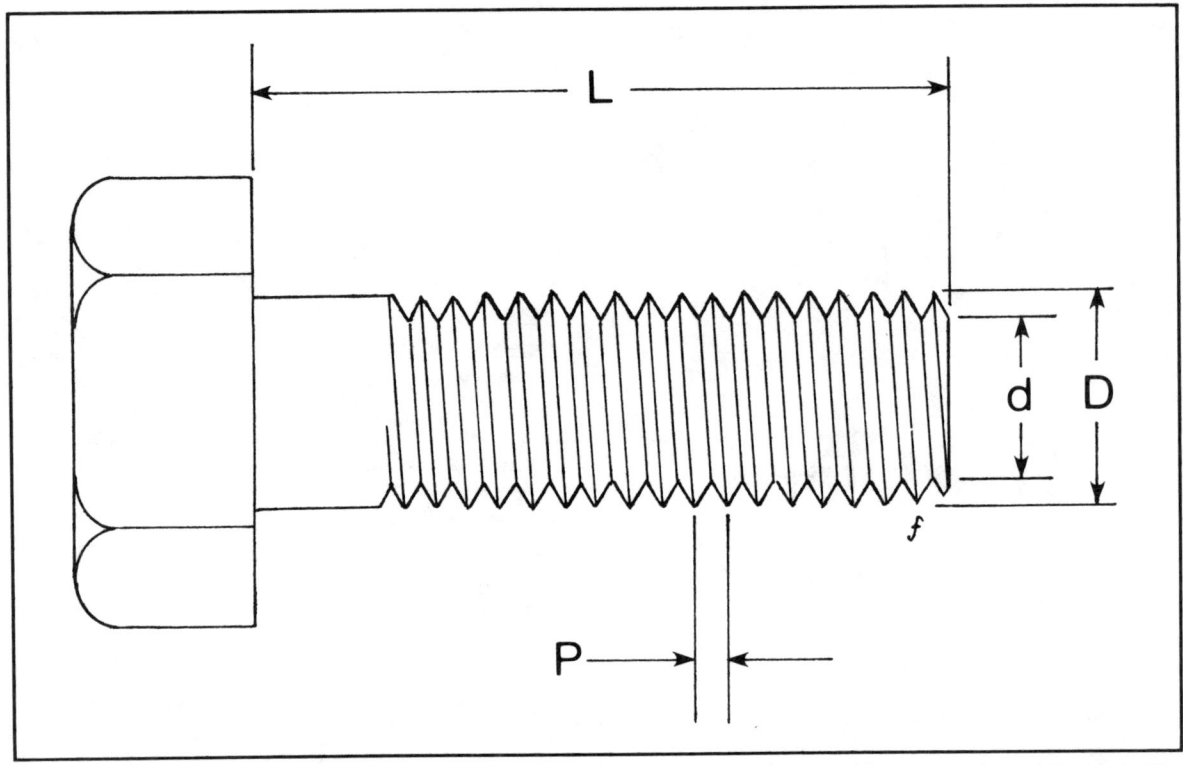

Fig. 15-1. Bolt measurements include shank length (L), major diameter (D), minor diameter (d), and pitch (P) or number of threads per inch.

length is the entire distance.

Nearly all threaded devices used on cars have threads in one of two pitches:

☐ Coarse—also known as United States Standard (USS) or Unified National Coarse (UNC).

☐ Fine—Society of Automotive Engineers (SAE) or Unified National Fine (UNF).

The USS and SAE designations are standard in the automotive trade. General machinists prefer UNC and UNF.

Why two pitches? In certain applications, the USS/UNC style, with its coarse, deeper-cut threads, provides substantially greater strength. This is especially true when the bolt threads directly into a metal component, without using a nut. Bolts attaching a cylinder head to the engine block is an example. They're also less likely to "strip" when threaded into cast iron or aluminum. For other purposes—particularly when used with nuts—SAE/UNF hardware, with a greater number of threads making contact, offers more holding power. Fasteners with *very fine* threads are also available for special installations.

A bolt in a given diameter, then, is available in a choice of thread patterns for different applications. A 5/16-inch bolt, for example, might have either 18 (coarse) or 24 (fine) threads per inch. A #10 screw can be purchased with 24 or 32 threads per inch. Table 15-1 lists thread counts for commonly used hardware in fine and coarse styles.

Bolts and screws are identified by a three-part number—diameter, thread pattern, and length—in that order. A 3/8-24 × 2 bolt has a 3/8-inch-diameter shank, 24 threads per inch (fine thread), and is 2 inches long (excluding its head). An 8-32 × 1/2 machine screw is .164 inch diameter with 32 threads per inch, 1/2 inch long. Nuts are specified by the outside diameter and pitch of the

Table 15-1. Dimensions of Fine, Coarse, and Metric Threaded Bolts.

American—NF & NC				Metric (common U.S. sizes)			
Size	O.D (in.)	Threads per inch		Size	O.D. (in.)	Pitch (mm)	Threads per inch (approx.)
		Fine	Coarse				
#0	.060	80	...	M1.6	.063	0.35	74
#1	.073	72	64	M2	.079	0.4	64
#2	.086	64	56				
#3	.099	56	48	M2.5	.098	0.45	56
#4	.112	48	40	M3	.118	0.5	51
#5	.125	44	40				
#6	.138	40	32	M3.5	.138	0.6	42
#8	.164	36	32	M4	.157	0.7	36
#10	.190	32	24	M5	.196	0.8	32
#12	.216	28	24				
1/4	.250	28	20	M6.3	.248	1.0	25
5/16	.3125	24	18	M8	.315	1.25	20
3/8	.375	24	16	M10	.393	1.5	17
7/16	.4375	20	14				
1/2	.500	20	13	M12	.472	1.75	14.5
9/16	.5625	18	12	M14	.551	2	12.5
5/8	.625	18	11	M16	.630	2	12.5
3/4	.750	16	10	M20	.787	2.5	10
7/8	.875	14	9	M24	.945	3	8.5
1	1.000	14	8				

bolt to which they can be attached.

Various other thread patterns have been used over the years, including the Whitworth system that was universal on British vehicles until the mid-1960s. Older vehicles could have hardware with Acme threads or were manufactured under the old American Standard system.

Until recent years, most automotive fasteners installed on American vehicles were manufactured to the familiar "inch" measurements. Metric hardware was used long before that on foreign cars, and has gradually come into widespread use on those sold and made in America. Many cars contain both.

Metric is certainly simpler when dealing with bolt diameters and wrench openings, which are given in even (non-fractional) millimeters. It's immediately obvious that an 11-millimeter wrench is larger than a 10mm. Determining whether 11/32 is bigger or smaller than 3/8 demands a quick calculation.

Metric bolts are specified in a similar way: major diameter followed by pitch (distance *between* threads), both stated in millimeters. A 10 × 1.5 metric bolt has a major diameter of 10mm, with 1 1/2 millimeters between threads. Metrics come in both fine and coarse thread counts, but coarse is most common in autos. A prefix *M* in the number shows that the ISO Metric designation is used.

MEASURING THE THREAD

How can you determine thread type and size when you have to purchase replacement fasteners or mate new nuts with old bolts? Just buy a thread pitch gauge. It is an inexpensive gadget with several marked leafs, and one of the leafs will match the threads on your unidentified bolt. Equally handy is the hole gauge. The size of the smallest hole into which a mysterious bolt or screw will fit is its major diameter.

Lacking either of these devices, measuring threads is still no problem. A vernier caliper or micrometer gives the diameter. You can measure the thread count with a ruler, actually counting the number of threads along a 1-inch segment. With metrics, count the number of threads in a 20mm length, and then divide 20 by that total to derive the correct pitch.

With a bit of practice, you'll be able to tell the difference between fine and coarse threads by sight. It's always wise to measure them to make sure. Remember, too, that while nearly all automotive fasteners have right-hand threads, a few are left-hand (especially on some wheel hubs).

FITTING THE NUT

Obviously, a bolt has to match its intended nut in diameter and pitch. That doesn't mean every bolt of a given size fits every nut in the same way. Some are designed to fit looser than others, depending on how much friction is desired between the two. Sometimes, quick and easy assembly (and disassembly) is the goal. Elsewhere, staying together through heavy vibration may be more important.

This fit is shown by *thread class*: an indicator of the clearance between a nut's internal thread and the bolt's external thread. There are three classes:

☐ Loose fit—made for easy assembly/disassembly.

☐ Accurate fit, but not overly tight (common in autos).

☐ Very accurate fit—seldom used in cars, but essential in aviation applications.

A symbol denoting class is sometimes (definitely not always) given at the end of an identifying number, whether standard or metric.

THREADED FASTENER STYLES

Machine screws are small in size, and their diameters are normally identified by the 0-through-12 number system. They come with a variety of head styles: round, flat, countersunk, panhead, etc. Heads are slotted or indented for either a blade or Phillips screwdriver. They're usually used with a hex nut or speed nut. Stove bolts are similar, but identified by a fractional diameter, and they are typically supplied with a square nut.

Hex-head bolts are commonly available in sizes from 1/4 in. diameter up to several inches, and with lengths from 1/2 to 6 in. or even more. The longer sizes are often threaded for only part of the shank length. When intended for threading directly into a tapped hole in a component, they're often referred to as "cap screws" or "hex screws." Bolts may have a square or Allen (internal hex) head rather than the familiar hexagon shape, but hex heads are far more numerous in automobiles.

Sheet metal (self-tapping) screws are identified by a "number" diameter and fractional length. All types are tapered, and must be used in a pre-drilled hole. They cut their own threads as they're tightened, and use no nuts or other affixing devices.

Carriage bolts have a round, unslotted head and a square upper shank that fits into a square hole in one of the components to be attached, preventing the bolt from turning. A nut is used to hold the second part in position. They're used where a hex head would be unsightly (bumper-attaching bolts) or access would be difficult (as in some shock absorbers).

Studs are essentially bolts without heads, threaded at both ends. Some have coarse threads on one end, and fine on the other (where the nut goes).

Most nuts in cars are hex-head. Square nuts are used for some hose clamps and a few other applications. Various "locking" nuts, designed to stay in place without a lock washer, are found in later-model cars.

TENSILE STRENGTH

Nuts and bolts of the same size are not all alike. They come in a progression of grades that are capable of withstanding a specified force. A bolt's grade is based on its metallurgical content, and the degree of cold working or heat treating. This is known as the SAE tensile strength rating—a resistance to forces in the direction of the bolt's length—given in pounds per square inch (psi).

Bolt heads have two or more embossed "dashes" to indicate their grade (Fig. 15-2). A head with no markings means you have a Grade 0, 1, or 2. That's the kind sold in the corner hardware store, made from low carbon (mild) steel, and rated about

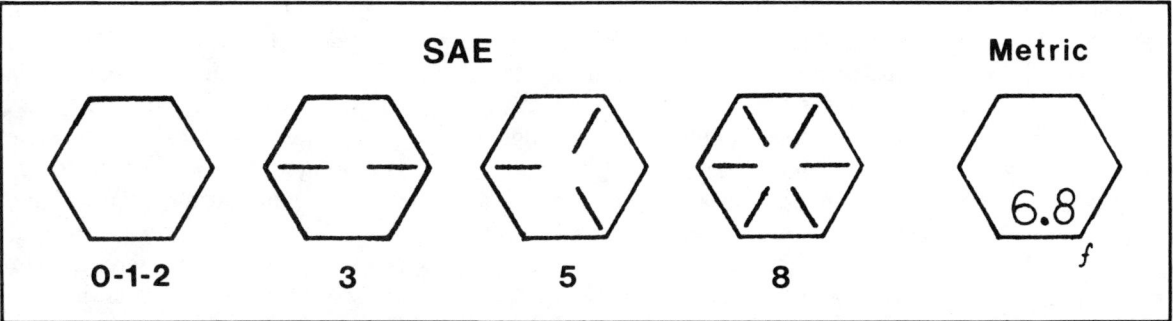

Fig. 15-2. SAE bolts have embossed dashes to indicate grade; metric tensile strength is shown by embossed number.

64,000 psi. Grade 3 is made of medium carbon steel, and is rated around 100,000 psi. Grade 5 is the same, but heat treated for a rating of 135,000 psi; these are used in many automotive applications. Grade 8 (medium carbon alloy steel, quenched and tempered) is more common in heavy-duty trucks.

Machine screws have no markings, but are the equivalent of Grade 0 (at best). Stove bolts are generally rated even less than zero, as are many carriage bolts. Allen-head cap screws are usually Grade 8 or more.

Metric bolts have a grade marking stamped on the head, such as 4.8 or 10.9. The higher the number the stronger the bolt. Metric grade 8.8 is about equal to SAE Grade 5; metric 6.8 is nearly equal to SAE 3.

Nuts and washers often are unmarked; their strength must be determined when they're purchased. Metric nuts often have ISO strength markings like those on bolt heads, or a pattern of nicks around one side.

Even when a fastener isn't marked or the marking isn't legible, its color gives a clue to its grade. Untreated steel parts are gray (one of the lower grades). Zinc-plated or cadmium-plated fasteners are silver color. These are relatively low in grade, but a bit higher than unplated. Heat treated nuts and bolts—SAE 5 and up—are dull black.

Of course, not all threaded fasteners are made of steel. We have screws of brass, aluminum, and other metals. Nuts might be made from fiber or plastics. Most of these special types are rather soft and much more prone to thread damage. They are rated at a far lower tensile strength than even their mild steel brethren. Special care must be taken when using them.

PIPE THREADS

Many temperature sending units and other sensors that screw into the cylinder head or engine block have a pipe thread size. Pipe threads are tapered so that the mating parts fit together much more tightly after the inner one is screwed in by only a few turns—not necessarily all the way. Some are designed to produce a pressure-tight joint, and others simply ensure a rigid mechanical connection.

You don't necessarily need to know the thread size of a sensor, but it's important for brass fittings like those that attach a carburetor's fuel line. Table 15-2 spells out the details.

SPECIAL THREADS AND SUBSTITUTIONS

When you need a cap screw with special threads,

Table 15-2. Pipe Thread Data.

Nominal Size (in.)	Pipe O.D. (inches)	Threads per inch
1/16	0.3125	27
1/8	0.405	27
1/4	0.540	18
3/8	0.675	18
1/2	0.840	14

Standard taper: 3/4 inch per foot.

to be installed in an already threaded hole in a major component, you have a problem. It happens with older cars. When the customary supply sources can't help, a machine shop is the only alternative.

A specialist is also the only possibility when you need a hardened thread of any kind, and can't find one ready-made. Armed with an appropriate tap or die, you can always create your own threads from a rod of steel stock, but you can't do the hardening yourself. The process uses highly toxic chemicals and demands the services of a specialist.

For a specially threaded nut and bolt, you can easily substitute a standard thread of the same diameter and length. Same thing with unusual head styles and other unique characteristics. As long as the new nut and bolt fit through the hole, and the bolt protrudes about as far as the original, the exact thread style probably doesn't matter.

One exception is any bolt and nut that attaches a crucial part. You hardly want to mount a leaf spring, for example, with anything less than original-quality hardware. Another exception arises when you are restoring an old car to authentic appearance. Hardware counts during show judging.

Believe it or not I've covered only the most significant facts about threaded fasteners. If you're really impressed by the subject, check out the handbooks for machinists at your public library. They contain dozens of charts, tables, drawings and diagrams that spell out the most minute details of thread sizes and angles, head widths and thicknesses. It's enough to satisfy the most avid threaded-trivia enthusiast.

How Tight is Tight?

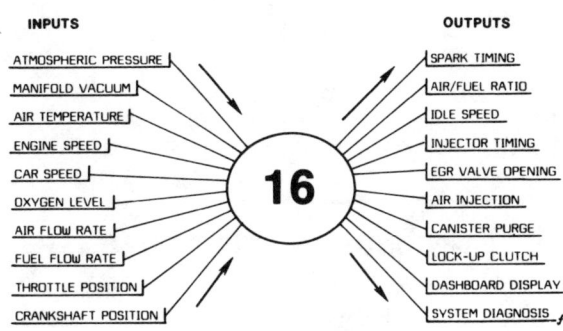

EVERY COMPONENT MOUNTED BY A THREADed fastener has a desired torque rating. Only the most important ones (Table 16-1) are given in spec tables of multimake manuals. Not even the factory manual carries a torque figure for every single part or piece of hardware on the car. That would total thousands of figures. Some components should always be tightened to the recommended tension and many others deserve similar attention by the thoughtful mechanic.

Torque is defined as the force required to produce a specified degree of stretching in a bolt. Yes, all bolts stretch as they're tightened down even though it's not visible. The bolt and nut take a "set" against each other. If they didn't, they wouldn't be able to hold much of anything, and certainly not a cylinder head or wheel hub.

Tightening with a torque wrench, rather than by guesswork, controls that stretching to the precise recommended level. Done properly the bolt will resume its original configuration when the tension is released—even after many years of "sitting tight." Overtightened past its elastic limit, though, the bolt stays in stretched position after it's loosened. Worse yet it's prone to breakage at any moment.

Undertightening is no better, of course. We hardly want to risk having a major component loosen or fall off as a result of ordinary vibration.

Naturally, we don't have to concern ourselves with the exact infinitesimal distance a bolt stretches as it's "torqued down." Engineers have made that calculation for us by expressing the amount of tension that's needed as a torque specification. What the torque wrench actually measures is a bolt-and-nut combination's resistance to turning—its "friction," you might say—in terms of the amount of force applied.

Torquing down bolts, nuts, and parts is a sometimes ignored art; but one that's vital to the longevity and continued efficiency of both engine and chassis components. Increased use of aluminum, which is softer than steel or iron, makes torque readings even more crucial.

159

Table 16-1. Typical Engine Tightening Specifications in Ft-Lbs.

Spark plugs	Cylinder head bolts	Conn. rod brg. caps	Main bearing cap bolts	Crankshaft pulley or vibration damper	Flywheel to crankshaft	Manifolds		Rocker cover bolts
						Intake	Exhaust	
22	65	45	75	60	60	30	30[4]	45[1]
10-15	65-72	19-24	60-70	70-90	75-85	23-25	18-24	3-5
20	60[2]	35	47	58	60	200[1]	150[1]	168[8]
25	130	42	80[3]	200-310	90[7]	40	25	7
22	65[5]	41	58[6]	181	65	18	18	50[1]
25	115	40	90	Press-fit	75	30	35	24[1]

[1]inch-pounds. [2]Plus 1/4 turn more. [3]Rear main, 120 ft-lbs. [4]End bolts, 20 ft-lbs. [5]Cold setting; 80 ft-lbs when hot. [6]Rear socket head cap screw, 47 ft-lbs. [7]With automatic transmission, 60 ft-lbs. [8]Camshaft bearing cap bolts (inch-lbs).

FOOT-POUNDS AND NEWTON-METERS

The foot-pound (ft-lb) is a torque unit denoting the application of 1 pound of force at a distance of 1 foot from a bolt or nut's center (the pivot point). You'll recall from Chapter 5 that the other measurement of torque, to indicate an engine's rotational force, is measured in pound-feet. In the one case, you measure what the engine is trying to do. Here it is what your muscle is accomplishing with torque wrench in hand. To distinguish between the two, tightening torque should be given in foot-pounds and engine torque in pound-feet. The rule is seldom followed.

Ten pounds of force applied with a 1-foot wrench would equal 10 foot-pounds. Ten pounds with a 2-foot wrench, 20 ft-lbs. Thirty pounds of force applied to a 6-inch wrench? That would be 15 ft-lbs. The longer the distance (wrench length), the less force is needed to produce a given amount of tension.

Parts tightened with a small amount of force may be measured in inch-pounds (in-lbs). One inch-pound is equal to 12 foot-pounds. There's even an inch-ounce measurement, but automotive parts rarely are fitted that loosely.

Metric torque figures are less common in the spec tables. When given, they're normally in Newton-meters (N·m); or in older tables, kilogram-meters (or meter-kilograms; these styles get to be a battle). Same idea but different units. A Newton-meter is the tension applied with a force of one Newton, to a lever (wrench) one meter long. One N·m equals 1.356 ft-lbs. A wrench reading 0-150 foot-pounds is equivalent to 0-203.4 Newton-meters.

TORQUE WRENCHES

Several torque wrench styles are available. The deflecting-beam wrench is the least expensive. A pointer moves along a calibrated scale to show the torque reading you've reached during your twisting. Its main disadvantage is that, when working in tight areas or poor light, you can't always see that pointer position clearly. And for proper accuracy, the scale must be viewed from directly above.

A rotary-dial torque wrench works in a similar way, but has a circular dial instead of the long moving pointer. These are somewhat easier to read.

The "clutch" micrometer-type wrench has a knurled sleeve on its handle. You use it to preset the desired torque against a calibrated scale. It releases tension as soon as you reach the recommended torque spec. The "click" style (Fig. 16-1) gives an audible signal when the preset value is reached. Both can be used without watching a scale.

Today's torque wrenches are calibrated in both foot-pounds and Newton-meters. Some have a scale in meter-kilograms as well. They come in several ranges, with either 1/4, 3/8 or 1/2 inch socket drive. Your best all-around choice is the 0-100 or 0-150 foot-pound version in 1/2 inch drive. If you expect to do much precision, low-torque work (on carburetors, for instance), a smaller wrench reading in inch-pounds is a necessity.

How accurate is a torque wrench? Most are guaranteed within 1 or 2 percent. They are that accurate only through the center portion of their ranges (80 percent at the most). A 0-150 foot-pound wrench offers excellent accuracy when measuring torque values from about 35 to 115 ft-lbs; adequate readings can be obtained for as far as 15 and 135 ft-lbs. It's far less precise outside those limits.

PARTS THAT MUST BE TORQUED

Certain parts must be tightened with a torque wrench every time. No exceptions. As a rule, these are the parts listed in every manual's torque spec table. They include:

☐ Cylinder-head mounting bolts (cap screws) or nuts (on studs): from under 50 to more than 150 ft-lbs.

☐ Main bearing cap bolts: typically between 50 and 100 ft-lbs.

☐ Connecting rod bearing cap bolts or nuts: normally under 50 ft-lbs.

☐ Crankshaft pulley or harmonic balancer (vibration damper) bolt: as little as 50, up to 300 ft-lbs or more (some are press-fit, not relying on bolt tension).

☐ Flywheel-to-crankshaft bolt: probably under 100 ft-lbs.

☐ Intake and exhaust manifolds: nearly always under 50 ft-lbs, sometimes under 15.

☐ Camshaft bearing caps (overhead-cam engines): comparatively low tension, sometimes shown in inch-pounds.

In addition to these, any part for which you have a torque spec deserves the torque treatment. It doesn't take that much longer than working with an ordinary wrench.

As always, pay close attention to table footnotes. A few specs might be in inch-pounds rather than foot-pounds. Some of the bearing caps might

Fig. 16-1. This easy-to-use torque wrench gives an audible "click" when the preset torque is reached. (Ammco Tools, Inc.)

demand a different torque reading than the others. Even cylinder heads sometimes require extra tightness on certain bolts. Depending on whether the head is hot (warmed up) or cold, they might have two specs.

PARTS THAT SHOULD BE TORQUED

Several parts have a torque spec in most service manuals, but in real life, they don't always get tightened down as you might like. Spark plugs is one example. Tension is important for proper sealing of the combustion chamber; overtightening can change the plug gap. Many a mechanic—including some who work on cars every day—rarely uses a torque wrench on plugs. Don't be one of them.

Wheel bearings, too, should always be tightened with a torque wrench. Carefully follow instructions. Often, the wrench is applied while the wheel spins slowly. It may have to be tightened, then loosened, and tightened again.

Multimake manuals don't carry specs for too many other parts. There might be one for rocker cover screws, water pump mounting bolts, rocker arm studs, and perhaps mounting hardware for one or two other components.

Factory manuals have dozens of additional torque specs for all the major mounting bolts and nuts that hold vital parts in place. Being realistic, most of them are ignored much of the time. When you are reassembling a precious vehicle, take the extra time to look up and use the torque specs because it pays off sooner or later in long engine life.

What can you do when you'd like to give a bolt the correct tension, but no spec is available? In general, the larger the bolt diameter, and the higher its tensile strength, the greater the torque value to which it should be tightened. There are exceptions to the rule. Only the manual knows for sure.

GUESSING AT TORQUE

When should you guess at torque? Not very often. It's true that, with practice, you could develop the knack of coming fairly close to desired torque readings by "feel." Still, estimating crucial torque values without that precision tool in your hand is risky no matter how long you've been around cars.

Obviously, it's never acceptable for bearing caps or cylinder heads. On the other hand, guesswork nearly always is essential for small screws and bolts. This is especially true when they're hard to get at with an ordinary wrench, much less the larger torque wrench.

The fact that ordinary box-end and open-end wrenches with larger openings are longer than those that fit smaller nut sizes does offer a rather primitive means of avoiding overtightening. Nevertheless, there's no substitute for the torque wrench used with a table of recommended readings.

As a rule of thumb, you can figure that giving a pretty firm push to a standard 3/8-inch drive socket wrench delivers torque somewhere in the 25 ft-lb neighborhood. You can produce similar tension with a regular 9/16-inch box-end wrench with a firm hand. The trouble is how firm is that? What's a good solid twist to one person is a gentle tug to another, and an energetic (even aggressive) shove to someone else.

RUST, DIRT, AND OIL

When looking up a torque spec, it's important to know whether the suggested readings are for a clean and dry thread or a lubricated one. Unfortunately, that information isn't always supplied. Therefore, you often have to make an educated guess.

Just bear in mind that a bolt lubricated with oil or grease might require only two-thirds of the force needed for a similar, but dry bolt to reach the same degree of stretching. When lubricated with graphite and petroleum mixtures, it could need even less.

One thing you can be sure of is that no torque spec is intended for use on a dirty, rusty thread. Clean them up thoroughly or your readings will be far off the mark.

Once in a great while, it's actually permissible—even desirable—to tighten a nut and bolt to less than its recommended torque value. This is true when the parts are not as strong as they were originally, but it's a very tough decision. Inexperienced torque-wrench wielders should stick to the book figures.

TORQUE TRICKS

All fasteners should be tightened with a regular wrench first, up to the final turn or two. Then use the torque wrench to complete the tightening process, doing it in steps: first about 25 percent of the final value, then 50 and 75 percent, and finally the stated reading. Brand-new fasteners should be torqued down once, then loosened, and re-torqued. Don't do it with new cylinder-head cap screws, for example, where a gasket is being compressed at the same time. It's generally a good idea to retighten any bolt after a brief period of use; they all tend to relax a bit after they're tightened down.

Whenever several fasteners are used to attach a component, they should be tightened in sequence a little at a time. With cylinder heads, a specific sequence must be followed exactly to avoid warping the head. It's equally important for water pumps, thermostat housings, fuel pumps—every part with more than one mounting bolt. Where more than three bolts are used, tighten them in a criss-cross pattern (not clockwise or counterclockwise). With two bolts, tighten one part way, then the other, then the first a little more, and so on. Do this properly every time and you'll never crack a casting.

Because torque recommendations are normally given for nuts, the reading should be increased slightly if you're tightening from the bolt end. If a range is given (say 40-45 ft-lbs), use the higher value in such cases. Fine threads will accept tighter torquing than their coarse equivalents, but that's been taken into account to compute the values shown. Plated bolts take less tightening force than unplated to produce the same tension; the plating has an effect similar to lubrication.

Unfortunately, there's no sure way to check whether a nut or bolt is torqued adequately after the job has been done or after it's been mounted for a while. If in doubt, all you can do is loosen it a half or full turn, and then re-torque. As a rule of thumb, about 10 percent more torque is needed to loosen a nut than to tighten it, but you can't rely on that figure. This is especially true if the threads are even the slightest bit dirty or rusty.

Overtightening not only stretches a bolt or stud excessively and makes it more likely to break in use, it makes them extremely difficult to loosen without snapping in half. It's not uncommon to find wheel lug nuts, in particular, that feel as though they must have been tightened by the neighborhood muscleman, using a super-long wrench. The culprit, though, probably was a minimally muscled garageman wielding an overpowered air-impact wrench.

Those wheel lugs have a recommended torque too, incidentally. If you abide by it, you'll never need two large men standing on the end of a 6-foot breaker bar to loosen them (and probably snap one off in the process).

The thousands of nuts and bolts that you find around the engine and chassis might not be very stimulating, but they're holding the car together. So it pays to wield that torque wrench wisely.

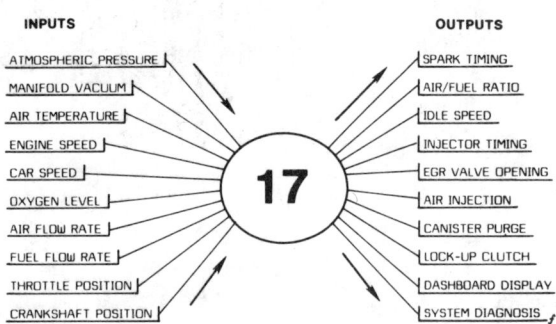

Fluid Capacities

EVERY VEHICLE IS FILLED WITH PRECIOUS fluids (Fig. 17-1). We have fuel in the tank, oil in the engine's crankcase, and coolant circulating through the radiator and block. There's hydraulic fluid in the brake system, transmission fluid or lubricant in the gearbox, and gear lube in the differential.

Some fluids have no specific capacity data, but are simply poured or injected into the vacant space until it's "full." For others, there's a definite maximum, as shown in Table 17-1. Most manuals give similar capacity data.

MOTOR OIL

No engine can go far without a plentiful supply of oil in its crankcase, circulating throughout the internal workings. Some small AMC motors hold only 3 quarts of oil. More typical capacities run between 4 and 6 quarts, and sometimes 7. Back in the 1930s, though, a few monster-sized V-12 and V-16 motors took in 11 or 12 quarts of oil with each change. A few engines of the Fifties also had oversize crankcases.

Most spec tables state that one extra quart (sometimes half a quart) should be added when a new oil filter is installed. Why? Because most filters hold nearly a quart that doesn't flow out during an oil change unless the filter is removed. Some earlier filters, though, are mounted so their oil content does flow out; the same amount of new oil is added whether a new filter goes on or not.

We all know about the dangers of running with too little oil. Too much is no better. The surplus can cause foam to develop that will impair overall lubrication. It's also important to guard against the possibility that a dipstick reads full when the crankcase really isn't. There could be too much condensation (moisture) inside, taking up space that belongs to motor oil, and giving a false dipstick reading.

For many years, motorists were advised to change oil every 1000 miles. In the early days, oil changes every *hundred* miles were often the rule, and oil had to be added even more often.

With improved lubricants and sealing, oil and filter change intervals lengthened to as much as

Table 17-1. Typical Fluid Capacities for the Engine and Chassis.

Engine/model	Engine crankcase (qts.)*	Transmission (pints)			Drive Axle (pts.)	Fuel tank (gals.)	Cooling system (quarts)	
		Manual		Automatic			With htr.	With A/C
		3-spd	4-spd					
350 diesel	7	---	---	6[1]	3.5	19.8	---	17.2
Escort 4	4	---	6.1	16.7	[2]	14	8.1	8.1
Cadillac	6	---	---	6[1]	4.25	27	23.7	23.7
Front WD	4	---	2.65	13.0	2.4	13	6.0	6.0
Gremlin	3.5	---	2.4	14.2	3	--	6.5	---
Barracuda	4	4.75	7.5	16.3	4.5	16	15	15
Ford V-8	5	3 1/4	3 1/2	20	4 1/2	20	19	---
Hudson	7	2	---	22	3 1/2	20	18 1/2[3]	---
V-16	11	2 1/2	---	---	6 1/2	26 1/2	30[3]	---

*Add 1 quart for new oil filter. [1]Not including torque converter. [2]Included in transaxle. [3]Without heater.

10,000 miles. Always this was with the proviso that for severe driving conditions more frequent changes were advisable. In the mid-1980s, some factories began advising a shorter interval, on the order of 3000 miles. It's now believed that the longer periods without a change may have been harmful to engines.

OIL VISCOSITY AND CLASSIFICATION

Spec tables say nothing about oil viscosity, but every owner's manual gives a recommendation. Viscosity is the resistance of a liquid to flow (its tendency to stay put, rather than spread out freely). Pouring in oil of the correct viscosity—and manufactured to the correct classification—is just

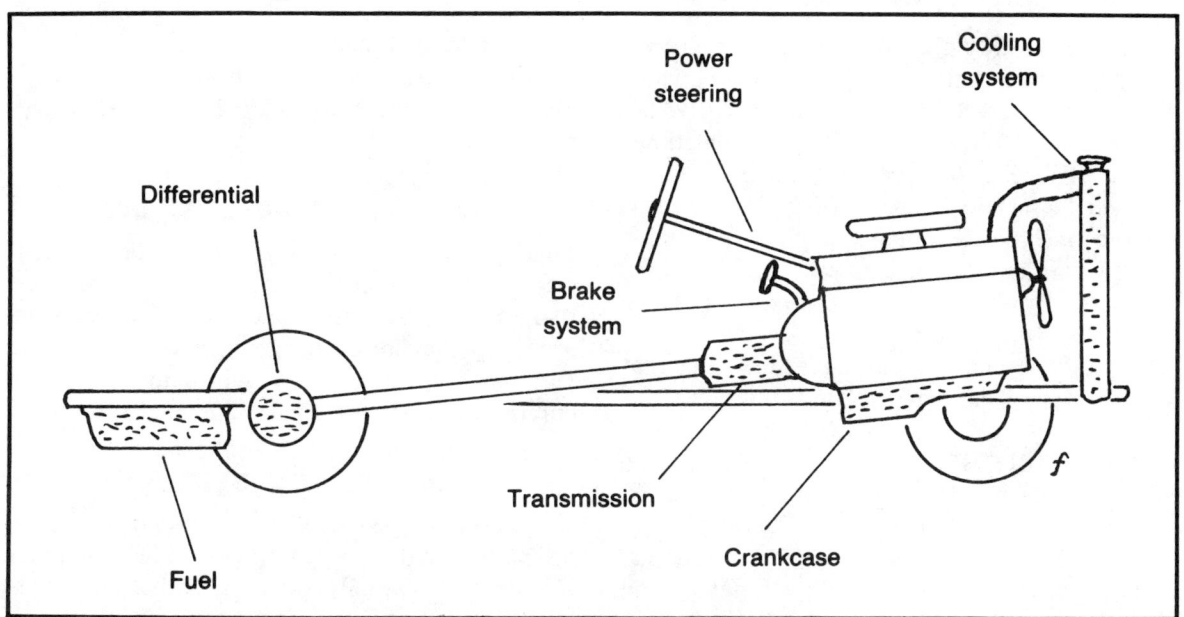

Fig. 17-1. Fluids are found in several receptacles in the engine and chassis.

as important as having enough in the crankcase.

Viscosity is an oil's "weight" as graded by SAE (formerly called the Society of Automotive Engineers). Single-weight oils have an index number between 5 and 50. Those with a low number flow most readily, and are "lighter" oils.

Most common for automobiles are numbers 10, 20, and 30. SAE 10W is the lightest, suitable for cold-weather driving, and SAE 30 is heavier, better for summer use. SAE 20W is a compromise between the two. SAE 40 is also available for use in very hot temperatures and occasionally in old engines that burn a lot of oil. It's very thick in order to fill up those overgrown bearing clearances (or so the clunker owner hopes).

Logically enough a lighter oil flows better through a cold engine, making starting easier. All oils become thicker—more resistant to flow—when cold and thinner when hot. When oil is too thick, it doesn't spread thoroughly and rapidly enough. When oil is too thin, its friction-cutting quality may be inadequate.

Multiviscosity oils were developed, in the 1940s, to give the best of both worlds: easy flow in a cold engine, but not becoming dangerously thin when hot. All cars made since 1968 should use them.

These multiweight oils have two (or three) viscosity numbers, giving the total range for which the oil can be used. Most common are 10W-30, 10W-40, and 20W-50. A 10W-40 oil (sometimes graded 10W-20W-40) is created to act like number 10 when it's cold (for winter starting), but performs like the much thicker number 40 when the engine is fully warmed up. For unusually cold climates, multiviscosity oils with a 5 as the first figure (such as 5W-20) are available.

The "W" following any figure indicates that its viscosity was measured at 23°F or less: 14° for 20W, −4° for 10W, −13° for 5W. All other tests are made at 212°F (100°C). 10W-40 meets the SAE 10W test at −4°, plus the SAE 40 at 212°F.

All oils also get an American Petroleum Institute (API) classification. The old API designations began with the letter "M": ML denoted oil for light service; MM, medium; and MS, severe. Today's categories begin with an "S" for standard gasoline (spark ignition) engines in passenger cars or a "C" (compression ignition, or commercial) for diesels. The gas-engine classifications are:

SF: recommended for vehicles made in 1980 or later.

SE: for 1972-79 cars and light trucks.

SD: for 1968-70 vehicles (some from 1971-up).

SC: for vehicles made between 1964-67.

SB: for engines operating under mild conditions.

SA: for very light operation (contains no additives).

Classification SF is intended for all recent autos. No other type should ordinarily be used. Those lower grades conform to the specifications that were current during the stated period, but SF rarely does any harm to earlier models and often lubricates better. Some owners of antique vehicles (older than the 1950s) do prefer to use lower-grade oils with few, or no, additives. Other old-timers are running around in good health, with the latest multiweight, detergent-type oils circulating in their motors.

Synthetic oils are manufactured to the same SAE and API classifications. Their advantage? A high viscosity index so they don't thin out as fast as the petroleum oils.

Diesel classifications go from CA to CD. All 1980 and newer diesels can use the best (CD) heavy-duty oil.

GASOLINE AND DIESEL FUEL

Fuel tank capacities are given in gallons. They range from less than 10, in some tiny cars, to more than 25 in the full-size models. Large tanks were especially common back in the days of the guzzlers. Dashboard gas gauges used to be notoriously inaccurate, but modern ones are far more precise.

THE COOLING SYSTEM

Cooling system capacity, as given in spec tables, normally includes the space in the radiator, engine block, hoses, and all related parts that hold coolant. In short, total capacity. A separate figure, in quarts, is usually given for cars "with heater" or "with air conditioning." There may also be a separate column for cars with heavy-duty (large capacity) cooling systems.

Some tiny engines hold as little as 6 quarts of coolant in their entire systems. Big V-8s may have a total capacity of more than 20 quarts (5 gallons). An old Packard V-12 held a massive 40 quarts, and the flathead Lincoln V-8 of 1949-51 vintage held nearly 35 quarts. That's a lot of antifreeze to pour in for a winter season.

As anyone trying to add antifreeze to an engine without draining the block probably has discovered, the radiator often holds less than half the total. A few spec tables spell out the capacity of radiator and block separately, but most do not.

DRIVELINE AND CHASSIS FLUIDS

Automatic transmissions use fluid of a specified type. GM and most other automatics require Dexron II. Older Ford products take type F, while newer Fords with heavy-duty transmissions take type CJ (similar to Dexron).

Early automatics came with recommendations for Type A, Suffix A fluid. Surprise! It hasn't been made for years. Motorists owning early models have shifted to either of the two standard types, depending on the transmission. If in doubt, it is best to consult a specialist on your make. Chrysler's old semiautomatic transmissions, incidentally, used ordinary gear oil.

Capacities are listed in pints. Most automatics hold a total of between 12 and 20 pints while some hold as much as 25. A few specs, though, show a much smaller figure. Chances are that's the capacity of the transmission itself—not including the torque converter—that may be drained separately. Front-wheel-drive vehicles have a combined figure for their transaxle rather than separate transmission and drive-axle capacities.

Manual transmissions today generally use SAE 80W-90 gear oil that is similar in "weight" to No. 40 motor oil. Some require SAE 140. Cars of 1930s vintage and older might need No. 600 or some other grade.

Gearbox capacities in the spec tables are normally shown in pints. Some older specs are given in pounds. Capacity could be as little as 1 or 2 pints of lubricant or more than 7 pints for a 4-speed or 5-speed transmission.

Measuring fluids isn't often necessary for either automatic or manual transmissions. Lubricant or fluid is simply added when the automatic-transmission dipstick shows "low" or you feel nothing when inserting a finger through the manual's filler hole.

Another column in the table shows the capacity of the drive axle (differential), typically 3 to 5 pints. An old Willys holds only 1 pint. Some big differentials hold nearly 7. Many take regular SAE 80W-90 gear oil. Be careful to use the correct type for limited-slip differentials.

Most other fluids are simply added to reach the "full" mark on a dipstick or reservoir. This includes brake fluid and power steering fluid. No spec is ordinarily given, but if you're really interested total capacity might be found somewhere in a factory manual.

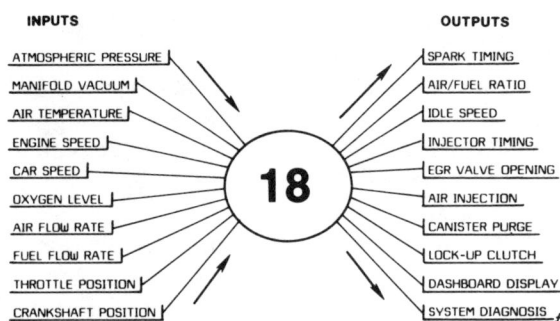

Driveline Data

NEARLY ALL THE VALUES AND MEASUREments discussed so far relate to the motor. Once the engine has produced its quota of horsepower and torque at the flywheel, its output passes through a couple of geared devices before getting down to the road to produce some real work. Power is transmitted first into the transmission, and then through the driveline, reaching the drive wheels by way of a differential.

Each of these components has a few ratios, dimensions, or other measurements of interest. Most of them don't come up all that often in service work. Nevertheless, the engine/transmission/drive-axle combination plays a major role in determining the car's acceleration and fuel economy, as well as driving ease.

TOTAL GEAR REDUCTION

Engines run at fairly high rotational speeds. Cruising down the highway, a typical motor turns at roughly 3000 rpm (give or take a few hundred). The car wheels aren't rotating anywhere near that fast. At the legal speed limit, they might be rolling at well under a thousand rpm.

Total gear reduction is the amount of speed change that takes place between the engine's flywheel and the car wheels (Fig. 18-1). Part of the reduction occurs in the transmission, and the rest in the differential. Each has a set of gear ratios that contribute to the total.

Example. An engine running at 2000 rpm, with transmission in high gear (1:1 ratio—no reduction), and a 4:1 axle ratio. The drive axle turns at 500 rpm (2000 divided by 4). Drop the transmission into second gear, with a 2:1 ratio, and driveline speeds are cut in half (1000 rpm at the transmission output shaft, 250 at car wheels), while the engine turns at the same speed as before.

Why is gearing needed? To produce the best possible torque output at the drive wheels. Unless the overall gear ratio closely matches the engine's torque/horsepower curve, performance will suffer. Gearing can deliver a torque boost, when the car needs it, while accelerating or climbing a hill. But it does so at a cost of speed. Torque can increase only if speed goes down. This principle of torque

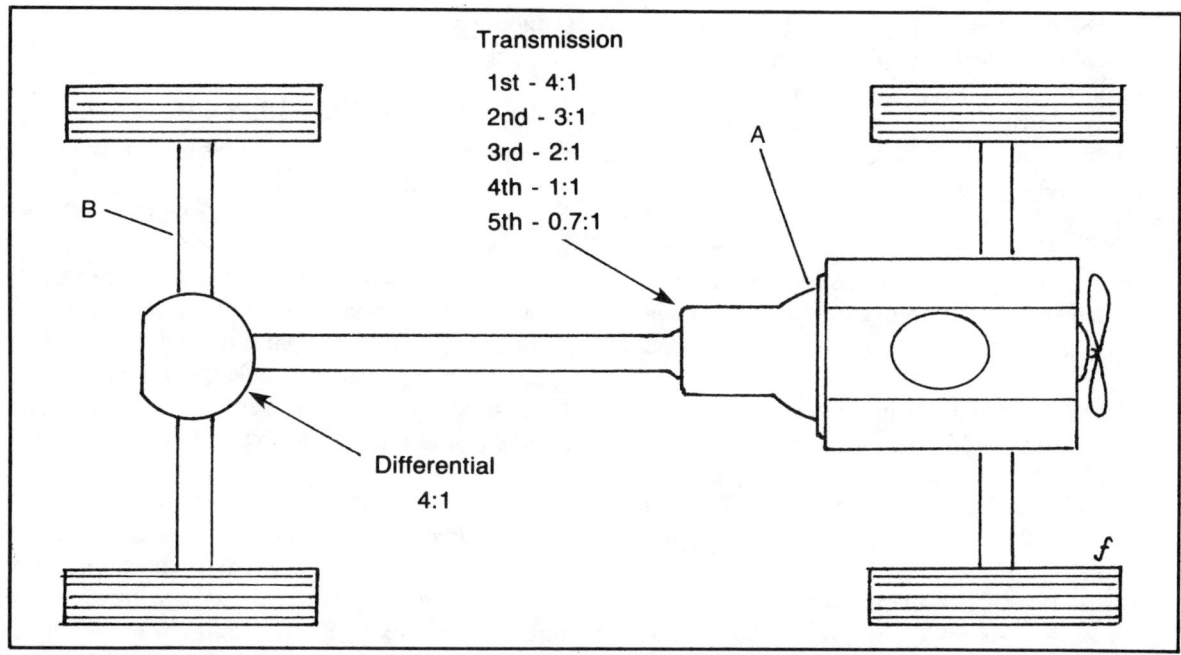

Fig. 18-1. Total gear reduction refers to speed change between the engine's flywheel (A) and drive axle (B). Reduction occurs in transmission and differential gears. In the example shown, total reduction in 2nd gear would be 12:1 (3 × 4); in 5th gear (overdrive), 2.8:1 (0.7 × 4).

multiplication is crucial in setting a car's performance limits, and its need for frequent downshifting.

CALCULATING A GEAR RATIO

Back in Chapter 1, it is noted that a ratio is a comparison between two units, expressed with the smaller unit as "one." If A is three times the size (or weight, or whatever) of B, the ratio of A to B is 3-to-1 or 3:1.

Same thing with gear ratios; they are determined by the number of teeth in each mating gear. Any driveline gear ratio is a numerical expression comparing the relative rotational speed of an output shaft to the speed of the input shaft. It shows the relationship between the driven gear's speed and that of the driving gear.

Example. If a ring gear has 38 teeth and the driving pinion 10 teeth, the gear ratio is 38/10 or 3.8:1. (Divide both parts of the fraction by the bottom number.)

Whenever the driven (output) gear is larger than the input gear, output speed is reduced, but torque potential climbs. That's torque multiplication. A large gear driving a smaller one does the opposite: less torque, more speed.

FINAL DRIVE: HIGH OR LOW RATIOS

In the differential, that ratio between the ring and pinion gear is called the *final drive ratio*. It used to be called "rear axle ratio," but the rising popularity of front-wheel drive cars with transaxles (differential integral with the transmission) demands a more general term.

Final drive, then, is the ratio between the driveshaft speed (coming out of the transmission) and the drive-wheel speed, both in rpm. In automobiles, final drive ratios vary between about 2 1/2:1 and 4 1/2:1. That means the driveshaft might be turning anywhere from 2 1/2 times the wheel speed to more than four times that speed.

There's always been some confusion between "high" and "low" drive ratios. The numerically largest ratio is actually considered "low" geared, giving the most reduction (slowest output). The numerically smallest ("high" gearing) delivers the least speed reduction. A 4.11:1 drive ratio is considerably "lower" than a 3.07:1 ratio.

In theory, at least, a "high" (numerically small) final drive ratio produces higher top speed and gas mileage, with less engine wear—but poorer acceleration. How come? Because the engine turns slower to deliver a given road speed. Conversely, "low" drive ratios deliver fine acceleration and hill-climbing ability, but at some cost in speed and economy.

The difference is not proportionate, however. Changing from a 4.27 to 3.85:1 rear axle ratio (10 percent "higher") might give only a tiny improvement in top speed (perhaps 1 or 2 mph). You could lose the full 10 percent in acceleration and pulling strength.

Circa 1949 Chevrolets, for example, were known for low gearing. Their rear axle ratio was 4.11:1. Some ratios of that era were lower yet. Sports cars and performance cars may be geared low for best acceleration. Pickup trucks are geared so that they can carry their loads and still manage to get away from stoplights. Today's minipickups have ratios of 4.5:1 or more. The general trend in recent years has been to keep drive ratios high, for economy's sake (Fig. 18-2).

WHAT SIZE IS THE REAR END?

No, that's not an indelicate question. In the days before front-wheel drive grew so common, final drive ratio was often called "rear end ratio." The differential/axle assembly was the "rear end." Ratios still are spoken of as a "four-eleven rear."

Either the actual ratio of the ring and pinion gears, or a code number that can be translated using a chart in the manual, is found somewhere on most differential or transaxle housings. It might be stamped right on the housing or on a tag attached to one of the bolts.

Years ago, many car makes came off the assembly line with only one possible rear-end ratio. As the performance era blossomed, choices became the rule. One ratio might be used with the standard engine, another with high-power versions, others for automatic transmissions or overdrive, and so on.

Computing the actual ratio isn't difficult. Just jack one or both drive wheels off the ground (up on safety stands), and put the transmission in neutral. With chalk, place mating reference marks on the drive shaft and on the axle housing. Chalk

Fig. 18-2. Even this minivan represents the modern trend in gearing. The front-wheel-drive transaxle has a "high" final drive ratio (2.56:1), plus two overdrive ratios in its five-speed manual transmission. (Chrysler Corp.)

another pair of marks on both tires and their fenderwells.

Then, while someone is under the car watching the drive shaft, rotate a wheel by hand through one full revolution. The number of times the drive shaft rotates equals the rear end ratio. If it turns about 3 1/2 times, the ratio is close to 3.5:1. Looking at the published figures, you can see which ratio offered for this car model comes close to your estimate—maybe 3.47:1 or 3.56:1.

MANUAL TRANSMISSION GEARING

Well, final drive is only part of the story. The other part of the overall reduction comes within the transmission. Why do you need several gears in every transmission? It's all a matter of torque again. Whenever you want to accelerate the car, or its load increases in any way, you need more torque than is presently available. But remember how we boost torque? By cutting speed, that's right. Use a set of gears to reduce the speed, and we can raise up that torque output as high as we want—well, to a point, at least.

Moreover, having several gears lets the engine keep turning at a speed sufficient to produce its highest level of torque. If rpm is permitted to fall too much, response and performance dwindle.

That's the purpose of recommended shift points. By changing from one gear to the next at the optimum time—the ideal engine speed, that is—the engine is allowed to keep producing torque at its peak level. Close to it, anyway. (Remember those torque/hp curves back in Chapter 5?) Shifting too soon, the engine has not yet reached its maximum torque output. Shift too late and you've passed the peak point, and you will not be taking full advantage of the engine's potential.

Close ratio gears make it easier to shift at the best possible moments. Each gear is fairly close in numerical ratio to the next one in sequence. First gear might have a ratio of 2.5:1, second gear 1.8:1, third 1.3:1. Therefore, little speed is lost during each shift (perhaps only 600 rpm or so). Close ratio gearing is most often found in sports and high-performance cars. Transmissions in conventional autos may have gears spaced so a drop of three times as much occurs during some shifts. Pickup trucks have ratios even more widely spaced.

The *number* of gears needed in the transmission also depends upon torque requirements. Low-torque engines require more gear ratios to keep pace with changing needs. High-powered motors can get by with fewer. The move toward smaller engines brought with it the 5-speed transmission.

As shown in Table 18-1, total gear reduction varies considerably. First off, the final drive ratio differs from one kind of vehicle to another. So do the number of gears in the transmission, and their ratios. First gear in some cars offers a gear reduction of 4:1 or more; in others, it is well under 3:1. Second gear delivers less reduction, third gear less yet, and so forth.

During the 3-speed years, high (third) gear was direct drive (no reduction at all, a flat 1:1 gearing). In 4-speeds, fourth was direct. Reverse is usually "lower" than first gear. Remember, overall reduction depends on the combination of transmission gear and final-drive gear.

Overdrive transmissions go beyond a 1:1 ratio. They produce faster output than that which comes in through the engine flywheel. Overdrive was introduced on the 1934 Chrysler, but after fading in popularity during the guzzler era, it's back in full swing again. In fact, some 5-speed transmissions have third as their direct (1:1 ratio) gear; both fourth and fifth act as overdrives.

THE AUTOMATIC TRANSMISSION

Shifting was a battle in the early days of automobiling. Gears were unsynchronized. Transmissions were nicknamed "crash boxes" for good reason. Getting the gears to mesh without horrid grinding demanded an expert touch on accelerator and clutch. Double clutching was essential. To downshift, drivers had to speed up the engine while the clutch was momentarily engaged so that the about-to-mate gears would be rotating at the same speed. Not easy at all. Nevertheless, many motorists became quite adept at gear changing.

Attempts at a workable automatic transmission came early. The 1904 Sturtevant had one, but the first memorable version didn't arrive until 1933

Table 18-1. Selected Examples of Transmission and Final Drive Gear Ratios.

Year/Model (Transmission)	Transmission Ratios					
	Final drive	1st	2nd	3rd	4th	5th
1985 Camaro IROC Z28						
Automatic:	3.42:1	3.06	1.63	1.00	0.70	- - - -
Manual:	3.73:1	2.95	1.94	1.34	1.00	0.63
1985 Corvette (MT)	3.07:1	2.88	1.91	1.33	1.00	- - - -
(overdrive ratios)			(1.28)	(0.89)	(0.67)	
1985 VW Golf (MT)	3.67:1	3.45	1.94	1.37	1.03	0.75
1985 Saab Turbo 900	3.67:1	4.53	2.56	1.72	1.24	1.00
1984 Plymouth Voyager						
Automatic:	3.22:1	2.69	1.55	1.00	- - - -	- - - -
Manual:	2.56:1	3.29	1.89	1.21	0.88	0.72
1984 Isuzu Trooper*						
High range:	4.56:1	3.79	2.17	1.41	1.00	- - - -
Low range:	4.56:1	7.08	4.05	2.64	1.87	- - - -
1984 Honda Civic	4.27:1	3.18	1.82	1.18	0.85	0.71
1984 Buick Electra T	2.84:1	2.92	1.57	1.00	0.70	- - - -
1984 Continental	3.27:1	2.40	1.47	1.00	0.67	- - - -
1961 Tempest (AT)	3.55:1	1.82	1.00	- - - -	- - - -	- - - -
1958 Edsel (AT)	2.91:1	2.37	1.48	1.00	- - - -	- - - -
1940 Cadillac (MT)	3.92:1	2.39	1.53	1.00	- - - -	- - - -
1937 Chevrolet (MT)	4.22:1	2.94	1.68	1.00	- - - -	- - - -

*Transfer case gives eight forward speeds.

(Reo's Self-Shifter). Oldsmobile offered an optional semiautomatic on its 1937 model. It was the forerunner of the GM Hydra-Matic, introduced on the 1939 Olds.

Hydra-Matic and its successors changed the face of motoring, making driving far easier—indeed possible—for millions who never quite got the hang of gearshifting. The synchromesh transmission, which first appeared on the 1928 Cadillac, had made manual shifting a lot easier (and quieter). Improved clutches helped. The automatic, though, eliminated that irksome clutch completely.

After World War II, the true torque converter arrived. Buick's Dynaflow and Chevrolet's Powerglide carried the car forward from a standing start with no gearshifting at all, automatic or manual. Other automatics combined the torque converter with various automatic gear-change mechanisms, operating on hydraulic/pneumatic principles. That's the automatic transmission as we know it today. Your car might have a transaxle, but those same principles make it perform.

EFFECT OF TIRE DIAMETER

Actual road speed depends not only on engine rpm, transmission gearing, and final drive ratio, it also varies with the size of the tires.

Going back to the example that led off this chapter, we had an engine turning at 2000 rpm, transmission in direct drive, and rear axle (and attached wheels) rotating at 500 rpm. How fast is the car moving?

If the tires are 24 inches in diameter, their circumference (distance around) is 75.4 inches: pi times 24. That's how far the car rolls with each axle revolution. Multiplying out, the car is moving at 37,700 inches per minute (500 × 75.4). That comes to 3142 feet per minute (37,700 ÷ 12). Finishing up, we get 35.7 miles per hour: 3142 times 60, divided by 5280.

This computation can be simplified to a matching pair of formulas, illustrating the relationship between engine and road speed, in terms of total gear reduction and tire size:

$$\text{mph} = \frac{\text{tire diameter (in.)} \times \text{engine rpm} \times 0.002975}{\text{total gear ratio}}$$

$$\text{rpm} = \frac{\text{mph} \times \text{total gear ratio}}{\text{tire dia.} \times 0.002975}$$

Whenever you see a constant like the 0.002975 in the above formulas, it's probably derived by multiplying and dividing several common figures. In this case, it's pi (3.14) times 60 (minutes in an hour), divided by 12 (inches in a foot) times 5280 (feet in a mile). Nothing to it, right?

Increase the tire diameter and the car moves faster for a given engine speed. Logical enough. But you also have greater rolling resistance; therefore the engine might need more fuel to reach that same speed or you might not get there at all.

GEARING DOWN FOR PERFORMANCE OR ECONOMY

No combination of engine size, transmission gear ratios, final drive ratio and tire size is "right" for every car, or even for one car model. Certainly not for every condition. The selection is nearly always a compromise.

High final drive ratios give better economy and engine life. While one driver is willing to accept the reduced acceleration that goes with it, another might be disappointed. A low final drive offers improved performance, but also requires more shifting of gears.

When considering the options during purchase of a new car, think about what's lost, as well as any gain, if you select a nonstandard transmission or drive axle. Same thing when deliberating about installing a different rear end or better-geared transmission. If your driving is nonstandard, you may well need something special, but most of us are better off with the compromise combination.

CLUTCH SPECIFICATIONS

Not all collections of spec tables contain clutch data of any kind. If you're into drag racing, however, clutch disc diameter and spring pressure become more relevant than for the everyday motorist.

In brief, the larger the clutch the better its "grabbing" power. Why? Simply because it has more surface area of contact between the disc and pressure plate. As a rule, clutch size is fixed (changeable only by major surgery).

Street rodders more commonly install heavy-duty clutches that may be the same *size* as original, but contain heavier springs. Again better grabbing. Most of the time, spring pressure of about 12 pounds is considered the maximum.

The force needed to depress the clutch pedal depends upon spring pressure and pedal travel. The farther the pedal moves the greater the pressure that can be applied with a given amount of force. A clutch pedal may travel 3 inches, but move the clutch mechanism only one-tenth that far. That's mechanical leverage of 10:1. If it didn't exist, no one would be able to release that clutch without power assist.

DRIVELINE ADJUSTMENTS

Only one adjustment is needed regularly during driveline servicing: clutch free play. This isn't usually mentioned in a spec table. Other specifications, like those in Table 18-2, come up only during disassembly of a drive axle.

Clutch Free Play

Total clutch travel isn't adjustable, but the amount of "play" in the clutch pedal is crucial to disc life and smooth engagement. This free travel is the distance the clutch pedal moves before disengaging the clutch (before the throwout bearing actually touches the clutch release fingers, separating the pressure plate from the disc).

You want as much clearance as possible inside the clutch—between throwout bearing and release lever—but not an excess of pedal play. If play is too great, shifting might be difficult because the clutch doesn't disengage fully. (With pedal all the way down, the clutch facings still touch slightly.) Too little free play often causes the clutch to slip while never engaging with full force.

How much is right? Usually between 1/2 and

Table 18-2. Typical Drive Axle Specifications.

Ring Gear and Pinion Backlash		Pinion bearing preload (in-lbs)			Differential bearing preload (in-lbs)		
Method	Adjustment	Method	New brgs.	Used brgs.	Method	New brgs.	Used brgs.
Adjust[1]	.006-.008	Spacer[2]	20-35	10-25	- - -	[3]	- - -
- - -	.008-.015	- - -	16-29	8-14	- - -	.016[4]	- - -
Shims	.005-.007	Spacer	22	5	Shims	Slipfit +	.004
Shims	.005-.010	Shims	20-40	15-25	Shims	.015[4]	.015[4]
Shims	.005-.008	Spacer	20-25	10-15	Shims	35-40	20-25
Shims	.006-.008	Spacer	10-25	8-12	Shims	35-40	20-25

[1]Threaded adjustors. [2]Collapsible. [3]Correct when ring/pinion backlash is properly adjusted. [4]Case spread across differential.

1 inch. An adjustor mechanism is usually found in the linkage between pedal and clutch housing.

When shifting is a problem, you might also search for specs that apply to the (manual) transmission linkage. These will either be clearances between specified points or distances a shift rod should travel as the gear selector moves.

Differential Backlash and Preload

Backlash is the amount of "play" between gears. Any mating gears. It's the distance one gear can rotate back and forth without moving the gear it meshes with. In other words, the clearance between two meshing teeth, which would allow the driven gear to rotate backward—opposite to its normal direction.

Differential backlash values are given in thousandths of an inch (usually under .015). Most are adjusted by changing to a different shim thickness, and some are adjusted by threaded adjustors. Unless ring/pinion gear backlash is within limits, you're likely to wind up with gear whine or worse.

Two preload figures are typically given: one for the pinion bearing and another for the differential (side) bearing. Preload means adjusting a bearing for zero clearance, and then tightening a trifle further. This puts the bearing under slight initial pressure, preventing looseness from developing as the unit is set into motion. Thus, the parts remain in their desirable positions—without shifting.

Some preload specs are given in thousandths of an inch. Most are given in inch-pounds of torque: the amount of pressure applied to the torque wrench that causes the drive pinion (or other specified part) to begin to rotate. There may be different figures for new and used bearings.

Pinion bearing preload is normally set using a collapsible spacer, and sometimes by changing ordinary shims. Side carrier preload may be adjusted by nuts or shims. Preload is sometimes assumed to be within spec whenever ring/pinion backlash is correctly adjusted.

FORGOTTEN SPECS

There's virtually no end to specs that can be found somewhere, should the need appear. *Pinion nose angle* is an example. This rather obscure measurement shows how much the engine/transmission assembly tilts downward at the rear compared to the upward tilt of the differential. It makes quite a difference to smooth driveshaft operation.

Transmissions have their own set of specs: gear backlash and the like. Should your transmission have to come apart such figures become crucial. For steering gears it's the same thing.

We'll leave the driveline at this point, secure in the knowledge that—if we understand the more common measurements—others are merely variations on the very same theme.

Chassis and Body Measurements

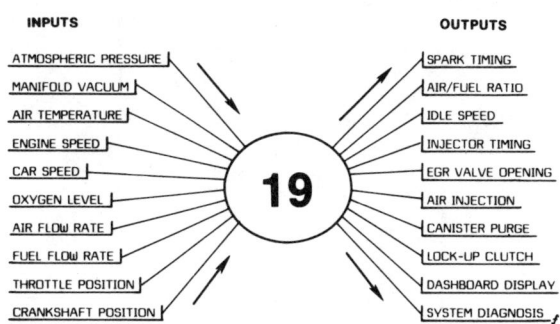

AUTOMOBILES STARTED OUT SMALL. THEY soon grew in every dimension, and some became gigantic. Not until the recent down-sizing did the average car shrink back to small again.

From the Teens through the Sixties, bigger was better, and biggest was better yet. The big car was popular for large families, for politicians, for gangsters, for corporate titans, and for anyone who wanted to impress the neighbors. Standing next to one of yesteryear's dinosaurs, today's Cadillacs and Continentals are downright tiny.

After a few false starts that included the early Fifties Rambler, the Henry J, and Hudson's Jet, the compact age began to bloom in the 1959-60 model years. Subcompacts took another decade to hit their stride. Miniature imports had arrived at American shores in rising numbers through two decades, but went largely unnoticed until the looming gas shortages of the early 1970s. Who wanted a small car when gas was inexpensive, engines were enormous, and status depended upon the size of one's transportation?

To be honest, most motorists don't need to know very much about auto size. Neither do mechanics. Even car enthusiasts aren't always so conversant with chassis data as they are about horsepower, cubic inches, and similarly inspiring mechanical facts.

Table 19-1 compares some important chassis/body sizes for cars of varied vintage. Similar tables don't appear in the general information sections of all service manuals. More often these specs turn up in tables, describing the newly introduced car models, in popular automotive magazines.

VEHICLE SIZE: WHEELBASE TO TRIM HEIGHT

Wheelbase is the distance between the front and axles—the most often cited chassis dimension (Fig. 19-1). Measurement was a bit more obvious when cars had actual axles at both front and rear. Even with independent suspensions and front-wheel drive, though, wheelbase is measured the same way: from the center of a front wheel to the center of the rear, on the same side of the car.

A handful of cars, like the Renault 5, are asym-

Table 19-1. Selected Examples of Auto Body Dimensions.

Year	Car model	Wheelbase	Dimensions (inches) Overall			Track		Weight (lbs)
			Length	Width	Height	F	R	
1949	Willys	104	175	69	72	55 1/2	57	2845
	Chevrolet	115	197	74	66	57	58-3/4	3075
	Mercury	118	206.8	76.9	64.8	58 1/2	60	3430
	Buick 70	126	214	78 1/2	66	59	62	4205
1959	American	100	178.3	73	57.3	54.6	55	2476
	Belvedere	118	208.2	78	56	60.9	59.7	3405
	Hawk	120 1/2	204	71.3	57.4	57.3	56.3	2810
	300F	126	220.9	79.5	56.5	61.2	60	4290
	Cad limo	149.8	244.8	80.2	59.3	61	61	5570
1970	VW 1300	94 1/2	158.6	61.0	59.1	51.4	51.2	1742
	AMX	97	179	71.6	51.4	59.7	57.0	3126
	Barracuda	108	186.7	74.9	54.8	59.7	61.3	2985
	Fairlane	117	206.2	76.4	53.1	60.5	60	3216
	Continental	127	225	79.6	55.7	64.3	64.3	4663
1984	Honda CRX	86.6	144.6	63.9	50.8	55.1	55.7	1713
	Mustang	100.4	179.1	69.1	51.9	56.6	57.0	2664
	Thunderbird	104	197.6	71.1	53.2	58.1	58.5	3037
	Voyager	112	175.9	69.6	64.2	59.9	62.1	2911
	Gran Fury	112.7	205.7	74.2	55.3	60.0	59.5	3585
	Rolls Royce	124.5	211.8	74.3	58.5	60.6	60.6	5040

metrical: longer on one side than the other. Otherwise published wheelbase is a single figure. Like all the figures in this section, it's measured in inches or millimeters (or both).

Overall *vehicle length* is self-explanatory. It's the biggest bumper-to-bumper dimension you come up with, from the tip of a protruding front bumper guard to the farthest reach at the rear. *Overhang* is the distance between the rear (or front) axle and the tip of the car.

Wheelbases have ranged from well under 100 inches to at least 150. Crosleys around 1950 measured in at only 80 inches (extending just 145 inches overall). A Cadillac 75 limousine in the late '50s had a wheelbase of nearly 150 inches, and stood a massive 245 inches long (over 20 feet!). Some monsters of the prewar era were even longer.

By the mid-1980s, "big" cars weren't so big at all. An Oldsmobile 98, for instance, measured only 196 inches from stem to stern in 1985. That was 2 feet shorter than the previous year. In fact, it was a full inch shorter than the supposedly compact Chevrolet Nova produced 10 years earlier.

Track (tread) is the distance between the centers of tires at the same end of the car: left front to right front or rear to rear. It could differ between front and rear so separate figures are given. The term became most familiar when used by Pontiac to promote its "wide-track" models in the early '60s. They were indeed wider than before and a bit more stable because of it.

Overall width is the widest dimension of the body. It is the size of the narrowest passageway the car could squeeze through. You might also find a spec for width with the car doors open.

Trim height (riding height) is the distance between the ground and some specified point on the car. Often the point is a body panel to the rear of the rear wheel. Unlike most other dimensions, this one is measured during servicing. It affects wheel alignment and handling. Cars with torsion bar suspension have height adjustment (as described in Chapter 20).

Vehicle height is the overall measurement with the car unloaded. Cars used to be tall as well as long. A 1950s model is easy to spot in today's parking lots. A prewar car might stand out a mile away. Nowadays, low, short and lean is the rule.

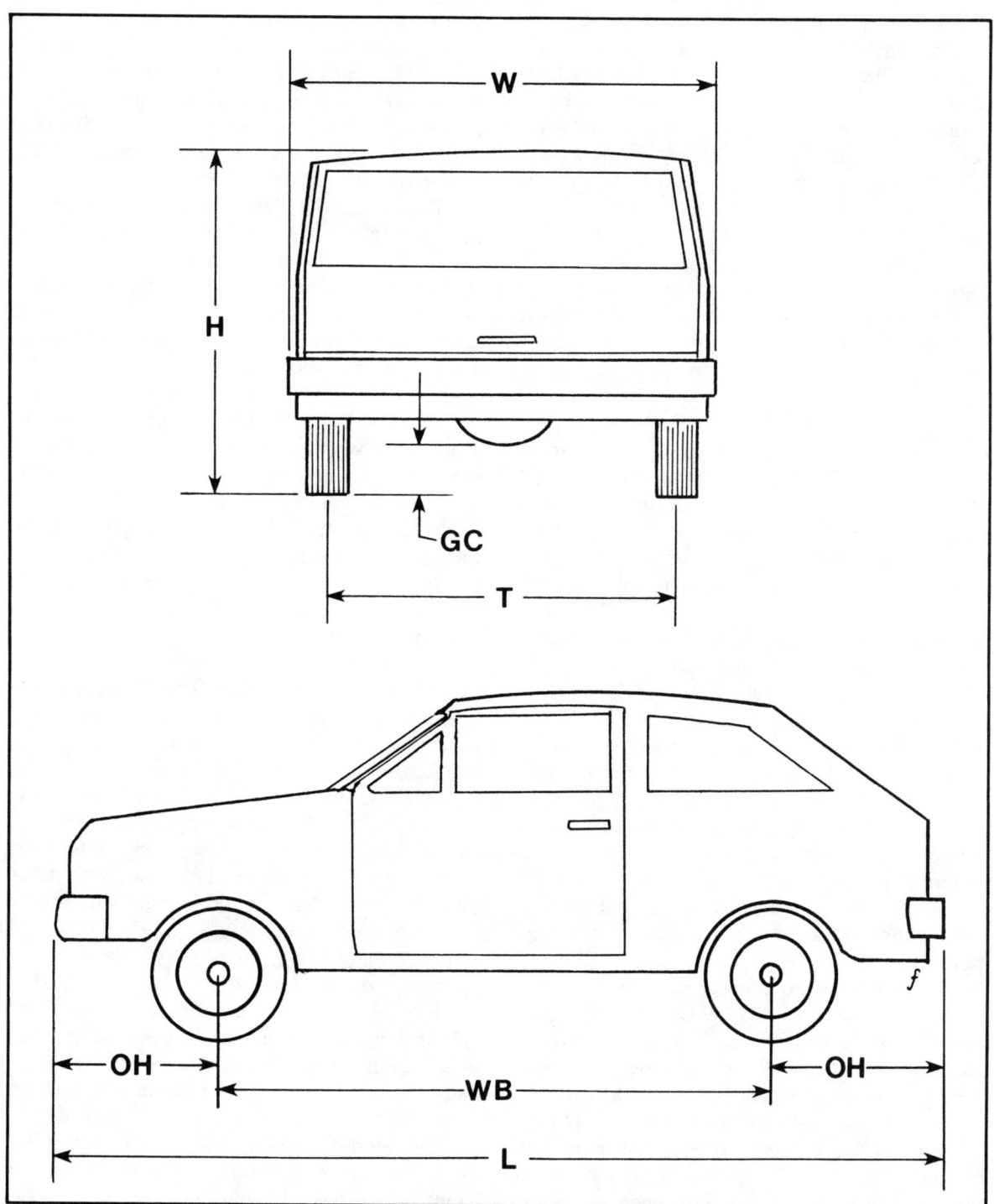

Fig. 19-1. Important body dimensions include wheelbase (WB), front and rear overhangs (OH), overall length (L), overall width (W), overall height (H), track (T), and ground clearance (GC).

Ground clearance (road clearance) is what you need to know when buying an unusually low, sporty type car. This is especially true if you ever have to travel along muddy or rutted roads. Clearance is the distance between the ground and the lowest part of the vehicle's chassis. RV's have enormous ground clearances while some old British sports cars have almost none, virtually scraping the ground.

You might also come across a figure for *axle-to-frame height*. This shows how much space there is above the axle at the rear. Too small and the car is likely to "bottom" on bumps; the axle actually hits the frame as the spring compresses.

VEHICLE WEIGHT

Curb weight is the most common measurement found in specifications for new cars. It's the weight of a car ready to roll, including spare tire and gasoline. *Shipping weight* is for a vehicle without fuel, coolant, and certain accessories. The difference could be as much as 150 pounds. Both weights are given in pounds and, for modern cars, kilograms. Trucks have a *maximum gross vehicle weight* (GVW), which includes the load.

Along with their small size, today's autos tip the scales very lightly. Some subcompacts weigh little more than a ton. Even the heftiest new models have lost a lot of weight; they seldom top 2 tons.

Years ago the heavy car was highly prized by Americans. Many of us falsely believed that extra weight offered protection in case of a highway accident. Average weight went from under 2800 pounds in 1930 to over 3400 in 1955—and then fatter yet. For extra traction, someone might even have tossed a few heavy sacks into the trunk.

Quite a few early models hardly needed any more bulk. The boatlike 1959 Cadillac, for example, weighed in at an elephantine 5570 pounds in its 9-passenger version. In the same year, Ramblers amounted to a mere 2435 pounds. The little two-passenger Nash Metropolitan weighed under 1800 pounds in 1957, but even that was far more than the earlier Crosley. Those early day miniatures hit the street at barely over 1100 pounds.

If you ever watched a couple of ordinary men pick up the front end of an old Volkswagen Beetle, you were observing an example of good *weight distribution*. For decades, the typical front-engine, rear-wheel-drive American car was notorious for its poor distribution. As engines grew in size (and weight), the front ends were just too heavy for proper traction and handling.

That ubiquitous Beetle, on the other hand, exhibited rather good traction because of its rear engine combined with rear drive. Saabs of the 1960s and 1970s were known for superb handling, especially in ice-racing events, largely as a result of front-wheel drive and front engine placement.

In 1953, the seldom-seen Volkswagen had 56.5 percent of its weight right over the driving wheels. A Dodge, typical of the new V-8 powered middleweight cars, was exactly the opposite: 56.5 percent of the weight above its non-driving (front) wheels.

Modern cars have improved quite a bit. This is especially true for those with front engines and transaxles. The lopsided distribution of years gone by may have provided a fluffy ride, but also contributed to the American car's sad reputation for marginal handling.

You might come across references to *sprung weight* and *unsprung weight*. This factor, too, has a significant effect on handling and ride. Sprung weight includes the weight of all parts that are supported by the suspension system: above the springs, torsion bars, MacPherson struts, or whatever form the suspension takes. That includes the car body, frame, engine, and almost everything else. Unsprung weight includes the car's wheels, tires, hubs, brake mechanism and, in cars with a rigid rear axle, the differential and axle shaft housings. It's everything that is not supported by the car's springs. Too much and you get a harsh, rough ride.

Figures for weight distribution and sprung/unsprung weight aren't so easy to find. For good handling qualities, engineers try to create a balanced distribution with as little unsprung weight as possible.

One more figure is the *horsepower-weight factor*. Found in some spec tables, it shows the relative capability of the car/engine combination. The figure is nothing more than the engine's peak

Table 19-2. Typical Brake Specifications for Disc and Drum.

Disc Brake Rotor				Disc brake caliper	Drum Brakes		Wheel cylinder	
Nominal thickness (in.)	Minimum refinish thickness (in.)	Parallel Variation (in.)	Max. Lateral Runout (in.)	Bore Dia.	I.D. (in.)	Oversize Limit (in.)	Bore Diameter (inches)	
							Disc	Drum
1.040	0.980	.0005	.004	2 1/2	9.5	.060	2 1/2	3/4
.880	0.815	.0005	.003	2.6	9	.060	2.6	0.94
.433	0.374	.0003	.005	1-7/8	7.87	7.899	1-7/8	0.69
1.250	1.215	.0007	.005	2-15/16	12	.060	2-15/16	15/16
1.285	1.230	.0005	.005	---	11	---	2-15/16	1
0.35	---	---	.006	---	8.0	8.05	---	---

horsepower divided by the car weight. In some tables, it is just the opposite; weight is divided by horsepower, sometimes called *power-to-weight ratio*.

BRAKE SPECIFICATIONS

Several figures showing brake sizes, similar to those in Table 19-2, are found in service manuals. Some are dimensions that don't change or cannot be adjusted. Others are needed for brake machining work.

Brake drum diameter is needed when a drum has to be "turned down" on a lathe because of wear. Drums must only be ground to a certain point beyond their original diameter; otherwise, they become dangerously weak. The size is given in inches. Another column often shows the regrinding limit, either in additional thousandths of an inch (often .060), or as a maximum diameter.

For disc brake systems, *nominal rotor thickness* and the accompanying *minimum refinish thickness* serve the same purpose. They show how far you can go with grinding. The machinist also needs to know the figures for maximum *runout* and *parallelism,* to be sure the refinished rotor is true within acceptable limits.

Specifications are also given for *cylinder bore diameter* of both master and wheel cylinders. Those for disc or power brakes may differ from drum type. These sizes would seem important for installing new internal parts in the cylinder, but pistons and seals are usually purchased by part number anyway, not by their actual dimensions. *Caliper bore diameter* is another size that's seldom needed in practice.

Even more rare is the need to know the *lining area* (in square inches) of a drum-brake system or its length/width/thickness dimensions. The larger the area the more effective its brakes, but there's not much to be done about it after the car is made. *Brake shoe clearance* figures, however, are essential when adjusting some very early model drum brakes.

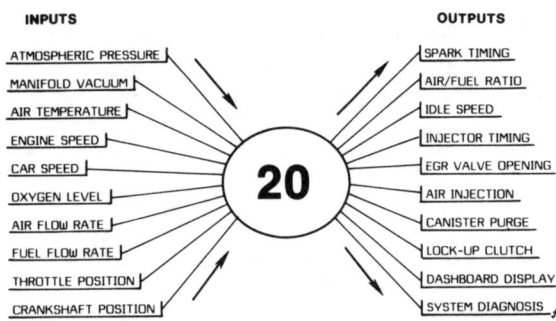

Aiming the Wheels

WHEEL ALIGNMENT REQUIRES ATTENTION to several angles and dimensions (Table 20-1) that make up steering geometry. Alignment is a practical application of the geometric basics. Proper alignment keeps the car rolling straight, tires responding to the steering wheel's commands, and rear wheels tracking the fronts without deviation. It assures easy steering, good stability, and comfortable ride with minimal tire wear. Even though most amateur mechanics (and quite a few professionals) have alignments done by a specialist, all of us should know what the specifications mean.

WHEEL ALIGNMENT GEOMETRY

A basic front wheel alignment job includes checks on caster and camber angles and measurement of toe-in, but several other angles and dimensions play their part in maintaining the car's geometric balance. These include its steering axis inclination, toe-out on turns, and suspension height. Each specification affects the crucial relationship of the angles between each front wheel, its mounting parts, and the road below.

No alignment should begin without first checking trim height (as mentioned in Chapter 19). *Front suspension height* is generally measured from the ground to the lower control arm. Either may affect alignment accuracy.

Chrysler products with torsion-bar suspension have adjustable height. Measurement is sometimes made between ground and a cross member, frame rail, or other chassis point. Some adjust by bolts and others have an eccentric cam mechanism. Cars with air suspension might also have an adjustment, but most vehicles do not. Some low measurements may be caused by weak springs and others by frame damage or bent parts.

A suspension height spec is easy enough to find for those adjustable Chrysler suspensions, and a few other models. Trim height may be given for selected makes/models only. If a chassis manual has no specs, check the factory's body repair manual. Even if no adjustment is possible, knowing height is way off the mark prevents a lot of futile effort.

Table 20-1. Typical Front Wheel Alignment Specifications.

Caster angle (degrees)		Camber angle (degrees)		Toe-in (inches)	Steering axis inclin. (deg)	Toe-out on Turns (deg.)	
Limits	Preferred	Limits	Preferred			Outer Wheel	Inner Wheel
1 1/4 to 3-3/4	2 1/2	−1/4 to 1 1/4	1/2	0 to 5/16	8	18	20
10 to 13	- - - -	0 to 1	1/2	3/64	- - -	- - -	- - -
−1 1/4 to +1/4	−1/2	−1/2 to +1	1/4	0 to 3/8	6 3/4	18 3/16	20
−5 1/16 to 15/16		9/16 to 1-9/16		3/16 - 1/4	7	32 1/2	36 1/2
1 1/2 to 2P	2P	1/4N to 1/4P	0	1/8	8	22[1]	25[1]
2 1/16 to 2 1/4P	2 1/8P	0-1P	1/2P	0 to 1/8	3 1/2-4 1/2	20[1]	23[1]
1/2P to 1 1/2P	[3]	1/2P to 1 1/2P	[3]	1/16 - 1/8	7.1	20[2]	24 1/2[2]
1/2N to 1/2P	0	0 to 1P	1/2P	1/8 - 3/16	3 1/2-4 1/2	20[1]	24[1]

[1]Wheel pivot ratio. [2]Turning radius. [3]Equal within 1/2 degree.

Caster Angle

On early vehicles, each front wheel's steering knuckle was wrapped around a solid steel pin called a *kingpin*. The wheel pivoted around its kingpin's centerline. Kingpins remained in use even after the introduction of independent front wheel suspension in 1934.

The arrival of ball joints in the mid-1950s didn't change the steering principle, but now the steering knuckle (and wheel) pivoted around an imaginary line—a line between the upper and lower ball joint. This imaginary line is called the *steering axis*. A more recent term, *strut axis*, identifies the centerline of a MacPherson strut, as used on many small cars.

Caster is the angle the steering axis makes with the vertical: how far it tilts away from straight up-and-down, when viewed from the side (Fig. 20-1). You can't see the ball joints with the wheel mounted, of course, but you can imagine that axis line.

Positive caster means the axis tilts backward from vertical. The upper ball joint is slightly to the rear of the lower. That seems the "natural" way (rather like a bicycle's fork). Actually most cars do have positive caster. It gives the best stability and control with least steering effort. The wheels tend to keep pointing straight. Moreover, the steering wheel has good *returnability*, returning quickly to straight-ahead position after a turn. That's especially desirable for power steering.

Some heavy cars, and others with manual steering, have the seemingly awkward negative caster: the axis actually leans forward slightly. In either case, the angle usually is small. Most of the time the angle is between about 1 degree negative and 4 degrees positive. Many are set at or very close to zero. A few imports, such as Renault's Le Car, have caster values of 10 degrees or more, but they're the exception.

Spec tables typically give a permissible range as well as a "preferred" or "desired" setting. Acceptable limits could even go from slightly positive to a trifle negative.

Overly positive caster gives hard steering, overreaction to road shock, harsh snap-back of the steering wheel after a turn, and maybe a little shimmy, too. Too small a positive caster and you could have instability (wandering and weaving). This would be especially true at higher speeds. When caster doesn't match between left and right wheels, the car probably will pull to the side.

Camber and Steering Axis Inclination

Camber is an angle not of the steering axis, but of the tire/wheel. It shows how much the tire's centerline inclines away from vertical, viewed from the front (Fig. 20-2). Camber is positive when the top of the tire leans outward and negative when inward. You might picture a negative-caster front end

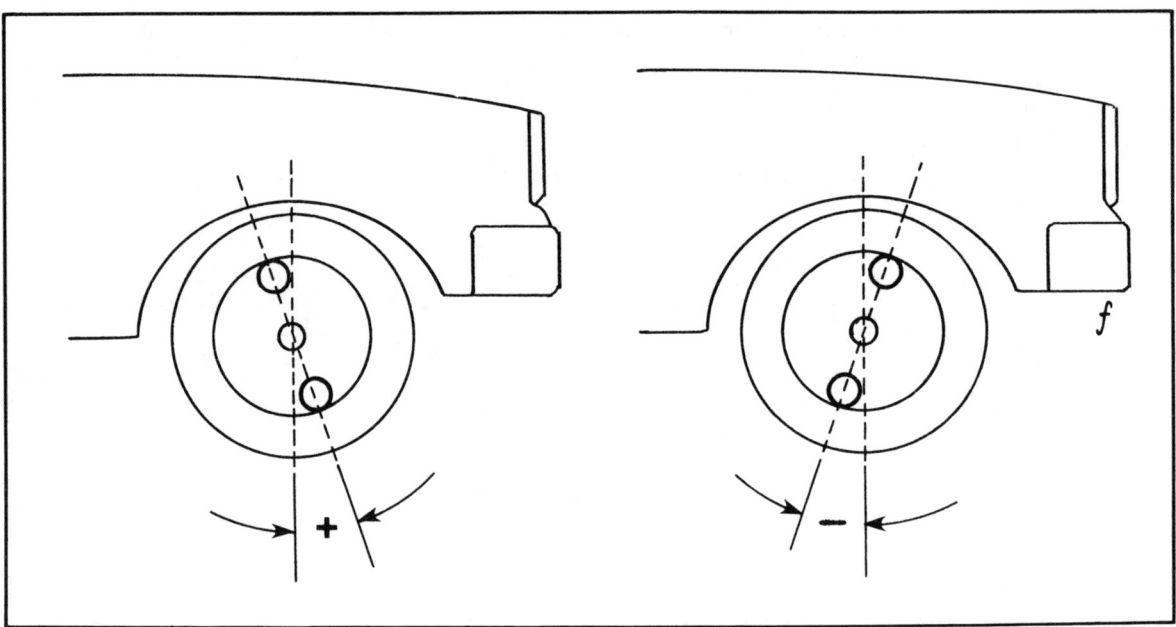

Fig. 20-1. The caster is positive (left) when the steering axis tilts backward (at top) and negative (right) with forward tilt.

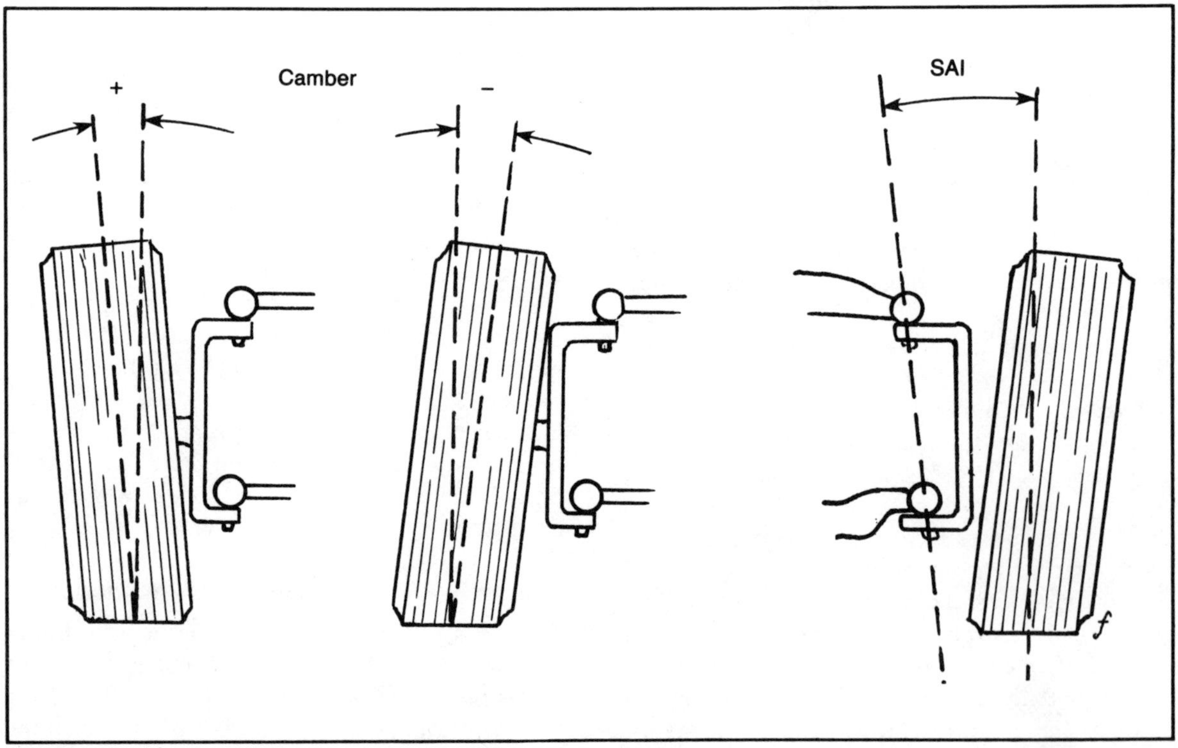

Fig. 20-2. Camber is positive when the top of tire tilts outward, and negative when it tilts inward from vertical. Steering axis inclination (SAI) angle reveals the degree to which the axis (center line between ball joints) leans inward.

as being knock-kneed and positive as bowlegged.

The normal goal is to have zero camber when the car is loaded and moving so that the tire contacts the road squarely. For that reason, most cars should have slight positive camber (tires tilting outward, usually less than 1 degree). Because specs are given as a range, however, very slight negative camber is often permissible.

Improper camber has its most obvious effect on tire wear. When you see a tire worn badly on one side of the tread, it probably came off a car with camber set way off. Adjusted correctly, camber helps keep the car going straight without pulling, makes steering easier, and minimizes wear to ball joints and wheel bearings. Wrong camber on both wheels leads to hard steering, instability, and road wander. Unequal camber produces low-speed shimmy.

Although most specs are intended for both wheels, setting camber about 1/4 degree more positive on the left side is often recommended. Some specialists do so whether recommended or not. How come? It compensates for the crown in the center of most roads, preventing the slight rightward drift, or pulling that might otherwise occur.

Steering axis inclination (ball joint inclination, kingpin inclination, or kingpin angle) seems related to camber, but has nothing to do with the tire. It's the angle the steering axis itself tilts inward from vertical as seen from the front. A specification is ordinarily given (in degrees), but SAI is not adjustable. When caster and camber are within spec, SAI should be OK as well.

SAI contributes a lot to a car's stability, steering "feel," and returnability. Autos may have slight negative caster to make steering easier, but remain stable anyway because of properly engineered SAI angles.

You might also come across the term *included angle*. This is the combination of camber and SAI angles. It is the angle between the steering axis and tire centerline.

Caster/Camber Adjustments

The traditional method of checking caster and

Fig. 20-3. Checking wheel alignment with the latest equipment, way back in 1931. (FMC Corp.)

camber uses spirit-level (bubble) testers that mount magnetically to each hub (Fig. 20-3). Other testers mount on the wheel rims, and produce a light-beam display. Not surprisingly, modern equipment operates electronically. Some instruments even reveal caster/camber settings dynamically as the wheel spins.

Both readings are in degrees (positive or negative). Left and right wheels are evaluated and adjusted separately. Depending on the car, adjustments are made in several ways. They include:

☐ Rotating one or two eccentric cams (at inner end of upper control arm).

☐ Removing or adding shims (at upper control arm shafts).

☐ Shifting inner control arm shaft through slots in frame.

☐ Loosening nuts or bolts to move a camber plate.

☐ Rotating the ball joint.

☐ Moving the tire itself, after loosening strut mounting bolts, or moving a MacPherson strut mount.

☐ Shortening or lengthening a control arm strut rod.

The same operation usually affects both caster and camber. Adding shims equally to both sides of the shaft, for example, changes camber; adding to one side only affects caster. Similarly, turning both cams the same way changes camber; turning in opposite directions changes caster. Even though steering axis inclination isn't adjustable, it can be read on most gauges.

Not all cars have adjustments for both angles (or either). Some MacPherson struts have an adjusting cam for camber only. Recent small Ford models have no adjustments at all.

Trucks and prewar cars with I-beam axles are tougher to align. Some have shims to change the caster angle, but many adjustments require bending the axle. It is not a job to be taken lightly.

Toe-in Settings

Toe-in is the third major adjustment. Measured in a fraction of an inch, toe-in shows how far the wheels point inward. In other words, it shows how much closer the fronts of the wheels are to each other than the rear portions (Fig. 20-4).

It isn't much. Toe-in is typically about 1/8 inch and seldom more than 1/4 inch. Some imports' specs are given in degrees.

Ideally, you want zero toe-in as the car moves forward so that the tires are perfectly parallel. Because the tire fronts tend to spread apart when in motion, this small amount of initial difference is important. It affects tire wear considerably. Certain front-wheel drive cars should be set with slight toe-*out*: tires closer together at the rear.

How is toe-in measured? The traditional way uses what amounts to a high-accuracy tape measure, comparing the front distance to the rear. Modern testers use a light beam projected onto a screen or instant electronic evaluations.

Some alignment specialists don't bother about toe-in settings at all. Instead, they insert a special spring-tension device that forces the tire fronts outward. It simulates the spreading that occurs on the road. Then toe-in is set to zero no matter what the spec table says.

Toe-in is adjusted by loosening and rotating the tie rod adjusting sleeves, altering the length of each tie rod. Adjustment also affects the steering wheel's position. One tie rod may have to change more than the other in order to keep the steering wheel centered when the car wheels point dead ahead.

While on the subject of the steering wheel, I should mention one figure that isn't ordinarily in the spec table: *free play*. There's no absolute maximum, but looseness of more than an inch or two means something is amiss in the steering gear. Some older steering gears are adjustable to take up some of the slack but most are not. Therefore, excess play suggests the gears are wearing down or other parts are weakening.

Toe-out On Turns

Toe-out is the final figure given in alignment spec tables (another one that's nonadjustable). Toe-out on turns (turning radius, turning angle, wheel pivot ratio) is measured in degrees, on turntable-type gauges. It's the degree to which the inner wheel

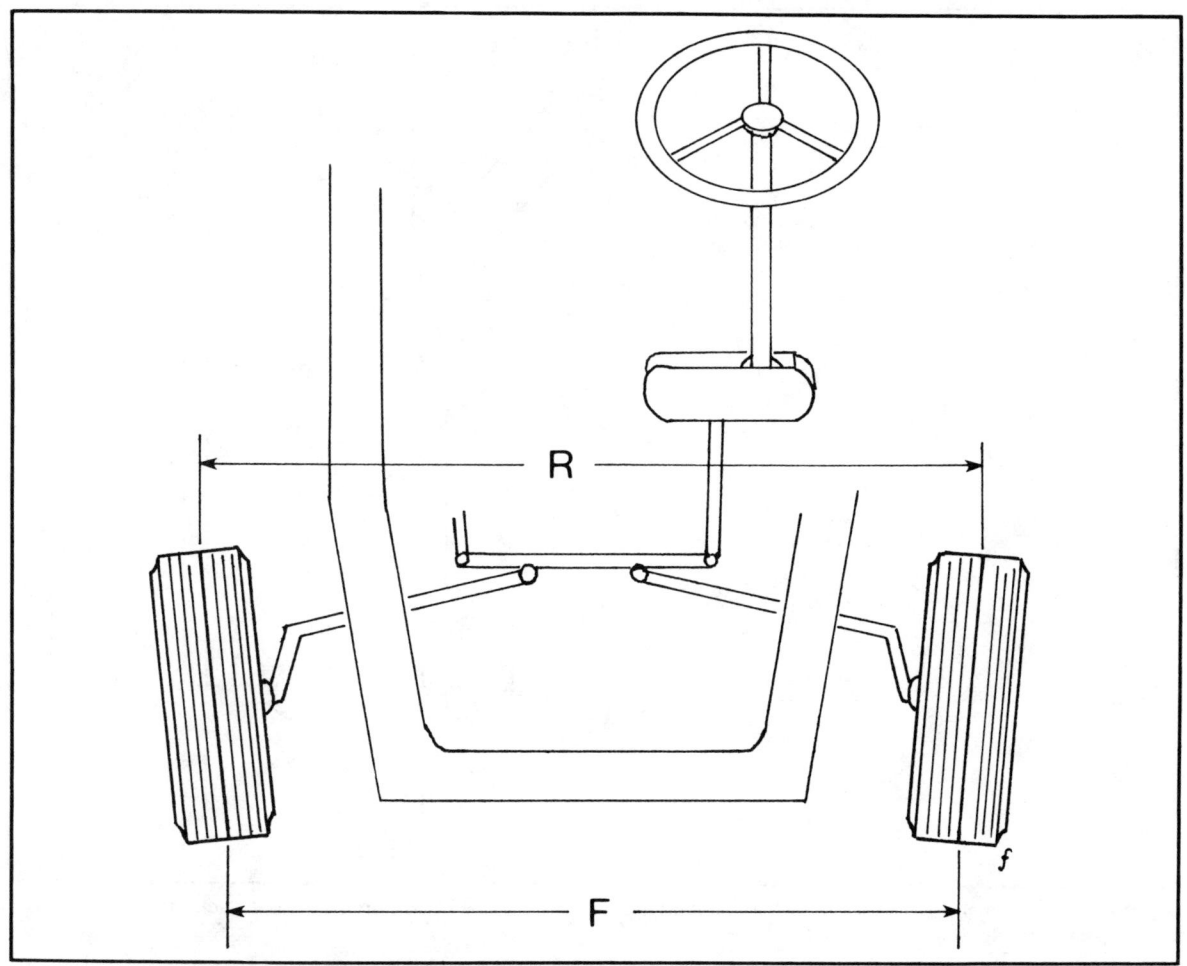

Fig. 20-4. Toe-in is the difference of the distances between left and right front wheel, measured at front (F) and rear (R).

turns more sharply than the outer when going around a curve. Specifically, it is the difference of the angles formed between each front wheel and the car frame during a turn (Fig. 20-5). The inner wheel always follows a circle of smaller radius so its angle is always larger than the outer.

The figure given for the inner wheel is often 20 degrees. For the outer wheel, the figure is about 2 degrees less. Some imports and early models have much different figures. An out-of-spec reading warns that a steering arm or tie rod must be bent.

REAR WHEEL ALIGNMENT

Corvettes and other cars with independent rear suspensions may also have alignment specs for the rear wheels. Adjustments are possible for camber and toe-in; caster may be fixed.

Correct alignment ensures proper tracking with rear wheels following the fronts as they should. This is important for all cars (not only those with independent rears). If any car tracks in a cockeyed manner even after a front wheel alignment, an investigation for bent parts at the rear, or improperly mounted springs, is in order.

UNDERSTEER AND OVERSTEER

Understeering and oversteering aren't specifications, but the terms appear quite often, and many

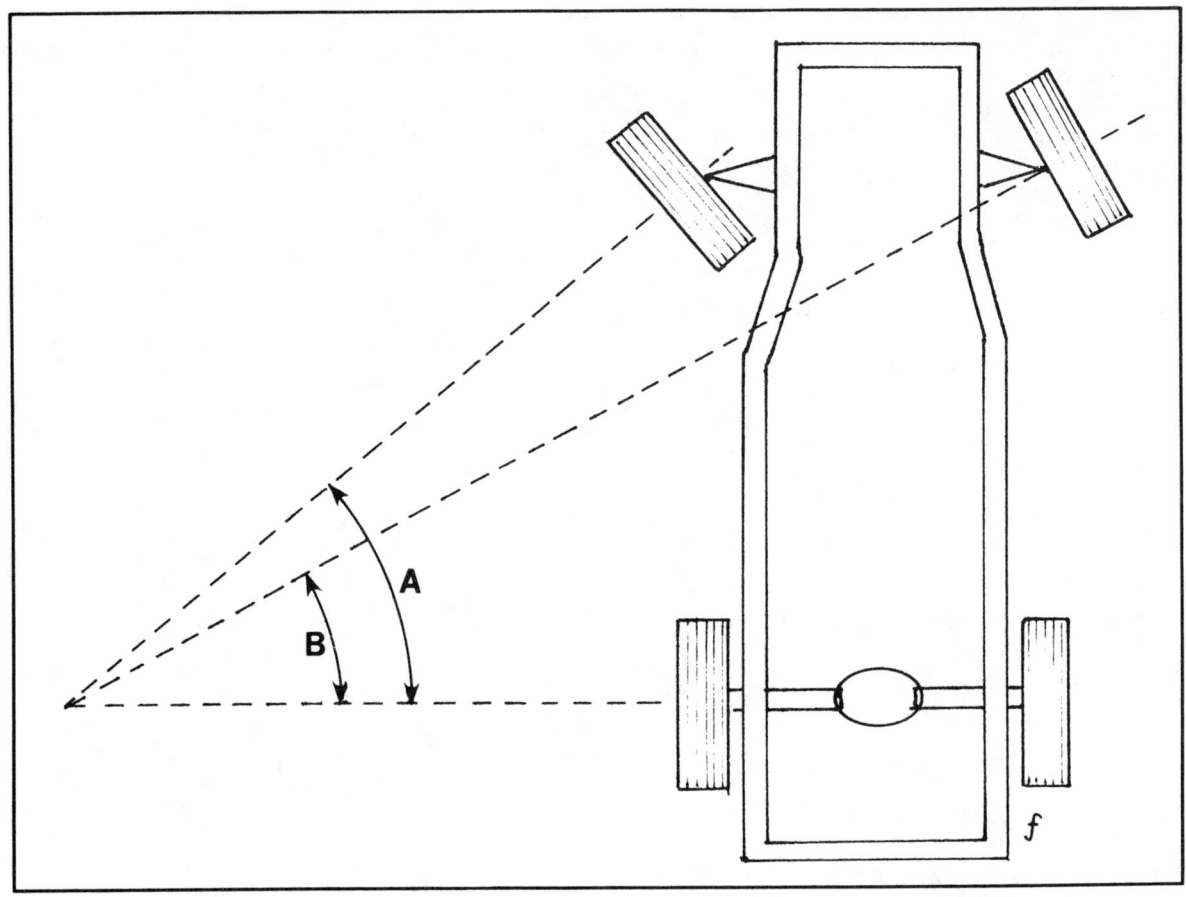

Fig. 20-5. Toe-out on turns is nonadjustable but important. It's the difference between the angles each front wheel makes with the car chassis while turning (A-B).

motorists seem uncertain what they mean. A car is said to *understeer* when its front tires slip, more than the rears, in tight corners. To complete the turn, you must turn the steering wheel a bit more than seems reasonable. The rear wheels don't seem to follow along as rapidly as they should.

Oversteer is just the opposite. The back tires tend to slip more so that the rear end slides into a tighter turn. Sometimes the turn is surprisingly tight, and you have to move the steering wheel back in a hurry to correct the car's trajectory.

Most conventional autos have slight understeer. Sports cars and some imports might tend to oversteer. It matters a lot on the race course, but the average driver probably cannot tell the difference (unless the tendency is severe).

Before leaving the steering system, I should mention a couple of additional terms you might encounter. *Turning circle* is the diameter of the smallest circle in which a car can turn around. Either a curb-to-curb or wall-to-wall figure given in feet might turn up. Some cars can turn in a 30-foot circle; big cars may need much more space.

Steering ratio is found more often in older specs. This is the number of degrees you have to turn the car's steering wheel in order to move the front wheels 1 degree away from straight-ahead. A figure between 20 and 30 degrees is typical. Another figure occasionally found is *turns lock-to-lock*. That tells how many complete rotations the steering wheel makes going from all the way to the left to full right.

WHEEL BALANCING

If you've ever felt the frightening vibration of a seriously out-of-balance wheel, you can appreciate how important a job balancing is. Wheels may be balanced in two ways:

- ☐ Statically, on a bubble-type balancer.
- ☐ Dynamically, on the car.

No specs apply to balancing. Either a wheel is in balance or it isn't. The machine shows how far out of balance it is, which size weight must be added, and where it should be placed.

TIRE SIZES AND RATINGS

Many years ago, tires were designated by their overall diameters and rim widths. A 28-×-3 tire was 28 inches in diameter (overall), mounting on a 3-inch rim.

Then came a system that gave tire width, but diameter of the wheel (rim). A 6.70-15 tire was 6.7 inches wide (in cross section), fitting on a 15-inch diameter rim. A ply rating gave its load limit. This style is still used for truck tires such as 8.00 × 16.5.

Next was an Alpha-numeric load rating system that is still in use. It consists of a letter followed by two 2-digit numbers. For example:

GR78-14

G = Load carrying capacity/size. *A* is the smallest (least capacity), *L* the greatest, for standard auto tires.
R = Radial (no letter for nonradial).
78 = Aspect ratio (height to width ratio): in this case, the tire height is 78 percent of its width. A low ratio describes a wide tire (squat in cross section).
14 = Rim diameter (usually 13, 14, or 15 inches).

The P-Metric (international standard) system is used to identify many modern tires. The number shows the type of vehicle, section width, aspect ratio, tire style, and rim diameters. An example:

P155/80R13

P = Passenger car (T = temporary spare; C = commercial).
155 = Section width (millimeters).
80 = Aspect ratio (profile).
R = Radial (B = bias-belted; D = bias ply).
13 = Rim diameter (inches).

An *M*, *S*, or *MS* at the end of the number denotes a mud, snow, or mud/snow tire.

Finally, we have the full metric system used by some imports. It shows width, inflation pressure, and peak load. For example:

190/65R-390

190 = Tire section width (millimeters).
65 = Maximum inflation pressure (kilopascals).
R = Radial.
390 = Load rating (kilograms).

Tires manufactured since 1981 also display a rating from the federal Uniform Tire Quality Grading System. This gives the expected tread life, traction rating, and temperature resistance. One example:

100 A B

100 = Comparative anticipated tread wear: a tire rated 150 gives 1 1/2 times the wear of one rated 100 (the range is 80 to 160).
A = Traction rating (ability to stop on wet pavement): *A* is best, *B* next, *C* third.
B = Resistance to heat buildup: *A* is best, *B* next, *C* third.

Modern tires also have a load rating: *B* indicates light load, *C* middle-range, and *D* heavy-duty. Recently made tires may instead be rated *SL* (standard load) or *XL* (extra-load, which is higher than the former D rating). These designations replace the letter prefixes (A through L) that showed tire load and inflation limit and the old ply rating.

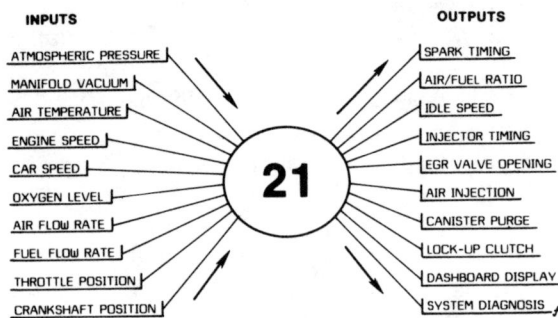

Performance

AFTER ALL THOSE IMPORTANT, BUT NOT EXactly thrilling, figures throughout the car, we come at long last to some that hasten the heartbeat of many a motorist. For a few years, as cars grew smaller and—in many people's eyes—duller, performance was nearly forgotten. The ads talked about economy. Gasoline prices, and the possibility of shortages, became more significant than acceleration times and top speeds.

By the mid-1980s, performance was back in vogue. The big engines were gone. Cars were lean, efficient, far different in size and style from the Sixties GTO's, Chargers, and Cougars. Still, new-car buyers again were paying more attention to the statistics predicting what the car would do on the road than to its miserliness at the gas pump.

Besides, turbocharging and electronic controls have helped produce car/engine combinations that not only deliver impressive gas mileage and shoot out far fewer nasty pollutants. (Economy and emissions are part of an engine's performance, too.) They also boast plenty of potential in the acceleration and speed departments.

WHAT DO PUBLISHED ROAD TESTS TELL US?

Road tests came into their own in the years following World War II. Magazines like *Motor Trend* and *Hot Rod* sprang up to sate the appetites of returned veterans who took a new interest in the performance of their hot rods or family sedans. Teenagers, too, succumbed to an irresistible fascination with speed and "pickup."

From a Standing Start

One factor that stood out was 0-to-60 acceleration. Quarter-mile times were standard on the drag strips. For the teenagers and young adults who made up most of the performance-minded public, who did their (illicit) dragging in impromptu contests on the street, 0-to-60 was the figure they looked for first in the magazines.

What is it? The number of seconds it takes to reach 60 miles an hour from a standing start. It didn't matter how much rubber was burned and left behind on the street or on the strip; those standing starts were the way to go.

As far back as the early 1930s, a supercharged Duesenberg could reach 60 in a swift 12 seconds. Such cars were owned by oil men and stock manipulators, and not by working folks. Ford V-8s of that era could get to 60 in about 18 seconds. It doesn't sound very fast today, but in the '30s that was really moving.

Rodders, naturally, produced some far swifter acceleration figures. By the late 1940s, six-second times were possible on street or strip, but the average car off the assembly line was lucky to make it in less than 20.

The new overhead-valve V-8 changed that. The first one could propel the 1949 Oldsmobile to 60 in what then seemed a neck-snapping 13 seconds. The renowned 265-cid Chevrolet of 1955—equipped with 4-barrel carb, dual exhaust, overdrive and a 4.11:1 rear end—was able to reach 60 in under 10 seconds. The 1955 Chrysler 300 reached 60 in about nine seconds.

A fuel-injected Corvette set the 1957 record at 6.6 seconds, according to *Car & Driver*. By 1964, it was a Pontiac Tempest GTO turning 60 in a startling 4.6 seconds. The next year, a Pontiac Catalina 2+2 reached 60 in a phenomenal 3.9 seconds. It's a record that's rarely been approached since. Through the 1970s, Porsches and similarly exotic machines took the number-one annual stoplight prize.

Today's performance vehicles are no slouches when the gas pedal goes down hard (Fig. 21-1). One version of Chrysler's 1985 LeBaron GTS with an overhead-cam four could get to 60 in just eight seconds. So could the '85 Fiero with a V-6.

Passing Power: Accelerating for Safety

What does 0-to-60 mean to the ordinary motorist? To be honest, not much except for the fact that a car with a rapid 0-60 time is also likely to have a fairly speedy 20-50 or 30-60 time. That could mean a lot when passing.

Most of us, let's face it, have seldom (if ever) ridden in a vehicle that could hit 60 in six seconds or even 10 seconds. Many of us haven't really wanted to. The super-fast times have been set by machines that approach racing trim. Those power-pack options added plenty to the basic car price. Most Pontiacs sold in 1964, after all, weren't full-performance GTO's.

Quarter-mile times have been standard for sanctioned drag racing. They also became more common during the 1960s muscle-car era, but eventually subsided in popularity again. They come in two parts: the time (in seconds) to cross the finish line a quarter-mile away, and the actual speed reached as that line is crossed.

Some cars have fast times, but don't reach such an impressive speed (and vice versa). Serious drag racing enthusiasts insist on knowing the combined

Fig. 21-1. Sporty modern autos like this Laser XE combine good fuel economy and sharp styling with snappy performance, especially in turbocharged versions. (Chrysler Corp.)

result. To the casual observer, though, a statement that car A does the quarter in 20 seconds and car B in 15 says enough.

Published tests often include 0-to-30 acceleration time. A high figure here predicts painfully sluggish takeoffs from traffic lights. In the years before 60-mph speeds became commonplace, 0-50 figures were standard. With today's 55 limit, acceleration times to that speed make more sense.

Triple-Digit Speeds on 55-mph Roads

Top speed is the fastest pace a car can attain on a test strip. The blown 1930s Duesenberg reached 120 miles an hour. Several American cars in the 1930s and 1940s could hit a hundred. Early Ford V-8s, in stock trim, reached about 80.

A 1955 Chrysler 300 delivered a top speed around 130 miles an hour. That was far faster than most motorists ever wished to travel. In the guzzler years, some auto makers installed 160-mph speedometers in their performance-equipped models. The seemingly timid family sedan of the 1950s and 1960s, with a plain old V-8 under the hood, often had a top of well over 100 miles an hour just in case dad ever felt like unleashing all the horses on his way home from work. Speedometers may read only to 80 mph nowadays, but top speeds in three figures are back in style.

FUEL ECONOMY: FROM GUZZLERS TO MISERS

In 1925, not many Americans worried about gas mileage. The average car got about 18 miles per gallon. Gas was fairly inexpensive and certainly plentiful. Gushers were rolling in. Prosperity was surely here to stay. Shortages? Not a chance. Oh sure, a few pessimistic "experts" gave a dire warning now and then, but their words went unheeded by motorists and automakers alike.

Just as the bottom fell out of the economy and the Great Depression began, average mpg dropped under 14. By 1941, the average was up to almost 19 again. It stayed near that level for the next 15 years. Well, the guzzler era that began around 1955, and lasted nearly two decades, took care of those figures (Fig. 21-2). By 1974, the domestic car average fell to barely 14 mpg.

Many individual models did far worse. *Popular Science* magazine eked out only 10.2 mpg from a 1969 Ford Galaxie with a 351-cid engine. A 1969 Plymouth wagon delivered only 8 mpg. Owners of 400-cid Grand Prix Pontiacs reported median gas mileage of only 10 1/2 mpg for local driving (13 1/2 on trips) to *Popular Mechanics*. Instances of cars delivering only six miles per gallon, even less, were frequently heard. For high-mileage oldies, the figures were even more dismal.

EPA to the Rescue

In the wake of the 1973—74 oil embargo, amid rising concern about fuel economy and waste, the government took action. Title III of the Energy Policy and Conservation Act of 1975 demanded average mileage figures of 18 mpg for 1978, rising steadily each year to a 27.5 mile-per-gallon level in 1985. Those Corporate Average Fuel Economy (CAFE) figures are the ones each automaker must achieve, when an average is taken for all the car models it produces.

Not all have made it. As the Seventies drew to a close, overall averages weren't matching the government requirements. Both GM and Ford fell short in 1983 and 1984. Still, the initial goal of improving the 1974 average by 40 percent was reached by 1980. Average mpg may not have met CAFE standards, but it's risen significantly each year.

In 1984, the estimated overall average for American-made cars was 25.6 miles per gallon. Most frugal in 1985 was Honda's CRX HF, reaching 54 mpg (highway). Even a Cadillac Fleetwood delivered 20 mpg on the road in that year.

Every motorist has learned, of course, that the Environmental Protection Agency (EPA) estimates, as posted on new cars, rarely are achieved on an actual road. They never were intended to predict mileage. The tests are conducted primarily to determine auto emissions. As the warnings in the ads state clearly, EPA mileage estimates are for comparison only.

One consulting firm has advised that a more

Fig. 21-2. Tiny Nash Metropolitan wasn't a big seller in the mid-1950s, with the horsepower race in full swing, but economy would become a major selling point a decade or two later.

realistic estimate might be achieved by multiplying the EPA figure by 90 percent. (If EPA says 30 mpg, expect about 27.) Many observers have felt even that correction is too conservative.

Beginning in 1985, the EPA gives adjusted city and highway mileage estimates. Engines are run through two tests on a dynamometer (not on an actual road) to simulate city and highway driving. Figures are then reduced by a certain factor (0.9 for city. 0.78 for highway) to give more realistic published values.

Dwindling Mileage: Is It the Car or the Estimate?

Countless motorists have discovered that their cars' fuel mileages don't come close to the EPA figures or to any other published estimates. Are all the estimates wrong? Probably not. So many factors contribute to individual gas mileage that it's difficult to say what's at fault.

In a test using a 1984 Ford Tempo with 2.3-liter four-cylinder engine and 3-speed automatic transmission, *Popular Science* achieved some striking results. First was the fact that, in initial testing, their car produced mileage (25.75 mpg) slightly *higher* than the EPA figure. Then, in a series of experiments that intentionally caused the engine to perform poorly, the precisely tested mileage fell considerably.

When ignition timing was advanced or retarded by 6 degrees, the Tempo suffered a loss of up to 4.75 miles per gallon (18 percent). Widening or narrowing its spark plug gap by .020 inch cut mileage by 25 and 19 percent, respectively. Other alterations, including a slight boost in idle speed rpm, using a partly clogged air filter, and disconnecting the engine vacuum hose, produced less startling results: a drop of 2 mpg or less in each case. But several small flaws can add up to a massive drop in fuel mileage.

Of course, you could always change cars, switch engines, or change differentials. As a rule, changing the drive axle ratio by 10 percent brings an economy boost of less than half that amount.

Reducing engine displacement by 10 percent might give 6 percent better mileage.

A 4-speed manual transmission delivers around 5 percent better economy than a 3-speed automatic—provided it's shifted by an adept gear handler. Overdrive? That might bring an extra 3 percent over the manual transmission and closer to 10 percent better than an automatic.

One sure way to boost mileage is to increase tire pressure. Low pressure increases the tire's rolling resistance, and requires more power to propel the car at the same speed. Be careful not to exceed the tire's maximum limits and be prepared for a rougher ride.

Driving habits contribute far more to poor mileage than many motorists realize or choose to accept. In one long-term Ford test of 20 Escort vehicles engaged in courier service, actual mileages ranged from 26.1 to 32.9 mpg. The cars covered the same terrain each day, endured the same traffic, and received the same maintenance; only the drivers changed.

The widespread unpopularity of the 55-mph highway limit has caused many drivers to disregard evidence that greatest economy is achieved at moderate speeds. A 1978 test of heavy trucks clearly demonstrated the connection. Only six out of the 32 drivers, all trying to show that high speed was OK, were able to produce better fuel mileage at speeds over 55 than at the legal limit. And they cheated a bit, too, by driving in low gear ranges at 55 but using the highest (most economical) gear possible at higher speeds in order to maximize the difference. On average, however, each mile-per-hour reduction down toward the 55-mph limit saved 2.2 percent in fuel.

BRAKING DISTANCE

We don't always think of it as a mark of performance, but braking distance—measured in feet for a "panic stop"—is surely a factor worthy of attention. Moreover, it's one that need not deteriorate with the passing of time or accumulation of miles. A thorough brake job should return the car close to its original published spec. You probably won't take it out to the road for an actual test, but you'll be pleased when those brakes once again feel solid and firm.

More than most of the figures we've studied in these chapters, braking distance is one performance specification that just might save your life one day.

Appendix

Sources for Service Manuals

INFORMATION ON AVAILABLE MANUALS CAN be obtained by writing to the addresses below. For recent vehicles, though, the first source to try is usually the local dealer who sells that make of car. The dealer's parts department can often order factory manuals for you, with a minimum of bother.

Ford, Lincoln and Mercury
Helm, Inc.
Publications Division
P.O. Box 07150
Detroit, MI 48207

Chrysler, Dodge and Plymouth
Chrysler Corporation
c/o Dyment Distribution Service
Service Publications
20026 Progress Drive
Strongsville, OH 44136

Chevrolet, Pontiac and Cadillac
Helm, Inc.
Publications Division
P.O. Box 07130
Detroit, MI 48207

Buick
Tuar Company
P.O. Box 354
Flint, MI 48501

Oldsmobile
Lansing Lithographers
P.O. Box 23188
Lansing, MI 48909-3188

AMC, Jeep and Renault
Order directly from local dealer or write:
American Motors Corp.
American Center
27777 Franklin Road
Southfield, MI 48034

Datsun/Nissan
Pendant Industries
P.O. Box 387
1648 West 240th Street
Harbor City, CA 90710

Honda or Subaru
Order manuals directly through local dealers only.

Toyota
Toyota Service Publications
P.O. Box 6668
Torrance, CA 90504

Volkswagen and Audi
Robert Bentley, Inc.
6 Bigelow Street
Cambridge, MA 02139

Chevrolet, Ford, Pontiac and Cadillac (early models)
Helm, Inc.
P.O. Box 3518
Highland Park, MI 48203

Original or reprinted factory service manuals for other early model autos are available from literature dealers. They advertise in several magazines devoted to antique and special interest vehicles, including:

Old Cars Weekly
700 East State St.
Iola, WI 54990

Cars & Parts
P.O. Box 482
Sidney, OH 45365

Hemmings Motor News
Box 100
Bennington, VT 05201

For information on popular multimake manuals, write to:

Chilton Book Company
Radnor, PA 19089-0230

MOTOR Publications
555 West 57th Street
New York, NY 10019

Manuals for professional mechanics are available from Chilton and MOTOR, as well as:

Mitchell Manuals, Inc.
A Cordura Company
P.O. Box 26260
San Diego, CA 92126

Index

A
accelerating for safety, 189
air supply
  boosting, 113
air/fuel ratio, 115
alternating current, 12
alternator and regulator data, 75
alternator and regulator specifications, 76
ampere, 12
amps
  volts, and ohms, 65
angles
  ratios, and proportions, 10
atmospheric pressure, 101
automatic transmission, 171
axis
  steering, 181, 183
  strut, 181

B
barrel, 12
battery ratings, 73
bearing clearances, 136, 150
body styles and models, 33
bolt sizes, 153
bore and stroke, 37, 40, 41, 44
brake drum diameter, 179
brake specifications, 179
braking distance, 192

break lining area, 179
breaker arm spring tension, 90

C
cable resistance, 84
calipers, 147
camber, 181
camber adjustments, 183
camshaft and crankshaft journal wear, 141
camshaft lobes and valve lift, 131
candlepower, 12
carburetion, 107
carburetor
  vacuum inside the, 111
carburetor adjustments, 116
carburetor capacities, 112
carburetor specifications
  typical, 116
caster adjustments, 183
caster angle, 181
centrifugal advance, 88
charts and manuals
  non-factory, 16
chassis and body measurements, 175
chassis and driveline fluids, 167
choke settings, 118
circuit
  secondary, 65

circuits
  electrical, 63
  parallel, 64
clutch specifications, 173
codes
  color, 32
coil resistance, 84
color codes and stickers, 32
combustion and compression, 103
compression
  boosting, 48
  rise and fall of, 48
compression and combustion, 103
compression ratio, 12, 37, 46
compression testing, 95
computer control and testing, 120
computer diagnostics
  on-board, 123
computers in the shop, 125
computers under the hood, 120
condenser capacity, 90
coolant pressure, 105
cooling system
  the, 166
crankshaft and camshaft journal wear, 141
crankshaft data, 135
cubic centimeter, 12
curb weight, 178
current, 65

alternating, 12
alternator field, 77
direct, 12
current draw, 83
current output, 76
cylinder arrangement, 37
cylinder bore diameter, 179
cylinders
  number of, 38

D

dashboards
  future, 123
data formats, 18
dc generators, 78
decimal and metric equivalents, 4
decimals versus fractions, 3
degree, 12
dial indicators, 149
diameter, 6
  inside, 12
  outside, 12
diameter and length, 4
diesel data, 100
differential backlash and preload, 174
direct current, 12
dirt
  rust, and oil, 162
displacement, 40, 42
  engine, 43
distributor data, 90
distributor point gap and dwell angle, 82
distributor retard, 90
distributor shaft, 142
distributor specifications, 89
drive ratios, 169
driveline adjustments, 173
driveline and chassis fluids, 167
driveline data, 168
dwell angle and distributor point gap, 82

E

electrical circuits, 63
electrical power, 69
electrical values and measurements, 63
electronic ignition, 90
emissions, 107
emissions control, 118
engine
  identifying your, 27
  inside the, 127
engine CID/liter, 36
engine code, 29
engine cycle, 38
engine displacement, 43
engine identification, 32
  when you're not sure of, 34
engine identification plates, 29

engine identity problems, 33
engine overheating, 106
engine pressures and temperatures, 101
engine size and style, 36
engine specifications
  typical, 37
engine styles, 37
engine temperatures, 105
engine vacuum
  uses of, 111
engine wear, 142
engines
  sizes of, 43
EPA, 190

F

factory service manuals, 14
fastener styles
  threaded, 156
feet per second, 12
fluid capacities, 164
foot, 12
foot pound, 12
foot-pounds, 160
fractions versus decimals, 3
free play, 184
fuel
  gasoline and diesel, 166
fuel and other pressures, 105
fuel economy, 190
fuel injection, 118
fuel pump pressure, 94
fuel supply, 111
fuses and shorts, 72

G

gasoline and diesel fuel, 166
gasoline octane, 115
gauges
  feeler, 150
  hole, 147
  plug, 147
  small-hole, 147
  telescoping, 147
gear ratio
  calculating, 169
gear reduction
  total, 168

H

hardward, 153
horsepower, 37, 44, 52, 178
  adding, 61
  brake, 50, 54
  chassis, 55
  gross versus net, 54
  observed, 55
  taxable, 50
horsepower and torque values
  typical, 51
horsepower race

the fifties, 60
horsepower ratings, 54
horspower, 12

I

idle mixture, 94
idle speed
  curb, 93
  fast, 94
idle speeds, 93
ignition
  electronic, 90
ignition coil
  the, 82
ignition system
  the, 79
ignition timing, 86
ignition tune-up specifications, 79, 80
inch, 12

K

kilogram, 12
kilowatt, 52
kingpin, 181

L

length and diameter, 4
linear clearance, 8
liter, 12

M

manual transmission gearing, 171
manuals
  auto service, 21
  factory service, 14
  footnotes in, 23
manuals and charts
  non-factory, 16
measurements, 63
  area and volume, 6
mechanical efficiency, 59
metric and decimal equivalents, 4
metric system
  the, 3
microfarad, 12
micrometer
  reading a, 145
micrometers
  inside, 146
  outside, 144
mile, 12
mileage, 191
miles per hour, 12
models and body styles, 33
motor oil, 164

N

Newton-meters, 160
numbers
  large and small, 1
  nice, 1

numerical style, 12
nut
   fitting the, 156

O

ohm's law, 67
ohms
   amps, and volts, 65
oil
   dirt, and rust, 162
   motor, 164
oil pressure, 37, 104
oil pump, 142
ounce inch, 12
oversteer, 186
oversteer and understeer, 185

P

percent, 12
performance, 188
piston and cylinder wear, 140
piston and ring specifications, 133
piston clearances, 132
piston pin, 140
piston pin fit, 133
piston ring gaps and clearances, 134
pistons and rings, 132
point gap, 82
polarity, 84
pound foot, 12
pounds per square inch, 12
power, 51
power and work, 50
power loss
   efficiency and, 59
power/torque relationship
   the, 56
precision measurements, 9
proportions
   ratios, and angles, 10

R

ranges and absolute values, 11
ratios
   proportions, and angles, 10
rear end
   what size is the, 170
rear wheel alignment, 185
regulator and alternator data, 75
regulator voltage, 77
rev's, 50
revolutions per minute, 12
ring and piston specifications, 133
rings and pistons, 132
road tests
   published, 188
rust
   dirt, and oil, 162

S

screw sizes, 153

shims, 150
shorts and fuses, 72
solenoid, 75
spark plug firing order, 84
spark plugs, 80
spec problems
   early model, 25
spec tables, 24
specifications, 14
   clutch, 173
   crankshaft and connecting rod, 136
   drive axle, 174
   front wheel alignment, 181
   ignition tune up, 79
   ignition tune-up, 80
   piston and ring, 133
   tune up, 25
specs
   forgotten, 174
   sources of, 14
   starter, 74
   timing, 87
specs you'll need to know, 20
steering axis inclination, 181
steering ratio, 186
stickers and color codes, 32
stoichiometric fuel mixture, 115

T

tensile strength, 156
test instruments, 67
thermal efficiency, 59
thread
   measuring the, 155
threads
   pipe, 158
threads and substitutions
   special, 158
timing gears, 142
timing light
   using a, 88
tire sizes and ratings, 187
toe-in, 184
toe-out, 184
tools
   precision, 143
   special measuring, 151
torque, 37, 50, 51, 52, 161
   guessing at, 162
   principle of, 53
torque test
   resistance or lock, 75
torque tricks, 163
torque wrenches, 160
transmission
   automatic, 171
tune-up
   diesel, 100
   finishing the, 93

U

understeer, 186
understeer and oversteer, 185

V

vacuum, 107
   normal and abnormal, 110
vacuum advance, 90
vacuum inside the carburetor, 111
vacuum pressure, 107
vacuum readings, 108
values
   absolute, 11
   electrical, 63
valve clearance, 96
valve face and seat angles, 128
valve faces, 139
valve lift, 131
valve lifters, 130
valve seat, 140
valve spring, 140
valve spring height and pressure, 128
valve stem-to-guide clearance, 129
valve structure, 38
valve timing, 96
valve train wear, 139
valve trains, 128
vehicle identification code chart, 30
vehicle identification number, 28
vehicle size, 175
vehicle weight, 178
VIN, 28
VIN categories, 30
VIN code, 36
voltage, 65
   induced, 83
   operating, 76
   primary, 83
   regulator, 77
   secondary, 83
voltage drop, 69
voltage drop as a troubleshooting technique, 71
voltage regulator, 78
volts
   amps, and ohms, 65

W

weight
   curb, 178
   shipping, 178
   sprung, 178
   unsprung, 178
   vehicle, 178
weight distribution, 178
wheel alignment geometry, 180
wheel balancing, 187
wheels
   aiming the, 180
wheelbase, 175

Edited by Steven Bolt

Other Bestsellers From TAB

☐ **CUSTOMIZING YOUR VAN—3rd Edition—Girdler, Revised by Calati**

Panel, carpet, and personalize the interior of your van—add portholes, skylights, roof vents, fender flares, and dozens of other improvements—without spending a fortune at a professional conversion shop. You can give any van a new look that rivals the most elaborate of the "California Customs," and save money by doing it yourself! All the information—the techniques, the materials, and the step-by-step guidance—is included in this newly updated, and revised version of a classic handbook on van customizing. 320 pp., 258 illus.

Paper $12.95   **Hard $18.95**
Book No. 2142

☐ **INSTALLING SUNROOFS AND T-TOPS**

Here's the complete illustrated guide to customizing almost any vehicle with a sunroof or T-top! Written by an automotive customizing expert, it covers everything from factory-installed units to luxury after-market conversions to do-it-yourself techniques. Packed with practical advice and professional tips, it includes a complete listing of sunroof and T-top models and manufacturers for dual and electric sunroofs! 176 pp., 154 illus.

Paper $14.95   **Book No. 2132**

☐ **BASIC BODY REPAIR & REFINISHING FOR THE WEEKEND MECHANIC—Calati**

With this illustrated, step-by-step repair and refinishing guide at your side, you can take on almost any basic bodywork and come out with professional-looking results! Using only a minimum number of hand or power tools you can keep your car in like-new condition . . . or refurbish and restore that old car to an almost-new appearance! There's even a list of sources for materials, tools, and parts. 192 pp., 230 illus.

Paper $13.50   **Book No. 2122**

☐ **CORVETTE: THE COMPLETE STORY—Tilton**

Here's the whole Corvette story: history, vital statistics, and restoration techniques! There's information on car options and specs. You'll find tips on routine maintenance and adjustments, and extensive restoration techniques covering engine and transmission removal and inspection, body rehabilitation, fiberglass repair, cosmetic repair, structural repair, painting methods, and more! 224 pp., 111 illus.

Paper $14.95   **Book No. 2107**

☐ **FORD ESCORT/MERCURY LYNX CARS (1981-1984): DO-IT-YOURSELF CAR CARE**

This guide covers all bases on maintenance and repair within the realm of the automobile owner . . . shows you how you can do it all yourself without the use of expensive or specialized tools and equipment. Reviewed in detail are engine, transmission, electrical and ignition systems, brakes, chassis, suspension, tires, air-conditioning systems, exhaust systems, winterizing, and more! 240 pp., 233 illus.

Paper $11.95   **Book No. 2133**

☐ **CHRYSLER K-CARS (1981-84): DO-IT-YOURSELF CAR CARE—Carley**

This guide is written for the person who wants to maintain his or her car as well as possible, at as little expense as necessary! Covered in this handbook are detailed instructions on: Checking vital fluids, Tune-ups, Winterizing, Checking ignition system, Emission control, Air-conditioning, Brakes, Chassis, Suspension, Tires, Exhaust System, Transaxle, Drive Shafts, Electrical System, and more! 240 pp., 299 illus.

Paper $11.95   **Book No. 2123**

☐ **TURBOCHARGERS: THEORY, INSTALLATION, MAINTENANCE AND REPAIR—Curless**

Now, this well-written, clearly illustrated, and exceptinally thorough guidebook gives you all the information you need to decide whether or not a turbocharged car is for you . . . how to install, maintain, and repair a turbo addition to your present auto . . . and how to choose a production model turbocharged car. Leading off with a clarification of how turbocharging works, the author covers such application factors as air-to-fuel ratios, turbo lag, controlling detonation and preignition, ways to tell when a turbo is overcharging (and damaging) an engine, and more. 176 pp., 129 illus.

Paper $11.95   **Book No. 2111**

☐ **CAR DESIGN: STRUCTURE & ARCHITECTURE—Norbye**

Here's an inside look at the steps involved in automotive design—from the drawing board to the showroom floor . . . from the horseless carriage to the compact cars of the '80s! This book examines the reasons behind the positioning of the seats, engines, and other necessary elements, and how these choices affect the body styling freedom of the body designer. 384 pp., 327 illus. 7" × 10".

Paper $20.50   **Book No. 2104**

*Prices subject to change without notice.

Look for these and other TAB books at your local bookstore.

TAB BOOKS Inc.
P.O. Box 40
Blue Ridge Summit, PA 17214

Send for FREE TAB catalog describing over 1200 current titles in print.